Integrated Ego Psychology

by
Norman A. Polansky

ALDINE PUBLISHING COMPANY
NEW YORK

Copyright © 1982 Norman A. Polansky

All rights reserved. No part of this publication may
be reproduced or transmitted in any form or by any
means, electronic or mechanical, including photocopy,
recording, or any information storage and retrieval
system, without permission in writing from the publisher.

First published 1982
Aldine Publishing Company
200 Saw Mill River Road
Hawthorne, New York 10532

ISBN 0-202-26090-9 cloth; 0-202-26089-5 paper

Library of Congress Catalog Number 81-67974

Printed in the United States of America
10   9   8   7   6   5   4   3   2

Preface

Whoever wants to help people, but doubts s/he has been anointed a Special Personality, realizes that s/he needs a system, a theory to guide his/her work. After a century of development, psychoanalysis offers the most complete and general theory of personality available. Formed in the course of trying to relieve psychologically induced pain, its applicability has always been one of its strengths. Moreover, customarily taking us beyond common sense, it even dares to contradict it from time to time. So, for many of us, it contains the most important set of concepts and laws we have found useful for helping people.

Ego psychology is in turn the part of psychoanalytic theory with the most immediate relevance to clinicians. This book is intended as an introduction to the very large literature on the subject. It will have done its job if the person who has studied it ends up well grounded yet still stimulated to move on to more advanced writings; I hope there will not be much to unlearn. With this aim in mind, I have avoided special pleadings or unusual positions within psychoanalysis in favor of generally accepted ideas. The beginner does well to believe enough to learn; having learned, he may then proceed to disbelieve. This is the perspective I have tried to implement in this book.

An author is wise to keep in mind the audience to whom his writing is addressed. This book is intended for graduate students in social work, and for advanced undergraduates interested in acquiring a basic theory of personality. It should prove useful, also, to students of clinical psychology and personality theory, those in counseling programs, psychiatric nursing, music therapy and psychiatric occupational therapy. Colleagues some years out of academic training who want to refresh their knowledge of the field or to pick up on new developments should also find this book useful.

The present volume is offered as a successor rather than revision of my earlier *Ego Psychology and Communication* since it has been so extensively rewritten and has undergone a change of focus. After some years of using the earlier book in the classroom, it became evident that my assumption that most graduate students would come to this course with a general knowledge of analytic theory was not fully justified. Hence, I have inserted a chapter on basic analytic concepts before addressing the main topic of the book. The space devoted to the Theory of Object Relations has been increased, and related theories are covered more thoroughly—and more critically. Other additions are in discussions of the psychogenetics of ego development, group psychology, and possible contributions to be incorporated from humanistic psychology. Communication, *per se*, has received considerably less emphasis. Hence, the change in title. At the same time, some parts of this version—several whole chapters in fact—have been taken over from the first. I could not find a way to say the same things better, or at least enough better to justify rewriting.

As in my first effort, I have tried hard to make the presentation readable. No one acquires a sprightly style simply by willing it of course, but I have tried to present expositions of some rather abstruse ideas in plain English. In this effort, I have been encouraged by moral support from a generation of students. As one remarked, some years ago, "What this field needs is some new clichés!" Who will argue with that?

Having in mind the student struggling to gain a foothold in analytic theory in order to help his clients, I have at times found it advisable to treat conceptual issues as more settled than they really are. Even the thinking about affect, or emotion, so important in analytic work, has varied over the years. Affect has been treated as causing behavior, at first, and then as accompanying it; its formulation as signalling drive state was evidently a later development. Traces of all three usages survive. I have tried to steer a course between confusing the newcomer, on the one hand, and oversimplifying the theoretical issues involved, on the other. Like other teachers, I have opted for providing a systematic, relatively uncluttered statement as a first approximation to the fuller understanding the student will eventually acquire through reading and further training. In the interests of compression, an effort has also been made to give examples of theoretical points which also elucidate an event or problem likely to be encountered in practice. Clinical examples, too, nearly always permit of more than one interpretation. Describing ego psychology in a form which will be unexceptionable may well be impossible, yet most of it fits together very well, and mine is offered as a workable version.

As before, I would like to thank Dean Charles A. Stewart and my colleagues at the School of Social Work, University of Georgia, for providing the support and the freedom of time to continue scholarly work. Mrs. Anne Hurst has helped by typing the whole of this manuscript. John Wander, of Aldine, has been a most supportive editor, throughout this process. My greatest debt, however, is to the well loved person who shares most closely in the throes of any undertaking, my wife, Nancy.

Acknowledgement is gratefully made to the following publishers and individuals for permission to include the following: *American Journal of Orthopsychiatry*, "On duplicity in the interview" (1967, vol. 37, pp. 568-79); copyright the *American Orthopsychiatric Association, Inc., Psychiatry*, "Psychodrama as an element in hospital treatment" with Elizabeth B. Harkins (1969, vol. 32, pp. 74-87). Faber & Faber and Harcourt, Brace & World, Inc., for permission to reprint lines from "The Love Song of J. Alfred Prufrock" and "Whispers of Immortality," *Collected Poems 1909-1962* by T. S. Eliot, copyright 1936, by Harcourt, Brace & World, Inc.; copyright © 1963 1963, 1964 by T. S. Eliot.

Athens, Georgia
February 1981

Table of Contents

To the Carbondale Polansky's

Celia Kaplan
Joseph Joel
Adele Lillian
Nancy Finley
Grace Rachael Vaughn
Jonathan Rolfe
Laura Smith
James Harrison
Benjamin Joseph
John Michael

CHAPTER 1
A SPEED READER'S GUIDE TO
Psychoanalytic Ego Psychology in Clinical Work

Good theory compresses the wisdom accumulated in a field. By reasoning from *general principles*, you can go beyond your own experience. Theory makes it possible to *predict* events and exercise *control* in behalf of the client. *Analytic theory* is attractive because it makes sense of behavior that seems unreasonable, even *self-destructive*. It offers suggestions about how to help. *Ego psychology* is a branch of psychoanalytic theory.

To evaluate this new theory, we first look at how good theory is constructed. Practitioners need one that is *parsimonious*, that strives for simplicity and so is easy to keep in mind. Yet, it must cover the variety encountered in clients. For prediction and control, theory must be *dynamic*, concern itself with events. It must be *communicable* among adequately trained professionals. A modern *theory of personality* should contain conceptions of *energy, structure, learning*, and *coping*. It should relate to the *organic* side of man, and describe his *executive* functions. Psychoanalytic theory stands up well by these criteria, better than any other

Ego psychology, in turn, deals with the following topics: the *defense mechanisms, object relations, characterology, adaptive apparatuses* and various expressions of the *synthetic function*.

Psychoanalytic Ego Psychology in Clinical Work

1

Ego psychology is the aspect of psychoanalytic theory concerned with how people adapt to the demands and possibilities of their worlds in accordance with their inner requirements. All substantial theories of personality refer to adaptation, but there are several features special to ego psychology. It offers by far the most elaborate picture of the adaptive apparatus and of the varied devices humans have for negotiating among their drives and their life situations. More than any other theory of psychology, it emphasizes the complicated transactions that go on in people's minds, of which many are outside conscious awareness. Ego psychology lays bare how much the adaptation is to oneself. Indeed, it shows how large a share of present mental activity has to be devoted to dealing with marks left on the person from past efforts at adaptation.

Few who are, or aspire to be, caseworkers, therapists or counselors will come to this book innocent of all the ideas contained herein. Much will seem familiar from previous training and from experiences with people. The "ego," after all, is the part of the client's personality which the practitioner most immediately confronts. Moreover, many Freudian terms have been adopted into the working vocabularies of all educated people. Words like instinctual drive, defense mechanism, anxiety, guilt, conflict, unconscious, and the like, are used all the time in estimating each other. One task of this book, therefore, will be to lend such terms precise meanings; another will be to show the logical connections among them. When the ambition is not simply to discuss the patient but to help him, precision in expression and thought become essential. Amorphous theories of treatment will not do.

Psychoanalytic theory has been evolving for about a century, and some "grand simplicities" have finally emerged. A further aim of this book is to show how modern ego psychology makes clients' and patients' seemingly unrelated behaviors and moods fit into understandable patterns. Those with little previous training will find some Freudian conceptions unsettling, surprising, and rewarding. An analyst's success in making sense of the complicated doings of people affords a very high intellectual pleasure.

This book, for practitioners, rests on my conviction that we all require a theory to guide our work if we are to help people effectively. The theory must be elaborate enough to cover a very wide range of human activity and it must meet certain other standards as well. Moreover, we must be disciplined enough to commit ourselves to one consistent line of theory if we are to harness reasoning to go beyond what we can directly observe. The bases for these convictions are the subject matter of this chapter. I begin with the alleged romance between one of my own fields of practice, social casework, and psychoanalysis.

Why the Choice of Psychoanalytic Theory?

Social work has been involved with the psychoanalytic theory of personality for over half a century. My participation during much of this affair between the disciplines provides an opportunity to review its true history. According to one version, several outstanding teachers underwent personal analyses in the 1920's and 1930's and proceeded to act out their unresolved feelings toward their analysts by preaching psychoanalytic theory to other social workers. Under the impact of the theory, social work lost sight of the role that circumstance plays in our lives, and came to assume that clients' troubles all stemmed from within. It took a major upheaval in the 1960's to "put the social back into social work" and free it from bondage.

The image has some basis in fact but is terribly overstated (Alexander 1972; Hamilton 1958). In the first place, the 1930's were the years of the Great Depression, which did not relent until we began mobilizing for World War II. Along with their other troubles, most people we saw were very poor. The hunger and suffering was staggering. One fellow student went to see an elderly woman to offer her agency help since neighbors had reported she was starving. The woman refused to discuss her needs, she "could not accept charity." Still concerned, the student went back to visit two days later and found her dead.

Regardless of our political philosophies before entering the field, nearly all of us were at least to some extent radicalized by it. "There has to be a better way to run a country" was a truism. Many were attracted by views comparable to those of the British Labour Party and the European Social Democrats. Quite a few had a fling with Communism, but typically renounced it after experiencing a demand for absolute loyalty to Josef Stalin and his wildly fluctuating "party line." Yet, in the midst of our experiences with very real clients and experiments with politics, many of us also became fascinated with Freud's personality theory. Nor were we unique. A number of writers of that era—Waldo Frank comes to mind—as well as artists, philosophers and others became interested in both Marxist economics and Freudian psychology.

On the one hand, the leadership of the Communist party regarded analysis as conflicting with Marxist doctrine. The burden of its complaint was that attitudes are really determined by man's objective situation, whereas Freudian theory assumes the opposite. The Communists, who devote great efforts to propaganda, are inconsistent in their stated devotion to *materialism* in metaphysics. In any event, they have always seemed to be more influential as astute adventurers in power than as thinkers, so their opposition to the Freudian point of view seemed another move toward thought control. We social workers, in any case, were not that interested in ideological argument, but in helping our clients.

On the other hand hardly anyone I knew became engrossed in Freudian theory either. It was amusing two decades later, therefore, to hear ourselves described as having been ambitious to be junior psychoanalysts, working to get our clients to "adapt to the system."

Freudian theory did not extend into social work by overcoming a competing set of ideas; it stepped into a hiatus. The majority of those doing the work were operating from a combination of concern, intuitiveness about people, and accumulated wisdom about clients passed on, largely by word of mouth from supervisor to younger worker.

At the School of Applied Social Sciences of Case Western Reserve University, where I was trained in psychiatric social work, I clearly recall two courses, one in adult psychiatry, one concerning disturbances in children. The courses were simply descriptive. If asked why epileptics so frequently adorn themselves with bracelets and trinkets—a "fact" that no longer seems a fact—you were told coldly that it was in their "nature" to do so. Such an answer provided absolutely no leads about how to help such a person, and the process of traditional diagnosis had about it a deprecating quality that we, who had defied our families to enter this field, found offensive.

Insights gleaned from courses with other psychiatrists and from teaching by the case method were simply handed over like presents. Oddly, it made you feel more helpless to receive your wisdom about people in such fashion, for unless you were similarly gifted it appeared you would never be able to generate such understanding yourself. And yet, I remember a course with Alan Finlayson, a local doctor trained in psychoanalysis. His course revolved heavily around the Oedipus Complex and other concepts associated with the Freudian theory of that day. It aroused so much enthusiasm that a delegation went to persuade the Dean to add a second course, and he did. Why the excitement?

First, Finlayson consistently dealt with human motivations and emotions, with *why* people do what they do. Second, he attempted generality, providing concepts and principles by which we, ourselves, could try to deduce what would happen in a given case, even if we were not either uniquely perceptive or ancient—like 40 years old, Lord love us. Third, the connections he described had about them the ring of truth, even when they did not accord with common sense; they were more interesting than common sense, filled with marvelous paradoxes.

I have left for last, however, the biggest attraction that analytic theory had for my generation. Then, as now, we had clients whose patterns were baffling. There was the alcoholic who stole his wife's hard-earned money, beat her, and disappeared for days on end; nevertheless she found him "loveable." There was the alcoholic, warned that his liver would kill him unless he stopped drinking, who paid no attention to the news. There was the rebellious adolescent who, after two arrests and much effort by his family and the settlement workers to have him placed on probation, continued to court trouble with the law. There were the elderly who needed immediate medical care, but seemed unable to discuss any kind of planning to get it.

In each case, regardless of the client's own statements, the behavior seemed self-destructive. We were at a loss as to how to help. Social workers half a century ago may not have known all we do now, but they were not idiots. By trial and error, they came to understand that arguing or reasoning with people locked into destructive life courses does little good and any may end the worker's involvement with the situation. We had to conclude either that "people make no sense," or else that the laws about human motivation lay at a level deeper than we had plumbed. Freud's theories made at least some irrational behavior understandable. And, it held the hope that, using it, we could find ways of helping that would work.

Kardiner (1945) has remarked that any theory which cannot explain masochism is a very incomplete psychology. Psychoanalysis had the attraction that at least it tried to deal with such a phenomenon. At the time, most psychology departments were completely engrossed in experimental work on vision and audition, long sessions with memory drums and nonsense syllables, and studies of the Norwegian white rat. A leading journal published this morose letter, "Gentlemen: I have recently received the Ph.D. in Psychology from X University without having had contact with a single human being—with the possible exception of the faculty." Nowadays, students have other theories to choose from which also attempt to deal with the parts of man that do more than see, hear, taste, or regurgitate nonsense, but in that day a man like my tutor, Gordon Allport (1937), who wrote a book on personality, was regarded as "soft." And since our training threw us directly into contact with clients from the first week on, we were clear that there was much we did not know about people or how to help them. Those of us with a scientific background were sure that improved methods of working with clients would require better theory.

Such a theory would explain *why* people think and behave as they do. Large segments of the population are completely incurious about such a question. I have known men who could tell you in boring detail the purpose and function of every part of the auto carburetor but who, when asked why a relative was depressed, would ponder for a full minute and reply, "That's just the way he is." Even people who plan to be clinicians give answers like, "I guess it's just a habit," which says the same thing but sounds better. To them. If people are in difficulties and we do not understand *why* they got into them, how can we help them extricate themselves? We do not ask the question why about all the behavior we see—but, then, we do not look into our auto's engine when it is running well, either.

The Role of Theory
What sort of theory of personality do we need? Let us remind

ourselves of the aim of the game. The aim of having a theory, in the helping professions, is to improve our ability *to control events* on behalf of clients. Anyone who enters our profession is expected to want to ease the lot of others and to make them happier. But, more than good intentions are needed; they have to be expressed in actions that have the desired effects in clients' lives and emotions. Choosing the actions to take requires knowing their consequences, for the sake of those we want to help.

Another reason for wanting to control events becomes more pressing as one matures in the field; it has to do with pride of workmanship. It becomes important to see that the bridges one has built in the lives of others are able to bear weight and can be used in daily trafficking. Unless one is unlucky, the ability to build strong structures for others increases gradually with experience, from one's own direct learnings. Intelligent craftsmen learn from experience, with and without having a formal theory that directs their knowledge. Indeed there is no substitute for hands-on experience in the development of a first-rate clinician. But, why limit oneself to one's own direct contacts and one's own lifetime? A good theory puts at the worker's disposal the gist of what preceding generations have been able to glean and does it succinctly.

Theory that markedly increases our ability to make things that we hope will happen to happen, has certain characteristics. First, it deals with sequences among events, enabling us to *predict*. Second, good theory *simplifies* our lives. After four decades in the field, it is a pleasure to be able to write the latter sentence, for I believe it. But, I doubt it is believable to many of my readers. In social work, the beginning student may founder under a mass of precepts, injunctions, formulations, undigested facts, not to mention agency regulations and policies. How can learning another set of ideas simplify this life? Before entering clinical training, the student had conversations all the time, enjoyable conversations. Now with the giving up of conversations for interviews, all pleasure is lost. Tongue-tied, s/he watches the client like an Indian snake charmer, making furtive notes (written and mental). The student can hardly wait for the end of the hour; neither can the client. To the weight which the worker already carries, all s/he needs is to add "theory."

Yet, an interview is a conversation with a purpose. And this makes a crucial difference. It is not forbidden for client and worker to enjoy themselves, but immediate enjoyment is not enough. Something useful is supposed to come of their talk. The practitioner who aims to help primarily by talking treatment must know how to use conversations to make things happen. S/he must know which conversational keys to play on, which to let alone. Above all, s/he has to know what to attend to while watching the client and listening. There are so many facts after all, from the client's age, to hair color, to a mother's depression at age forty-one. Which facts make a difference? Or, more precisely, which matter most in deciding how to help? Let us face it, raw reality is simply chaotic; we need a basis for judging relevance. Therefore, a cardinal aim of any worthwhile theory is to *reduce the chaos of raw experience.*

A good theory consists of statements that are actually dependable predictions about sequences among events. If A happens, B will follow—if not always, at least usually; if not immediately, eventually; if not at all, for good reason. Let us call A the *cause* and B the *effect.* The clinician who wants to produce a particular effect will be alert to see whether s/he can introduce its cause. That is all that is meant by a *planned intervention.* Planned intervention rests on *dynamic* theory, a network of highly dependable predictions about changes or tendencies to change.

Not all theories have this dynamic quality. For centuries, people thought that a theorist had nicely reduced the chaos of raw experience by finding a way to arrange ideas (usually), objects (sometimes), and events (seldom) into neat, mutually exclusive pigeonholes. As an undergraduate, I was taught that there were three types of itinerants: the tramp, the hobo, and the migratory worker. Each had particular features, so I dutifully memorized the textbook definitions. Later, I had experiences I strongly doubt the writer of our textbook ever had. For over two years, I was a caseworker in military and civilian prisons; I interviewed a host of "Veterans Administration bums" (dependent personalities by act of Congress); I worked in family agencies and in mental hospitals. Never did I find use for those distinctions in trying to help. So, theory that merely results in classification is of scant use. It may put to rest an obsessiveness within the textbook author, but it does not ease the mind of the practitioner who has to act.

Of course all abstracting involves classifying, and a *concept,* the building block of theory, is a term or symbol for a class of objects or events having something in common. It is not hard to invent concepts. Select any two objects at random in the room and demonstrate to yourself that you, too, can think of an abstraction, a "concept" that will subsume both. For example, a blackboard and a chair are both pieces of classroom equipment. Similarly, it is relatively easy to erect a terminology by which to categorize people, or their expressions, or their behaviors. We have all heard the man, who has acquired age without wisdom, pontificate, "Basically, my friend, there are two kinds of people..." At the age of seventy-five, he still cannot count to three?

So, setting up systems for classifying is almost too easy. What is hard, in theorizing, is finding just that system for classifying that best reflects the regularities among happenings. This is the dynamic theory that enhances our ability to predict, and therefore to control, to some extent, events involving our clients.

The Rule of Parsimony

Those who devote their lives to building theory have evolved a set of precepts about its construction, based on rules that have worked well in the past, such as the rule of parsimony. To simplify rather than clutter our working lives, theory should be parsimonious. Briefly stated: the ideal is to encompass a maximal range of phenomena with a minimal number of statements.

If a student in the Middle Ages asked, "Why does water run downhill?," the answer would have been in terms of the "essence" or the idea of water. "It is of the nature of water to run downhill." If Newton asked why an apple fell from a tree, he would be told that it was "in the nature" of apples to fall from trees. Predicting which objects would fall required a very large amount of memorizing. We owe to the genius of Galileo and Newton the single principle of the Law of Gravity. Indeed, at a more general level the law explains not only falling bodies, but predicts other phenomena as well. It states the attraction between any two bodies, the force drawing them toward each other, so the falling apple is but one illustration of this force's operation. Moreover, the strength of the attraction is directly proportionate to the weights, or masses, of the two bodies, and inversely proportionate to the distance between them. This is hardly a thought that makes one awake and shout with glee every morning. But if you are in the business of making objects move through space—which seems to be one of mankind's morbid preoccupations—the Law of Gravity is a convenient thinking tool. Certainly, it is simpler than remembering a long list of objects, each of which has it in its essence to run downhill.

Note, however, that the simplicity was found when physicists went beyond superficial similarities—for example that apples are often red, that they are fruit—to the observation that nearly everything falls toward the center of the earth, *as if* there were a force pulling in that direction. The force, if there is one, cannot be seen, nor heard, nor felt. Yet, if we go beyond the directly observable to what might be imagined or *inferred*, we suddenly arrive at a great regularity. If we construct a mental model of the world, *as if* there were such forces present, a very large number of specific predictions can be drawn and, in fact, proved true. Concepts used in such mental models, known only by inference, are called *constructs* (Polansky, 1975). As we shall see, Freud employed a number of constructs, often using analogies from other sciences, in erecting his models of mental functioning. But, because such a model does not always bear an obvious correspondence to the way things seem at first glance, we have to use other standards for deciding whether to rely on it. We ask: "Does it help us to predict?" And, since we are practitioners, "Does it help us help our clients?"

A principle in psychology that has shown a rewarding facility for reducing the chaos of nature is *the organism will seek to re-establish internal equilibrium*, closely related to one in physiology, Cannon's (1932) principle of *homeostasis*. Cannon was able to explain a number of symptoms by following the notion that the body strives to re-establish the equilibrium it had before some insult or injury occurred to it. Very similar processes seem at work in group psychology. What happens, for example, in a group of people who are cohesive, closely bound to each other, when one is seized with an idea at variance with an attitude important to the others in the group? The first effort of the group will be to pressure this individual to change his mind and to resume thinking like the rest. Should this fail, the group will eventually withdraw from the person, or even eject him or her from the group. In so doing, the group returns to a state of minimal internal tension by redrawing its boundaries so as to contain only like-minded persons. Of course, the group could accomplish the same thing if the majority would change to resemble the deviant, but this would require more change: S/he would have to be very important for this to happen.

Talking about individual reactions, we refer to tension reduction and *drive reduction*, shorthand ways of saying that the person behaves in order to achieve an equilibrium with minimal tension. So, we eat to reduce hunger pains. More interesting is the manner in which psychological symptoms follow the same principle. A psychological symptom may be very painful, but it would not be there unless it were keeping the person in an equilibrium in some way preferable to the psychological state without it. *Equilibration* is a model of human responses unusually powerful in its ability to organize and simplify a broad range of happenings.

The formulation of each major principle in psychology reflects an act of genius. How such a breakthrough occurs to a particular individual remains something of a mystery. But much is known about the approach a whole science should follow to lay the foundation for a major breakthrough, and this is what is meant by the scientific method.

The *rule of parsimony* is accepted as an essential part of the approach, telling us to be stingy with theory, never to introduce a new concept or hypothesis without examining whether an established law will not cover the new case in point. Any science hopes constantly to add generalizations, covering more of the world about us, but the method requires us to give ground reluctantly. A new explanation offered to fit a single new instance is called an *ad hoc*, or "for this case," hypothesis. And often it is just as it sounds, a notion volunteered on the spur of the moment to cover an unanticipated research finding.

While *ad hoc* hypotheses are particularly common in the concluding chapters of student theses, they are not unknown among famous scholars. There was a psychologist, McDougall, who was strongly convinced that all behavior is purposive—a notion that is now generally accepted. McDougall (1932) was also fascinated with instincts, and when confronted with the need to explain some specific behavior, he was likely to call it an instinct or, later, a propensity. From him and his confreres we have such concepts as the maternal instinct, the paternal instinct, the filial instinct, often still discussed in literary psychology. It does not, however, simplify life if, whenever we are faced with a new behavior, we ascribe it to an "instinct," invented to fit the case. For example, Freud also used the idea of in-born drives, or instincts, to explain behavior. But, rather than proliferate them, he sought to come up with the smallest number absolutely required to explain all behavior. Eventually, he settled on two basic drives: pleasure seeking, or *libido*, and *aggression*.

But to many, Freud seems to have speculated too far beyond his data when he sought to raise his conception of the instincts to a very high level of abstraction and postulated two basic opposing forces in man, Eros (life force) and Thanatos (death instinct). One still occasionally sees reference to "death wishes" in popular writings, and even in clinical descriptions, but most practitioners find such notions too airy and non-specific to be of help with individual clients. They are like saying, "All men are mortal." The statement has been undeniably true, thus far, but faced with a person in one's office trying to find a way to pay his rent, our reaction is, "So what?" In other words, it is possible to violate the rule of parsimony by unnecessary elaboration of theory, but it is also possible to strive for parsimony so relentlessly that the theory loses applicability to individual cases, and one is left with empty truisms. So, another challenge to the theoretician is to hit on the right level of abstraction.

Scientists are Human

Science is of necessity a social enterprise. The systematic growth of knowledge has been the most impressive monument we have been thus far able to erect. To contribute to this growth is one of the few feasible ways to defeat mortality. Though the desire to discover a new principle is enormous, it is held in check by the rule of parsimony.

The Orthodox Freudian movement has been a history of schisms, ejections and secessions. Left out, finally, were Adlerians, Jungians, Rankians, Horney adherents and others. Because the ideas represented by these figures often foreshadowed elements of what we now call ego psychology, a word is in order about this aspect of the history of psychoanalysis.

Freud has been described to this author as the old bull of the herd, unable to tolerate competition from the younger men who gathered around him. Whether or not this describes Freud, the man, there was more at stake than his need to be boss bull. For example, Freud for a time insisted that the development of ego psychology be delayed until more had been uncovered about the id, the source of the great unconscious strivings, the primeval emotions and energy in the personality. And it was already clear that insights about the id were not at all popular. The temptation, therefore, was to pursue matters closer to the surface, often quite conscious, acceptable to the general culture. But, if analysts had submitted to their critics' shock and disapproval, they might well have re-repressed their hard-won insights into matters normally unconscious. The knowledge would have been lost, not because it was wrong, but because it was unpleasant.

I suppose in any event Freud felt particularly skeptical about ideas that seemed too readily palatable to be true. When Adler, for example, suggested that the need to overcompensate for felt inferiority explained a great deal of neurotic behavior, Freud is said to have remarked of this and kindred insights, "There will always have to be a psychology for the Hausfrau, and Adler has created it." The idea that the boy who puts on superior airs may be covering up deep feelings of inferiority was not news to most of us at high school age. It fits common sense, a most untrustworthy instrument, always in short supply. Common sense psychologies are not parsimonious and usually only contain explanations that the conscious mind can easily tolerate. They are boring. The simplicity inherent in an elegant theory is a great convenience to the busy or even to the slothful but it opens few doors to the simple-minded. So, another concern we must have about a system of theory is whether it offers the illusion of simplicity at the cost of failing to illuminate anything at all obscure.

All of which should not imply that Adlerian analysts were simple-minded. Adler's social philosophy required therapists not to use a language among themselves that was not to be used with their patients also, and this constrained the kinds of conceptualizations he developed. But the reason he was read out of the psycho-analytic movement had more to do with how sciences develop. In the earliest phases of theory-construction, all is in flux—the concepts, their definitions, basic assumptions, and so forth. After a time, however, it becomes desirable that things settle down, at least temporarily. One has to say, "Let us agree to define the 'ego' as such and such for the next few years, and see where that leads us in our attempts to build theory." Science cannot live in a state of permanent revolution.

The various schisms presented difficulties to the mainstream of psychoanalytic thinking because basic assumptions were constantly reopened to question, familiar terms were given new nuances, new terms were introduced, seemingly *ad libidem*—or at least without sufficient concern as to how they fit the rest of the theory. With a newly emerging theory, the danger is always that the chaos within the science will come to match that within its subject matter. When that happens, there has been no progress at all. Freud felt that the schismatics' preferred notions would interfere with the development of a parsimonious theory, with an agreement on the terms to be employed.

In research we are much concerned with the *inter-observer reliability* of any instrument we use because it represents the extent to which two or more observers, using the same method of observing, come up with similar pictures of the groups or persons they study. If the agreement is great, reliability is called high; when it is poor, it is termed low. Without reasonably high inter-observer reliability, communication among colleagues becomes impossible. No new knowledge can be added to the field. Disagreeement about the basic concepts of a science and their definitions would have made a shambles of Freud's effort to develop a consistent theory. I hope this digression into the logic of science helps explain why variants from the orthodox analytic tradition presented such a problem.

Nor is this all ancient history. In more recent years the founder of the highly publicized Transactional Analysis, Eric Berne, took himself and his approach to therapy out of the Freudian tradition in which he had been trained. And the brilliant attempt at synthesizing newer knowledge from other fields by John Bowlby, also a former practicing analyst, is also treated as being outside the orthodox tradition. Yet as we remarked, a number of the dissidents have offered insights of proven value to ego psychology.

The communicability of psychoanalytic knowledge is also an issue in the strongest criticisms leveled against it. Years ago, an elder colleague challenged me, "What is this *anxiety* you practitioners prattle about?" He said he would not know how to observe it, and certainly he, himself, had never experienced any. The man was a rigid person in poor physical condition, so there was no mercy in trying to demonstrate his own anxiety to him, on the spot. But if he rejected the notion of anxiety as an objective and observable phenomenon, how could one discuss any clinical issue with him? Does communicability require that a concept have high reliability regardless of *who* uses it?

The test of communicability need not be so gross. It does not really require that everyone who wanders down the pike must be able to repeat our results, no matter how he goes at it. No. Results are expected to be understandable to suitably equipped co-workers, to be replicable by persons adequately trained in the methods and concepts involved. The poor in spirit are always with us. To limit what we use to facts observable by persons obtuse about people would prematurely rule out the things we most need to know, leaving us a science of personality of little use in treatment. Of course, the obverse of all this is also true. Those incurious about *why* people do what they do will find a book like this of little interest and less comprehensibility. Ego psychology makes a poor playground for the non-psychologically minded, or those content to plumb their own shallows.

Which is not to say that those who have examined Freudian theory and found it wanting were all limited. The creators of the theory were men and women, just as were their critics. The theory is just that; it is not a system of religious beliefs. Many psychoanalytic propositions have proven wrong or not quite right in the past and have had to be modified. The same is undoubtedly true of widely accepted ideas which will be presented here. However, to test a theory one must withhold judgment long enough to learn it and try it out. If it helps predict and control events to better help our clients, then its acceptance is justified.

Elements Desirable in a General Theory of Personality
The following criteria suggest themselves as essential elements for a comparative analysis of theories of personality.

1. A conception of *energy*. What makes the engine go? Where is the source of psychological gasoline? Whether we speak of drives, instincts, needs or purposes, we have to be able to identify and differentiate the dynamic elements of personality that push for change, or the taking of action.

2. A notion of *structure*, which represents the part of personality that changes most slowly. We need to be able to finger structured elements to bring our job of prediction within tolerable, human limits, for by structure we refer to the elements of the personality we can treat as "held constant." In personality theory our main attention is on events, not things. Structural elements simply index events likely to recur. In sociology structural elements include institutions, values, social roles. In personality we speak of traits, enduring needs, attitudes.

3. A notion of *learning*, which at its most general refers to enduring change in the organism's pattern as a result of interaction with the environment. There has to be a principle, or set of principles, dealing with the circumstances under which learning is, or is not, likely to take place. In humans, learning is the major origin of structures. Without such a notion there can be no image of personality change in treatment.

4. A conception of *coping*. How does the organism respond to change, or even to threat, from the world surrounding itself? Better yet, is there also a recognition of coping with demands and threats that arise from within? What distinguishes adaptive reactions from maladaptive? How can we help clients cope?

5. An image of the relationship between the *organic* and the psychological, in order to understand the impact of physical illness; it is also needed even to recognize a need like hunger.

6. A description of the *executive* facets of the personality.

The image of the personality has to be sufficiently elaborate to describe how the organism itself operates to meet its needs; it must also be able to take into account individual differences in people's capacities. Theories that presume all people to be equally intelligent, well informed, able to make decisions, or to have intact sensory systems do not permit us to individualize clients. Theories that do not concern themselves with functions affecting *efficiency* in getting one's needs met are incapable of describing pathology, tracing its causes, mapping its remediation.

All of these elements are, in fact, present in the psychoanalytic theory of the personality; the same cannot be said for any other. Learning theory, for example, has an elaborate conception of how learning takes place; it deals, also, with motivation, and with some traits described as habits or conditioned responses. Humanistic psychologies are organized around propositions regarding human motivation. Their emphasis on free will presumes the patient to be an essentially normal person capable of exercising judgment in his own behalf.

Many-faceted clinical practice requires a theory of personality able to take into account the very wide range of people with whom we deal. Freudian psychology has been developing for a long time, nearly a century as I write this. It has had time to incorporate much of the complexity of behavior, which is a major reason for remaining involved with it and basing practice in large measure on the propositions it contains (Hollis, 1972). Others argue that the very grandness of the theory's design has become a disadvantage, that the essentials for helping people can be based on a less inclusive image of the personality. Students make up their own minds, eventually, based on experiences with helping people over a period of years.

In any event, it is far beyond the scope of a single volume to attempt to present the full psychoanalytic theory. This book deals with only a segment of the theory and is intended as an introduction to that. It begins with a compact statement of some essentials of the more general theory, for we have discovered that the majority of our students need this review. Most of the book, however, will concern ego psychology.

Functions of the Ego

One aspect of the psychoanalytic literature is delightful even though it presents a problem. Profound ideas are often explicated through rich figures of speech, parables, and paradoxes. While many of the authors were middle Europeans, more was involved than charm and *gemutlichkeit*. In the United States, we are accustomed to having our ideas conveyed rapidly, at a high level of abstraction, in the deadly style of some professional journals. But, does not presenting ideas so concisely rob them of associations which could contribute to grasping their meanings on unconscious levels also? The less formal literary style might, in fact, make the ideas it presents more vivid, more valuable, and more accessible.

For instance, a figure of speech employed in discussing the parts of the personality is reification: terms with abstract connotations are made real, given life, even human properties. Thus David Wineman might remark, "The super ego made a deal with the id, and was seduced." A concrete example of this kind of seduction may be found among certain religious fundamentalists. Most Americans do not applaud having more children than one can properly care for, but there are still those who believe no effort ought be made to control family size. When a man believes he can earn his way into heaven by activity in the marital bed, he has an unbeatable combination in which Id and Super ego have made a deal. The image we have is of two people negotiating, one knave and one sanctimonious hypocrite. It comes as a jolt to recognize neither Mr. Id nor his corruptible confederate are real persons, nor identifiable bits of the personality. Each is, in fact, an *abstraction*, a label given to a set of mental processes and operations. In the case of the ego, we refer to the *functions* subsumed under that concept (Stamm, 1959; Wasserman, 1974).

Within the corpus of Freudian theory itself, ego psychology is to be distinguished from id psychology, the first area emphasized in developing the theory. As we shall see, the id has to do with drives, instincts, emotions, the energies that impel the personality. Ego psychology has to do with *adaptation;* the usual description of the ego is that it mediates among the id, the super ego and the environment—external reality. But, if the id refers to a multitude of sins, what is the role of the ego? The following specific adaptive functions, commonly taught as ego psychology, seem to me to be of greatest importance for clinicians.

1. *Defense mechanisms and the formation of symptoms:* Even if they come from undergraduate anti-Freudian departments, nearly all students have some acquaintanceship with defense mechanisms, for these mechanisms have passed from their original auspices into general knowledge. Terms like rationalization, reaction-formation, projection are listed and defined in most basic textbooks. A knowl-

edge of the logic of the defenses is useful to anyone undertaking to help others through interviews, for the defenses are among the mental functions most immediately visible when one first meets a client. We shall begin our examination of ego psychology by discussing the nature of defense and its role in symptom formation.

2. *Object relations:* The theory of object relations contains many of the most exciting advances associated with ego psychology. What is the theory of object relations? As might be expected in a field where the Latin word *ego* was chosen as the English for the German *Ich*, objects are typically people. (By the way, a nice reversal of some dehumanizing trends in our general culture.) Under object relations, we study the attitudes clients have toward others, and how these influence facets of their living beyond those we term, sometimes euphemistically, "human relations."

3. *Characterology:* In common speech, the term *character* has value connotatons. Someone "has character," or she is "a woman of character." The implication is that the person can be relied upon. In analytic usage, the term is value free. It refers to aspects of the person that are pervasive and color the whole. Bigots can be relied on for bigotry, narcissists for selfishness, caring people for helpfulness. *Character refers to traits that hold steady over time and in varying situations.* Ego psychology examines whether there are patterns of traits or character-structures that recur among people that help us simplify our predictions and guide our efforts in treatment. Whether the structures we find are "good" or not is another question.

4. *Adaptive apparatus:* A number of personality functions have been of interest to all psychologists, including the non-Freudian: perceiving external reality; perceiving oneself, including one's own motivations and patterns of response; cognitive functions like learning, remembering and thinking; processes of coping with one's social and physical realities. This listing, seeming to encompass a large chunk of all human behavior, was not traditionally of concern to Freudians. They were, after all, engaged primarily with diagnosing pathology and treating it. In my own experience, the average medically trained psychoanalyst knew no other psychology than the Freudian. Thus, for example, attention would be drawn to emotional "blocks" deterring learning, with only a limited understanding of physiological conditions which also interfere with ability to learn. More recently, however, a group of distinguished Freudians has argued the importance of such "normal" processes and the "conflict-free" spheres of the personality (Hartmann, 1958). Analysts have extended their efforts in two directions beyond those first

envisaged: on the one hand, they deal with patients much sicker than those originally served; on the other, there has been a steady increase in the effort to apply their learnings in prevention and in helping people to use their full capacities.

5. *Synthetic functions:* It must already be apparent that the headings of the various ego functions are not mutually exclusive but simply convenient handles by which to grasp an interdependent network of ideas. The *"synthetic function of the ego"* is involved in many other processes, including the ability, indeed the tendency, to try to bring one's thoughts, motives, and in the final analysis one's life into a coherent whole. The reader may already have encountered the "tendency toward closure" among the Gestalt principles of perception: a circle that is not quite closed will be seen, at quick glance, as a circle. A similar idea is contained in Festinger's (1964) well-known theory of cognitive dissonance in social psychology, predicting, among other things, that once a decision is taken, relevant perceptions will be weighted selectively to justify the commitment. At a grander level, the synthetic function is implicated in Erikson's (1950) concept of Ego Identity. The principle may be simply stated; its ramifications are manifold. The clinical orientation of Freudian theory makes it possible to recognize that the synthetic function is more in evidence in some types of clients than in others. As we shall see, its strength or weakness affects treatability.

This book emerged from the conviction that there is by now a body of psychoanalytic theory that can be fairly readily grasped and which will greatly help a beginning social worker, therapist or counselor. Most of the theory presented here is a synthesis and reformulation of ideas I learned from others. Some, naturally, rests on my own observations in doing treatment, in research and in teaching. Scarcely a week passes that something is not added to what I thought I knew, but my intent is not to give *my* version but the one generally accepted as fundamental in knowledgeable circles. Any area of knowledge as large and complicated as ego psychology is highly vulnerable to interpretive biases, to the selective attention and inattention of the presenter. One would disqualify himself as a Freudian if he presumed his own version were magically immune to these universal psychological processes. Nevertheless, the person receiving an introduction to the theory needs a reasonably balanced overview, one that is fairly noncontroversial. Special points of view and argumentation are matters for later study. The book will have done its job if it permits the student to later elaborate his knowledge of theory contained here without having to make major retreats from what he has learned.

The later chapters, drawn from my own work on verbal communication, group psychology and the like present claims not yet widely accepted in the field; such parts, pretty much pure Polansky—and I know it—will be so labelled.

CHAPTER 2
A SPEED READER'S GUIDE TO
Basic Freudian Conceptions

Ego psychology is a branch of Freud's larger theory. Its basic terms and assumptions derive from it, so we must summarize the larger whole.

Freud's theory emerged out of day-to-day work: the focus was as much on patients as ideas. Growth was not always logical; concepts evolved and were put in order later.

Analytic theory can be organized in terms of *metatheoretical conceptions*, or points of view about personality. *Ideas* and *images* in the mind are the subject matter of psychoanalysis. They may be divided in terms of accessibility to *conscious attention*. Viewed *topographically*, ideas are *conscious*, *preconscious* or *unconscious*. Many unconscious *impulses* are *repressed* to spare us *anxiety*. *Guilt anxiety* arises from an impulse for which you anticipate punishment; it represents *conflict*. *Separation anxiety* will be discussed later. Freud surmised that much *neurosis* stems from inner conflicts.

The *structural approach* evolved in part to describe conflict within the mind in terms of ego, superego and id. The *id* has to do with *instinctual drives*, *sex* or *libido*, and *aggression*. The *superego* contains the conscience. Sources of *psychic energy*, its *channeling* and alterations are discussed as the *economic conception*. *Raw drives* visible in infants rarely appear in adult behavior; rather, we see *drive derivatives*. Besides the drives, *anxiety avoidance*, *survival needs* and *stimulus hunger* are other sources of energy. Most behavior is *overdetermined*, has more than one source. Energy is discharged as *behavior*, *ideation*, *affect* or in some combination.

We will discuss the *genetic* and *psychosocial* conceptions later.

Basic Freudian Conceptions 2

I frequently find myself defending the Freudian movement. Whether it deserves this defense is arguable; that it has needed defending at times is not. Especially against some of its adherents.

Many psychoanalysts who taught colleagues in other professions were the psychiatric equivalents of general practitioners, not the investigators and scholars who created theory, but the technicians who applied it. Most of us rather uncritically adopted the fragmented version of analytic psychology that pervaded social casework practice twenty-five years ago, which had not been very profoundly explained to us.

One result of this naïveté was that what should have been taught as a science was purveyed as a religion. With no real grasp of the issues involved in theory construction, our teachers nevertheless demanded respectfulness and reverence. The disciples of a charismatic rebel like Freud always busy themselves in establishing a new orthodoxy in his name. But the disciples of disciples are the most sectarian generation, and we were in contact with these men and women.

It is typical of such ideological movements that the area of strictness shifts from substance to form. Because many of our teachers did not fully understand analytic theory, they were most rigorous about details of clinical practice, particularly the classical technique then in vogue and still usually associated with psychoanalysis. The patient lies on a couch in a quiet, darkened room, with the analyst seated in a chair at the head of the couch, outside his/her realm of vision. The patient is then instructed to follow "the basic rule," saying aloud everything that comes into his mind. This is a ridiculous injunction. Often two or three thoughts enter one's mind at once, some of what enters is in the form of images that are not verbally communicable anyhow, and so forth.

These *attempts* at free association had led to a number of profound inferences about human behavior. The analyst typically remained relatively silent, even noncommunicative, except to encourage the patient's flow of speech. From time to time, however, s/he might make an "interpretation" of what the patient seemed to be unfolding. The idea was that a better conscious understanding of one's motives and emotions would gradually lead to cure. The material provided by the patient was grist for the analyst's inferential mill. If the analyst—having examined his/her own thoughts, the last few articles read, and intuition—made an interpretation, the patient was supposed to accept it as a revelation of his/her unconscious. Not to accept it was said to be "resisting," and the reasons for this resistance must then be analyzed. Obviously, at fifteen dollars per hour, a large sum of money to a caseworker earning sixty-five dollars per week, it was important to try not to resist, but to hurry up and get better. Even the private mythology of dream interpretations, custom-crafted at tedious expense, was to be accepted gratefully.

Now, there is a lot that is right about the classical technique, and few who used it were fools or charlatans. But, in my judgment, and that of many others of my generation, it cannot be regarded as a form of treatment that yielded substantial results for our friends or ourselves. There is now grave doubt whether it was appropriate for many to whom it was so slavishly applied. Some famous social workers, who brought the fruits of their own experience of psychoanalysis into our field and whose work is part of its history, continued to be unpleasant, narcissistic, and downright odd, even as they questioned whether anyone should be trusted to do social casework who had not had the benefits of a personal analysis!

But the rigidity of the Freudians was accepted as at least better than the absence of any standards at all which pervaded so much of American psychiatry in those days. Patients were financially drained; lonely patients seduced their psychiatrists and vice versa; psychiatrists involved wealthy dependent patients and ex-patients in joint business ventures; therapists and patients moved from professional to buddy relationships; patients became cheap institutional labor or disciples of the "great doctor." All these things went on, and continue to go on, of course. They also went on among the Freudians. But there was less of it.

The worst by-product was an inability to discriminate between intellectual curiosity, or scientific skepticism, and resistance. I still recall my experience in the first (and only) Freudian seminar it has been my privilege to attend. Our teacher was the senior, distinguished analyst in town, a member of Freud's original Viennese circle. Although he was a Gentile and married to a baroness (who also practiced lucratively), his teaching style recalled the methods employed in the rabbinical seminars of Europe. To learn theory, one person would read aloud from Freud's famous seventh chapter in the *Interpretation of Dreams*, where he sums up his theory. Then the meaning of the section was propounded, sentence by sentence. The room was crowded, the chairs uncomfortable (if you did not end up on the floor). For me the whole thing was a conflict. On the one hand, I was unable to stay away because it was supposed to be a great privilege to be allowed to attend if one were not a medically trained therapist. On the other, it was tedious, confused, and a strain to maintain the aura of sanctimony. Torn between narcissism and stinginess, I used to recall Lord Chesterfield's advice to his son, "As for carnal relations, the pleasure is momentary, the expense is out of all proportion, and the position is ridiculous."

One evening we came across a section in which, in terms of my recent doctoral training, it seemed evident to me that Freud had declared a serious error in logic. Rousing from my fear of being revealed as the tyro I was, I piped up and said so. Dr. X destroyed me utterly. After all, I had now been *analyzed*, a state of grace otherwise reserved for those whose grandfathers also had attended Harvard or the holy men who wash in the Ganges. Dr. X stared at me through his prominent spectacles and in cold dismissal remarked, "Well, if you do not accept this statement, then you do not accept any of it." The class then adverted to a written report on the forthcoming night's reading from one of its bright boys who had summarized Freud into 1.7 times his original length. I broke into a cold sweat, and my "transference cure" was never again the same.

I do not now think it is good for patients, or for anyone, to accept statements made by therapists on faith. A patient should understand what he is able to with *all* his faculties, including his critical ability and his adult suspiciousness if he is to grow up and become more integrated. It is especially dangerous for a practitioner to accept a theory of treatment on the basis of the prestige of its author or its current popularity in his field.

As we now embark on what may be the most important set of

propositions a caseworker can learn from the Freudians, I want to make one point clear: these are not ideas to be accepted on faith. Neither is one expected to skip over gaps in logic by appealing to intuition. Once the premises underlying a theory are accepted as plausible, or at least conceivably true, the rest should follow openly, clearly, and logically. Freud was not a new messiah, but simply a scientist having unusual difficulties in gaining acceptance because of the propinquity of his unpleasant discoveries to thought itself. The fact that their observations were unwelcome lent a conspiratorial air to the deliberations of the earlier Freudians which some of them must have enjoyed, because long after their theory had swept the field in psychiatry they continued to regard themselves as a beleaguered band of revolutionaries. But these social processes should have no consequences for the student's learning what he can of the intellectual outcome of the movement.

Clinical Beginnings

To those who have never worked on constructing theories, they must appear to arrive in this world fully developed. After all, one does not publish one's gropings and confusions. Concepts are identified and defined; assumptions are clearly stated; laws are expounded. The whole has a coherence and polish that makes it seem to have been born fully clothed and toilet trained. In fact, only the theories that emerge from armchair musings have developed so suddenly. Theories that try to order the happenings of the real world typically come into being after many false starts, turnings and reversals.

Certainly, this has been true of psychoanalytic theory. To understand it, it is useful to have a notion of the circumstances surrounding its birth. For good and for ill, these have left permanent marks on the undertaking. An awareness that the theory has by now had nearly a century of development helps keep the student aware of another aspect. When one asks, "What is Freudian theory?" the answer has to take into account the follow-up, "Of what era?" For some critiques of the theory do not recognize that its proponents also became aware of defects in it, and have long since moved to clarify or correct them.

When he invented psychoanalysis, Freud was not setting out to write a general theory of personality. For one thing, he did not regard himself as a psychologist. He was a fairly young physician, recently married and starting a family. He had been well trained in neurology, and was setting up his practice in that discipline. As a specialist, his livelihood depended on referrals from other doctors. And, in this respect, he had some disadvantages.

The time was a century ago, the place Vienna. When we think of this capital of the Austro-Hungarian Empire, we think of lovely ladies and resplendent cavalry officers dancing to the music of the Strausses; we think of kitsch and pastry, charm and wit. But, Vienna was also the seat of the Hapsburgs, so expert at marrying into kingdoms, so poor at defending them. Spain has still not fully recovered from their dour and fanatically conservative rule. Underneath the bemedaled tunics beat many a bigoted heart. The aristocrats who dominated the power structure were not the brightest minds of Europe, but their status-happy socializing was adopted throughout the society. Sigmund Freud was a Jew, and not even a rich one. No social favors were to be curried by referring patients to him. So, his best hope was to acquire expert prestige, to make a reputation by linking his name to important medical discoveries. Freud was not wanting in brilliance or ambition, but major discoveries do not come easily. He had already, for example, enthusiastically described the anesthetic powers of cocaine—but had to retreat when the addictive potentiality of that drug became apparent.

Of the patients sent to Freud for neurological consultation, a number were diagnosed as hysterics. Such a patient had symptoms for which no physical cause could be found, but which seemed very real to him or to her. Some of the syndromes described in those days are now rarely or never seen, such as "glove anesthesia," an inability to use the hand or even feel anything in an area starting at a fairly neat line around the wrist and ending in the fingers. A moment's reflection will convince us that, of course, the nerves to the lower arm and hand do not follow such a neat configuration, but patients with vague notions of anatomy found it easy to believe themselves physically disabled.

How to treat such a condition? Progress had been made by some French physicians, including Charcot and Janet. It had been found that if the patient were hypnotized, the symptom could often be eliminated by a strong suggestion, during the trance, that when the patient awoke it would be gone. It had also been noted that many a patient could recall under hypnosis the shocking or frightening events which precipitated the hysterical reaction, even though these were gone from the patient's memory in a normal waking state. So, the powers of what some were calling the sub-conscious mind, in literature and philosophy as well as in psy-

chiatry, were receiving speculative attention. During his neurological training Freud spent months in France, and was acquainted
with the ideas involved.

There were, however, limitations to the use of hypnosis. Fore-
most was the fact that not everyone is susceptible to hypnosis,
which meant a substantial proportion of patients could not be
helped by this technique. Freud also had misgivings about a
method of treatment in which the patient took so little active part
Given such acquiescence, what was the gain in self-knowledge?
And, why might not the patient replace the symptom removed by
suggestion with another? He sought other ways of trying to bring
to light the buried reasons for the symptom, and hit on the use of
free association. The "classical technique" has been alluded to
earlier in this chapter. The purposes of having the patient relaxed
in a quiet room with even the physician out of the range of vision
and otherwise inactive was to encourage the flow of associations,
uninfluenced by the therapist, unselected by the patient. The hope
was that by listening closely to the patterns of associations one
could grasp the hidden dynamics of the condition.

All this story is, of course, simplified for exposition and tele-
scoped in time. But, the important thing to note is that psychoanalysis was invented as a treatment tactic by a man whose living
depended on finding cures. Far different from the armchair speculation of much of current academic psychology, the theory was
based on daily observations of patients and tested against the
pragmatic criterion: Does it work? The appeal to busy social workers
of a psychological approach founded in daily practice is obvious.

An important assumption in Freud's work was that mental contents are real and influence behavior and bodily states. The subject matter, as one listens to associations, is the patients' mental
imagery, as well as he or she can report it. Therefore, the contents
under scrutiny by psychoanalysis are the *ideas, images* and *impulses
in the patient's mind*. These ideas and images may have a relationship to "external reality" as others perceive it, but the two are not
the same. Even if the patient's world view is distorted, every idea
that s/he has of it is *real*, and affects current life and health. Freud
was not indifferent to the patient's physical condition and processes. After all, his basic training was in medicine, and he thought
that some day the physical bases of neurosis might well be discovered. As that was not possible in his day, he distinguished
between the *psi* system, the mental, and the *phi* system, or physical.
Psychoanalysis concerns the former.

It is important to keep the epistemological position in mind. It differs from that of a number of theories in economics and sociology. Some take it for granted that the image you have in your mind is an exact reflection of your "objective" situation—which is a naïve idea, of course. Marxists, for example, propound that a person's idea of the world and the world as it actually is (who decides that one?) are not the same. The Marxist position maintains that people adjust their beliefs about the world to fit their objective and material realities, so that those doing well in a capitalistic society, for example, naturally support that system. The mental processes by which such self-serving adaptations take place are not examined in Marxist theory, for after all, the same analytical tools might be turned against the theoretician. In any event, in theory, mental content is considered the dependent variable, physical reality the independent. Psychoanalysis, on the other hand, does not assign weights to the mind/body dichotomy. While recognizing their interdependence, it is primarily concerned with analyzing mental content.

The Topographic Conception

Freud sedulously followed free associations to discover hidden causes of symptoms. Thus, he began by sorting the ideas he was hearing into three categories. The criterion for this first categorization was whether the patient was able to bring the idea he seemed to have in mind under the spotlight of attention. Some ideas and images were, in fact, being currently attended to; these Freud labelled *conscious*. Other ideas could be focused on at will but were not being attended to at the moment. Most students, for example, can recite their parents' telephone numbers, even if their thoughts have just been on something else, like psychoanalytic theory. Ideas thus readily brought to attention Freud called *preconscious*.

The third category represented a major theoretical advance. Freud posited a set of ideas, images, impulses, present in the mind which the patient cannot bring into the full light of conscious attention even if he wants to. These he labelled *unconscious* as distinguished from the older, vaguer term, *sub*conscious. This unconscious was surely a strange notion of Freud's. His information came entirely from the patient; he was discussing the patient's ideas, not his own. Yet, he said there were ideas in the patient's mind that the patient could not directly report because he could not bring them to consciousness. How, then, did the analyst decide such content existed?

The decision was based not on direct reports, of course, but on *inferences* drawn from listening to and observing the patient. At first glance, clinical inference seems a shaky basis for thinking about patients, but it is not really so tenous. I can explain it best, I think, by asking the reader to keep in mind the expression "as if" (in Latin, *qua si*). Take this homely example. You have been seeing a patient for four months and are usually scrupulous about keeping scheduled appointments on time. Today, the client arrived eagerly, the secretaries say, and ten minutes early. But, you have had an emergency, and are fifteen minutes late. The patient flounces into your office, is seated, leans forward, and begins, "I'm not sure why I came today. I don't really want to be here." Which shall you believe, the actions or the words? What hypothesis or "model" will fit what is going on?

It does not take great imagination to suppose that the client wanted very much to see you but is now reacting to feelings of unrequited love. So, you ask if the upset is because you are late. This is denied, "I have just been wondering about this whole treatment business." So far as you can tell, s/he is not angry, that is, s/he is not aware of feeling anger. But, the reaction is *as if* s/he were angry. Indeed, inferring rage offers the most parsimonious explanation of the attitude.

Some scientists object to clinical inference. They prefer explanations in terms of observable events. However, since even behaviorists began to accept such notions as "intervening variables" (Tolman, 1932), the proportion of pure empiricists has declined. Others simply cannot hold complicated sets of information in mind and test them against "as if" models in their heads. They, too, cannot use psychoanalytic theorizing. For, when Freud identified unconscious impulses to action, he was utilizing *constructs* (see Chapter 1).

The evidence of the existence of unconscious ideas and impulses comes from a variety of sources in addition to patients' free-associations—from humor, slips of the tongue, and dreams. It is thought that one determinant of what makes a joke funny is whether it facilitates the sudden emergence into conscious attention of an impulse previously kept unconscious. A friend of mine once introduced a colleague he thought rather stuffy by ending a complimentary set of remarks with, "And I know of no one less qualified to speak on this subject than Dr. Luftmensch." So, slips of the tongue sometimes reveal thoughts that have been suppressed or actually repressed.

From the wish-fulfillment function of dreams also we learn the role of needs in affecting the ideas that come to mind. Not all dreams serve this function, be it noted, but some dreams portray wishes carefully kept unconscious when the person is in a waking state. Some examples are even simpler and clearer, like dreaming of going to the bathroom to urinate, on a cold Wintry evening, only to awaken just in time to realize the call of nature. The dream made it possible to "satisfy" the need without facing the cold room.

The types of "consciousness" referred to above were, of course, adjectives. Except as descriptors of specific ideas, they had no referents. It was not long, however, before Freud began to use them as nouns. He spoke of the Unconscious, the Preconscious and of Consciousness as if they were place names in the mind. Why the reification? It provides a kind of shorthand. Instead of speaking tediously each time of unconscious images, ideas, impulses. . . . Such a shorthand was needed, for Freud rather soon began to attempt generalizations that went beyond why a specific idea was unconscious to why *any* idea might be in that status. Besides, the possibility cannot be discounted that the founder of psychoanalysis had his moments of grandiloquence.

So there was now a model of mental landscape as a hilly country, viewed in a setting sun. The highest ground remains vivid; parts of the hillsides are fairly visible in reflected light; all lower areas and valleys are hidden in darkness. Perhaps because of such imagery, the first tripartite division of mental content is known as the topographic conception.

But to label mental ideas in terms of their accessibility to attention was only descriptive. Certainly, it explained little. Trained in the determinism of his day, Freud could not assume the state of consciousness was accidental, that it just happened, as a poet might. The next important step was to assume that *mental events also follow cause/effect relationships*. This assumption, too, was a major breakthrough. Even among psychologists, few had grasped that what we think or feel has to be explained as rigorously as what we do. The idea is staggering to many of us, as it was to philosophers like David Hume (1890). Not only do we notice that we are thinking about thinking, but now we must ask *why* we are thinking *what* we are thinking about thinking. And, why we were thinking about thinking in the first place. Once convinced the last two sentences are not nonsense, one must fight the temptation simply to give up the issue. Among its other consequences, Freud's determinism makes it necessary to live with the knowledge that the most important tool we have for understanding the world, our thought process, is both the subject and the object of study.

To explain why some ideas are unconscious, Freud drew on imagery from mechanics. If one tried to recall an event but could not, even though it seemed on the tip of the tongue, some mental—or psychic—force must be preventing its becoming conscious. He spoke of the idea as being *repressed*, and the process by which something once conscious becomes unconscious as *repression*. We also refer to the *force of repression*. The conception of forces at work led to another logical step. If you are trying to remember, you are exerting a force to recall the idea; if you cannot, there is an opposite force that is, at the moment, somewhat stronger. The opposition between these two forces represents a *conflict*.

Freud used the conflict model at various points in his developing theory. It represented an important advance in recognizing complexities in motivation. Take for example, an instance of amnesia, the inability to remember. A victim of rape might be totally unable to recall her attacker's appearance. This might be interpreted as meaning that the memory was erased by the chemistry of shock; one might also guess that the victim was afraid to attract further attack. The truth, however, could be that she consciously wants to describe her assailant to the police, but something inside her cannot stand to image his face again. Writers have always envisaged people in conflict, usually between themselves and outside forces. The author of Hamlet depicted contending forces within the person; Freud emphasized that one of these forces is often unconscious.

One knows intuitively that even when no action results, to be in a state of conflict uses psychic energy, just as opposing muscle groups against each other takes physiological energy. We also know that concentrating, paying close attention, is an expensive form of psychic energy, rapidly running down our psychological batteries. But it is also an effort *not* to let yourself attend to something, not to notice it. From the conflict model we are reminded that keeping an idea repressed takes energy too. The guess that maintaining repression uses up energy was to have important meaning for the Freudian theory of treatment.

Note that *suppression* has a very different meaning from repression. By suppression we refer to a state in which the person is quite conscious of an idea, but does not want to talk about it. All of us withhold critical thoughts we may have about others' dress or manners as a matter of ordinary courtesy, and there is probably more danger of letting such thoughts slip out if they are repressed rather than suppressed. Distorted reports by clients sometimes represent outright lying, of course, but lying drops out entirely as most treatment relationships continue. More often, distortions are the facts as the client is able to know them.

The Structural Conception

At some point, the theoreticians of psychoanalysis began to group their terms along the lines they called *metatheoretical* conceptions. Now, metatheory means beyond theory; it is not a theory of human behavior, but a theory about how to build theory, like General Systems Theory. The various Freudian "conceptions," which Rapaport called points of view (1960), refer to differing angles from which to examine mental processes. Put another way, it is always the same cake you are cutting. But the stroke of the knife yields different kinds of information about it. A vertical cut makes the layers stand out; a horizontal one makes its roundness apparent.

The topographic conception supported the effort to surmise what was going on behind the patient's symptoms, but it also raised more specific questions that demanded elaboration of the theory. If there was conflict within the patient, how should it be depicted? Conflict between what, or between whom? It would be circular to say that the patient's Conscious was in conflict with his Unconscious, and therefore an image was repressed and became unconscious. More terms were needed. Over a period of time, Freud evolved the concepts subsumed under the *structural conception*: the *ego*, the *id*, and the *superego*.

By *id*, we refer to the great instinctual strivings, "the ultimate drive determiners" within the personality (Rapaport, 1960, p. 54). To personify it, you might call the id the "dirty old man" of the psyche.

The *ego*, on the other hand, also enters into every piece of behavior, but its function is to assist *adaptation*. Traditionally, it has been described as operating to synthesize the demands from the id, the superego, and external reality. The ego, then, is a general term given to a complicated organization of psychological functions and abilities, including perceiving the world, processing information, learning and using skills, steering behavior, regulating drive discharge, helping the personality find ways for discharging drives, relating to other people, and—as we shall soon see—coping with internally created problems like anxiety. The ego covers a very wide range of all psychological functioning; its psychoanalytic study is still in the early stages. The part of the client's personality that the social worker first becomes aware of is naturally that subsumed under the ego. For that reason I now feel the student's introduction to Freudian theory should be via ego psychology, rather than the study of the drives, as in my day.

The *superego* is meant to be something very like the conscience, but without certain overtones. Some people flaunt their consciences, saying, "My conscience is shinier and stricter than yours." The biological function of the conscience, however, is to keep one out of trouble so as to maximize pleasure and minimize pain. In this sense, the superego also serves to help adaptation, so it is really to be seen as a specialized segment of the ego. The ability to acquire a superego is not limited to humans. A dog who has "had an accident" while you are out will slink around looking sheepish, to mix a metaphor. The ability to develop a superego is an enormous convenience for humans, since so much of its content is taken over from other people. While this may limit one, in that an adult may still feel bound by a mother's injunctions that realistically applied only to a three year old, adopting other people's standards also means we do not have to learn all dangers from our own experiences. Taking it for granted that "We do not touch the stove" can save many a burn. The processes by which the superego and indeed all controls become internalized, as part of the person, will be discussed in Chapter 4.

During the development of these concepts the term ego (in German, *Ich*, I) was used somewhat interchangeably with conscious, to express the sense of selfhood, the "I" in the personality. The id was identified with the unconscious. Remnants of this older confusion are still found in texts offering diagrams showing overlaps among the terms. Actually, a bit of thought will demonstrate that while much of the id is usually unconscious, it certainly is not totally so. For example, one commonly knows when one is sexually aroused, or hungry, or needs to go to the bathroom. Nor is the ego all conscious, by any means. One of its major functions, as we shall see, is to help us cope by keeping certain thoughts and impulses repressed. In short, the two metatheoretical conceptions of the mind are to be thought of as independent. Hence, it would not be talking nonsense to say that an idea was repressed by the ego, that is, made unconscious, because it was associated with an impulse from the id which the superego found intolerable. It might not be saying much, but it would not be circular nonsense.

The Economic Conception

The economic conception concerns the energies fueling the personality. If the structural viewpoint describes its engine, the economic conception refers to the source and fate of the gasoline we put in the car. We may say that it has to do with the drives and their vicissitudes.

The psychological drives, also called instinctual drives or basic drives, are *sex* and *aggression*. Two seemed to Freud the minimum needed to explain behavior. The *sexual* drive has to do with what we think of as sex, of course, but it also refers to more general pleasure seeking and may be termed *libido*. Aggression has to do with impulses to attack and destroy, and the feeling or *affect* that accompanies this drive is often called *hostility*, although rage, anger and the like will also do. Although Freud's neurological training encouraged his seeking physical bases for psychological events, basic anatomy and physiology were not far enough along when these concepts were developed to permit such connections. They are thought of as psychological drives, born into each human because they had *survival value* in the evolution of mankind. The reader will recall from biology courses that traits have survival value if they contribute to the survival of the individual, and/or the continuation of the species. Those individuals who have useful traits reproduce, and in that sense are "fittest." The role of sex in the continuation of the race is not much in the minds of those practicing it most assiduously, but the potential is there. Many think of aggression as signifying an attempt "to push the world around" to get one's needs met, as when the enraged infant demands his bottle.

Influenced by Darwin, psychologists of the late nineteenth and twentieth centuries explained behavior in terms of inborn instincts. McDougall's (1932) hormic theory discussed eighteen "native propensities," including the acquisitive, the migratory, and the propensity to laughter. Such proliferation does not make for parsimonious theorizing and is believed by many to overlook learned behavioral patterns. Moreover, instincts are also constructs, distasteful to those who prefer to study things directly observable. But even the learning theorists who provide the base for behavior modification techniques have to assume at least some innate drives or tensions. How else can they account for why some consequents of action are "rewarding" or positively reinforcing (Skinner, 1969)? The assumption that there are inborn drives which seek expression or "drive-reduction" is not unique to analytic theory.

In addition to the instincts of sex and aggression, there are other sources of psychological energy encountered in Freudian theory useful for the student to identify separately. If one of your cases is involved in a behavior, and you find it impossible to imagine how it is giving pleasure, or expressing aggression, what else might you look for? The next most likely candidate when there seems to be no drive reduction in the picture is anxiety. Anxiety is *not* a drive but a feeling, an emotion, or an *affect* as the analysts call it. But, anxiety is so unpleasant a feeling that avoiding it becomes a quasi-drive; it acts as if it were a drive. The next most important source of energy might be called anxiety avoidance. The defenses are called into play for this as we shall see below.

Another source of energy seems more physiological than psychological. The human infant can live minutes without air, hours without water, days without food. In the study of early infancy, and in some other contexts, we have to take into account the energy source called *survival needs*. They are terribly at stake at times among clients we see, and so we have to take their existence into account in our theorizing.

For completeness, one must also include *stimulus hunger*. At times the human organism acts as if the sensory organs themselves ask to be stimulated or are "hungry" to be used. For instance, when a subject is placed for hours in a darkened room, sound-proofed, floating in a tub with water near body temperature, it has been found that hallucinations of sights and sounds may occur, and do occur among a minority of cases. Failing external stimulation, the sensory organs seem to fire of their own volitions. Stimulus hunger has also been noted in studies of very young infants. Contrary to early notions, Wolff (1960) observed that young babies have periods of alert wakefulness not because of hunger but more often *after* feeding. Some sociologists were carried away by similar observations to the point that they presumed everyone, without exception, needs things like change and adventure—a generalization that does not fit what others have termed the "imbecility of rural life." However, few of those we see in our offices or their homes receive no light, sound, odor or other stimulation. We include stimulus hunger in the list, but not with the thought that this motivation will very often be relevant for thinking about cases.

Let us now image psychic energy as water stored behind a dam, with the capacity to perform work, like dropping through a turbine to generate electricity. We need only harness the potential force to use the energy, which we do in part by leading the water through prepared pipes or channels. We may now ask, "Through what channels may psychic energy be discharged?" The question implies that needs and drives, aroused but unsatisfied, seek discharge; it also implies that *everything* that happens in the human personality involves the expenditure of energy, that *all* behavior is motivated. The latter is a specific case of the principle of strict determination discussed earlier.

The channels through which psychic energy is discharged can be listed at a highly abstract level. They reduce to three basic types of activity: action, ideation and affect. By *action* we have in mind the fact that one way we express a motivation is by *doing* something about it. When you are hungry, you find food and eat; when you are angry, you try to hurt the person you are angry with. The thought that behavior is motivated will not be new to the reader, naturally, although the assumption that no behavior happens that does not express a motivation takes some getting used to.

Less familiar to most of us is the notion that *ideation*, producing an image in the mind, or thinking about something, must also be seen as a way of discharging energy, if we follow strict determination. Thus, if one is hungry, but at the moment no food is available one *thinks* about eating. It is no accident that committees meeting from 4:30 to 6:30 so often talk about recipes. A rationalistic psychology gives the student the impression that action follows ideation: first you have a thought and then you act on it. But, Freudian theory implies that *both* the thought and the action stem from the same basic drive or other energy source. If you are hungry, you are apt to think about food and, given the chance, you will shortly eat.

Ideation, in fact, is regarded in Freudian theory as providing a channel which "substitutes" for action. Nor are the Freudians alone. "Them as can, do; them as can't teach" is an old American saying. Similarly, it has been suggested that all imagery and ideation begin when the infant, hungry but unfed, hallucinates the mother's breast in her absence while making sucking gestures with his lips. Unable to get the breast, the baby "detours" into ideation. To regard ideation as a substitute declares it second best for discharging energy. Can thinking about sex make up for having none? In the U.S. Army during World War II there was a well-known joke which confirmed the substitution, while answering the question in the negative, "Sex is something you can get farther behind on, and caught up faster on, than anything else." To the

GIs involved, ideation was clearly an unsatisfactory form of *sublimation*, but there are many people who are, in fact, willing to settle for thinking without taking action. Some of them will be discussed later when we encounter the *character types*.

The use of *drive reduction* in these examples should not mislead the reader; anxiety avoidance also energizes ideation. Often, what we worry about is meant to distract us from other issues that would be even more uncomfortable. I once knew a man weighing three hundred pounds who, in his early thirties, was diabetic and had ominously high blood-pressure. His wife told us that he saw no reason to diet, because he was convinced he had cancer—for which there was absolutely no evidence!

In ordinary living, most of us do not burden ourselves with misgivings about why we are thinking what we are thinking. However, in the classical analytic situation, it will be recalled, much of what the therapist had to work with were the patient's reports of the ideas and images passing through his or her mind. The presumptions that these thoughts were, in the first place, not accidental and that, in the second, they probably reflected motivational patterns which were enduring facets of the patient's makeup, made it possible for the analyst to use the associations as clues to the unconscious sources of the patient's symptoms. As the Sherlock Holmes of psychic mysteries, it was natural for the analyst to ask, "I wonder what was meant by that?" And, "Why *this* recollection so closely on the heels of the last one?"

Perhaps even stranger for the reader is the notion that energy may also be channeled into *affect*. By affect is meant emotion, or feeling. We naïvely presume that first we are angry, and then we strike out at the person we hate, that the feeling "causes" the behavior. But in this theory, affect is often an epiphenomenon; like the handle of the teacup "it is there but not in it." So, the model is that the aggressive drive becomes aroused, and this in turn gives rise to thinking about how to hurt, to trying to inflict the hurt, *and* to feeling angry at the same time. The affect accompanies the rest of the package; it does not "cause" the action. Affect, like action and ideation, may also be harnessed to anxiety avoidance. Few of us who played football or boxed as young men experienced anxiety consciously during contact sports. Instead, we were likely to feel competitive or determined or even angry. In other words, there was the motivated use of one affect in place of another through a *defense mechanism* we shall later specify as *substitution*. Clients often try to conceal anxiety from themselves with anger.

The Complexity of Human Motivations

When I was being trained in psychology over four decades ago, we had a simplistic notion of human motivation and did not realize it. Thus, we would argue whether a man who was mean and sadistic inflicted pain on others because he found pleasure in watching them suffer, *or* because he made himself appear superior by humiliating them. In other words, true to our version of strict determinism, we sought *the* motivation for the action. But, our arguments were often pointless because we were not, in fact, dealing with an either/or relationship. Both motivations might be present and in many concrete instances both were. So the sadist was channeling more than one form of psychic energy into his activity. Not to mention the old quip that a sadist is someone who is kind to masochists. The phenomenon by which the person uses the same action—or idea or affect—to satisfy more than one need is called *overdetermination* in Freudian psychology.

The principle of overdetermination simply reminds us that the human personality is shrewd enough to get more than one satisfaction out of the same action. An example of this principle which we were taught early on was "secondary gain through illness." Having produced a leg paralysis, let us say, to solve an unconscious conflict, the young woman became the focus of affection from her whole family. So she now had *two* good reasons for keeping her symptom. Most patterns in people that persist over any length of time are enlisted by the personality to serve more than one purpose. It is not at all unusual for the purposes served to combine conscious and unconscious motivations. Typically, in the example given, the pleasure gained from familial sympathy is close to consciousness and the patient can see that readily, but the original reason for the symptom remains stubbornly hidden.

Freud took cognizance of the complexity in people when he identified conflicts. The little boy, momentarily furious because his father has punished him, has an urge to kick him. This urge "comes into conflict with" powerful feeling that one ought not, or dare not, attack a parent. Speaking generally, we might say that the hostile, forbidden impulse arose within the *id;* the impulse *not to* attack one's father, within the *superego.* In learning any new vocabulary, including the psychoanalytic, it is important to try to use terms precisely. This is especially important for students, since they have the remainder of their professional lives in which to obscure and forget what the terms mean; and they will have ample help from colleagues, including me, in watering down the precision of their language!

Let us remind ourselves, then, that a conflict implies *two* forces in opposition to each other. To say the person is still guilty because he or she had hostile urges toward a parent in childhood downplays the other side: that this youngster was also capable of wanting to restrain the hostility. Take the same conception from the other direction. To speak of a person as "guilt-ridden" may mislead us, in our compassion, from recognizing that the same person must be harboring impulses that he or she, at least, feels to be dreadful and forbidden. Would not real empathy require us to go the full distance with the client and be willing to discover the "bad" impulse along with the guilt it leaves in its wake? The *two* forces?

How may conflicts get resolved? Schematically, there are a number of possible outcomes. If the impulse is very strong, it overcomes the restraint, which can lead to murder and may be followed by guilt so strong that a murder/suicide occurs. (This, of course, is a very dramatic example!) If the restraints are very weak, if—as we say—the person does not have much of a superego at all, or has a Swiss cheese superego—meaning a conscience that can easily locate loopholes in its own legal code—then s/he may act on the impulse with little or no guilt. For instance, take the fellow who would certainly never steal your money but who, on the other hand, would make little effort to return lost money saying, "Anybody who would leave his wallet lying around deserves to lose it." Another outcome of a conflict happens when the restraints against an action are strong enough to stop it. Most growing children rarely attack their parents, even verbally, and not just because they are afraid of being beaten for doing so. It is worth noting at this point that while the theory's notion of conflict is very general and universally applicable, analysis does not assume that each person responds to conflict in the same way. The theory allows for individual differences in reaction; what happens "depends on" other factors about the person. To fill in these other factors requires a larger theory of personality, and a more complicated one, and we can already see that any theory that skimps too much for the sake of simplicity will be forced to overgeneralize about what people do.

But to return to our discussion. If the child does not permit himself to discharge his aggressive impulse directly into action, what happens to the impulse? A very nice maneuver would be for the ego to find a way to express the hostility, while keeping the conscience reasonably happy. An enraged little boy could go to the basement and holler at the furnace. Since speech involves discharge into ideation, and an element of taking action and expressing affect, this shouting spell (*catharis* or *ventilation*) might be enough. Another possibility would be to sulk in his room, thinking darkly about how he will grow up and become a war hero and they will have a parade in his honor when he comes home. Of course, he will not do anything gross like snub his father on that occasion; he will be gracious and dignified. But he will know, and his father will know, that between them lies an insult never to be forgotten, even by a man now as great and decorated as he is. The boy then becomes engrossed in the details of whom he killed to become a hero, discharging more aggression into ideation, so that he starts to forget what he was mad about. He really responds too cheerfully when his father invites him downstairs for ice cream. (That is one of the dangers of dreams of glory, is it not? No dignity around the house.) But, meanwhile the ego has been doing an expert job coping with opposing forces within the boy, finding compromises that work. Question: What sort of boy do you have to be, otherwise, to go this route?

Another outcome, of course, may be for the hostile impulse to grow stronger and stronger, perhaps because of repeated paternal insults, perhaps because this youngster was born with an unusually powerful aggressive drive. Yet let us imagine that the superego restraints continue to contain the drive and block its expression. The whole uncomfortable conflict and related imagery or, speaking loosely, the whole *complex*, may simply go underground and be repressed. The sullen little boy does not even know he is angry. But, the continued existence of a powerful forbidden impulse shows itself primarily in the form of *guilt anxiety.*

At one point, Freud thought that anxiety itself represents the conversion of drives not permitted expression. In some magical way, undischarged drives are converted directly into anxiety. This notion, which in retrospect seems rather silly, implied that the way to rear children without anxiety was to let them "express themselves," to do whatever they wished. Members of the movement who followed this conclusion seemed to like their children, but others found them intolerable, and the policy was abandoned long before it was unfairly attributed to Benjamin Spock, a great pediatrician and humanitarian, and nobody's fool about child rearing. Guilt anxiety means something else. Guilt means that you feel that if you do something hostile or forbidden, the person you do it to will retaliate strongly; you will be punished in accordance with the "Talion principle." The typical target of such anger in young children is of course the mother or the father, so the image includes the notion that the person doing the punishing will be your parent. Not only do you love your parents, you are totally dependent on them. And in sheer size, compared with you at the age of two let us say, they are enormous. So, the beginning of guilt anxiety as a discernible affect originally arises in the child-parent relationship.

The "Talion principle" takes its name from the Law of Talion, the Babylonian king who prescribed, "An eye for an eye, a tooth for a tooth." Many analysts believe that, regardless of how civilized and mature the person, deep within most is a conviction that if somebody hurts you, you should get even. From this it would follow that we expect others will want to do the same if we hurt them. Hence there is the expectation of punishment making up guilt anxiety. Since our discussion of defenses will require further elaboration about anxiety, we leave this for now except to note that guilt anxiety is a major source of psychic energy at the disposal of the superego.

Even though we have been discussing some of the "great instinctual drives," we are already involved with ego psychology, with ways of *adapting* to the drives, and helping them find satisfaction or expression. A reasonably normal adult, however, does not spend much of his day coping with drives in the form they are experienced by an infant. Take the libido, or pleasure-seeking. Some infants clearly get delight from smearing. They defecate and then decorate their cribs with the proud product. Are we to assume, therefore, that when a Leonardo painted the Mona Lisa he was motivated by infantile urges to smear? Or, was that the reason Michelangelo painted the Last Judgment? An urge to smear may, indeed, have been woven into the complex blend of purposes, but it would be a terrible simplification to assume this was the only or even the primary motive.

Michelangelo, for example, was from a family with minor aristocratic pretensions but little money. Throughout his career, he sent money to his father to restore the family estates of the Buonorratis, and kept most of his own funds in gold. He also had his nose broken when a young student and for various other reasons besides his appearance seems to have been a proud, fiercely competitive, suspicious and sensitive man. Michelangelo was also well trained and fascinated with his craft, probably the greatest sculptor of all time. And he was religious in his way. No, the motivations of a Michelangelo certainly cannot be reduced to one urge. To describe the fact that adult motives so often have roots in primitive drives, but become greatly altered, subdued, harnessed and blended with other motivations, the Freudians speak of *drive-derivatives*. The conduct of a fine, helpful interview by a social worker might, it is true, partly express his defiance in having persisted in this vocation despite parental objections, but such an interview requires other motives as well—including identification with supervisors whose work one has admired. Complex behavior then, may be expressing drives, drive-derivatives and resolutions of conflict all at once. Painting the Sistine Chapel or the "Last Judgment" was surely *overdetermined behavior.*

Genetic and Other Conceptions

Scholars and systematizers of analytic theory have identified other metatheoretical conceptions. Rapaport (1960) mentions the *genetic* conception. Since so many neuroses had their roots or some of their roots in childhood experiences, it was natural for the Freudians to try to erect an image of children's psychological development, with a special interest in the emergence of drives and affects. At first, their model of child development was obtained, nearly entirely, by inferences from the analysis of adult patients, using the classical technique. The accuracy of many of their formulations, given the way they went about collecting data, was remarkable. They put together the picture of *psychosexual stages of development* that has entered the general literature on child development.

More recent work has combined such inferences with painstaking direct observation of children by gifted child analysts. We look to the genetic conception, in part, to account for major trends in character resting, for example, in childhood *fixations.* Another body of work is also concerned with the origins of patterns and symptoms in the developing child's relationships with his caretakers and the images he may have generalized to all people as a result. The depiction of the person's unfolding which assumes that the human is "social" from birth is typified by Erikson (1959). Others have contributed exciting observations as well, and Rapaport (1960) refers to Erikson's point of view as the *psychosocial* conception. We shall have much to say about the genetic and psychosocial conceptions when we turn, below, to the theory of object relations as an aspect of ego psychology.

But, enough abstract theory for now. Though I have found it impossible even to discuss ego psychology without some grounding in basic Freudian theory, I am also aware that this chapter has been a very concentrated dose. So, let us turn from the origins and vicissitudes of the drives to an early nexus of ego psychology, the mechanisms of defense.

CHAPTER 3
A SPEED READER'S GUIDE TO
Symptom and Defense

Even a limiting and painful psychological *symptom* serves an unconscious purpose. It seems preferable to experiencing conscious *anxiety*. Symptoms are often defenses; they support repression of *unacceptable*, anxiety-inducing ideas and impulses. While there is a general structure applying to all defenses, many *mechanisms of defense* have been identified and are worth learning by name. Whether they produce *symptoms* requires a value judgment.

A symptom may be hard to dislodge because it is *ego-syntonic* and/or *overdetermined*. Like a lie that needs ever more elaborate bolstering, defenses typically exist in layers. *Uncover* a defense and anxiety comes to the fore; so may the impulse that was being concealed. Uncovering techniques include *interpretation, clarification*, and *interference with* or *refusal to go along with* a defense. But, while *insight* is often helpful, we do not lightly try to take away a patient's defenses.

Symptom
and Defense

3

Once I knew a woman whose life had a tragic outcome, though what led to it might otherwise have been amusing. Very simply, her feet hurt. She was not presently standing behind counters as a salesperson, nor running up and down hospital corridors, not even shopping for a bag to match her new shoes. It was hard to find an explanation for her discomfort in her daily life. Extensive medical studies were no more enlightening. All physical findings were negative, as they say, but the pain persisted.

Eventually she met a man who offered to do what no previous doctor suggested—operate. It was never clear to me whether he believed he would really find diseased tissue in the balls of her feet. He might, indeed, have been following an idea once popular among medical primitives in this country. The notion was that if a female patient complained continuously about abdominal pain, one could relieve her mind, at least, by surgically removing some organ not essential to life. For this, the surgeon was well paid, and he also retaliated against a patient he regarded as a nuisance. One might say the medical decision was overdetermined. This interaction between well-to-do patient and physician was sufficiently widespread at one time that it was rare to find a long-term, hospitalizable neurotic who had not lost various parts of her reproductive apparatus before finally seeking out a psychiatrist. So, we have no way of knowing whether the patient's doctor was carrying out such sadistic therapy. He claimed to have found something wrong with her feet, and to have rectified it.

The patient's reaction to the good news was most disappointing, but not surprising to students of neurosis. After surgery, her pain increased from bothersome to excruciating. She became suspicious and embittered toward the surgeon and tried to sue him. She also became anxious and depressed to the point that she could not remain at home, and was hospitalized because of the danger of suicide. Now, as I said, there was reason to doubt there was anything physically wrong with this person. But, even if there had been, removal of organic disease could have led to more emotional upset. Why?

As a first approximation, we may reply that the pain, bad as it was, must have been fulfilling some need or purpose. For, when the pain was removed, or one threatened to remove it by surgery, the patient's psychological state grew worse. One might have the further hunch that if the pain in the feet served some need, the patient would have to find another expression if it were given up, or put her pain elsewhere. Because of this rough reasoning, most well trained plastic surgeons are chary of the patient who is extremely insistent on his or her need for a rhinoplasty. If the patient has been living on the illusion that by shortening his nose he will escape his other life problems, a successful nose job may leave him even more despairing than before. Suppose that even with a great profile one still is not the life of the party?

Note that we do not say the patient was getting pleasure out of her foot pain, for that seems doubtful; we simply say that she had a need for it, that it served some psychic purpose. If the symptom is not pleasurable, and does not express aggression, maybe at some level of her being it seems preferable to another feeling she might have. We will call the advantage, if any, that the poor woman was getting from her symptom a *defense*. What does that mean? Let us define defense as any maneuver a person may undertake to keep something he cannot bear to see or feel out of his awareness. A defense may also be used simultaneously to prevent him from carrying out an impulse he regards as forbidden. In other words, the purpose of defense is to keep out of consciousness that which we badly need to control (i.e. to *bind*) and to keep unconscious. A defense is like turning our eyes away, or shutting them tight, or even fainting to keep from looking at a scene that fills us with horror. The horror could be a vision of something dreadful we imagine ourselves committing.

The generic term for the process of pushing out of consciousness that which we cannot bear to bring to attention is *repression*. The many actions or twists of thinking one goes through to *maintain* repression are called *defense mechanisms*. Defense mechanisms are also described as operating "in the service of repression." If this sounds as though I am relating all the defenses to repression, that is what I am trying to do. Defense mechanisms operate like keeping your eyes shut tight, like a reflex.

But, why the effort to keep from looking? Not to look itself takes concentration. If one were to look one would feel *anxious*. We may say that the energy behind any defense mechanism, therefore, is the need to avoid feeling anxiety. Anxiety in heavy doses is among the most unpleasant of all human emotions. Most readers will have experienced anxiety at least in the form of "butterflies" in the pit of the stomach before an important interview or examination, but examination panic is mild compared to the sensations of deeply disturbed patients to whom anxiety comes in the large, economy-sized package.

It is understandable, therefore, that the woman with sore feet might *resist* the removal of a defense which was doing its job holding down her anxiety. It is equally understandable that, should the defense be penetrated or even, as we say, *threatened*, there will be an automatic response either to try to strengthen it or to find another mechanism to replace it. Should all fail, and the dreaded images with their attached dosages of anxiety come to consciousness, the patient may be overwhelmed.

Some friends of mine, working skillfully with extremely neglectful mothers, encountered a couple of women who, having given up messy life styles and tried to organize their child care and housekeeping, suddenly had psychotic episodes. It was as if they needed to be living in external chaos to stay internally comfortable. To repeat, if a client has a persistent way of acting, thinking, feeling, or some combination among them, and you cannot imagine what pleasure it is giving or what aggressive purpose it is serving (i.e. the pattern's usefulness for drive reduction), it becomes reasonable to ask whether the pattern might not be a defense. Labelling the pattern a defense is a plausible hypothesis to keep in mind while collecting other facts about the case to see if they confirm or disprove it.

We remarked earlier on this theory's emphasis on events within the mind, but that does not mean things happening in the environment play no part. In the present instance, the patient's feet felt even worse after surgery. Even if the surgeon had been a capable man, correct in his diagnosis, the results could have been the same. For if the foot pain was a defense, removing it would be resented. That is why we say, again and again, that the conscious perception of "external reality" inevitably represents a compromise between what there is to see, and what we need to see or can stand to see. Any image enters the mind first through the physiological apparatus, in sight the lens of the eye and the optic nerve; and the workings of these parts of the body are unconscious. So any perception is first unconscious. Will it come to consciousness, then, and if so, in what version? Passing from unconsciousness to consciousness a perception goes through what Freud called *censorship*. So it is not surprising to find that the "objective" facts about a patient's life change as he gets better. Even the way a patient describes the people s/he is living with may alter. A husband may shift from beast to hero to middle-aged slob to kindly old fellow. Hence, we cannot take at face value our patient's complaint against her surgeon as a charlatan and sadist. She could have been right, but it would not help a gullible caseworker to accept as true a tale the patient later corrected. The best we can know, at the moment, is that this is how the surgeon seems to her, now.

Once the history was available, the defensive foot pain actually seemed to represent the outcome of a conflict. The patient's husband had overexpanded his business and had severe losses after early success. She had to do things like drive up to a gas pump in her Lincoln Continental and ask for two gallons of gasoline since that was all the cash she had. She also had to give up the lifestyle they had achieved and return to clerking in his store, which she found humiliating. Her anger at his lack of judgment hardly made her feel cooperative but, at the same time, she could not stand to see herself as a mother too proud and pouty to help earn her daughter's college tuition.

She wanted to spite her husband, and she did not want to spite him, and both wishes were strong. Developing a physical complaint which disabled her as a salesperson, and whose treatment cost her husband more of his dwindling funds, presented a nice compromise among her conflicting impulses. But it was important to the side of her that was decent and loving that the illness be "real." Since her husband had noticed her pain seemed to lighten if they were going out to a party, and said so, she had to make her symptom spread over more of living as time went on, seriously limiting her fun and depressing her even further. Looked at from the outside, we might wonder if the defense was worth the trouble, but there were parts of her, largely unconscious, which found it the best way out.

It is typical of defensive symptoms that they spread; it is also fairly typical that they make the client's life worse, rather than better, although this is not always so. Much of the figuring the ego does that remains unconscious is shrewd but lacking in foresight. One task of therapy or casework is to decipher defensive solutions that dig the patient in deeper while relieving his immediate crisis, and to bring them to the attention of the more mature part of his personality.

The Mechanisms of Defense

Anna Freud followed her father in making the study of emotional disorder her life work. Her book, *The Ego and the Mechanisms of Defense* (1946), is regarded as a landmark. Her greatest contribution was to therapy with children and training child analysts.

In beginning to picture defenses it is well to bear in mind that while the term sounds like a wall set in place to hide a dismal scene, such an image would be misleading. Closer to the idea would be terminology from football, in which they refer to the standard moves made to defend against the screen pass, let us say, or "the long bomb." In chess, there is talk about classical defenses against certain well-known openings; in tennis, about protecting against the lob. In other words, defenses have more to do with things done than with states of being (Siegal, 1969). As in all energy discharge, defenses may utilize action, ideation, affect or some combination of all three. I suppose it was natural for the analyst, trying to enlist the patient's help to intrude into matters unconscious, to feel on the attack—and often foiled by things the patient did. Hence, the term "defense."

According to the *Psychiatric Glossary*, defense mechanisms are, "Specific intrapsychic processes, operating unconsciously, which are employed to seek relief from anxiety. Conscious efforts are frequently made for the same reasons, but true defense mechanisms are out of awareness (unconscious)" (1969, p. 27). The reader might want to check this definition against the examples we shall be giving, for it does not seem to me that the defense mechanism, itself, is always or even usually unconscious. Very often, the client is well aware of what he is doing or saying; what he does not know is *why* he is doing what he does. In other words, keeping the purpose hidden from oneself is the more critical issue in defensive workings.

The myriad ways people have invented for achieving and maintaining repression never cease to astound me. Fortunately for the beginner, however, a certain degree of order has been found among these responses. Hence, one can at least commence learning about defenses by memorizing the names and definitions of a number most frequently encountered. In the first edition of this book, I did not list specific defenses, feeling that once one grasped the general principles, their names were irrelevant. From subsequent use, however, I decided I was wrong. Learning the standard names seems to be necessary to becoming so familiar with these processes that one no longer names the defense, but only specifies its function for the particular client. To my knowledge, there is no standard listing, so I list the following defenses as useful to know by name and definition. Anna Freud enumerated nine methods of defense to which, "We must add a tenth, which pertains rather to the study of the normal than to that of neurosis: sublimation or displacement of instinctual aims" (1946, p. 47). For our own listing, we have drawn heavily on the 1975 edition of the *Psychiatric Glossary*.

Of *repression*, the *Glossary* says it is a defense that "banishes unacceptable ideas, affects or impulses from consciousness or that keeps out of consciousness what has never been conscious" (1975, p. 135). Anna Freud included repression as one of the defense mechanisms, though its purposes seem typical of most others as well. However, when confronted by a motivated lapse of memory, repression or "massive repression" is the only term that seems applicable. Repression is not to be confused with *suppression*, which simply means that the client knows what he or she thinks but prefers not to say it.

Projection is the mechanism whereby you take something that you find unacceptable about yourself and attribute it to another. It may be a trait, an impulse, even a feature of your face or body. If you are angry at your friend, but feel no anger and instead think s/he is angry at you, that is projection. Your suspicious feeling is not projection in this instance; rather the suspiciousness rests on the fact that you attribute your hostile urges to another. Thus, people constantly on the alert against attack while living in the same world as the rest of us, are probably projecting their own hostility. Otherwise, why do they perceive so much danger in their environments? Some clients live in settings that are dangerous, but this does not mean they do not project. To the current saying, "Just because you're paranoid doesn't mean people aren't out to get you," one may also append "And vice versa!" Nor is it projection when you find an acceptable reason for hating your friend: that is *rationalization* (see below).

Most reasonably mature people find it rather hard to carry out gross projection, since both the *reality-testing* and *self-observing* functions of the ego question what they are doing. Flat out *denial* is also of little use to mature egos, since the *Glossary* defines it as "disavowing thoughts, feelings, wishes, needs or external reality factors that are consciously intolerable" (1975, p. 41). Years ago at one hospital, I met several middle-aged ladies who, when sober, were extremely tight, polite and oblivious of how angry they were. "No, young man, I certainly am not angry. I am just very tired, and my doctor sent me here for a rest. I have no idea why he chose this psychiatric hospital. Why don't you ask him?" The local diagnosis? "Good Christian dowager." One woman had faced a tragedy in which her first child was born severely retarded. Since she had never mentioned more than "My two boys," I was taken aback when her husband told me confidentially about the drain he faced in keeping the eldest in a private institution, and the strain from his wife's appearing not even to know the child existed! One can easily imagine the woman's conflict—terrible guilt about putting the child away; terrible needs to be relieved of the burden. Wiping the child out of consciousness alleviated all this, but it did require that she remain uninformed about the family's finances. The mother in a family in which father-daughter incest has been going on might, as we used to think, be *unconsciously* encouraging the escapade. But, think of this: if she lets herself know consciously what she has started dimly to suspect, she has a *disturbed* child, a husband she *despises*, a total explosion of her whole way of life. When the denial breaks down, there is often recall of all the clues that had been received but disregarded and forgotten at the time. Such information reached the margin of consciousness, but was kicked back downstairs. An expression applied to such experiences, as well as to our rapid forgetting of dreams and fantasies, is *repression in statu nascendi*. Literally, repression of the thought "in the state of being born." What the client verbally denies to *you* is not necessarily denial; denial concerns what he is doing to his *own* awareness.

Reaction formation, on the other hand, may take elaborate forms: the person adopts attitudes or behaviors the opposite of impulses s/he is trying to repress. Thus, we are put off by people who are syrupy sweet, suspecting them of being far more critical than they let on. Similarly, exaggerated humility may be used to cover illusions of being better than everyone else. A student has also pointed out that *detachment*—a mechanism without which we could not stand the repeated separations in our lives—is a kind of reaction formation against *attachment* (see Bowlby, below).

Most readers have heard of *regression*, representing "partial or symbolic return to more infantile patterns of reacting" (*Glossary*, 1975, p. 134). Mama brings home a new baby from the hospital who gets all her attention, and the three year old forgets her toilet training. It is as if she were saying, "Things are bad now, so I'm going back to a time when I was happier." An old friend, John D. Patton, taught me that we also see a good deal of defensive *progression:* "I'm going to jump ahead to an age at which I'll feel safer." This defense is found, for example, in the eldest daughter in a neglectful household who has, when herself only seven or eight years of age, been given responsibility for the care of three younger siblings. Flattered to be called "Mama's little helper" and even to compete with Mama for dominance, she is still in a scary position. People who have utilized defensive progression as youngsters often develop a pattern called *pseudomaturity;* they act more dignified and stately than people who developed more gradually find necessary. It is risky to skip stages of development. As a teen-ager, the pseudomature youngster may find herself used as an advisor by friends whose exhilirating love lives s/he would rather emulate than hear about. Defensive regression and progression are both found among clients who have experienced early deprivation.

Several defenses have to do with altering the direction of drive or the like to alleviate anxiety and, in fact, their definitions show considerable overlap. Most generally, one speaks of *substitution* "by which an unattainable goal, emotion or object is replaced by one that is more attainable or acceptable" (*Glossary,* 1975, p. 145). Feeling anger instead of anxiety would be an example of this. Feeling anger instead of fear, as athletes often do, is a more intricate process, for fear is not anxiety and so does not fit our conception. Rather, to experience fear would be unacceptable to a young football player since, if it became known, he would probably be rejected by his mates. The anxiety about experiencing and especially showing fear is probably *separation anxiety.* The need to avoid it leads him to substitute anger, determination, or other *macho* affects. One may also substitute one objective for another. The physician who proved not to have the brilliance for a research career can concentrate on extending services to people in need.

Displacement involves turning one's impulse aside from its original unacceptable target to one that involves less anxiety. In the Freudian scheme, we speak of the *object* of a drive or drive derivative. Thus if infants associate the mother's breast with feeding, their imagery will have the hunger drive connected (i.e. *cathected*) to the thing that satisfies it, namely the breast. The object of hostility would be the person you fantasy yourself hitting. Displacement, then, deals specifically with substituting a safer object for the original. A man angry with his employer who does not dare express it may take it out on his family, or he may kick the cat, or handle his car savagely. Or, he may displace his rage onto himself, producing *depression*.

Most readers will have heard of *sublimation*, which the *Glossary* nicely describes as a mechanism "by which instinctual drives, consciously unacceptable, are diverted into personally and socially acceptable channels" (1975, p. 145). Sublimation is a defense, in our conception, when the reason the original channel was "unacceptable" involved anxiety. A child, angry and defiant toward his father, who also loves him and was reared in a family where such mixed feelings would produce enormous guilt, cannot let himself be conscious of the defiance. He may sublimate the impulses into opposing authority more generally, like becoming a lawyer who prefers to fight for the underdog in our society. But, as I quoted from Anna Freud earlier in this section, sublimation need not always be defensive. If you are not pretty enough to be the heroine, could you not enjoy a major supporting role? Among the adaptive tasks of the ego is finding a way to meet one's needs, and if you decide that half a loaf is better than none, you may be sublimating, but warding off anxiety is not the issue.

Rationalization has to do with justifying to yourself something you have done or are doing which otherwise would be intolerable and make you guilty. Excusing your misbehavior to another is not rationalization; excusing it to yourself is. If you are evading the issue, as in protesting, "I was only joking," that is not rationalization unless you believe it yourself. Rationalization may, of course, be combined with other defenses. A classic that students recount is the woman who says of the flagrantly unfaithful boyfriend with whom she still lives, "I can't leave him; he needs me." In this gesture, the person conceals from herself her inability to leave, because she would have so much separation anxiety at breaking off even an unpromising relationship, by giving herself another reason for clinging. At the same time, she projects her own needfulness onto her partner, onto whom it does not fit very well, to salvage her pride.

Self-abasement is a process whereby through criticizing, blaming, or otherwise derogating the self, the individual seeks to allay anxiety. In academic textbooks on personal adjustment, one used to encounter descriptions of the patient whose problem was a "poor self-concept" or feelings of inferiority. You knew it was true because s/he acted that way, and s/he said so, constantly describing personal inadequacies or being otherwise self critical. The author implied that when you had identified the low self-esteem, you were at the core of the problem. But to feel like a nothing is really devastating. Why would anyone who felt that way keep reminding him or herself of the fact? It would make more sense to try to cover it up with other people, and certainly to oneself!

Academic writers seem to overlook something that strikes you very hard as a clinician. Clients with low self-esteem find it difficult to give it up. They find it hard to accept compliments, and greet them with suspicion; they screen evidence about themselves to put things in the worse possible light. "Yes, I got a 90 on the examination, but I missed some really obvious questions." As with other exercises in masochism, the thought occurs that nobody would put up with what the client self-inflicts unless it seemed better than some alternative. Self-abasement may be a reaction formation against feelings of *omnipotence*, that one is all-powerful. Grossly immature people sometimes use self-abasement the way dogs use submission: "If I lie down, and expose my throat, then your dominance is established and you will let me alone." Their unconscious, alas, may be too optimistic about people as compared with dogs. If you expose your throat in human circles, somebody may step up and finish you off. So self-abasement is not, objectively, a very adaptive mechanism, which is all the more reason for questioning whether, after you ferret out a low self-concept, you have come to the core of the client's problems. Psychological health, after all, seems to reside neither in high nor low self-esteem. Rather, when one is functioning well, energies are too invested in doing, loving and living to spend much time in self-evaluation.

A general characteristic of any defense is the tendency to use it over and over, even if it does not seem to succeed in resolving one's problems. Freud, early on, referred to this as the *repetition compulsion*. At first the repetition compulsion was accepted as a given, general feature of all human functioning. Later, ideas were advanced about the specific purposes of repeating patterns. The repetition compulsion comes to mind in respect to the next set of defenses.

A *compulsion* is "an insistent, repetitive, intrusive and unwanted urge to perform an act that is contrary to the person's ordinary wishes or standards" (*Glossary*, 1975, p. 35). Not to perform the act leads to open and conscious anxiety. However, if you block a person from his compulsion he will probably attack you. I once had an in-patient who used compulsive defenses constantly. We were trying to block him from them in the hope that by doing so whatever was being covered up by them might come to the surface. The nurses noticed that in one corridor the young man always stepped on a particular black spot in the tile design before turning the corner. Indeed, if someone else were there, and had his spot covered, he would loiter around waiting for the person to move so he could go on. The nurses "ordered" him to give up the gyration —which he did, in his usual smiling fashion. Afterwards, they noticed that if he had to make the turn, and only the black spot on the floor was open to him, he would not move. He now had an anti-compulsion compulsion!

An *obsession* is like a compulsion, except that it is channelled into ideation rather than action. The *Glossary* (1975, p. 110) calls an obsession "a persistent, unwanted idea or impulse that cannot be eliminated by logic or reasoning." Many have experienced worries in the middle of the night about matters that will not go away and yet about which absolutely nothing can be done at the moment. At such a time, it seldom occurs to the worrying client that he may be "obsessing" about one topic in order to *avoid* thinking about what is really bothering him. Sometimes the obsession is used to cover an impulse, itself unacceptable. There are *rescue fantasies* in which one feels a terrible need to help another person escape an awful fate. Most fairy tales involve such fantasies. Note, however, that the story teller, before introducing the brave young prince who snatches the maiden to safety, first puts her in the claws of the dragon. Those of us who like to help others in trouble are accused by some analysts of displacing our rescue fantasies from, let us say, younger siblings we would have liked to be rid of, to clients whose sad plights we magnify. I am sure this interpretation does not usually apply and that in any event socially useful motivation is often better left unexamined. Analysts often would be more admirable if they showed more.

Many connect Hamlet with his obsession concerning his father's death, and his compulsion to revenge it. Lady Macbeth's ritualistic hand washing also comes to mind. What was she expunging? The blood of the man she murdered. Many compulsions are tied to another defense mechanism called *undoing*. In undoing, we try symbolically to reverse, take back, un-do something we regret. Of course, we can only do this in symbols, for the past is dead and the present perishes each moment. But on driving away from a party, it is common to think about one more comment by which you would have won an exchange of repartée. A husband, having tarried too long during happy hour, brings home something to mollify himself, as well as his wife, *undoing* his thoughtlessness. Indeed, compensation offered for psychic damage can be pleasant to receive for it is ridiculous to think that being in love means never having to say you are sorry. Indeed, the older one gets, the more one gives up on virtue and the more willing one is to settle for a decent hypocrisy.

And what about the patient with the sore feet? The defense in her case would be labelled *conversion*, meaning the emotional pain was "converted" into a bodily form. Conversion symptoms, however, imply that the illness is "functional," that is, there has been no discernible change in organ structure. Most of the patients with whom Freud began would, at one time, have been diagnosed as "conversion hysterics." *Psychosomatic* symptoms, by the way, are something else. In these, there is actual bodily change which has been linked to emotional distress, as with stomach ulcer, colitis, some forms of hypertension and the like. When the anxiety expresses itself by producing, among other things, actual physical illness, we may say the patient is *somatizing*. True, somatization may operate in the service of defense, but it is not usually referred to as a defense mechanism.

There are other defense mechanisms in addition to those discussed here. A number will be described in relation to other topics as we go along. But those given will provide a beginning vocabulary of the subject and they serve to illustrate the principles involved. The defenses, clearly, are not things; they are repetitive patterns of doing, feeling, wanting.

Structure of a Typical Defense Mechanism

Is there a reasonably simple schema underlying most defensive operations? By simplifying a bit we can abstract a set of events common to most defenses that work. By "work," I mean hold down anxiety by repressing images that would cause anxiety if they became conscious. When anxiety is provoked, the personality takes refuge in a defense mechanism, and repression results. What may stir anxiety? What forms of anxiety are commonly at work? What is the chain of events?

I have constructed Figure 1 as a mnemonic device with misgivings since nearly all attempts to diagram psychological events only add to the clutter.

Figure 1

TYPICAL DEFENSE SEQUENCE

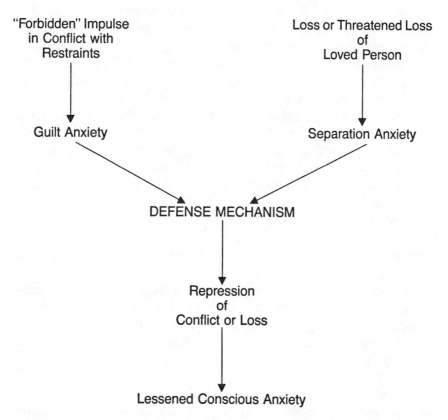

One possible source of anxiety is conflict between an unaccept-able urge (like all urges, presumed to arise in the id), and a force within the personality (which can be said to come from the super-ego) seeking to check the urge. I note in passing for clarification, that the checking force does not act until needed to stop the unacceptable impulse. It is like the floor under you, exerting no upward pressure until you step, putting downward weight on it. The superego functions to keep you out of trouble by producing the expectation that, if you indulge in the forbidden, you will be punished. In a nutshell, this is the foundation of guilt anxiety. The "signal function of anxiety" arises since it can act as a warning signal. The net result is that the "bad" impulse stirs up a countering force, there is a conflict, and there is guilt anxiety to be handled. The ego may employ a defense mechanism to "bind" or contain the impulse and to repress it all. If the defensive operations performed produce symptoms severe enough to be termed neurotic, the left-hand chain in Figure 1 also provides a rough diagram of the "conflict theory of neurosis."

Not all anxiety can be understood as representing this kind of conflict. Many examples brought in by my students may be more directly conceptualized as representing *separation anxiety*. The latter may be viewed as a reaction that arises, automatically and instinctively, when you are left, and especially when you feel abandoned, by someone you love (Bowlby, 1961). Even the threat of losing a person to whom you are attached may stir this anxiety. For instance, the young man desperately trying to conceal his own unattractiveness from himself could be concealing feelings of inferiority, but inferiority, or shamefulness, is not an anxiety. The danger of inferiority is that it may *make* you unlovable, and so more likely to be abandoned and left alone. In the case of a young infant, survival itself is involved, so the issue of being lovable is of tremendous importance to the human psyche and will recur throughout this book. In the present context, it is more parsimonious to presume that the anxiety energizing defenses may also derive from fear of abandonment. If you doubt it is actually more parsimonious to assume *two* origins of anxiety, try explaining someone's concern about being short as a form of guilt!

Once we grant anxiety, however, the sequence is similar. A defense mechanism is likely to be called into play, and repression of the anxiety and of the threats it represents should take place. Earlier we asked, what part of all this is unconscious? As I said, the defensive operation is often quite conscious—in obsessions, compulsions, rationalization, and so on, but the purpose of the operation must be hidden for the defense to work. Will the anxiety also be repressed? What is your observation? Sometimes it is gone completely; often there is still visible anxiety. In other words, defenses do not always do their job perfectly.

And, defenses use psychic energy. When this was first noted, it probably seemed to be another abstraction. But to glance back at some of the examples—hours of worrying; repetitive compulsive rituals; rationalizations put together in great detail that need to be added to from time to time as the unconscious truth tries to surface; painful gyrations *not* to know what you know—is to remind ourselves that defensive maneuvering may entail a lot of effort, including physical work. Like all else in life, the ego provides nothing for nothing. Defenses may perform marvelously in helping us keep afloat, but they may also take forms we term symptoms, the mixed bag which is our next topic.

When is a Symptom?

Painful feet, a conversion symptom, distracted one woman from a major life problem while providing a compromise among her conflictual urges. A defense became necessary because she was capable of guilt. Had she simply been selfish, and not rejected such feelings in herself, she would have had little reason to blind herself to her spitefulness. In the latter event, we might not have liked her as a person, but she would not have had her symptoms. The fact that in addition to her childish rage she was also a decent human being made her defense necessary. Still, her compromise was extremely costly. It warded off some anxiety, but at great discomfort to herself and burden to her family, and we think of her as having had *symptoms*.

Not all symptoms result from defensive operations of course; and not all defensive operations result in symptoms. Each of us is constantly at work warding off anxiety. It would be unwise to label all our efforts symptoms. So we ask, when is a defense a symptom?

At one time, I worked in a private hospital catering to "the carriage trade." A large proportion of the patients were adolescents; many came from families that were not only wealthy but talented. Proficiency in the arts was not unexpected, and musical ability was especially prevalent. I was struck by the number of excellent pianists. Why the linkage? Why were there so many fine pianists with emotional difficulties?

A violinist's impulse might be to say that if they had chosen a fretless instrument, nearly impossible to play in tune, they would have had enough troubles without emotional problems. But listening to their histories, I became aware that for them their skill came from a talent they had developed. At some point in the life of almost every such young man or woman, s/he had practiced assiduously, even compulsively, for three and four hours a day. It soon appeared that what appeared to be devotion to the instrument was overdetermined by its convenience as a defense. An unhappy and phobic youngster could achieve the same sense of mastery others were seeking on the ballfield or in the theater without having much contact with other human beings. Many of us clearly recall what an unpleasant, duty-laden task practicing was. For these neurotic children this onerous task became an island, a healthy outlet for reasonably useful motivations, within a situation that did not expose them to competition or even to the other social contacts that made them anxious.

To return to our question. Was their practicing a "symptom?" If it fit into their withdrawal, of course. Yet they were also able to master an instrument for pleasure; and, in a few cases, for profit. When the young Mozart practiced and composed equally assiduously, no one thought of him as having symptoms. Schubert, living in terrible poverty, wrote melody after melody, ofttimes on butcher paper, as songs crowded his mind. Was this obsession evidence of disturbance, or genius, or both? At least one violinist, Viotti, gave up in disgust after a couple of financial disasters and became a wine merchant—which did not make him rich either (Wechsburg, 1973).

Accordingly, what we term a symptom cannot be defined on the basis of specific behavior. If it serves a defensive purpose, that does not necessarily make it a symptom. What we call symptomatic involves more inclusive criteria than the specific motivations in question; the criteria also involve us in value judgments.

Generally, clinicians regard as symptomatic behavior whose cost to the person outweighs the benefit gained in reducing anxiety. The youngster, locked in his room with his beloved piano because he had not matured in a way that permitted him to get along, may become both a more comfortable teenager and a proficient musician. Skills learned in the service of neurosis need not disappear when the neurosis recedes. On the other hand, if a youngster sat all day rambling through vague and discordant sequences while being a recluse, one might question whether what he has been learning about disharmony has been worth it.

A person's whole situation may influence the evaluation. The news is filled with stories of some quite dreadful people, but how about everyday heroes. In my early twenties one of my very good friends had a form of pericarditis which was usually fatal, until the discovery of sulfa drugs some six months after his death. On furlough from the Army during World War II, I visited him in the hospital where we spent an hour telling jokes and otherwise pretending nothing much was going on in our lives. As I left, I could not help but ask him, "Sid, how are you doing? When will you be out of here?" He stared at me soberly and said, "Well, the doctors say I have a fifty-fifty chance. But I say it's sixty-forty."

And then the punchline, "But there I go again—sentiment entering in." Of course his partial denial was a defense, but who would treat it as a symptom? There are many instances of denial we rather regard as courage. And so, another factor comes to mind, the place of the particular defense in the context of the total personality. In reasonably well put together individuals, the defenses are apt to be integrated into their total personality functioning, and to add to their ability to cope.

In terms of integration with the personality two other terms apply to symptoms. Those acceptable to the rest of the personality, unquestioned by the client himself, are called *ego syntonic*. An alcoholic's use of liquor to allay anxiety and make it easier to socialize may be symptomatic. But if he or she, like most alcoholics, denies the degree of dependence ("I can stop anytime; I just don't want to"), the client does not even recognize the problem. Furthermore, the denial frees him from another piece of information that would give the rest of us pause. We might realize that our bodies, including our brains, were deteriorating, but the alcoholic secretly believes such natural laws do not apply to him. If other facets of the personality recognize the symptom and want to be rid of it, it is *ego dystonic*.

Part of a good caseworker's skill lies in the ability to "start where the client is," noncommittally accepting ego-syntonic attitudes and behaviors that we think self-destructive. Gradually, in some course of interviews, the symptom may move in the direction of becoming ego dystonic. Far from rebuffing help, or evading it, the client may now actively seek it out and pay for it, if he can. At the point at which the patient finally sees a problem, movies commonly have an elderly analyst announce, "Ach, und now ve shall begin." Caseworkers do not live such sheltered lives, alas. We begin, shall we say, before the beginning?

We see, then, that the requirement that the patient be "motivated for treatment," for which some private therapists and agencies hold out, may be off the mark. Among many of our clients, ego-dystonic symptoms and clients motivated to get rid of them mean the road to recovery has begun. Should an orthopedist refuse to see a man with a broken leg because he is unable to get himself to the office? Lack of motivation is, itself, only an aspect of what is wrong. Unfortunately, people without sufficient surviving ego capacities —for example, the capacity for self-observation—to know they need to change are much harder to treat. Indeed, the effort may well fail. Infantile people, for example, do not usually recognize anything wrong with how they function. Our knowledge and skills for dealing with folks who start so far behind the eight ball is not what it should be. But, in principle, arousing sufficient motivation to keep the treatment going is our technical problem—not the client's. Hellmuth Kaiser, who will be described later, pointed out something else: as the treaters, the responsibility for success or failure is ours. Failure of the treatment, then, is ours; for the client, it may well be a life tragedy. Nothing is gained, therefore, by blaming the client's lack of motivation for the failure, if it is used as a defense against feelings of inadequacy by the therapist.

Just as their symptoms are often ego acceptable to our clients, so the notion that the way out of one's difficulties is to try to change oneself does not come naturally to many. They seek, instead, what are termed *alloplastic* solutions, meaning literally, "change the other." A recognized need to change oneself tends to be more characteristic of people who are, in general, more confident, mature, and ready to seek *autoplastic* solutions, meaning change of oneself. Of course, one can also play games in the realm of self-observation. In *Portnoy's Complaint* Philip Roth achieved a high point of satire in describing Portnoy's mother who said, in effect, "I know I'm not perfect; I have faults. For instance, I'm too good. Everybody tells me I'm too good."

Etiology of Symptoms

With the human organism we can usually count on an attempt at self-healing. When we cut our finger, we usually need only try to prevent infection. Likewise with psychic insults the ego tries to heal itself and usually succeeds. Most mild depressions, for example, are self-limiting; like a common cold, the personality throws them off. A defense is like a home remedy the person applies to his own psychic wounds.

It is as if one had a cut leg to which antiseptic is applied but which otherwise is permitted to heal itself. A scab forms to stem the flow of blood and protect the exposed underlying tissues against further infection. Eventually, the cut heals and you forget where it was. Usually, this is what happens, but alas, not in all instances. Sometimes the scab is accompanied by scarring. In some severe wounds, the scar tissue becomes disfiguring, or so large it may interfere with free use of the injured part. If the scarring, then, is too bulky or uncomfortable, you may be in some ways worse off than you were with the open wound.

Kaiser once remarked to me, "The child puts on a suit of armor to ward off the immediate danger, and it works. But he is unable to guess that years later, when his friends are running and leaping ahead, he will be dragging along in the rear, still weighted down by the same old armor." This is a useful way of looking at the etiology, the historical causes, of neurotic symptoms. They represent the outcome of home remedies that proved ill-advised. But then what can you expect of a little girl aged four or five who becomes aware only that she is somehow "different?" Where would she get the perspective to realize that her chosen solution, trying harder to *act* like everyone else because that is how you too become a person, would leave her twenty years later with an "as if" personality (Deutsch, 1942)?

Another frequent question is, why the particular symptom? Why did the client somatize and have a heart attack, let us say, rather than develop a compulsion? The question is reasonable, but we are still not able to answer it very well. We do know something about types of personalities more likely to develop one sort of symptomatology rather than another; many clinicians are very adept at providing plausible explanations for why the symptom was chosen—after the fact. But a really good theory would enable us to take a set of facts about a person and predict not only that his/her level or anxiety will rise—which reflection will show is really very easy—but also what the *symptom choice* will be. Such prediction remains an uncertain business. The same may be said for choices of defense by the way. Quite possibly, events very early in life now being examined more closely, even constitutional factors, play roles not yet included in our theorizing.

Layering of Defenses and their Uncovering

Defenses typically exist in depth and are referred to by a term which has considerable relevance to practice: *layers of defense*. Take, for instance, a Mr. Z, younger than Messrs. X and Y.

Mr. Z begins contact by telling a caseworker the importance of his associates. Dropping a name here and there, he also maintains a gracious but subtly condescending manner. Should the worker proffer a comment, Mr. Z considers it judiciously, accepting or disregarding it with easy casualness. A terribly busy fellow, he may or may not have time for his next appointment. The caseworker learns that he maintains this air of studied superiority in most human contacts. As a result, he is something less than appealing as a person; indeed, his attitude interferes with his livelihood.

It is not necessary to have a master's in social work or a doctorate in something or other to draw the conclusion that Mr. Z seems to be "overcompensating for feelings of inferiority." Adler, one of the earliest students of ego psychology, wished to make this mechanism the keystone of a general system of psychology (Adler, 1917). But as observed earlier, it was not exactly news around the ninth grade, either. The superior attitude is a *reaction formation*. Mr. Z acts superior to conceal how inferior he feels from others and, most importantly, from himself. Only dimly aware of the consequences of his manner, he knows that people tend not to react positively to him and is vague about why they are turned off.

One consequence is that people are not really people in his life. In most contacts, he is alert primarily to whether the other fellow helps bolster his sense of superiority, or threaten it. He needs to be acknowledged, to be treated as special. Ordinary teasing and banter are impossible for him because he is so sensitive to criticism. The stakes are too high. If the verbal barb strikes home, he reacts with a deep sense of degradation. As he is very careful not to invite others into such give and take, the result is that he comes across as stuffy and literal. Mr. Z naturally prefers to spend time with those he regards as clearly his inferiors, like servants or some of his clients. In these limited relationships he feels safe and can even unbend slightly. But in most others, getting to know you is a series of gambits on his side to test out who is going to be on top. Relating to women has been a problem. On the one hand, he would rather date someone he thinks would be honored to have him; on the other, a girl who is less than a great beauty is hardly someone to parade in public.

The caseworker thinks that to get at Mr. Z's feeling of inferiority would give him some relief from the way life has been closing in. Whatever *childish remnant* is hounding him should dissolve in the light of conscious attention and adult judgment. In fact Mr. Z does become aware that he thinks of himself as low on the totem pole, dogged by a constant sense of failure. His caseworker, fortunately, too shrewd to be put off by generalities, asks for specifics. It turns out that one of Mr. Z's failures was to rank third in his college class. He used to claim to be bothered by examinations, but this was not true. What bothered him was the fear that he could not get honors. In short, feelings of degradation were secondary to more competitive strivings. As it would be embarrassing to admit one were competing and lose, he professed to be humble about his chances of passing. What we have is a sandwich of defenses, if you will, a virtual Dagwood creation of salami on cheese on lettuce on white fish, with all the maneuvers he has to go through as garnish.

Defenses typically exist in depth because the first one often solves one problem only to create another to be defended against. Furthermore, a defense usually contains some unreality. To keep the whole thing from breaking down, the ego has to buttress one defensive thought with another. It is like telling a white lie. Of course you assure your mother you love the purple and brown tie she bought you, but you have to account for why you never wear it. You cannot slip and claim you *lost* it. That would blow the whole game, would it not? It may take an efficient ego to erect defenses in depth, protecting an original distortion with a series of secondary and tertiary elaborations. It requires a very busy ego, as well, for maintaining defenses in depth takes even more psychic energy. Might it not be better simply to let the whole house of cards fall, and deal openly with the original, core problem even if it makes us anxious? The notion sounds plausible but is also reckless. While a complicated defensive structure contains pathology, recall that it may also be in use for other purposes, like drive discharge, or earning a living, easing the way socially and so forth. How much of a collapse can a client tolerate at any one time?

Fortunately, and unfortunately, most people within reasonably normal limits do not easily abandon their defenses, as becomes apparent when we try to use methods called *uncovering* techniques. The intent in uncovering is, as it sounds, to strip off a layer of defense so that the material being repressed becomes open to conscious attention. *Insight* has various connotations, but in the tradition of ego psychology it means that something previously unconscious is now conscious.

The uncovering technique many associate with psychoanalysis is one in which the analyst, having begun to put a number of pieces of information together, tells the patient what is going on in his unconscious, that is, what needs, feelings, and so forth he is covering up. Such a directive attempt to break through repression is called *interpretation* (Bibring, 1954). Because the defense mechanism serves to bind anxiety, removing it entails the probability that the person will feel anxious. Many do not want to give up repressions. This unreadiness to deal with repressed content is called *resistance*, and one can easily imagine an early generation of analysts proffering insights to patients who greeted them with disbelief, making the analyst feel his efforts were being resisted.

But, whereas resistance originally had to do with refusal to accept an interpretation, the term is now used in social work, at least, to refer to all efforts clients make to avoid an unpleasant insight. Of course, the phrasing of an interpretation affects its chances of being acceptable, and some phrasings will increase, others decrease, the anxiety. Proper timing is crucial. Interpretation is well used when the patient shows critical issues are already coming close to consciousness. For example, he may express the insight as a "slip of the tongue," or as a joke. The "interpretation" then might simply consist in taking his words seriously. Interpretation helps speed the process of insight while putting things into perspective.

Most caseworkers do not make interpretations, if only because our cases are typically seen weekly, rather than daily, and so we have to be chary of releasing anxiety we will not be in position to deal with. But insight may also come from *clarification*. By this we mean a process in which patterns, or new connections, are found among facts, all of which are conscious, but not yet seen in this relationship. The term means, on the one hand, something the therapist may do for the patient; it is also used to refer to a resulting clarification in the patient. An insight, the recovery of something repressed, often occurs out of a process of clarification. An example follows.

> I recall always wanting my grandmother to like me and was careful of what I said and did in her house. As she was sensitive to slights, I spent a lot of time placating her, even offering excuses for my sister's never coming to see her. It was a strain. You know, I'm starting to wonder if I really liked her all that much. I guess I loved her for what she did for me, but she really wasn't a likable person. I blurted this out to my father, once, and he told me to shut my mouth or he'd shut it for me. Why was he so defensive about her? Did he feel the same way, do you think?

This client is working along nicely, uncovering her feelings at a tolerable pace. The therapist just has to be there to reduce anxiety by accepting what is reported, while supporting the self-observing function by providing an audience to reinforce the importance of the work through paying attention. In other instances, of course, we may take a more active role in clarification: "You said this, today, but last week you said something that sounded contradictory with it. What do you think you mean?"

Uncovering can also be accomplished by *interfering with the defense*. The patient in group therapy who needs to sit in "paranoid corner," with his back and sides protected can be shaken up by the therapist's taking the seat before his arrival. Hospitalization may be used, in part, as a major intervention to interfere with defensive maneuvers like drinking, or making suicidal gestures, or picking up sex partners in bars, or squandering one's money (outside psychiatric channels). *Refusal to go along with a defense* is a very common mode. One can simply decline the gambit of the client who uses the put down. Rather than submitting or getting angry, the caseworker may simply relate an observation of what is happening with a smile. To refuse to react to a child accustomed to getting his parents fighting with each other—which makes her feel in control and assuages her separation anxiety—can help in uncovering (Ganter, Yeakel and Polansky, 1967). Indeed, the difference between sophisticated treatment and hack work may lie in whether the therapist sees interfering with the client's acting-out as possibly leading toward insight, or he interferes simply because what the patient does is morally offensive to him.

The penetration of defenses nearly always releases anxiety that they were binding. We do not release anxiety simply for the sake of doing so because, "The patient is not anxious enough and needs to be motivated." The release of anxiety is indicated when there is no choice in trying to get at what is being covered. A diseased appendix requires the pain of cutting through perfectly healthy skin to get at the inflammation. No benefit results from entering the main body cavity, but there is presently no other way to treat acute appendicitis. We must realize that even learning about defenses affects nearly all students by shaking theirs and making them anxious. I regret this because it has not been my experience that anxiety is a good motivation for learning. I regret it even more because the process often makes me be visualized as the source of anxiety. Not infrequently, like the bearer of evil tidings, the teacher becomes the target of anger released.

We must remember that when something results in a blast of anger from a client, it is possible that you have been unkind or unfeeling or untactful. On the other hand, perhaps the client was already filled with rage which your attempt to help uncovered. As the nearest available person, you became a convenient target though you did not "make" him angry.

The logic of defenses is simple and straightforward, once a few unfamiliar propositions are accepted. The resultant theory is conceptually powerful, integrating a large number of observations and suggesting a whole therapeutic approach. The same logic may also have ominous implications.

For example, certain neurotic symptoms generalize and spread if untreated. The phobic initially afraid of the subway becomes afraid of transportation he cannot leave whenever he wants, ruling out all public conveyance. Later he may find himself unable to leave his neighborhood. In the Jewish tradition this is called, "building a fence around the law." Dietary laws such as Kashrith derived from the Biblical injunction against cooking a kid goat in its mother's milk. To ensure that this would not occur it was first forbidden to eat meat and milk at the same meal, then meat and any milk product, such as cheese, or butter. Then one had to be careful that no *traces* of either were left on utensils used for the other sort of meal, so all Orthodox families had two sets of dishes, two sets of silver, two sets of cooking pots and pans. (I once visited a family who maintained two complete kitchens, one *milchik*, one *flaischik*, as they said in Yiddish.) Phobias and compulsions tend to spread similarly, becoming both hobbies and tyrants.

Similarly, some people become troubled by their own violence or hostile feelings as youngsters and determine to stop expressing them. The youngster who puts a stopper on the bottle of emotions little reckons that, having plugged the bottle of rage and hatred, he may also stop feelings of love, joy, pleasure, fun. No wonder, therefore, that many untreated neurotics, in addition to their specific symptoms, come to us discouraged and depressed.

CHAPTER 4
A SPEED READER'S GUIDE TO
Sources of Resiliency

The strength or weakness of the ego depends on (a) the availability of *free psychic energy*; (b) the ability to mobilize energy for useful work by *synthesizing* one's motives and by *structured channels* that control *drive discharge*. Energy then is central; it may be drained off into sustaining defenses, for example, *narcissism*. The free energy needed for concentration may be dissipated in *chronic indecision*, an inability to synthesize. *Looseness of ego boundaries*, which are internal organizational structures, may lead to unwanted eruptions of *primary-process thinking* and to *impulsiveness*. *Characterological looseness* often reflects failures in personality development, resulting, for example, from having only an impulsive parental model to identify with, or being given *unconditional love*. Looseness of boundaries may be *situationally* caused by fatigue, illness, or sustained deprivation of externally supportive stimuli.

Successfully responding to challenges requires *coping mechanisms*. Two general modes of coping, *repetition* (e.g. the *repetition compulsion*) and taking an *active* stance, both occur in various specific defense mechanisms. *Grief work* provides a good illustration of coping: turning the anger of object loss *against the self* is an attempt to cope but leads to *depression*. *Crisis intervention* involves offering *ego support* to people in difficult straits and may include suggesting coping mechanisms they can use. Depression may be treated by *ventilation, restitution* and *working through*.

With these basic concepts we can begin discussion at a more advanced level. Still new and confusing, many of the same terms will be applied repeatedly as we look at the next nugget of ego psychology: the study of character types.

Sources
of Resiliency

4

W e have been discussing drives, conflicts, anxiety and the occasions when a defense leads to morbid symptoms. Many students now notice that the theory that applies to clients also applies to us. The attempt by the Freudians to erect a universal theory could be reassuring, but leveling is seldom thought elevating. Awareness that all of us use defenses is experienced as a comedown and we react with resolves to give up such nonsense. Alas, like the conscious decision to be sincere, premature self-analysis is a contradiction in terms. How can we penetrate an unconscious which, by definition, is closed to us? We need outside help if only because the other person is probably not repressing the same content. Perhaps all one can do is to join in my clinician's prayer, "And forgive us our defenses as we forgive those who defend themselves against us."

The formation of a symptom represents the outcome of an attempt to heal oneself that proved ill-advised. Most such efforts have better results. Many symptoms, in less exaggerated form, seem highly adaptive. To be unclean is to be a slob, perhaps, and to put yourself in danger of infection. But, what are we to make of the person who will not touch a doorknob without gloves?

The Case of the Rejected Suitor
There are many pithy comments to be made about marriage. George Bernard Shaw remarked it to be a successful institution because it combines a maximum of temptation with a maximum of opportunity. There is a French saying that a bachelor lives like a king, but dies like a dog; a married man lives like a dog, but dies like a king. Such thoughts are not typically in the mind of an enamored young

man. He knows only that he loves, a state still not adequately described by ego psychology or any other. Being in love is marvelous but it has its vicissitudes. Let us begin to study resilience in the ego with a series of tales about an all too common happening: being jilted.

This could be the story. A college student during World War II was attracted by a lovely girl. He pursued her avidly for, like most of us, he was resistible. After a time, she returned his affection, and they were engaged. Fate willed that they could not marry at once. The ardent lover had to go away for many months on what was then being euphemistically called "government business" in the Army. While he was gone, his beloved found that being without current and pressing attentions was hard to bear. At first, she was seen socially, then she was seen often, and finally she was not seen nearly as much because she was with another young man. She became pregnant by this fellow and decided to marry him. When her fiancé returned the following month with hopes of eternal bliss, she spent an evening with him to give him the news. She was tender and sober, as befit her condition. One might say she handled her part of their interview very well, considering that hers was not a lovely situation to be handling.

Now, this was not one instance, but several, for rejection happens all the time. Here were the reactions of four disappointed young lovers, each of whom had experienced irretrievable *loss of the object*.

Tom took the news without losing his composure. He said, "I see," swallowed hard, and left. He went home, wrote an oblique and gentlemanly note about failing at all he tried, and shot himself.

Dick was also a gentleman born and bred. He managed a wry grin as he said he understood. Barring a caustic remark or two on the idiocy of building hopes on the constancy of women, he was not really offensive. Shortly thereafter, he joined the Foreign Legion where he spent several years riding camels.

Harry was a different sort of man. He became insulted and threatened both his ex-fiancée and her new lover with great bodily harm. Not only did he make crude statements about his ex-lady's morals, he was not above demanding the immediate return of a ring and a fur coat or two she had naturally assumed he would not be needing. Afterward, he went to visit his drinking buddies, in whose companionship he made vile comments about his erstwhile girl friend. It is not known how long he remained despondent beyond the second week after the encounter, for he left at that time to take a position with a construction firm. Later he married and reared three children, one of whom was last seen wearing braces on her teeth.

George had still another reaction. As he was receiving the news, he became totally silent and pale. Then, he made one or two blundering attempts to entice his pregnant ex-fiancée into returning to him. After leaving her house, he went to a bar where he met several college acquaintances, and became so drunk he had to be taken home by two of them. Although he cried several times while in his cups, he never did reveal what was bothering him. Subsequently, he dated other girls, off and on, but broke off with each when he seemed to be getting seriously attached. George is now an alcoholic, who never married. His mother, who provides him with money to live on, and for occasional skirmishes with psychotherapy, blames his lifetime of troubles on his having been rudely mistreated in his first romance.

These are varied ways of responding to the same life crisis. Which is to be thought the healthiest? With the suicide, we know the ending without ever finding out how the life story might have come out, so we can discard that one. But, which of the rest would one choose? Regardless of your answer, and mine, we will agree that some personalities are obviously better able to roll with life's punches than others. If the ego deals with adaptation, it must be in the ego that one absorbs—or fails to absorb—the punishment that happens to all but the luckiest among us. Social workers, who spend so much of their lives helping others cope with losses and other stress, need concepts to describe, and to account for, people's differences in ability to rally from disaster.

We sometimes speak of "ego strength" or "ego weakness" but these are vague terms. They have the advantage of sounding less judgmental than calling someone a strong or weak person, but otherwise they simply describe the person as good or poor at adaptation. As for *explaining* variations in general ability, I find it useful to organize my thinking around two general issues: (a) how much psychic energy is "free" and available to be marshaled on demand; (b) how well the personality is structured so that the energy available can be channeled where it is needed, so that psychological effort can be organized and synthesized. In discussing these two general determinants of ego-strength, I will try also to put in order some other concepts related to each, as well as ideas that have accumulated about the events in a person's life that affect resilience.

Availability of Psychic Energy

To say that a person's resiliency depends in part on the psychic energy free for solving the problems of the moment has a couple of implications. It suggests that each of us has a fixed quantum of energy to start with, and that how effectively we operate is affected by how much of the resource stays available for loving, working, living, and how much is dissipated or "lost." Loss of energy would be one approach to explaining general differences in ego strength.

One Freudian model of energy disposal does, in fact, resemble a hydrostatic or hydraulic system. You start by assuming the person has a kind of reservoir of psychic energy resembling a water tower in a town located in flat countryside. The psychic energy is pumped to the tank primarily by the drives. The model does not presume we all have the same amount of energy; there is speculation that some are born with stronger drives than others. However, variation as to how much energy each person starts with is not nearly as significant as individual differences in its effective use.

Now, the liquid below the water tower is under pressure from the weight of the water at the highest point in the system. "Water seeks its own level" and the water in a closed system piped down from the water tower will try to flow up nearly to the same height as the water in the tower. So, pressure in a water system can be very great. By analogy, we assume that the psychic energy in the personality is constantly seeking discharge, or expression.

Sometimes the expression comes out in what is called *raw* or *primitive* form, as in sex or greedy eating or murderous outburts of rage. However, this kind of direct expression is more typical of very young children, of people who have failed to mature psychologically, and of those who have regressed under stress. In the course of *normal maturation*, the drives become *modulated*. Their force is reduced. They are expressed in ways unlikely to get you into trouble with your superego or society. The *objects* of the drives, the targets involved in their expression, also become redirected in accord with reality, and socialized. Thus, the incestuous feelings presumed present at the resolving of the *Oedipus Complex* are generally not expressed, nor even thought about. At most, they will be shown in a preference for a mate resembling the parent of the opposite sex—"I want a girl just like the girl who married dear old Dad." Or, more guardedly, they may be expressed as a reaction formation, that is carefully steering sexual feelings to people very *unlike* the "best parent, opposite sex" (as they say at dog shows).

The modulation of drives and their cathexes to realistically acceptable targets is learned by nearly all of us in the course of growing up. These processes are at work in the creation of *drive derivatives* (see Chapter 2). *Sublimation*, another related concept, may operate in the service of defense, but may also simply represent the normal developmental process of modulating and redirecting drive-expression. An older child says, "You are being a pain in the neck," where the younger one says, "I'm going to chop your head off and throw it in the garbage can."

If the water entering your house were under the same pressure as at the pumping station, it would probably damage your plumbing, perhaps burst the hot-water tank. Likewise, drives that are too raw, too powerful are dysfunctional for civilized living. Repairing the leaks they cause— like having to apologize to your friends for outbursts—can take a lot of energy. Most people develop internal apparatuses that reduce drive pressure. Such devices work like pressure-reducing valves in a home plumbing system, and make up one facet of our *internalized control system*.

Of course, we start learning controls when we are very young. But, the ability to learn controls and other adaptive devices is present at birth in humans. As Rapaport put it, "In animals of lower evolutionary levels the instincts are the guarantee of reality adaptedness; man's drives have lost much of this role, and thus his inborn adaptedness is more a potentiality than an actuality; processes of adaptation outweigh inborn adaptedness" (1960, p. 60). The ego becomes the primary organ for adapting to what Hartmann (1958) termed "an average expectable environment," the kind of world into which human children are typically born. Hence, most of the ego functions we described are thought to come with the package, at birth, but only as buds. They require nourishment and maturation to grow to fruition. Although this process is frequently termed "normal development," as we shall see repeatedly there is nothing inevitable about it. One often encounters clients whose ego functions have been stunted in one way or other.

Presuming that controls are internalized as the child matures, the drives become related to reality and modulated. Much psychic energy may then be seen as *neutralized* (Hartmann, 1956). Love of one's mother can be generalized to concern for all mankind, and further reinforced by a reaction formation against anger toward one's father. In dealing with a person with such a mature motivation, it hardly matters for practical purposes that the energy may originally have come from an Oedipal conflict. Gordon Allport (1937) had a related notion in his conception of the *functional autonomy of motives*. In fact, if we were to ask where the energy used by the ego in maintaining the controls comes from the answer would be that this, too, is drive energy diverted to the ego's purposes.

So, we have a working model of the individual's "economics." At any time s/he has a certain amount of psychic energy that is personally typical and that is probably not very different from the amount the rest of us have. Available energy is constantly being replenished from the well-springs of the drives. Flowing through the personality under pressure, the drive tension seeks "reduction" or discharge. Freud suggested a *drive-reduction* theory of motivation. In untamed form the energy is not available to be efficiently employed. But, if it flows in modulated, neutralized, socially and physically adapted fashion, it is readily harnessed. Therefore, when we encounter a client who strikes us as "a low-energy personality" or generally ineffective, what do we guess? We assume that either energy is being wasted or that the person's apparatus for harnessing energy does not function very well, which amounts to the same thing.

Blocking and Inability to Concentrate

Two problems with which any student is all too familiar will serve to illustrate how this energy depletion appears in daily living. Most of us have periods when we experience troubles concentrating; most of us also have times when our inability to learn something specific, which we ought to be able to master, confronted us with an unfamiliar sense of stupidity.

At a time when I was practicing psychotherapy with considerable license, a young man came into my office and announced, "I've been reading a *book!*" Why the accent on the last word? We had been so occupied with more urgent troubles that a key matter had never come out. I doubt he thought of it as a symptom, but for years the patient had been unable to get involved in reading anything longer than a newspaper or magazine article. "As soon as I'd read more than a couple of pages, I'd forget what I'd been reading about, and have to start over."

There are a number of possible explanations for such experiences. The particular subject matter may be conflictual, as with the four year old who removed a girl's pants and was severely punished. He did well in high school biology so long as the class studied amoebas and plants. When it reached the vertebrate reproductive system, he could not remember anything, even about frogs, which confused him because he had repressed the early episode. As fish reach up to drag down unsuspecting birds, old conflicts may reach up and repress new information that threatens to expose them to consciousness. In such cases, the act of reading has been "invaded by conflict" or "invaded by neurosis."

The explanation for my patient's inability to read was simpler and more general. He could not sustain attention. Attention, as we have noted, involves an expensive use of psychic energy. It waxes and it wanes. Any experienced teacher knows that while one segment of the class follows a discussion, another is at least momentarily wool-gathering. To keep all together, it is necessary to find an unobtrusive way of saying important things twice. Similarly, good teaching does not remain always at the same dead level of abstraction, but mixes principles with concrete examples, sometimes commencing with one, sometimes with the other. Rhetorical questions help. But, for persons who are distracted all the time, no teaching device can work very well. One would expect that people whose psychic energy is constantly draining away into maintaining defenses would show it partly by an inability to pay attention. Difficulties with concentration are so common among neurotics that they may not be specifically recorded.

Chronic Indecision

A phenomenon that seems related represents another leak in psychic energy; the inability to *integrate one's motivation* or make up one's mind. T. S. Eliot gave us J. Alfred Prufrock:

> I grow old...I grow old...
> I shall wear the bottoms of my trousers rolled.
>
> Shall I part my hair behind? Do I dare to eat a peach?
> I shall wear white flannel trousers, and walk upon the beach.
> I have heard the mermaids singing, each to each.
>
> I do not think that they will sing to me.

Elsewhere in his lovesong Prufrock says sadly, "I have measured out my life with coffee spoons" (1963, pp. 118f.).

My first academic advisor occupied one of the oldest, most prestigious chairs established in his discipline. To write a famous

commentary on Spinoza, he had searched out and read everything the great philosopher had, himself, ever studied, in the
original Greek, Latin, Hebrew or Aramaic. Fresh from a small
town and with no study habits, I was soon flunking out under the
program of studies this advisor arranged for me. So, my mother
came to look into things and went to talk with him. But she
quickly dismissed him as of no help, and we found the solution to
my course load elsewhere. Forty years later, I met another expert
in the same field who knew my professor and recounted his reputation for setting doctoral students in his department standards
that kept rising and were impossible to meet. The great scholar
was famous, even in my day, as his own version of Prufrock. With
cowboy movies his major recreation, in conversation he was likely
to draw you into his ruminating about whether he should buy a
pair of blue or brown socks! Yet, within the protected setting of a
great university, he made a career of obsessive doubting by raising
questions where none had been seen to exist, and then seeking
their answers. "What did Spinoza *really* mean by this?" On the
other hand, Bertrand Russell, another admirer of the philosopher,
dismissed his "proofs" as tedious gestures Spinoza felt he had to
go through (Russell, 1945).

Indecision as a symptom and as a defense will recur in this text.
We find it as an accompaniment to depression; it is central to the
obsessive compulsive's controlling of hostility; commitment anxiety is widespread among schizoid people. For the moment, however, let us note the costs in psychic energy. For some people, it
means having to do everything double—taking a master's in social
work *and* in biology, let us say. Now, gifted people are very often
gifted in more than one direction. It is possible to say, "I love
English as a field, but I cannot see trying it as an occupation, so
I'm going to work out my fascination with people in social work."
That is different than, "Well, if ever I get the chance, I'm going to
try to become an English professor. This is just a stand-by." Or, "I
don't know what I really want."

A major task of the ego is putting things together. This includes
refereeing conflicts among competing urges. Perhaps the student
can find a way to use both his social work and his biological
training in a public health job? But such urges may be mutually
contradictory. It is unusual to eat all you want and still keep a
svelte figure after thirty. Or, a therapist might say, "Again and
again, you attack someone and then you are drowned in guilt.
Which do you want to do? Stop attacking, or stop feeling guilty?"

In other words, the synthetic function cannot always help you wriggle around until you have it all. It becomes the job of the ego to set priorities, to help the person settle for one choice and give up the others. Motivational juggling acts waste energy.

Along with a tendency to integrate, the synthetic function, most people have a need to appear integrated to themselves, as well as to others. I suppose that is why discussions of energy loss through chronic indecision are so often taken as preaching. Not to be able to make up one's mind is looked down on. Indeed, some clients are prone to hasty actions because they cannot stand to appear indecisive. Their decisiveness is a reaction formation. Should you really choose to be decisive? Aren't there two (or three) ways of looking at this issue?

Loss of Energy in Defenses

In Chapter 3 it was remarked that all work uses energy including the acting, thinking, feeling used in defenses. It even costs energy to ward off emotions thought to threaten the defenses. Though the point was illustrated before, I would now like, as an example, to introduce a defense not mentioned earlier because it makes the loss of energy so graphic and is often misunderstood. Just as social work students—most of whom are straightforward people —commonly underestimate the presence of spite as a motivation in clients, they also overlook *narcissism*.

In the Greek myth of Narcissus a beautiful boy was wandering in the woods and came upon a still, clear pool. Gazing into the water, he saw his own image, which he had never seen, reflected. He fell in love with the beautiful creature, reached down toward the water to embrace him, and drowned. So, *narcissism* is taken to mean, in a general way, self-love. *Primary narcissism* connotes the self-involvement of a young infant not yet aware of a world separate from himself at all. *Secondary narcissism*, on the other hand, is a defense we see all the time in our work that comes from disappointment in love. The child who has begun to treat its mother as a special object associated with satisfying needs for pleasure and survival represents a later developmental stage than primary narcissism. If the child has felt attached and then feels abandoned, how may it react? We say the child *reinvests* the love in itself, using substitution as a mechanism. Having experienced loss and separation anxiety, and needing a defense, the child reacts with "If nobody loves me, then I will."

Moderate use of this maneuver is a source of normal *pride* or *dignity.* Pride helps us survive insults and rebuffs; to lack pride is to be extremely vulnerable. But heavy doses of narcissism are not functional. Therapists often recommend, "You have to love yourself before you can love other people." Even among clients addicted to self-depreciation this advice is so gladly received that we have to conclude it goes along well with a defense present in most neurotics. Freud has remarked that "as long as a man suffers, he ceases to love." The image is of a hurt dog lying in a corner, licking his injured paw. Narcissism is an expected defense among victims of psychic wounds; its side-effects are often noxious.

To be in love with an image for yourself is hardly a way to become popular. For one thing, you promise so little consideration to those around you. It is obviously fatuous to build hopes around a narcissistic person. Yet, the pattern is much more misfortune than sin, severely limiting and crippling its victim. Take a mother living in a small house on a limited income. This morning, she has the two preschoolers in the backyard while she begins her thrilling day of washing dishes, scrubbing floors, dusting the living room. Every few minutes, she looks out the window to assure herself the children are safe—one more chore! Still, from time to time she catches them in a really joyous mood, giggling over the sandbox or spinning in the swing their father made of an old tire. As she sees their pleasure, she feels cheerful herself. The ability to gain satisfaction vicariously goes along with loving. After a little while, she calls them in for mid-morning peanut butter snacks.

Compare this mother's day with a narcissistic woman's. As far as she is concerned, her morning is absolutely nothing. Unable to gain gratification from the happiness of others, she is reduced to her own experiences. In the midst of an otherwise dreary morning, a caseworker may also get pleasure from seeing an assisted family now looking cheerful. The pleasure is not just self-congratulatory, but an enjoyment in seeing them happier for their sakes. Excessive narcissism narrows one's range of pleasure.

There are other prices. An overconcern with your image exacerbates feelings of shame. Some cannot even ask a question, for not to know is to admit being less than perfect. Others cannot acquire skills. To practice a sport means living through a long period of looking bad. "Can you ice skate?" "Don't know. I've never tried."

Obsession with an image of yourself can make you so sensitive to criticism that ordinary give and take is humiliating and you avoid people. It also becomes enormously important never to anger anyone lest, in retaliaton, they puncture your tender balloon. Doing the best you can to be agreeable, you gain a reputation for being a person of no convictions, or two faced. Teenagers trapped with this defense certainly cannot be loose and spontaneous. Their woodenness hardly make it fun to know them; they tend to be left out of social doings. Since, to them, a friend is important not as a person, so much as a thing from which to milk support for their self-image, the lack of social facility makes the isolation worse.

What is extreme narcissism a defense against? It is often meant to bolster against feeling abandoned. But, the upshot of the defense is to end lonelier than most people. It makes one sad to penetrate the unpleasantness at the surface to the vulnerability beneath, and I think the sadness reflects what we see in the client. But which would be worse? To admit one's sadness and anxiety to consciousness or to continue the game?

Looseness of Ego Boundaries
The client bustled into the office and brushed back a wisp of hair from her eyes. This was rather futile, because the hair soon fell back, and indeed, her whole appearance was slightly bedraggled. She was not dirty; she was not clean, either. She hunched forward in her chair, breathed a deep sigh after having hurried up the stairs three minutes late, and said:

"Well, it's the same old sixes and sevens at our house. The children are driving me wild, now that school is out, and I don't know if I really do want to go on living with him. Last night was the living end. Well, everything sooner or later comes to an end. And that reminds me. I've got to get the toes repaired on those blue shoes of mine... we were planning to go to Sylvia's wedding... weddings are so nice. If I had only known... What do you think? What would you advise?

"About what?"

"Would you let him take me to the wedding, when I'm sure he'll just get sloppy drunk, and spill cigar ashes all over the car. And then he'll want to sleep with me. Boy, I never seem to get enough sleep. It is my aristocrasis acting up."

"Your what?"

"My aristocrasis. At least that's what I think it's called. They call and we fall. Tall against the wall. I should never have let him maul... you never tell me what to do."

By now the caseworker is a bit groggy. This lady has him on the ropes. He has been carefully schooled that one should "start with the client where she is." But where *is* this lady? The worker feels helpless, inadequate—if only he were more sensitive and skilled. Undoubtedly the client is communicating something besides general restlessness and some complaints against life. It is the worker's job to pick out signals being passed even in a language not generally understood by laymen. But there is something else he should be aware of. This client seems unable to formulate her thoughts into any systematic sequence of ideas. She talks, it is true, in what sounds like complete sentences. But the sentences do not follow, one from the other. There is evidence at times that her thoughts are easily distracted. One or twice we note that the client seems to have been carried away by the sheer rhyming quality of what she said. She used a word that is not a word at all. Either she has misheard it from her doctor, or it is a word she just invented, a *neologism*.

When it is this difficult to understand a client, two major hypotheses are to be considered. Perhaps the client does not wish to be understood. Or, perhaps the client is *unable* to sustain a logical train of thought, which is then reflected in his speech. When this is true, we say that he sounds *loose*. This is an imprecise but descriptive term characterizing the kind of weakness in thought process we see here. That is, ideas are associated not so much in terms of a problem to be solved or a meaning to be communicated as in terms of "echoing" verbal sounds. Other associations may be quite mysterious to us. If we had the time we might discover that the client's basis for connecting images is that they remind him of things he once saw together—his mother stooping to scrub her front stoop, or some such event.

Another general characteristic contributing to loss of energy is *looseness of ego boundaries*. Describing a patient as "loose" refers to several phenomena: weakness of the synthetic function of the ego to which we have just alluded; difficulty in binding impulses or affects; and primary-process thinking. Looseness is not an all-or-none matter, but relative. Some people's mentalities are so rigid that, once they reach a conviction, they cannot change it. Their attitudes remain impenetrable to new influences or information. At the other extreme some are so flexible and permeable they cannot even keep clear distinctions among ideas, do not have values or motives so much as whims, and usually repressed images keep breaking into consciousness.

Freudians distinguish two levels of thought, the *primary* and the *secondary process*. Secondary-process thinking is characteristic of reasonably mature people. Connections are logical, abstractions are used; notions are realistic. Primary-process thinking on the other hand resembles that of the young child. Ideas are connected in ways not "logical" by adult standards; by gross similarities (bing goes with sting goes with sling); by temporal accidents (clocks go with streetcars because I saw the big clock the same afternoon I saw the streetcar); by irrelevant features (the bedtime pill and the locomotive are both dark green). Notions of causation are primitive and magical (Fraiberg, 1957). Some fit classical examples of fallacies taught in courses on formal logic. "You painted the house and the next day my dog was run over, so you caused my dog's death." This is an illustration of *post hoc ergo propter hoc*. "A hill is to climb," said Dr. Seuss, who understands this style of thinking very well. The primary process, then, is the way we thought when we were children.

It is theorized that the same style of thinking continues in parts of the mind hidden during the day which reveal themselves in dreams where anything can happen. Dreams are not bound by considerations of reality or causation. It is also believed that a lot of our unconscious thinking and fantasying is primary process. Naturally, that part of us that does not believe there *is* a real world can do only a poor job of looking ahead and planning for the future.

Few clients speak and think purely at the level of the primary process, but in some it seems to predominate over the secondary. Schizophrenics and other psychotics show a loss of the ability to "test" reality; primary process often emerges in intoxicated people. Each of us experiences primary process from time to time—in reverie, between sleeping and waking, or when very tired. Indeed, many creative people exploit primary processes to gain imagery or unexpected associations for humor or stories.

The structure of the benzene ring is said to have been imaged by a chemist who saw visions of snakes swallowing their own tails while gazing into a fireplace one evening. The atomic scientist Oppenheimer remarked, "If we do not dream by night, we shall have nothing to correct by day." The secondary process remains necessary to appraise inspiration and give it logical form; the ability to tap into primary process is called *regression in the service of the ego*, and is enormously helpful in conducting psychodrama (see Chapter 17). Voluntary regression can be difficult during periods of tension, perhaps from an unconscious fear that it may trap us.

Though defenses may become pathological, *workable* defenses are "normal." Looseness is also used to refer to instances when usually repressed ideas or impulses keep popping into consciousness which means the defenses are not holding. Now, if having fantasies of sleeping with one's mother after learning about the Oedipus Complex meant most students were "loose," our mental health statistics would be much worse. Fortunately, fantasies under suggestion are usually not in touch with real impulses.

But, you do encounter people who are aware of facets of themselves that startle you. For example, it used to be thought that a person terrified of heights was combatting an unconscious wish to throw himself down. What would you make of the client who, in the first interview, remarks, "I guess I want to jump and am afraid I'll carry it out." You are supposed to require treatment to have such insights. I now think that there is more to acrophobia, the unreasonable fear of heights, than this, that separation anxiety is also involved. But, the formulation, "The wish is father to the fear" is not a bad one to bear in mind when examining a phobia, for it often applies. The phrasing is not male chauvinism: the wish begets the fear; it does not directly bear it.

Failures of defense and other forms of looseness are also evident in what clinicians call *leakage*. Early in his practice Freud identified slips of the tongue as windows on the unconscious to peer through. "Don't you care what anybody says, you wear that dress," does not come out quite as you meant it, or does it? Twenty years ago, I was introduced to the wind-up luncheon of the Alabama Welfare Conference with the remark, "And now we come to the bitter end..." (I hoped it was a slip.)

People with reasonably normal defenses can slip up. People regressed in psychosis produce a "word salad," including *neologisms*, or completely new words. If you are Lewis Carroll, your neologisms may be memorable. My wife and I have a dog named Brillig as in "'Twas brillig and the slithy tove did gyre and gimble o'er the wabe." The poet Heine added words to the German language. James Joyce did the same for English although it is not clear we *needed* the new adjective in his phrase, "snotgreen sea." I guess the key issue is that psychotics and Mrs. Malaprop manage this without effort; it is ominous if you do not have to make one.

Finally, we think of "looseness" in connection with the inability to *control impulses*. Such failures lead people, like little children, "To want what they want when they want it." Once, we received a middle-aged patient at the hospital because severe business reverses had triggered a dangerous depression. His mood improved after a bit, becoming if anything too cheerful, and his unsuspecting doctor let him go to town for the afternoon where he bought a new Buick Electra to be delivered to the hospital, his local address. And he was in fact legally responsible for his actions. Looseness is also seen in casual violence. In large cities violence has many meanings, but on the individual level those committing it are very often "loose" personalities, as I learned working in prisons many years ago. The looseness of impulse buying or violence or shoplifting or unwise sexual escapades is usually accompanied by a disregard for real-world consequences. The lack of foresight is typical of childlike thinking. But an inability to control discharge or to think things over or save up to pay for what you want reflects deficits in the *superego*. The function of the latter, you will recall, is to keep you out of trouble. To a degree that I did not appreciate years ago, a healthy superego helps hold the personality together.

One might speculate that all this looseness would actually save energy, or at least make it available. One is no longer all tied up with denial, reaction-formation, undoing, or general condensation of affect. A bit of thought, however, will suggest that it wastes psychic effort. How efficiently can you meet your needs if you live impulsively, illogically, with little regard for the consequences? Besides, who would more need reaction formation, a person whose hostilities were under reasonable control and sublimated, or one living under threat of sudden outbursts? To paraphrase, "Looseness is the mother of rigidity."

Conditions Loosening Ego Boundaries

Why are some clients so much looser than others? As we so often must in social work, we distinguish between those whose *ego-deficits* are *situational*, who usually operate at a better level and can return to it, and those whose looseness seems *characterological*, part of the way they always are. Let us begin with the latter group. We start with their failure to develop internalized controls.

CHARACTEROLOGICAL LOOSENESS

Ego boundaries emerge with the differentiation of yourself from the rest of the world (see Chapter 8). At some point in very early infancy the baby becomes aware that he and his mother are not one. They have different wills and purposes. For instance, part of the blob you think of as you, your mother's breast, does not appear and offer milk whenever you want it. So one might say in a very general way that the beginning formation of boundaries has to do with the differentiation of the self from the non-self.

A second source of the formation of boundaries seems to lie in getting drives under the control of the ego. Analytic theory provides two conceptions of how the superego is formed and controls are *internalized*.

The first conception really follows Thorndike's *Law of Effect*, formulated in the 1890's and memorized in my generation as "Pleasure stamps in, pain stamps out." Pioneering students of memory assumed that associations between ideas form because of repeated encounters, but this did not account for which associations held and which were forgotten. The Law of Effect said that if the connection gave pleasure, the memory would hold. The same may be said for the formation of habits as well, so you can see that Thorndike's law is really basic to learning theory and the practice of behavior modification. Freudians rarely mention Thorndike, despite a very similar position regarding learning. In line with this principle they trace development as follows.

At first the child controls his impulse to avoid punishment. If you throw your milk, Mama, who is right there, will slap. Next, he controls his impulse to avoid anticipated punishment. Mama is not here, at the moment, but if you throw your milk on the floor, she will punish you when she gets back. A still later stage would be self-control in the anticipation of reward. If you do *not* throw your milk, Mama will praise you when she comes. Finally, if the external supports for the sequence are in place long enough, the child gradually takes over the reward and punishment himself. If I throw my milk, *I* don't like it. To the extent that the child sees himself as the source of his reward or punishment, we say he has *internalized* control. The trouble with most old-fashioned reform schools was that the last stage never occurred. The discharged delinquent youngster returned to his impulsive pattern as soon as outside controls were removed.

Failures in this aspect of superego development can be studied by listing the life events under which we know internalization is unlikely. If the infant has inconsistent caretakers, irregular in rewarding or punishing, the pattern will not form. Inconsistency can occur when the child is reared by his mother, if she is impulsive or distracted by other troubles. The parents may disagree, with a mother opposed to milk-throwing and the father thinking it funny. When caretakers are ambiguous in other ways, learning is deterred—for example, if it is not made clear which behaviors are approved and disapproved.

Of course, most babies are not literally slapped. They are mildly scolded, but they feel the mother's disapproval. Disapproval has to do with withdrawal of love, and that has to do with abandonment, so it is an enormously powerful threat to the vulnerable little being. Still, babies who have experienced little love do manage, but their detached invulnerability creates, besides other problems, persons with flimsy superegos. Studies have repeatedly described mothers of delinquents as indifferent and cold. You can readily imagine how all these processes are distorted among youngsters reared in a succession of foster homes.

For Freudians, however, the Law of Effect is not the only way to understand the development of controls. The other mechanism whereby internalization takes place is *identification*. I must say, it has taken me years of trying to teach about it to clarify what this concept really implies. It is easy to be misled, for the Freudians talk about concepts like *incorporation*, which gives you images of children swallowing their parents. The simplest way to look at the mechanism is to remind ourselves that identification is a defense. There *is* anxiety in the picture, when it takes place.

If you take your little boy to the zoo, and get near the lions he will be curious and interested. Suddenly, however, one of the lions lets out an enormous roar. The youngster screams, starts to cry, and cannot be mollified until you go off to the monkey house or some other neutral territory like the habitat of mouse deer. Yet what does the child do on you way home in the car? He starts to roar like the lion! Why? He is mastering his anxiety by what is called *identification with the aggressor*. He acts as if saying, "If I make you part of me, then I can control you—and you cannot hurt me." Naturally, he cannot make the lion part of him, but he does not have to since we are talking about ideas and images *in the mind*. It is as if he had a photographic negative of the lion and a similar image of himself, and he slid the lion's image under his so that they blended or combined in some way. Thus he "incorporates" the lion.

The other type of identification is *identification out of love*. If I love you and am attached to you, then the threat of your leaving me stirs separation anxiety. How can I handle it? In the same way. If I make your image part of my image of me, then "I can control you—and you cannot go away and leave me." So, identification out of love is really a shorthand way of saying identification out of the threat of *loss* of love, which is the usual form of identification operating in most families during the internalization of controls.

In taking over the parental image, the child also takes on the parent's values, attitudes, and controls.

As Rapaport implied in the quote cited earlier, humans are not born with these contents already in place, but with the capacity to form identifications. From an evolutionary standpoint, this is a lovely mechanism for, among other things, it means the human child does not have to learn everything about avoiding troubles by trial and error or reinforcement scheduling. We take over a lot of our standards "on faith," as it were.

Certain circumstances prevent a child from using this mechanism. Identification with a parent who has few controls and poor judgment is little help. Furthermore, the child in a cold relationship may not "need" to use this defense mechanism: if he is already unloved, what does he have to lose? Another circumstance, infrequently mentioned in the literature, also occurs. The child for whom no limits are set, given *unconditional love,* is under no threat. So there is no anxiety and no need to use this defense mechanism. And it is not necessary to have a rich mother to be "spoiled," as we used to call it. Parenting requires steering between being too demanding and too lenient. Fortunately, it seems the line must be fairly broad, for most youngsters acquire workable superegos.

When the controls are firm, well internalized, not too severe, they ease living. I can leave a ten dollar bill on the table and walk away from social work students and they feel nothing except, perhaps, mild curiosity about what I am up to. Delinquent boys and girls I have known, however, would have to make a conscious effort not to grab for it, or waste energy calculating how to get it from this stingy, quick old man. When the controls are "normal," as we say, they operate unconsciously, and relatively effortlessly. To return to our model of the water tower in the small town and the system under pressure, we are talking about the difference between holding a thumb over the end of a hose as compared with twisting the handle on a faucet. We have looked at looseness of ego boundaries as implicated in behavioral control. Without overloading the issue, we can see that other matters like thinking and perceiving reality might have similarly fortunate or unfortunate histories. In short, one condition affecting looseness is the client's enduring character structure.

The other, as we noted, has to do with the current situation. Under the impact of a major blow—a death, disappointment in love, business or job failure, injury to a child—most people appear less well put together than normally. Physical events often have similar psychological effects—severe fatigue, illness, intoxicants, drugs. Indeed, it is necessary to be able to tolerate looseness to fall asleep (regression in the service of the ego).

SITUATIONAL LOOSENESS

Ego boundaries weaken in certain life situations. Generations of social workers have learned there is nothing better than a good marriage and few things worse than a bad one. Two adults who were once in love can become so mutually irritating that they make each other sick, each becoming more and more regressed over months and years of intimate antipathy. Add to this the clinical saying that, "Sex repugnant to one of the partners is eventually destructive to both." You then have *a downward spiral of causation* as they say in General Systems Theory.

Boundaries also loosen in life situations lacking structure. Most readers will have heard of stimulus-deprivation experiments in which a subject is placed in a pitch dark tank at body temperature in a soundproof room. In one typical series, roughly a third of the subjects hallucinated at some stage. To be in a boring job with nothing much to do can have a regressive effect. What you welcome on a vacation you may despise in a vocation. Living under conditions of terror from unseen enemies, as in Israel, may bring out the heroic in a people, but also prove regressive.

Several authoritarian regimes, German Nazis, Russian Communists, Chinese Communists, have used a combination of stimulus deprivation, cognitive unstructuredness, and terror to break down the defenses and values of political prisoners and prisoners of war. The aim was to prepare them for "brain-washing." Such regimes do not like psychoanalysis but have a lot of practical experience in cowing people and dissolving their personalities which the Freudians understand from trying to reverse such processes. Bettelheim (1943) held himself together in a concentration camp in part by analysing the Nazis' rationale and observing the effects of their methods on his fellow-prisoners. So not everyone breaks down.

As Rapaport has suggested (1959), the ego is connected both with internal processes, the id, and with external reality. It maintains its autonomy from the id in part by continuing its responsiveness to external reality and stimulation. The more chaotic or ambiguous one's environment, the more necessary it is that ego boundaries be firm or even rigid, in order to retain essentially the same personality. It is not surprising, therefore, that Solzhenitsyn, who survived the Soviet prison system to carry on a self-imposed mission as witness for humanity, should prove critical of Western society too, after being exiled. On the other hand, persons whose ego boundaries have become loose may be helped by removal to the safety and routine of a hospital; indeed, many immature individuals function better in an all embracing highly structured situation such as the Army, a police unit, the staff of an institution, a university or another bureaucracy.

Let us summarize. We have been discussing what affects the ego's resiliency or "strength." We began by considering the kinds of things that may weaken the ego. If one way to conceptualize ego strength is in terms of the psychic energy freely available to solve current life problems, then the ego may be weakened in two general ways: (a) energy is being dissipated or wasted in some way; (b) energy is available but the machinery for putting it to use is inefficient or broken down.

Concerning the loss or unavailability of psychic energy, we mentioned the tying up of energy in maintaining elaborate defenses. A defense that afflicts many clients deprived in early life is secondary narcissism, a conception introduced to illustrate how time, work and sensitivities may be consumed by narcissistic attitudes which are bound to be unsatisfying. A second way of dissipating energy is through chronic indecision, which may express greed or reflect an inefficiency of the personality, namely, a deficit in the synthetic function of the ego.

This led us to a discussion of how the ego may inefficiently utilize energy because of lack of adequate structure. We illustrated this problem with a discussion of looseness of ego boundaries as, for example, expressed through lack of organizaton in the way one thinks—primary-process thinking and/or eruptions from the unconscious. Looseness is also reflected in the lack of internalized controls over impulses which work silently and relatively effortlessly in normal adults. To understand why some people are psychologically "looser" than others, we look to see whether the looseness is situational or characterological. With the impulse-ridden the cause must lie in failures of early parenting and a lack of development of normally internalized controls. On the other hand, any of us can show a kind of looseness under the impact of fatigue, illness, intoxication or life-stress. Indeed, the ability to get into contact with one's primary process at will can be advantageous for many who do creative work.

Coping

Readers too young to recall Damon Runyon's wonderful tales of racetrack hangers-on, may remember Nicely-Nicely from the musical, *Guys and Dolls*, given us twenty years ago by Frank Loesser. Adaptability is readily illustrated by heroic figures in history, of course. But it has always seemed to me that social workers also encounter impressive examples among those living on the margins of society. Their ability to survive is sometimes the more inspiring because they have so little to work with. Keeping going the best you can may also be referred to as *coping*.

So now I will tell you about Nicely-Nicely Jones, who is called Nicely-Nicely because any time anybody asks him how he is feeling, or how things are going with him, he always says nicely, nicely, in a very pleasant tone of voice, although generally this is by no means the gospel truth, especially about how he is going.

He is a character of maybe forty-odd, and he is short, and fat, and very good-natured, and what he does for a livelihood is the best he can, which is an occupation that is greatly overcrowded at all times along Broadway (Runyon, 1941, pp. 34f).

In practice, none of us deals with LIFE but with a long series of happenings. In these more limited episodes, we ask not only how generally resilient the person is, but how he deals with stresses and crises. Interest in *mechanisms for coping* has grown in recent years, as clinicians moved beyond their preoccupation with curing ills into prevention, and help with daily living. During World War II, for example, it was found that a soldier removed from combat for battle fatigue was impossible to restore to duty after he had gotten far enough to the rear. The *secondary gain through illness* became so powerful, there was so little wish to get well, that he was lost to his unit. Therefore, psychiatric treatment was offered right behind the lines, preferably in the battalion aid-station. The aim was emergency treatment until the man's own coping abilities could resume work.

The general function of the coping mechanism is to restore equilibrium or psychological homeostasis. Indeed, a lucky person copes in a way that leaves him better able to deal with stress than before.

There are many coping mechanisms. In a sense this whole book is about coping. For example, a form of coping with an obstacle is to stop and take thought as to how to overcome it. This detour into thinking starts when a person is very young. The energy cost of trying various routes past the obstacle in your mind, rather than with your steps, is cheap; the payoff in effectiveness, great. However, this kind of detouring is not at the disposal of chronically impulsive people, or those momentarily overwhelmed with anxiety. Therefore, when Perlman (1957) talks of the problem-solving process as universal, she seems to overlook a goodly proportion of the clients we see all the time.

It is natural to think of coping as dealing with events "outside" us. However, much of what we cope with is internal. If you are out of work and desperate, are you coping with the economy—or with your distress for your children. In other words, much and possibly most coping is with inner forces, some of which are stirred by external happenings. An emphasis on the detailed analysis of coping with *internal processes* distinguishes Freudian ego psychology from nearly all others.

Any person at all active, sooner or later does something about which s/he feels guilty, and the guilt is appropriate. What are typical reactions? Some consciously refuse to experience guilt by rationalizing the action. But this undermines the superego. Some are overcome with remorse in a dramatic, general way that leads to no specific learning (e.g. "I'm just a dirty, low-down person") and thereby evade the concrete issue. Some seek to carry out their own punishment, and so become depressed. The conscious absorbing of deserved guilt is a hallmark of maturity, so it is well worth considering how to counsel someone who has wronged another. But note that insofar as guilt anxiety is involved, the method of coping is familiar: it involves a defense mechanism. Indeed, we may say that the function of all the defenses is to cope with anxiety. Viewed in this way, the defense mechanisms are subsumed under the more general rubric of coping mechanisms. It is not always easy to decide when what we see is a defense mechanism, and when it is "realistic" coping.

Two rather general processes underlying defenses and other coping mechanisms seem worthwhile identifying at this point. The first is the ego's use of *repetition*. The need to do something over and over that causes unhappiness and anxiety is termed the *repetition compulsion*. At first glance, it makes no psychological sense. Yet, repetition is used by all of us at times to overcome fear. And it works. What is the advice after falling from a horse? Get back on and start riding. Repeated exposure to an anxiety-producing experience seems to help the ego master the anxiety, to "wear it out," as it were. To help a small child upset by her mother's going to the hospital, Fraiberg (1950) hit on the idea of getting down on the floor with her to play peek-a-boo. It has been said that when you have a nightmare that happens again and again, it must represent a strong wish. Such an interpretation can be shattering to a patient if her bad dreams concern injury to someone she loves. But, wish-fulfillment hardly accounts for the terror-laden dreams combat veterans suffer years afterwards. Would it not be more parsimonious to hypothesize that the ego is trying to "wear out" the anxiety by repetition? The same explanation would apply, of course, if the anxiety *were* related to guilt over an unconscious wish you find unacceptable. So, the use of repetition to assist mastery over unpleasant affects is one *general coping maneuver*.

A second rather general maneuver by which the ego tries to achieve mastery over experiences that threaten to overwhelm it is the *symbolic conversion* into activity of what has been passively experienced (Rapaport, 1967). Children abused at home are sometimes identified in the primary grades by their aggressiveness toward others. In the concentration camps described by Bettleheim (1943), many "old prisoners" who had been inmates for some time wore scraps of SS guards' uniforms and prided themselves on their toughness and military bearing. Analysands often yearn to become analysts. All these may be called *identification with the aggressor*, but that seems a specific form of the general mode, *converting passivity into activity* to overcome feelings of helplessness. Is it not better to be borne away on the plane than to be left waving good-bye from the ground? To take action rather than suffer in silence? A most important rule in adolescent love is to try to be sure that you are in position to quit rather than being fired.

So both these general maneuvers usually help with coping, and we use them all the time in healthful ways. Yet, each may also be implicated in obsessions, compulsions, meaningless guilt, and repeatedly unsatisfying love affairs. From recognizing these maneuvers as attempts at self-healing we can make sense of their roles in pathology.

Ego Support

The term, *ego-supportive*, is widely used in the social work treatment literature. One might think it refers to praising or otherwise helping the client feel better about his/her self-image, though this is not what we mean. The term distinguishes a type of treatment that does not aim at change, so much as helping the person do the best with what s/he has. There is even a hint of derogation in the term, as if ego support is all you do when you cannot offer more definitive treatment.

It seems to me that what we call ego support has to do with helping the ego recover its ability to cope and/or do better than comes naturally. One task of the ego is certainly to find ways to meet needs. Having money is, itself, ego-supportive in this country since it removes so many obstacles and strains. But, if the client has no way of getting any, giving him funds is a form of ego support that removes an obstacle to getting food. A person who is hungry because shamed or threatened by being in a taking position may need ego support in the form of assurance that there are times in life when our usual values have to give way to other standards; this supports the ego in dealing with a tyrranical superego. Providing one's client with advice from your greater experience, or information from your special knowledge are supportive of adaptation. Deliberateness and good example may facilitate the client's detouring into thought for problem-solving. A great many clients are very lonely people who know no way out of their isolation. To them, our caring and being there are ego-supportive reassurance against feeling unloveable.

We try to reduce the overloading of the client's ego by offering the resources at our disposal. One type of resource we have are coping mechanisms that are free to borrow. When to make such offers and when to hold back, how to offer ego support in a way that enhances rather than weakens the clients' ability to cope in the future are skills one has to acquire. Here, I merely want to emphasize that social services thought of as financial assistance, or other concrete services are, from a psychological standpoint, ego-supportive. They enhance the adaptive power of the client just as surely as *clarification* supports the *self-observing* function of the ego.

This self-observing function refers to most people's ability to stand back from their acting selves and form an impression of what they are doing and what they look like. It is as if one part of the personality were able to move to one side, "take distance," to look at the rest. This capacity is much needed for most forms of talking treatment. In fact, the process of therapy brings this function to the fore to a degree that may make a client temporarily very self-conscious.

Which part takes distance and observes the remainder? It is a separate organization, probably formed out of identifications with people whose judgments you have respected earlier in life. But the process of casework can itself support the self-observing function. After a person has been some months in treatment, it is common to hear, "Well, I got into it again with my wife, but then I seemed to hear what you would probably think I was up to. So I stopped and asked myself what I was so mad about." The client has begun to internalize the casework process, the worker's attitude of inquiring into *why* he does what he does. Identification with the worker, in his current life, provides another form of ego support.

On-the-spot aid to people in danger of becoming overwhelmed has been called *crisis intervention* (Parad, 1965). Suppose we made observations on how a series of people faced with a particular life-stress or disturbance handled it. We would then be in a position to know what ways of coping are typically used to overcome the stress successfully; we could even identify coping mechanisms that make things worse. This would put us in a position to offer cogent advice to anyone presently experiencing the same life-crisis. Indeed, the advice should be better than drawing only on our own coping techniques, which might not fit our client well at all.

A number of the principles involved may be illustrated with the process of *grief*. In my junior year at Harvard a terrible tragedy struck Boston. On a busy evening, the Coconut Grove, a nightclub jammed with students from surrounding universities, caught fire and—as has happened since in other places—because exits were stuck over a hundred lost their lives. There were grieving families all around the Boston area. Erich Lindemann, an analyst on the faculty of the Harvard Medical School who was helping develop the field we call Social Psychiatry, thought to contact all the psychiatrists in the Boston area to see how many families sought help, and to make a study of their reactions. The results of that survey were reported by Lindemann (1944) and his classic paper is available in the book edited by Parad (1965).

Lindemann was able to ask the question: What reactions to grief are "normal?" That is, what widespread responses and symptoms do we see among those suffering grief, including those persons we did not previously think of as neurotic or emotionally ill? The results of his survey, and of his shrewd thinking about the facts, led Lindemann to speak of *grief work*. By this he meant, that following the loss of a loved person (the *love object)*, the ego typically starts to work in various ways to absorb the blow, and to heal the wound. Some of the initial reactions commonly found do not appear to be efforts at recuperation. For example, precordial pain, pain over the heart, sighing, or an inability to make decisions seem to be reactions to the stress. On the other hand, a variety of other reactions make sense when viewed as attempts at coping.

Loss of appetite, in grief, symbolizes "I can't swallow this." Early waking and insomnia are thought to be ways of evading terrible dreams. Depression and irritability are nearly universal. One is angry at the person for dying. At funerals one often hears, "How can you go away and leave me?" But of course one would feel guilty to attack directly; and besides, the object of the anger is inaccessible. So, one *displaces* the anger, putting oneself in the place of the missing object. Hence, we have the formulation of the classic dynamics of depression as "Anger turned against the subject." The irritability is general, too. One is also apt to displace the rage against others around—the doctor who attended the relative who died, friends who wander into one's view, and so forth. Preoccupation with images of the deceased may endure for many months, leading one to believe at times that you have seen the person, or heard him. By keeping images active in one's mind and by putting pictures of the person in prominent places, one tries to hold onto him. It would be expected that identification be used also, and survivors sometimes show this by assuming the work and causes of the deceased—or, less healthily, by believing they are suffering from the same illnesses. Restlessness or pacing is common in grief as in *agitated depression;* some believe these movements represent instinctive attempts to find the missing attachment object. In other words, once one assumes that the ego is trying to cope "the best it can" seemingly unrelated behaviors prove to be aspects of the same underlying process.

It is common in grief to encounter guilt. "If only I had gotten up one more time during the night to check on mother, I would have saved her." "Did we really do everything we could have?" When the guilt is quite unrealistic, which it not always is, we used to look for an unconscious wish that the person should die. After all, if the daughter had waited on her dying mother hand and foot for four straight years, worrying and neglecting her own family, an impulse to be released from bondage would be quite expectable—and *un*acceptable. Often the statement "I could have done more" represents an attempt to turn what was passively suffered into activity. Not only must the ego withstand the loss, it must even deal with its helplessness to do anything. As a defensive maneuver, it denies this, trying to think, "There must be some way I had control over what happened to me." But, having used this device to master the anxiety, the price demanded is the reply, "You had control, and you let it happen."

Successful coping with grief seems to require, among other things, that it be consciously felt when faced, and that the person express his feelings as much as possible through talking, crying, clutching or whatever. Grief unexpressed at the time of loss leaves behind the threat of *delayed grief reaction*, which can lie like a blight of chronic depression, sometimes for years. All therapists have encountered this in clients and patients, sometimes five or ten years after the event. So, far from encouraging "a stiff upper lip," which is usually done because the hearer cannot stand the tears, we encourage weeping and full expression. Successful grief work seems also to require going over and over some of the reactions, wearing them out and, as we say, *working them through*. Finally, successful grief work leaves the person free to shift feelings of love and attachment to other objects. Even if no one can really replace the one who was lost, it is evident that those who are able to fill their lives with others have the best recoveries.

The processes and dynamics of grief are very close to those of *reactive depression*. This is understandable, for the majority of depressions we see in clients stem from what we call "loss of the object." Brown and Harris (1978) have given us a remarkable study of types of events that preceded onset of depression among working class women in London and rural Britain. They found the following: separation or threat of it, such as the death of a parent, or a husband's announcing he was going to leave home; an unpleasant revelation about someone one had loved that changed the relationship to that person (e.g. husband's unfaithfulness, homosexuality of a lover, criminality of a loved one); a life-threatening illness to someone close; major material loss or disappointment, such as unemployment; enforced change of residence. As noted earlier, analytic theory assumes that rage against the person who abandons you cannot be expressed because of guilt or because the real target is absent or indifferent. Accordingly, the anger is displaced against the self, or "against the subject," as in "I am mad at me and I'm going to make me suffer."

But that is only the simplest formulation. Next, we might note that when we love, we probably have incorporated an image of our love into our image of ourselves, through *identification* out of love. So, we can further assume that with absence, we try to attack that image *in ourselves*. One might say that the full formulation would encompass love of the object, incorporation of the object, loss of the object, rage, guilt anxiety, displacement of the hostility against the subject. (See Bibring [1953] and Rapaport [1967]).

Depression is very widespread among those we try to help because of the dreadful things that keep happening to our clients— some of which are the reasons we know them at all. All social workers, therefore, need to have up-to-date knowledge of depression. Most reactive depressions are self-limiting, the ego will cure itself after some time. We all do this with the blues, and with worse. Some need another's assistance. First-aid treatment of depression should be within the ability of any trained caseworker. It involves the trilogy of *ventilation, restitution*, and *working-through*. In this introduction to ego psychology we are not concerned with discussing all the modalities of treatment. We have described the application of principles from ego psychology to treating reactive-depression in clients elsewhere (Polansky, DeSaix and Sharlin, 1972). A fine, advanced discussion of ego-supportive and related techniques of treatment has been published also by Sidney Wasserman (1974).

CHAPTER 5
A SPEED READER'S GUIDE TO
Character as Personality Structure

In a dynamic personality theory, *structural* concepts, called *traits*, identify patterns of recurring behavior. *Characterology* searches for *syndromes* (or clusters) of traits. Character diagnosis does not imply forcing clients' personalities into pigeon-holes. And, it would be too bad to fall into *labeling*. Our system provides *condictability*, projecting from traits known to be present to others likely to be; and it is geared to underlying dynamics that help us choose among possible modes of *treatment*.

Abraham and others grounded their initial characterology in *psychosexual stages* that can be quickly reviewed. *Oral* characters display marked oral drives and *remnants; anal* characters show anal traces and *reaction formations* against anal *expulsiveness; phallic* individuals show competitiveness. Such older formulations are still used as a verbal shorthand. *Infantilism*, for example, is useful to sum up a syndrome of developmental failure and early *fixations*. It usually reflects deprivation, identification with infantile parents and/or having been *infantilized* that is, encouraged to remain childlike and helpless.

Character As Personality Structure

5

M any trivia have been written about how to behave in order to make a good initial impression on a prospective employer. The advice is often beside the point for professionals who need cogent advice about how to size up the person doing the hiring. After all, anyone you spend one, two, or ten years working for will be in position to have an enormous impact on your career.

Let us suppose you have been in correspondence with the dean of a school. He has expressed interest in you; you have expressed interest in his job and have driven hundreds of miles to visit. You arrive promptly for your appointment, but then are kept waiting—not five minutes, but twenty. From the first exchange, you are let know, "who is in charge around here." He brushes aside questions about working conditions to brag about his skills in bridge, golf, riding. In short, it is apparent within fifteen minutes that this is a difficult little man, no one to whom you want to entrust your chance at a productive work life.

But, internal warning bells go off immediately about turning down a job offer from this person. Since he is only aware of his own needs, he will be furious if you reject an offer from him after he has deigned to make one. Your refusal challenges his control and is taken as a personal affront. He will have an urge to get even. If he is infantile enough, and has enough control, he always carries out his retaliatory impulses.

I once had such an interview. I agreed to visit for two days to look and to be looked over; after the first few minutes it was clear to me that I could not stand to work there. Still, to avoid embarassing anyone I went through the motions for the agreed time.

It also occurred to me that if I immediately made my disinterest known, I would never be reimbursed. Returning home, I waited a full week after receiving my travel check, and wrote albeit with misgivings. Perhaps I had estimated him incorrectly. Some years later a colleague revealed that the Dean would behave exactly as I predicted. A mutual friend had courteously immediately told him that she was not interested and was never reimbursed for her travel.

Among the most important facets of ego psychology is *character-ology,* the study of character. Indeed, greater experience can only deepen our impression of the efficiency of concentrating on the characters of those about whom we must make predictions. From a knowledge of character, one can derive crucial guidelines for helping our clients. We will begin our discussion of this topic with some general principles of characterology and illustrations of character types.

Structure

As commonly used, the word "character" has a strong value con-notation. To say a man has character is to imply he has morals and acts in terms of them. Indeed, a fixity which can approach rigidity is implied. It is in character for a man of character to stand by his principles, as long as they are characteristic.

Psychoanalytic theory also employs the word, but without the values. The emphasis is on continuity, on aspects of the person that can be counted on to reveal themselves again and again, even under changing circumstances. Put another way, character is the warp and woof of personality, the traits and values repeatedly in evidence.

The attention is on the fixed parts of the personality when, in fact, none are totally unchanging. The saying, "This too shall pass," is very old. In life, all is change; nothing stays constant. But, even while everything is changing, some changes are much faster than others. Relatively fixed parameters that change very slowly are referred to as *structures.* In speaking of groups one refers to the *power structure* to denote that some group members possess more influence than others. *Roles* too are structured, as they define how people are expected to behave toward each other. A group's *morale,* on the other hand, is expected to vary from day to day, on sports' teams it often alters from minute to minute.

In setting up a theory, it is convenient to use at least some concepts that refer to structured aspects of the field. For example, in order to predict how far a ball dropped from an airplane will have fallen in ten seconds, we use the formula taught in high school physics: $S = \frac{1}{2} g t^2$. The number of seconds is given us, and g is a *constant* whose value we know, so we easily solve the equation for S, the distance traveled. Elements in a situation that can be treated as constant, in other words, reduce complexity in making deductions. If you are low on cash before a Sunday outing, you can count on the fact that a stingy friend is not going to ease the planning by offering to buy beer for the crowd. He may not simplify your life, but what you know of his character simplifies the prediction. Knowing the social role of a first-year student in our school this fall, permits a whole series of reliable predictions. Regardless of mood, the weather, or minor illness, that person will very probably be in Aderhold 411 Monday at 2:20 P.M. So the discovery of recurrences we can rely on is a great convenience for theorizing.

And people do, in fact, tend to be structured. As time passes, they become more and more "set in their ways." We have already noted the usefulness of the repetition compulsion for wearing out anxiety, but there are other advantages of structuring for the personality. With a problem that resembles another familiar puzzle, following a well-worn solution is far less demanding than finding a new one. For one thing, finding a new solution requires attention, an expensive use of energy. Similarly, what we call "habitual" ways of doing things often represent defenses working reasonably well or resolutions of old conflicts. The ego is reluctant to stir matters up. Any pattern that becomes a part of *character* usually yields the person some kind of satisfaction, consciously or unconsciously. The ego is shrewd enough to rework any liability into a partial asset; even while warding off anxiety the person may also be getting other benefits. A young man "camps," caricatures women and mocks his mother, even as he renounces whatever he finds threatening about the male role.

When an action originally adopted in the service of defense becomes a channel for drive-discharge and gives pleasure as well, it is likely to become *structured* and a part of character, a *character defense* (Reich, 1949). Like a bureaucrat building a small empire, the symptom makes itself useful to the whole personality in so many ways that it is hard to dislodge—and not just because it has been around a long time. Old attitudes that are *not* thus embedded and ego-syntonic may be relatively easy to change. As the psychologist John McGeoch used to say, "Time *qua* time does nothing." He meant, of course, that the mere passage of time is not an explanation of anything; it is necessary to explicate the specific processes that go on while time is passing. He was right of course. Not all who age grow up.

Recognition that much of the personality is relatively constant was expressed in a tiered diagnosis that used to be universal in the more advance psychiatric setting in this country. The neurotic patient was given a label related to his immediate pathology, followed by a character diagnosis, and an etiological summation. For example, a new patient might present "a reactive depression in an obsessive-compulsive woman following the death of her daughter." The term obsessive-compulsive referred to structured aspects of the personality, unlikely to change. The rest of the diagnosis, however, had to do with *dynamics*, aspects of the person that change and are connected to change. The patient is not described as having been typically depressed; had she been, the phrase "in a depressive personality" would have been inserted.

Many therapists nowadays eschew character diagnosis entirely and do not regard it as useful. But, from my experience I must say that I find such diagnoses not only useful but essential. Working on the problem of why some parents neglect their children while others of similar economic and social background do not, we were repeatedly impressed by the significance of character as a variable (Polansky, *et al.*, 1981).

On Choosing a Characterology

Some of those opposed to character diagnosis are concerned about *labeling* people. Imagine a man brought to a mental hospital by the police one night. Drunk and depressed, he also showed signs of confusion. A rather sleepy physician hung the admitting diagnosis of paranoid schizophrenia on him. Three day later, feeling better, the patient approaches those in charge and demands to be sent home. Indeed, he cannot recall how he got to the hospital and is sure there is some kind of ridiculous mistake. What is going on around here? On his chart, the attendants enter, "Talking of anger and suspicions." Since nothing happens, the patient demands to see a physician. In this hospital, where the medical staff is mostly incompetent and totally indolent, even a well intentioned ward nurse cannot arrange to have the man seen in less than a week. The patient does not understand this, so he begins to wonder querulously who is out to get him? On his chart is duly entered, "Suspicions stated more openly; expressing ideas of reference."

According to labeling theory, the patient's treatment is determined by his label. Moreover, new information is simply fitted in by the staff to support an existing stereotype.

Fortunately for all of us, it requires an unusually indifferent staff for such a sequence to occur, but there have been such happenings. As a matter of fact, labeling theory may be seen analytically as a possible expression of the synthetic function of the ego. Still, it is possible to overestimate the relevance of these processes among competent and dedicated professionals. Taber has abstracted the literature and writes, "Many of the research reports support the idea that socially deviant people are tagged with negative labels which reinforce a negative valuation by society. On the other hand, the specific effects of negative or positive labels on behavior are not shown" (1980, p. 97).

Others who dislike diagnoses protest that each client is unique. Yet, a small voice answers that even though people are unique, they also have commonalities that make it possible to generalize about them. Otherwise, we should have to invent a theory of personality for each new client we encounter, which is neither humanly possible nor necessary. And if you cannot group people meaningfully, how do you decide how best to treat each one? Surely, the common cold should be treated differently from appendicitis; further, it makes quite a difference whether the person with the cold has a chronic lung condition.

What shall be the basis for grouping people? Shall we separate the extroverts from the introverts? The people with blue eyes from those with brown, grey, hazel? The chubby endormorph from the skinny ectomorph, and both from the muscular mesomorph? Will each of these schemes classify people? The answer is, yes. Then, by what criteria shall we choose *which* scheme to use?

It seems to me there are two relevant critieria: the scheme's *condictability* and its *treatment relevance*. The term *condiction* is from the writings of Gordon Allport (1942). In discussing the role of theory in our work the significance of prediction was stressed. Prediction involves going from what is known in the present to estimating what will occur in the future. But that is not what is usually at issue in character typing. Rather, we expect to be able to go from facts we already know, in the present, to other things about the person we do not know but which are probably also true at present. It is not very striking for our system to connect our friend's not buying beer to guessing that he gives nothing to charity; it is more impressive if one's typology successfully condicts that our stingy friend also finds it hard to accept a compliment and relates to girls by teasing them cruelly. We need *condiction* to make good guesses from traits we know to those we do not so we can handle clients skillfully. Besides, such accurate guesses, seemingly out of the blue, help one's prestige!

Related, and even more important, is the matter of whether your typology has *treatment relevance*. Does it affect choice of which mode of helping to use? Earlier, we described some means of uncovering defenses—interpretation, clarification, and so on. But, if one is dealing with a person whose ego boundaries are generally fluid, such as the client diagnosed *borderline personality state*, most Freudians would not work toward uncovering at all for fear of precipitating a psychosis. The character diagnosis dictates confining the treatment interview to material of which the client is already conscious, while helping him deal with external reality. Similarly, a depression in an obsessive-compulsive person should be handled differently than in another sort of personality.

Of course, diagnosis has no treatment relevance if the therapist or worker offers essentially the same treatment to all comers. And, a listing of those who do this finds some strange bedfellows: client-centered therapists; caseworkers trained in the Rankian or the problem-solving traditions; practitioners of transactional analysis; psychiatrists who rely solely on drugs. Behavior modification, regarded by some as a universal therapy, for instance provides no structural concepts that would permit differential diagnosis. Similarly, at a time when it was heresy among psychoanalysts to use anything but the classical, free-association method with all patients, it is no wonder many analysts concluded there was no point in formulating diagnosic statements. On the other hand, diagnostic social work believes that *treatment follows diagnosis:* what you do depends on what you are dealing with. And so far as the personality is concerned, *differential diagnosis* includes character type. Dynamics tend to be universal; anyone can be anxious or depressed at times.

Furthermore, the Freudian character types do not consist of neat categories; they are *syndromes*. Certain traits seem to go with certain other traits. They do this consistently, by and large, because the personality is a *gestalt*, a whole with interdependent parts. The traits, values and attitudes that "go together" have been identified largely from clinical experience. At first glance, clients' associations may not fit common sense, but there are basically two reasons for their coexistence.

The first is historical. An event in one's early life is likely to have far-reaching effects. The sequellae show up in various spheres of adult functioning—how you behave, how you think, how you relate to other people. If one knows the historical point at which a particular incident or distortion of development happened, one can predict, or at least understand, its varied adult manifestations. In other words the various traits in the syndrome are consistent because of a common *historical* root. As we shall see, this type of thinking was the conceptual rationale for the first Freudian attempt to compose a characterology.

The second reason for consistency among features of the personality is functional or, as Kurt Lewin (1963) would have said, a matter of *ahistorical causation*. Thus, a surgeon with sadistic impulses may show exaggerated concern for the suffering of his patients, but a merciless criticalness toward the nursing staff hired to care for them. His hostility creeps out around the edge of his reaction formation against it. Later attempts at contructing characterologies in the analytic tradition place more emphasis on the ahistorical sources of consistency.

Since character types are syndromes rather than a neat set of categories lying along a single dimension, they are not clean and mutually exclusive at the present stage of our knowledge. Each is to be thought of as an "ideal type," as they say in sociology. You may have a client who fits the type nicely, whom you may term without equivocation an "hysteric." Another fits the same description in most but not all respects and might be said to have "hysterical features predominating" or to show "many hysterical features." These verbal devices express the degree of fit with the ideal type.

An important limitation of the typologies we have had thus far is the substantial minority of clients who do not seem to fit any. Some appear to be mixtures of two types; others just do not fit the available labels. Obviously, to take a great deal of time simply to decide how a patient meets the scheme you have learned does little to help your efficiency and defeats the purpose of having such concepts. They no longer make the work easier. So, it is wise to learn all one can from the available diagnostic descriptions—but to take them with a grain of salt.

A Traditional Characterology
Karl Abraham (1927) is remembered for his early work on developing a psychoanalytic characterology. He thought he found pat-

terns of traits among adult patients that could be related pretty directly to their *psychosexual stages of development*. Most present-day students are reasonably familiar with these stages, for they have gone from Freud into the general literature of psychology. The key issue in the psychosexual stages is the area of the body highlighted, or attended to, as the main source of pleasure.

The first body area capable of giving pleasure when stroked or stimulated is the mouth, or *oral* zone. At first, the pleasure of the mouth is related to the lips and sucking responses. Called the *oral-receptive* stage, its occurrence at birth has an obvious function, individual survival. The second aspect of mouth pleasure actually comes from the gums, so we have the *oral-biting* or *oral-sadistic* stage. When the infant has had adequate oral satisfaction, he moves on to the next stage, the *anal stage*. In the anal stage there are again two subphases, the pleasure, associated with bowel movement, called *anal-expulsive*, and the pleasure to be obtained from holding back, the *anal-retentive* phase. Again, if there is enough, but not too much, anal satisfaction and the child is not handled in a way that causes conflict, he is ready to move on. As we say, the next *erogenous* (literally, "makes pleasure") *zone* becomes *libidinized* ("charged" or looked to as the main event in pleasure seeking). We come to the stage which (out of the male chauvinism of the early Freudians—creatures of their own time and place) is called the *phallic* stage. In a gesture toward including little girls in the theory, it has also been called the *urethral*, which represents real confusion! In any event, the gist is that stroking or touching or rubbing the genital area becomes charged with pleasure, the next main event for the maturing child.

I have found it important for students to note at this point that the phallic phase in youngsters of age three involves a different sexuality from what we regard as *mature genitality*. For one thing, phallic pleasure is essentially masturbatory; it lacks the mutuality and enjoyment of another's responses found in mature sex. And the *eroticism* involved is non-orgasmic. Instead of starting at a low level and building up to a peak, as in orgasm or ejaculation, infantile genital pleasure stays on a mildly pleasurable plateau. One thinks of the mildly exciting self-rubbing that a lonely, unhappy child might use to distract himself from his sadness. Anxious adults sometimes engage in analogous activity. Masturbation has been called, "the poor man's tranquillizer." Of course, there are veiled sublimations of masturbation too, termed *masturbatory equivalents*. Knitters are infuriated by such descriptions of their art, as are scholars who go in for endless statistical manipulations and re-examinations of research data.

The three stages of development thus far listed are sometimes referred to as the *infantile* stages, and they are expected to be followed at around five or six with the *latency period*. During the latter phase, the child's attention is away from erogenous zones and, normally, very much onto the external environment and achieving mastery of it. Little boys throw and catch baseballs and footballs endlessly, little girls ride bikes and begin to learn to sew, and so on. During latency, in other words, there is supposedly a truce or moratorium on sexuality. There may well have been one among the proper middle-class Viennese Jews who purveyed and purchased so much early psychoanalysis, but those of us experienced in the mores of lower- and working-class America have known many youngsters who do not seem to have a clear latency phase— in interest, if not ability! After latency, of course, come *pubescence* and then *adolescence*, which do not concern us at the moment. An authoritative recounting of the traditional Freudian description of infantile sexuality is available in Fenichel (1945). When one considers that as a matter of policy the original analytic group put this picture together primarily from the free association of adult *analysands* rather than from the direct observation of children, it was quite an integration.

While the specific age at which infants pass from one stage to the next varies from child to child, the *sequence* of the stages was thought universal, an inborn process of psychologicial maturation. Moreover, most infants were thought to proceed regularly through the stages. It was not, of course, that having passed to the anal stage, all oral pleasure was forever given up. Rather, oral pleasure remained available but was not the focus of attention for *libidinal gratification*. Indeed, traces of these forms of eroticism normally survive into adult life where they are called *remnants*. The pleasure of sucking survives in adult kissing, smoking and other *oral remnants*.

An unlucky infant, not given enough gratification at the crucial age, or given too much, might not move forward in erotic interest, but continue to concentrate on the mouth as the main source of pleasure. Such an individual would be said to have been *fixated* at the oral stage. It was later thought that such specific psychosexual fixations can have very general consequences for the personality. Finally, it was noted that some people appear to have progressed beyond a particular stage, only to have fallen back because of something traumatic or anxiety evoking. The return of libidinal interest to a stage already passed is called *regression*, which we listed earlier as a defense.

Traditional Freudian characterology was based on the model and related processes I have just sketched. The basic idea was that *the psychological consistency among the traits* found in a patient was due to the fact that *all were historically related to the stage of development* at which the person had been *fixated*. An infant given a great deal of oral gratification, let us say acts "as if" he had had no reason to move onward for other sources; an infant massively deprived acts "as if" he were still hungry for oral pleasure, unable to go on because he has unfinished business in the oral stage. I say "as if" because, of course, we cannot interview the tiny human, nor find out whether each carries on such a Benthamite calculus of hedonism in his mind.

The traditional characterology based in the id psychology summarized above has now been mostly given up by those working in the analytic tradition. Yet, many of the terms then used survive in their field and ours, and studying the older framework will help the student know what is meant. In truth, despite later advances in theory, some of the older types still provide good shorthand summations of fellow humans we encounter. And of course, personality descriptions that are now more in vogue (e.g. the *infantile* personality) presume one has previously learned the older typology (Reiner and Kaufman, 1959; Kaufman, 1963).

Oral Character
The outstanding characteristic of the oral character is greed, as shown in eating, drinking, and smoking patterns. It may even be found in work habits, a completely throwing of oneself into the job as if trying to engorge on work as otherwise with food. I once had an alcoholic patient, who was extremely successful. One reason for this was that he alternated several months of working twelve- to sixteen-hour days with a binge of a week or more, followed by a few days in a middle-class drying-out spa, euphemistically termed a sanitarium. One might say that he worked, as he drank, *addictively*. Indeed, students of alcohol and drugs have found it useful to identify an *addictive* personality.

If the oral character is primarily oral-receptive, he is likely to be quite *passive*, wanting the nourishment to be trickled into his mouth as he lies supine. The emphasis on passive receptivity is at variance with the standard requirements for males in our culture, and many men, who have such passive longings, do much to hide them from themselves and others. Just as all persons who act a part, they tend to overdo it, with a great show of ambitious striving in an effort to prove they do not really yearn for purely passive gratification. This discrepancy between the reaction formation and the underlying wish often produces a great deal of tension in such a person, especially when the desire for *oral supplies* is so great that he simultaneously has an inordinate need to please, to be liked. It is no wonder, then, that many persons thus constituted end up with ulcers or cardiovascular disease.

Fixation at the oral-biting phase is more likely to be represented in *demandingness*, also a frequent attribute of oral characters. This demandingness applies, of course, to food and other ingestible stuffs, but it is likely to go beyond that. Such persons frequently "get their feelings hurt," which is to say they are not able to get the *unconditonal love* they feel is their right, their need—or their preference. "Love me just because I'm me." Demandingness may also lead to an impatience with others, an "I want what I want when I want it" attitude. Perhaps it is for this reason that, Shakespeare to the contrary, life demonstrates few truly jolly fat men.

An oral-biting person may also be demanding in another sense. He is greedy for perfection. The best is never good enough. When this kind of perfectionism is turned toward one's view of himself, he may be as angry with himself for not performing up to what he requires as he might be toward an external object. From this derives depressiveness in its classical formulation: depression as aggression turned inward against the self.

This is but one of the dynamic constellations out of which depression may arise, but it is common to find that a chronically depressive person is also a covertly demanding one. Ofttimes, the first casework step in relieving depression is to encourage the demandingness to come out into the open, into free verbal expression. Oral-biting persons, by the way, often have biting tongues, although they are not the only ones with this characteristic. Perhaps it is no more than fair that if one has a biting tongue, he should so often put his own foot in his mouth.

In interpersonal relations, a man or woman with strong oral needs is likely to be recognizable from the way in which he tends to engulf others. The more passive person establishes a clinging, appealing sort of symbiotic tie: nevertheless, it is as firmly fixed as is that of the more obstreperously requiring man who *insists* on being taken care of. This feeling of being entangled, of being *incorporated*, derives from the steady flow of speech which, as it were, fixes your attention in its grasp, and will not release you even after—having still said nothing—you feel sucked dry.

A noteworthy feature in many oral characters we encounter as adults is their *expansiveness*. They are given to large schemes and big dealing; they have no patience for details and, in fact, may be so insistently optimistic as to exhibit questionable judgment. When such a promoter succeeds, he is hailed as a genius; when he fails, he is very susceptible to depression. Many creative people alternate the two. Expansiveness is often exhibited in smaller ways. Many fat people cannot reduce because they find it impossible to think in terms of losing a pound a week. They immediately set their goal at thirty pounds, only to become discouraged when, after a month they have "only" lost six or seven. The expansiveness, then, is to be seen as a facet of the all-or-none style of thinking and feeling that we associate with the oral phase of development. And this same oral-phase, all-or-none quality in thought will recur, in our discussion, when we mention the *splitting* within the ego that occurs when the child cannot integrate his love and his hate of the same person.

The study of orality serves to illustrate the guises and disguises by which the same basic drive may make itself variously evident in the same person. By orality we refer, or course, to the yearning for pleasurable sensations from the mouth's erogenous zones. We may find direct gratification, as in chewing gum or sucking and biting in sexual foreplay. The drive may be visible in modulated form among those who join gourmet clubs or lavish attention on cigars or assemble wine cellars to sample. Then, there are more symbolic manifestations of orality. Numerous red-blooded Americans take their pleasures passively, spending long football afternoons sipping beer in front of television sets. Oral passivity and demandingness may become more generalized and neurotic. The client feels put upon when asked to show initiative. "Something holds me back. I don't see why *I* should have to do anything." Derivatives of orality are often nicely sublimated into occupations. The literary critic spends his life sniffing and tasting others' productions; he then reports whether they stayed down when swallowed, or had to be regurgitated. Often quoted a decade ago was Dorothy Parker's book review of *Winnie the Pooh*, "Constant Weader fwowed up." A little nip taken out of A. A. Milne, also?

Strong oral needs may become evident, as noted earlier, through reaction formations against them. One meets people so abstemious of food and drink they seem to be fighting off urges to gobble the world. "I'm eating every bit I want to," they say, in stout denial of accusations no one else is making. One recalls the French saying that the trouble with chastity is its overemphasis on sex. Indeed, some therapists suspect strong, unconscious orality whenever evidences of oral remnants are too absent, but it seems risky to draw such conclusions. Tracing out the unfinished oral business of infancy in adults' myriad expressions can be a fascinating diagnostic exercise. Certainly, it gives more body to the cryptic phrasing that the economic metatheoretical conception has to do with "drives and their vicissitudes."

Occasionally, a whole series of facts make sense in these terms, even after the first interview or two.

The patient, a man in his thirties, was referred to me by a friend who feared he might harm himself. At one and the same time, he was breaking up his marriage and his job—an ominous combination. On interview, he was tense, perspiring with anxiety, at first somewhat disconnected in getting out his story. Under questioning, however, he confirmed several indications of at least moderate depression—early-waking; loss of appetite; blue mood; and so forth. There had been vague thoughts of self-destruction, but "I would never do such a thing."

Trouble with his wife came to a head the other night when, during intercourse, she asked him sarcastically "Aren't you finished yet?" Patient exploded; there was a violent scene and wife agreed to his leaving. In several years of marriage, wife had been consistently unresponsive. "I love you, but you don't turn me on." More recently she reported a slight flirtation with another, which did not help.

One cannot simply take it for granted that this situation would be aggravating "to anybody." What made it so hard for *this* man to bear it? Why the violence of his reaction?

The inability to induce a response from his wife was especially infuriating. Associated were thoughts indicative of need to be at center of attention: flaunting dating successes before friends; competitiveness in general. "I always had to be first." Jealous of his more easy-going brother, yet when younger would sometimes assume blame for brother's misdeeds. "I'd rather be punished than left out of the action." Felt stymied and worthless sitting in waiting rooms all day hoping to be noticed by the arrogant purchasing agents from whom he had to wheedle orders, a dreadful match between his job and his personality. Angry much of the time, dissatisfied, he is aware that, "I'm abrasive. People don't take to me easily." Also, more proudly, "People to me are either black or white. I'm for you or against you."

From his unusually perceptive mother, I was volunteered information regarding very early history. Very much wanted, this child was delayed at birth, had to be delivered by Caesarian. He was give a 10% chance of survival when they took him home. Feeding was a terrible problem at first until a more optimistic pediatrician simply increased the amount to be offered the infant. The sturdy, active fellow we knew had been a delicate, sickly baby, much fussed over by his parents. Mother was aware of his strong tie to his parents, his treating the family house as "home" even after marriage. Also, takes delight in aggravating his mother, using profanity before guests "To stir me up." A mess? Definitely not. The patient is scrupulous about the truth and others' money; very industrious; psychologically minded and able to look at himself; capable of gratitude; articulate and intelligent; and decent in dealing with ex-wife, after their split-up.

Among the various theories of social casework, the psychosocial approach (Hollis, 1972) requires taking into account both the person's character and situation in diagnosis and the planning of treatment. It is easy to see, in the man above, how a particular combination of situation and character became intolerable; how major aspects of his life were frustrating the marked oral remnants which survived in the mature personality. Of course he was "fed up" with both marriage and a job that violated his needs.

Treatment can be approached, psychosocially, from the standpoint of the character, the situation, or both. An obvious help, for the moment, would be to introduce the attentiveness and concern of the therapist. We have also discussed earlier, first-aid treatment of depression through encouraging verbal and emotional ventilation of rage and hurt. But, helping might also require shifts in the patient's typical modes of adapting. For a man like him, frank recognition of underlying oral needs would be unacceptable. Yet, it was impossible for him to make intelligent decisions about what he wanted or could tolerate in life without taking them into account. Would he be better off with a glamorous wife whom he can show off, or one that offers him more admiration and warmth? Can he emotionally afford a job filled with interpersonal rebuffs? In the long run, it would be very helpful if the oral demandingness could be directly treated. Since it keeps him chronically angry, his pattern pushes people away. Not only is this a career handicap; it works directly against his yearnings for affection and acceptance.

In passing I also want to note that, contrary to stereotypes many of us had in the past, such strong orality does not routinely imply having had an unsatisfying experience of mothering. As we can see, there are physiological accidents at birth which may have profound effects on the infant and on his anxious parents.

The Anal Character

The traditional mnemonic device for keeping what is meant by anal character in mind was the four p's. An anal character was said to be parsimonious, prurient, petulant and pedantic—see whether this does not apply to someone you know. These adjectives are not flattering and, indeed, there is little connotation of the cheerfulness we associate with the oral fellow, so indulgent to himself and others.

The parsimoniousness of stinginess in the anal character has usually been the facet most remarked upon in professional circles. A woman married to a stingy banker, accountant, lawyer, or psychologist might complain about his *withholding* in a number of other areas. Tight-lipped, such a person often withholds words: certainly, he finds it difficult—he would call it unnecessary—to be generous with demonstrations of affection. "She should know I love her. Don't I let her buy anything she wants?" In direct treatment one has a sense of *stubbornness,* also a marked facet of this personality type. Where some clients are stubborn about changing because they fear becoming nothing at all, the stubbornness I allude to here seems to derive from the attitude, "I won't give you the satisfaction." This person has resumed the battle of the potty which he fought with his mother, insisting on evacuating when and where he wants, and refusing to produce when *she* wants him to.

Prurience is visible in the tendency of anal characters to see things as dirty. Sex can be expected to be interlocked with bowel movements. Certainly, their view of sex is typically a matter for sniggering, leering, a "behind the barn" sort of approach. Sex is dirty, just as bowel functions are dirty. Although there may be great pleasure in little-boy sex jokes, the funny-bone is really touched by bathroom humor. Because this may be embarrassing, many anal characters avoid the danger of being exposed by showing practically no sense of humor. Hypocrisy is rife among such people, for they are preoccupied with questions of shame and blame.

Young caseworkers confronted by such intrinsically sullen folks are prone to credit them with somewhat more maturity than they have achieved. They will tell their supervisor, "I don't think he can be active and outgoing because he feels so guilty." The client may not have matured far enough for guilt, which is after all, a feeling that you have wronged *another person* and warrant being punished for it. The shame we have under scrutiny here is much more self-centered. It takes the form, "I have messed up my pants, and now I smell bad, and people will point and laugh and say 'Shame, shame on you.'" The relation of this feeling to toilet training is quite direct.

If anal characters are preoccupied with shame and blame, they are also often caught up in varieties of sadistic fantasies. They are likely to get a quiet pleasure out of criticizing, "For your own good," while joyfully defecating on the others' works. Meanness, in its implication that one is both small *and* nasty (like a Klan member in the deep South or a Hell's Angel in California), is common. Because of the tendency to withhold, the meanness seldom erupts in major outbursts of rage. It is as likely to be expressed in niggling ways, as *petulance*, carping, and nagging. Not a few elderly folks who may have had such traits well mastered in their healthier days regress to them under the impact of aging and the constant threat of death. They are then converted from people into "management problems" in nursing homes. The relation of the petulance and the prurience to taking malicious gossip into one's joyful embrace does not need spelling out.

We have sketched the manner in which the anal character used to be discussed, covering three of the four p's—parsimonious, prurient, and petulant. Our curiosity about the fourth tells us something about what is meant by *pedantic!* Along with being stingy, the anal character was also commonly said to be extremely orderly. If a person not only were willing but also seemed positively anxious to sort and file miscellaneous papers, we would immediately accuse him of being anal, although not so anal as if he saved money and kept his dictation up to date. The pedantry extends also to syle of speech, especially written communication. The anal character's great desire to control, and overcontrol, and generally exercise sphincters is closely related to his desire, and fear, that he will give way to his other urge, to smear feces. The practice of putting ideas or papers or objects into neat little boxes becomes part of enjoying the process of holding back. Not all anal characters are pedantic. Some are happy simply to wallow in disorder and filth and not only as a matter of laziness or even of defiance (which it very often is). It comes from the original urge to gain pleasure from one's bowel action. Sometimes impulse and reaction formation alternate. The person with an excessively neat desk may keep closets at home so jumbled that clothing is lost in them, for months on end.

Phallic Character

The third stage of development has been called the phallic. In the circles in which I was trained, this character formation was not so frequently alluded to as the former. Perhaps the phallic traits were too visibly present among those at the top in our training facilities?

Some years ago, while travelling near Florence, Italy, I visited the town of San Geminiani. Viewed from a distance, it is a most exotic place, for you first see numbers of steeples without crosses rising from the town. Indeed with few exceptions, each tower is secular, privately owned and rises from the house of a wealthy local resident. At some point in the town's history one man built himself a tower; and his neighbor then went him one better by building a slightly higher tower. Others joined the game, for the countrymen were nothing if not competitive, and their erections appeared all over the town. Since they were building in stone, it was not long before the local masons had achieved the maximum height, but one man was not stymied. To outdo his neighbors, he built two towers.

Nor are the San Geminianians unique. The wealthy Genoans are famous for their stinginess. Yet they too have found an arena in which they will spend any amount of money to outdo their fellows: the cemetery. The crowning Genovese achievement is interment in the most elaborate family tomb. Other Italians describe such goings-on with about the same mixture of amusement and admiration they might have for little boys testing who can urinate the farthest, or who has the longest penis.

The blatancy with which phallic remnants are expressed by supposedly mature men (and sometimes women) would be hilarious if it were not so often dangerous. In this country, for example, millions of dollars are spent erecting enormous towers to establish the prestige of great corporations, whatever rationalization is given the stockholders. They are almost always economically disastrous structures, appearing just after the corporation involved has passed its period of greatest growth and is about to start downhill: the Woolworth Building, the Chrysler, the Pan American come to mind in New York. Sears-Roebuck's management put up an enormous tower in Chicago while the company's stock dropped to a third of its previous value. Yet, we are all impressed by sheer height and many good people like to tell others how high up in a great hotel they stayed. So, intense competitiveness was a major feature associated with the phallic character, and sometimes connected with an obvious overcompensation for felt inferiority. Need more be said?

The same competitiveness is rife on campuses, where it is expressed as pride in sheer size, often at the cost of wrecking the scholarly process. And then, there are the "jocks" with their sedentary following that curses them when they lose and assumes the credit when they win. What did Senator Eugene McCarthy say? "Politics is like managing baseball: you have to be smart enough to understand the game and dumb enough to think that it's important."

Competitiveness and other needs to erect and project—e.g. shooting birds and animals, and exploding people—are not confined to males. A well tuned phallus is experienced as a powerful engine, and vice versa. Many young woman go through a phase of fascination with powerful sports cars. The majority of amateur riders at horse shows in our part of the country are post-pubescent girls, still innocent of heterosexual interest. Some women remain that way into their twenties, whatever life styles they choose. It is not from being anxious about heterosexuality so much as having not progressed to a more complicated developmental stage. The same may be said of many men as well, now living happily in singles' housing drinking with their buddies and playing macho games, while treating women as the aliens they are to all eleven year old boys. The games include the sexual capture of as many females as possible, and then talking about them!

Reaction formation against phallic strivings were not so frequently remarked among clinicians. However, I have myself had a number of clients and patients whose fear of competing was clearly in the context of rivalrous strivings so strong they could not bear to lose. And we might ask what causes the phallic fixation in the first place? Surely, in this culture it is rarely related to either deprivation or indulgence. The image of what happens was less concrete than in the case of orality, and had more to do with an unsatisfactory outcome of the Oedipal drama which occurs at about the same chronological age. More parsimonious formulations have supplanted talk of phallic strivings to explain rivalry and the like.

The Infantile Personality

A secret of the adult world to which most of us become privy only during middle age is that most people never really grow up. In the days when I was trying to use the characterology outlined above I encountered a problem that I eventually discovered was typical. Many clients did not fit their genotypic pigeonholes. A person with anal traits was very likely also to have some oral, and vice versa. Indeed, some folks seem to move through life with all their psychogenetic underclothing flapping in the breeze. Rather than a delimited syndrome, they just seem generally immature. Needs which ought to have dropped aside are still pressing; feelings which ought to have been repressed are still conscious. One hardly knows where to begin in trying to understand their difficulties. At one and the same time, they have no specific symptoms and a myriad. They behave oddly by most peoples' standards; they generate troubles for others—especially their children if they are parents —and for themselves. In the end, we recognize that whatever the manifestation at the surface, the gross immaturity is, itself, the "illness." These people have moved along chronologically and physically but not emotionally, and often not intellectually.

A variety of words is used to label them. Thirty or forty years ago, psychiatrists termed many of them to be in a *constitutional psychopathic state* until it became apparent that those favoring such genetic diagnoses were themselves constitutionally incapable of insight. Terms of more recent vintage include *character disorder* (Reiner and Kaufman, 1959), *inadequate personality* and *impulse-ridden character.* We resorted to these conceptions to sort out observations on parents implicated in neglect; we concluded that the majority may be termed character disordered, with the *apathy-futility syndrome* and *impulse-ridden character* accounting for the character types most frequently found (Polansky, *et al.*, 1981).

If one can overlook its deprecatory overtones, the conception that fits many of these clients best is *infantile personality,* a term introduced by Ruesch in 1948. The expression reminds us that the roots of the disorder lie in massive early fixation. Ruesch coined the term in trying to describe a person prone to *psychosomatic* illness. Children have limited views of the world and limited repertoires of responses available; the same is true of grownup children as well. Instead of dealing with interpersonal conflicts by discussing them and negotiating differences, the infantile personality is incapable of either (Hill, 1952). He remains angry and tense, his adrenals are active, his pulse and blood pressure both go up. These things happen to any of us under stress, but the difficulty that infantile people have with adapting and their failure to find realistic solutions mean they are under stress a good part of the time. And there are medical consequences—ulcers, hypertension, coronary thrombosis, cerebral "accidents," and the like. Colitis, or "nervous bowel," often occurs, and can become ulcerative. Where a more mature person might permit his or her anxiety to become conscious and try to do something about its cause, the infantile personality suffers from *low anxiety tolerance*. The patient can take only a little consciousness of anxiety before the ego begins to try to repress it through defenses that produce symptoms. Lest the student discount the impact of these ailments, functional in origin but physical in expression, all those listed above are potentially lethal. And if the client tries to assuage needfulness by falling back on oral greed, the consequent obesity may itself be dangerous to health.

The tension felt by the infantile person is based, very often, on a demandingness compounded by limited competence in dealing with the world. Because he "wants what he wants when he wants it" he has little frustration-tolerance or ability to delay immediate gratification. Not for him saving up to buy a car in order to avoid paying excessive interest rates, not for him standing back from a hard-to-climb fence to look for an easy way around it. Because of a foreshortened time perspective (Lewin, 1951), such a person has difficulty planning in general. Lacking such a perspective, it is hard for him to find the motivation to stick with a skill long enough to achieve great mastery of it. He is in danger not only of fearing that he is inadequate but of *being* inadequate. Interpersonal judgment is poor, grasp of reality limited. The infantile are often exploited by "hustlers" because of their suggestibility.

I have a biography of Picasso written by a former mistress—an acccount that cannot be taken as unbiased. Still, if any of it is true, Picasso in his daily life *outside his work* was a boringly infantile man. Yet he produced some work that is certainly great art, and even more that is calculatedly expensive. The same man who required to be coaxed out of bed and could not bear to be measured for a pair of pants, also survived one marriage and several long-term liaisons without dissipating more than a tiny fraction of his fortune. Even highly competent geniuses may have islands of infantilism.

Similarly, there are some impressively verbal, even verbose, people who are nevertheless infantile. The general trend, however, is a lack of verbal skill. They literally do not know many words. The words they know tend to be concrete, as one finds with children. They have neither the vocabulary nor the capacity for complex grammatical structure to support a complex train of ideas, and this further incapacitates them for long-range planning. The net result is kind of concrete-mindedness we associate with schizophrenia. This feature makes adaptation difficult, just as it limits what can be accomplished in therapy. All these are personality features which emerge from the *culture of poverty;* they are said to be attributes derivable from *cultural disadvantage.* I must note, *en passant,* that these are also features of the infantile personality, and one effect of severe *deprivation* is the production of markedly childlike people. Because of the limitations of ability and judgment mentioned above, we realize it will not be enough to put money into the hands of these people—necessary though that may be. There will be too many others around ingenious at taking it away from them!

In interpersonal relationships, the infantile personality can exhibit many things, but it is well to be on the lookout for *selfishness.* Mature love involves a giving and taking between two people who could exist independently of each other but prefer not to. Even though the childish person makes a fetish of "independence," this is not the way he relates. Attachments are apt to be a type of clinging and clutching which we call *anaclitic dependency.* This kind of sucking on the other person is bound to irritate sooner or later, so that the very needfulness of the infantile person eventually leads to rejection by those he has left drained. Because of the continued dominance of *separation anxiety,* the infantile person finds it uncomfortable to break off relationships, even after they have become unsatisfying to all involved.

Childish persons are, of course, not without urges to give, but the giving is always in danger of being impulsive, overwhelming, well-meant but insensitive. I recall the instance of a wealthy man in treatment with a psychiatrist who lunched with him between appointments at the clinic. Out of gratitude for the "help" he had received, he presented his doctor with a motorboat. I am glad to say the doctor refused it, pointing out simply the criticism to which he would be subjected if he took so handsome a gift from a patient. Of course the patient was not thinking so much of the effect of the gift on the recipient as of how good he would feel in making the present.

A frequent accompaniment to "giving" among infantile persons is the tendency to *infantilize* the beneficiary. This is especially true of their children, as in the case of the "Jewish mama," but the same sort of person encourages dependency and childishness in her husband as well. It is as if they cannot bear to see those dependent on them grow up, lest they become so mature they can walk away and leave. We recognize a closely related phenomenon in child guidance work when we see a mother who seemingly does well with her children until they have reached a developmental stage critical to the mother's makeup. She may be comfortable with a helpless infant, but the toddler is capable of more mobility and, we hope, begins to assert a mind of his own. At this point the infantile mother, threatened with both physical and emotional separation, becomes discombobulated (Polansky, et al., 1968). Many such women deal with the anxiety by having another child, and discarding rather abruptly the next elder when the baby arrives. In such families there is naturally sibling jealousy. And, women are not the only ones with problems in accepting their children's burgeoning personalities. The world is full of successful men, mature in many ways, who cannot stand to see their sons grow up. They are happiest with fellow-infants, and make far better grandfathers than fathers.

Childish people typically have spotty superegos. Many of their standards are thinly held and poorly integrated, and they sense this. Hence, we often find a reaction formation against the sense of being so easily corruptible. Such persons become extremely *rigid* in their standards. We can see a great deal of this in the Bible Belt where part of the population gets roaring drunk whenever it can afford the bootlegged whiskey, another part of the populace is rigidly abstinent, and a third part, the majority, alternates between the two positions!

A youngster whose mother was childish and impulsive is unlikely to have been held *consistently* to any set of standards to have sufficiently internalized them. Moreover, if one's parents are immature and have a limited ability to give love, another link in the chain, the chain leading to internalization is missing. The child is unable to respond to his parents' disapproval as if it threatened the loss of love, when he has never been that comfortably loved. For a variety of reasons, therefore, one can anticipate that the consciences of infantile personalities will be childishly oversevere, on the one hand, or corruptible and poorly formed on the other. Often they are both. The man who is absolutely reliable in business dealings may be a complete liar and cheat in his relationships with women.

Related to defects in internalized standards is the lack of ability to appraise one's personality and weaknesses. Using the term loosely, we say these patients have no *insight*, by which we mean the *self-observing function of the ego* is sadly underdeveloped. The capacity for self-observation, after all, also requires the internalization and organization of a set of standards that come from outside the self. For reasons similar to those involved in faulty superego development, the ability to appraise one's faults realistically is also impaired. Therefore, a distinguishing mark of any infantile personality involved in treatment, for whatever reason, is that he really sees nothing wrong with himself or with how he does things. Denial and projection are prominent.

The woman who eats herself into a state of grossness "cannot understand" why her husband's eye should wander; the man who works obsessively while rubbing up his own narcissism about success, sees no reason his wife should be unhappy. Typically, infantile people are in treatment because they have been forced into it by the threats of losing the comforts of married life, say, or by physical symptoms. To expect a childish man to want to change for the sake of his wife's happiness is ridiculous. The only thing that will induce an effort at change in such a person is a simple answer to an age-old query: "What's in it for me?" As soon as the threat of divorce is dissipated, for example, such a man is ready to stop further marital counseling. Although he may have made some grudging obeisances, he never really saw anything wrong with his way of operating. The same applies to the woman being seen for the sake of her child's treatment. A major evidence of growth for such people is the decision to change behavior (never type) for the sake of long-run comforts. Yet despite their obtuseness about others, they often expect great sensitivity where their own feelings are concerned. Infantile people are constantly "feeling insulted" in treatment.

Gross immaturity finds its reflections in the cognitive, interpersonal, affective and even somatic spheres. A bizarre blend of self-abasement and arrogance often accompanies the syndrome. We have mentioned the infantilizing mother, pointed out by Levy (1943) also in his unfortunately neglected work on maternal overprotection. We believe the child's self-regarding attitudes, his self-concept, are affected by what the mother communicates in actions and, at times, in words. For, he acts as if somewhere inside him an insistent voice were saying, "You are still part of your mother"; "You are fragile and easily damaged." But, the same voice is saying,

"You are—or should be—special" (Polansky, Borgman and Desaix, 1972, p. 145; Polansky, *et al.*, 1971). Identifying with the mother, clients seem to treat themselves as if they were weak and defective. Also, the price for gaining strength by remaining part of one's mother is to remain an incomplete person. No wonder such people have trouble with actual physical coordination, they have such distortions in their sense of the self. And because failure is not felt to be a learning experience but an insult to the defensive need to be perfect, the client is very apt to quit. As one of our patients used to say, "If at first you don't succeed, the hell with it."

Infantilism may be used as the noun denoting a state of being infantile. In most instances it represents fixation due to early deprivation. Such deficits of parenting, occurring very early in life, in this culture are from limits in mothering. Quite often, the inept parent, herself massively deprived, in addition to less than optimal care offers the child an immature object to identify with. In numerous neglectful and abusive families, for example, at least some of the children are observed to have reversed roles with childlike parents. In effect, the child becomes confidant and parent or big sister to the mother (Morris and Gould, 1963). So, the failure to develop may be concealed behind a brittle façade of *pseudo-maturity*. The child avails herself of *defensive progression*, as if saying, "This is hard and frightening; I will feel safer as a grownup."

As noted, one also finds examples of the person's having been infantilized, a process that can occur among low-income families as it does among the wealthy. But overprotection is not often the problem in the histories of the retarded, delinquent and emotionally ill most of us will see as caseworkers. We will encounter these issues in discussing the development of the ego as well as the theory of object relations.

My immersion in the notion of infantilism derives from a decade and a half of studies of child neglect (Polansky, *et al.*, 1981). Whether one uses this term or the closely related one, character disorder, the theme is the same: rather than specific symptoms, the client's difficulty is one of limited adaptability because of failure to develop.

CHAPTER 6
A SPEED READER'S GUIDE TO
Contemporary Characterology

Contemporary characterology puts more emphasis on adaptive style and the type of defense relied upon. However, for planning treatment, the *core conflict* being adapted to must also be understood. *Obsessive compulsives* stress *control* over *anal-sadistic* impulses through a variety of tactics, such as obsessions, compulsions and rituals of *undoing*. *Hysterics* seem to be dealing with an underlying *emptiness* that may be countered by a *craving for excitement*. In search of comforting, they show *histrionics* and *sexualize* relationships, in turn stirring up further conflict. So, they present defenses like *self-righteous indignation*, massive repression and the *conversions* for which this group of patients is known.

Paranoid characters have been angrily disappointed by their parents and feel weak and helpless. Such feelings are rigidly defended through *contempt for weakness*, projection and displacing aggression to "the enemy." Strong oral remnants have inevitably left *depressives* feeling disappointed and resentful but they are too needful of love to attack directly so they *turn anger against themselves*. Hence, their chronically low mood.

A relatively new conception, the *borderline personality*, seems to fit many clients with limited ability to cope. Characterized by *looseness* of ego boundaries and an odd uncertainty in their perceptions of the world and themselves, they appear *plausible* on initial contact but live with *chronic anger* and anxiety.

The syndromes associated with character types are useful because they explain present functioning and relate it to historical development.

Contemporary Characterology

6

Expressions like "oral-dependent" and "anal-sadistic" still survive in the verbal shorthand experienced clinicians use. To those with similar training, such comments briefly describe patients and sum up prominent dynamics, though taken with a grain of salt. It has been many years since I encountered a clinical setting in which such terms were used in formal diagnosis. Identifying a client's personality in terms of fixations in early development leaves too much unsaid about subsequent adaptation and current adult functioning. The later character types in Freudian psychology pay much more attention to predominant defensive operations and styles of coping.

The student could already infer, from learnings in Chapter 3, that the infantile personality would be apt to employ such defenses as denial, projection, self-abasement. What sorts of people use the more elaborate mechanisms and maneuvers, like rationalization and intellectualization? Clearly we have not yet dealt with such character-types under the rubrics derived from id psychology.

In this chapter, I will abstract some of the types often referred to in contemporary practice. Each may be seen as organized around a particular defensive mode or theme; thought has also been given to the underlying *core conflict* with which that personality is likely to be coping. I have chosen the character types most germane to our practice. There is a fair amount of debate in the field about several of these. For example, some diagnosticians may not accept that there is a borderline personality. However, those included here have seemed useful for thinking about treatment in my own practice and that of colleagues. So in order not to clutter the exposition, I have described each type in the way those reflecting it appear to me. For a more advanced treatment, it would be well to read Shapiro's (1965) excellent book.

Obsessive-Compulsive Personality

No adult can survive with reasonable comfort in this society who does not plan, keep most appointments, put papers and tools where he can find them, and think carefully about decisions. To be unable to maintain some order and caution in one's affairs may doom you to life under someone else's supervision. But, should the interest in order become more important than the purpose for which it is kept, it stops being useful and becomes a handicap. We have commented that there are ego functions which, "within normal limits," are adaptive and beneficial. The same coping operations, nevertheless, may be magnified into symptoms. Rarely is this principle illustrated better than in the bundle of motivations we have come to call the obsessive-compulsive personality.

Many splendid specimens of obsessive compulsives are to be found on college campuses throughout the United States; they were even more concentrated in European universites. The story is told of the German philologist who spent a long life studying the uses of the dative and ablative cases in Tacitus. Although well regarded by his colleagues, the scholar was given to self-doubts. On his deathbed, he moaned that he had accomplished nothing, finished nothing. His friends were anxious to reassure him. They reminded him of his numerous books, his many published papers, the footnotes he had enriched and the citations he had graced. The old man roused himself. "Ah, yes," he grumbled, "But think what I might have done had I confined myself to the uses of the dative, only."

The key to understanding the obsessive compulsive is his need to maintain *control*. Preoccupied ruminating is obsession, whose aim is to control thought. Compulsions, on the other hand, have more to do with externally visible, repetitive actions and rituals attempting to control behavior. Ritual does not always require burning incense, as I found in a class on descriptive statistics. The median, as most students learn, is a statistic offering a rough indication of the central tendency in a distribution of scores. Since the precise value of each score does not enter into its computation, the median is algebraically inert, useless in most further computation. Yet in the old days it was commonly calculated to five decimal places; one would do that even for IQ scores which, we knew, had a measurement error of as much as five full points.

The presence of an obsession or a compulsion does not by itself mean we should classify the person as an obsessive-compulsive personality. Either, or both, may occur as an isolated symptom in a person otherwise essentially normal. It is also common to find these symptoms in persons extremely ill psychiatrically. When, then, do we make the character diagnosis? When the emphasis on control and "playing it safe" has become a total way of life. Although no real person will fit *all* these characteristics, we can make a number of related statements about most obsessive compulsives.

We have alluded to the delight in orderliness and fascination with precision. Although this has its uses, it is frequently accompanied by an inability of the obsessive compulsive to look up from his worm's-eye view of the world—"He cannot see the forest for the trees." The military officer may claim that close-order drill produces discipline in an Army, despite the appallingly good fighters we have witnessed who do not salute. We become aware that he loves drill for its own sake. Moreover, he is aghast at any lack of skill in drilling. He is *rigid* and finds change extremely hard to take. This is because many of the disciplines by which he lives are set up to prevent his feeling anxiety. Change endangers a whole defensive system. While the rigidity is usually quite unconscious, and can be assessed only by the therapist, his *stubbornness* is not. Of this he is likely to be quite conscious, even taking a quiet pride in it.

At first glance, the stubbornness seems paradoxical, for it occurs in a person otherwise plagued by *self-doubts* and *indecision*. Only gradually do we understand that these seeming paradoxes in personality disorders represent a problem and an attempt to counter it. If it were easier for the obsessive to make up his mind, he would be less fearful of changing it. For change requires him to make a whole new decision.

Sensing that he has this trouble and thus appears weak and vacillating, the obsessive compulsive sometimes swings between extremes of indecisiveness and hastiness. Where another man might find it quite appropriate to stay a decision pending more information, an obsessive will sometimes busy himself with *appearing* decisive. The chief functions of commitments he makes at such times are to relieve him of the discomfort he feels at having things undecided, and the boost to his self-esteem which he experiences from having vaingloriously taken a stand. Reality may then run a poor third in influencing judgment.

The more typical stance, however, is to remain undecided and proceed with extreme caution. Psychologically there are several reasons for this. To begin, we have in mind the rather obvious derivation of this personality structure from fixations at the anal phase of development. There is some satisfaction in *withholding* decisions, especially if they affect other people, just as there is pleasure in withholding love, money, feelings in general. Commitment is like a hard bowel movement. But this describes only the part of the pattern derived from drive satisfactions in one zone. Rarely does a person remain immature in only one sphere of his psychosexual development. In my own observation, obsessive-compulsive personalities are typically extremely *oral* as well. They have difficulty in making up their minds partly because they are *greedy*, just as they are greedy for *perfection*. Most decisions require that in order to get one thing, you have to give up the other. The sort of person we are discussing has a secret notion that he can beat life at this game. He believes he will find a way to get both choices, and give up neither. So he stalls for time.

Finally, we note that the indecisiveness is also a defense. This is where ego psychology takes us beyond the original formulations on this character type. What is he being so cautious about? Despite his emphasis on orderliness, restraint, and containment, the obsessive shows signs from time to time not only that he fears he will make a mess but also that he wants to make one! This masking of a wish by experiencing it as a fear is termed a *phobic defense*. The strong emphasis on order derives not just from anal-retentiveness but from a desire to be anal-expulsive.

I once knew a young woman, an excellent pianist, who majored in piano in college. She found it impossible to pass the required recital as a music major because she froze when facing an audience, her fear was that she would "make a mess of things." It was true: she might well have. For she resented her mother's treating her successes as a personal triumph, as if her daughter had done nothing herself. The only way the patient could retaliate was to "make a mess of myself."

Making a mess of one's self has been graphically described in Rabelais as "beshitting one's self." True enough, the pleasures of anal-expulsiveness precede and accompany toilet-training, in life-history. No wonder, therefore, that meticulous persons, so ultra-refined in certain ways, should be a bit messy in others. These are not paradoxes, really. They are questions of the extent to which drive overcomes reaction formation, and what compromise has been worked out. In spending money it is not unusual that such a person will suddenly indulge in a major splurge after months of self-denying parsimony. Diarrhea follows constipation. The same may be true with his handling of rage, alternating passivity with outbursts.

It is not *de rigeur* to be indecisive in this culture, especially for men. There are, therefore, a number of screens that such persons put up to avoid facing the problem. They take pride in being judicious: "I like to see both sides of any issue." Or, as I prefer to put it, "I'm a man of firm convictions. One on each side of the question." Often, they simply avoid any situations requiring decision-making, and are spared having to face this disability in their personalities. The regulations of bureaucracy are welcomed by personnel who merely have to "look them up" to have made a decision. In social work this is known as "making positive use of agency structure." Sometimes it is. Life is similarly simpler for certain followers of Learning Theory in psychology.

Beyond questions of pleasure in withholding and greed, persons with this makeup are *fearful* of deciding. As one would expect of a person with an urge to besmirch himself, he is preoccupied with questions of shame and blame. After all, these are the levers primarily counted on by mothers to get young children to use the bathroom as they want them to. The fear is not just that a wrong choice will lead to financial loss. What is worse, he could be criticized for having had poor judgment. But, to reiterate, his anxiety is over being *shamed*. Because of this sensitivity, the obsessive compulsive hates to be held responsible for his actions. In conversation, for example, he may be a counterpuncher. He does not offer an opinion outright; he prefers not to deny yours too obviously. He does not argue, he only "qualifies." He is a great "Yes, but"...er.

Another way to avoid responsibility, or course, is to pretend that one never exercises an act of will, but only reacts. "Where are you rushing?' "I *have* to go down to buy a suit." "Why do you have to? Don't you own one? "Yes, but there is this terrific sale, and I can't resist sales!" "Oh, you *want* to buy a suit." "I suppose you could say that. Well, see you around. Got to go now." This poor victim of circumstances is about to be *forced* to spend money for a new suit, with a color that everyone is favoring, in a tweed that his wife likes, because *he* can't resist its appeal. How many burdens must one person carry? His arrive in Job lots, by limousine.

In order to side-step responsibility for a decision, the obsessive *feels forced.* Indeed, he prefers to feel forced, but this creates new difficulties which themselves demand solution. By avoiding responsibility and the danger of blame, the price he pays is to experience life as a long session of being pushed around. While overdoing exactly what he wants to do, he manages to feel coerced. He eventually becomes resentful, not to mention the backlog of frustration built up by withholding pleasure from himself. This, in turn, leads to more need to control himself, lest his angry feelings burst forth. It is no wonder, therefore, that so many obsessive compulsives are sardonic, slightly vitriolic characters who do not express hostility; they leak it. But, even these, if humorous, are easier to live with than persons who take refuge in an odor of sanctimony, like the frozen-faced, self-righteous politician protecting his cause behind the flag.

The obsessive is concerned with "moral responsibility" and, in a limited way, with shame. That is to say, he may otherwise be a moral man, but this is not part of his "problem." From the standpoint of those who have business with him, the obsessive compulsive is usually responsible; you can count on him and his word is good. This is not always true, however, and there is a subtype we label the *irresponsible obsessive.* He is an immature person, really indifferent to his wife and family, who will devote days to tracing a minor issue in his family's genealogy, tuning his sports car, and so forth. For many such a man, when the season is ripe for fishing, you might as well forget that he has taken the roof off your house. He *must* go fishing, and your house is your problem.

These are the absorptions of small boys playing games, not to be interrupted by the needs of others. A few such persons, incidentally, through special talents or luck become extremely successful at their compulsive hobbies, and support their families very well. They are used as hopeful examples by the women who marry them, to buoy up their spirits, but this is self-deluding. Most irresponsible obsessives are simply childish, and remain that way, without acquiring wealth except by inheritance. They usually live longer than conscientious compulsives.

There is a group of famous men whose habits represent an overdetermined form of irresponsible obsessiveness. These were the men, great artists of the printed page, who nevertheless were continually in debt, usually because they spent so recklessly that even their assiduous writing could not counter their extravagance. It has been common for their biographers to express dismay at the even greater things they might have written had they not been driven by their own profligacy into supposedly excessive productivity.

A fascinating instance of this is Balzac as portrayed by Andre Maurois in *Prometheus* (1965). Here was a man sufficiently versed in business matters that he wrote of them shrewdly and in detail. Yet he managed his own finances in such a way that he was constantly in debt, hiding from the sheriff, impoverishing his aged mother in her efforts to rescue him, and mortgaging his writing months ahead. All this because of his selfish, impulsive buying, his ostentation, and apparent lack of judgment. If one were to ask Balzac, he would undoubtedly complain that he wanted nothing but to rest and he wrote only to stave off bankruptcy. But this man who played so much the childish slob in his personal affairs spent as much as one hundred hours a month correcting proof; he is said to have rewritten supposed pot-boilers as many as ten times. It does not seem to have occurred to Maurois that Balzac wrote because he wanted to write, but that he also feared it. The financial need into which he trapped himself acted to spur his productivity *and* to permit his creativity. Only in a situation so maneuvered that he created under compunction could he defeat his fear of asserting his own ideas, lest they be criticized. He arranged his life to "force" himself to write. Of course there is more to the infantile side of Balzac's character. I merely want to assert an artistic advantage which the egos of such men as Dickens, Wagner, Scott, and Mark Twain may have wrung from the disaster of their poor handling of money.

It is possible to be a bit more precise about the chief mechanisms involved in the syndrome. The average obsessive is an intellectual ruminant. An idea gets fixed in his mind, and he cannot let it go; it turns over and over and he complains that it keeps him awake. Not all such rumination is wasted, of course. A poet quoted in this book, T. S. Eliot, often held up a poem for months until he had changed one line so that it satisfied him. This typical *conscious* worry is meant to prevent thinking about an idea he dreads will become conscious. It is a diversionary tactic by the ego to maintain repression. To listen to such conscious obsessions during treatment is at least polite; often they betray a hint of the real source of concern.

Rumination also performs the function of *undoing*. By going over and over an event in the past, we try to remold the memory of it to make ourselves look good. As a cow rechews her cud, we redigest a dismaying evening. Undoing is also at work in compulsive rituals, for which we earlier used the example of Lady Macbeth. Being caught up in undoing may take other forms. Some compulsives have a barely controllable impulse to spoil things at the end. Leonardo da Vinci had a dreadful time completing a work of art; others have simply destroyed their paintings. All teachers encounter at least some students who refuse to take the final examination in a course, or complete the thesis. Thereby they take back whatever steps forward have happened. Also typical of the obsessive is having the last word in almost any conversation, by appending one more "See you around" to your "So long," to actively control the parting.

Another facet of the obsessive compulsive is vacillation between *gullibility* and *suspiciousness*. The obsessive psychiatrist is apt to accept as true everything a tearful, angry wife tells him, if she is his patient. The social worker, in such a case, will have a hard time introducing the husband's version of reality into the therapist's mental processes. As a result, the therapist may join the wife in her neurotic machinations and stupidly permit a salvageable marriage, and a salvageable life, to go down the drain. Should you have such an obsessive in a position of authority over you, you must be wary. Because he believes the first person who gets his ear, and thereafter finds it extremely hard to hear new evidence, any liar on the staff can make your life miserable.

The suspiciousness is a defense against gullibility. The obsessive in his rigid, awkward way senses from time to time that "he has been had." Thereafter, he tries to protect himself by doubting everything told him, as indiscriminately as before he accepted all. Rather than alternating these attitudes in time, however, the obsessive is more likely to divide them among others. A female patient, having trouble with her husband, may decide that her therapist can say no wrong; her poor husband, whom she formerly treated as an oracle, now is never right. This arrangement often leads to a happy and prosperous treatment relationship in which, unfortunately, neither the patient nor her marriage recovers.

Entire books can now be written about this character type, once regarded as untreatable. Despite the difficulties his patterns create for himself and others, the person with this character, or with *many obsessive-compulsive features*, as we say, does much of the work of the world. It is possible to rank character structures from very primitive to quite mature. In any such ranking, the obsessive compulsive scores rather high.

When we find an obsessive more involved in analyzing than in being analyzed, we say he is *well compensated*. By this, we mean simply that his defense system is collaborating well enough with reality to keep him happy and productive. Should the defenses begin to collapse, we say he is *decompensating*. Decompensation is sometimes first visible through compulsions which become more and more frenzied, more and more life-encompassing—a small boy literally trying to stop a hole in the dike with his thumb, and then with handful after handful of mud. If an individual is put under enough pressure, and if his customary limitations in life style are interfered with, such decompensation can proceed to the point of psychosis. When someone with this character becomes psychotic, he is likely to experience paranoid states. There is reason to believe Stalin was a case in point.

Fortunately, most people with many obsessive-compulsive features remain reasonably well compensated and seldom become psychiatrically ill. However, the pattern is likely to be progressive. A somewhat perfectionistic and reserved young man may become a constricted, pedantic middle-aged one, who "never wants to go anyplace." The trim and well-dressed young woman who proved so good a housekeeper when first married may turn into the lady who makes her family remove their shoes before entering the parlor. We have already discussed some reasons why any defensive pattern tends to spread and become fixed. Why this particular character structure should be notable for its progressive nature into middle age, we do not fully understand. Neither is it clear why, in many instances, there is mellowing in old age. Perhaps the anger against which the syndrome is primarily erected becomes banked. And many older people do report their pleasure in no longer caring so much about being shamed in the opinion of others.

The Hysteric

Think, now, of a woman who exudes more allure proffering her cigarette for a light than Cleopatra managed floating in her pleasure barge. But, how shall I describe her without sounding ironic? If her actions are touched with charm and sensuousness, they must also at times be seen as more than a little ludicrous. Let me say, to begin with, that I find hysterics very likeable patients. Moreover, I regard the effort by some therapists to strip such folk of their flair, in the course of reducing their anxiety, as leading to an unsatisfactory treatment result. The flattened remnant of personality represents a waste of a natural resource.

Let me illustrate the personality type by a composite. I shall refer mainly to female patients in this section, but I want to note that many hysterics are men. Most of what I shall have to say seems to apply to them too, except that in our culture a number of pressures lead to important differences in the way the pattern expresses itself.

The patient was a thin-waisted, large-bosomed woman with lovely features and a skin that had not aged. She had finely formed legs, and helped me to be aware of this fact by wearing snug skirts. Some days she wore a blouse carelessly undone at the throat; other times, a sweater; occasionally a semi-bare midriff. Complementing the studied dishabille of her expensive clothing, her face was always meticulously made up; her nails were nicely polished in a unusual shade, above them flashed her boulder of a diamond with matching wedding band. Both arms were decorated with bracelets. Here, indeed, was a woman making the most of the physical equipment with which she had been endowed.

The patient's excitement communicated itself whenever she made her entrance for a conference. Her eyes shown; she spoke rapidly and energetically. Her feelings carried her away, so that she laughed, wept, scorned, raged, and depicted deep thought within the compass of fifty minutes. Her conversation seemed scattered at times, childish and illogical, as if one were dealing with a schizophrenic. But her judgment of reality was not bad, usually shrewd. Nor was the excitement confined to the patient's manner with me. If her life had been marked by tragedy, at least it had not been dull, and certainly she had not stinted living at high emotional stakes. To be her therapist was an invitation to a ride on her emotional roller coaster.

The *craving for excitement* is one of the most characteristic features of the hysteric, even if outwardly her life seems routine and decorous. One can make a desperate struggle out of sewing a dress; a polar expedition of going to the mailbox in the snow; a disaster of a child's sore throat. What is the excitement all about?

At one level, the excitement represents *displaced sexuality*. Indeed, it has been well understood for a long time that the hysteric is likely to be preoccupied with sex. Many readers will have heard already that the word hysteric is derived from the same Greek root as uterus. It has been said that if you scratch a compulsive defense, you will find rage underneath; scratch an hysterical symptom, and you will find conflict about sex. The excitement is seen as an attempt to discharge sexual stimulation in neutralized, sublimated fashion.

A number of characteristic features can be understood in these terms. If the hysteric is addicted to sex, she is also conflicted about it. She invites, and then she flees: she is a *tease*. The delight in teasing may be ego syntonic and conscious, when it has been displaced—like wanting to be coaxed to play the piano for guests. With respect to sex, however, the hysteric is surprisingly often only dimly aware of just how much of a tease she is.

The client who waves her exposed thighs at you may be evading her own seductiveness. If you point this out to her, you stand in some danger of being accused of making a pass at her! This would be in line with her tendency to *sexualize relationships*, that is, to experience sensual associations in otherwise matter-of-fact hetero-sexual encounters. Doctors, dentists, caseworkers, ministers have all learned this from experience, even though Freud, in his Victorian fashion, first resisted acknowledging it. As a result, he interpreted transference fantasies toward himself as real memories of child-hood sexual experiences with elder males in patients' families, thus committing one of the blunders of his career.

Professional men who tend to sexualize intimate contacts have been known to have affairs with hysterical female clients or patients. Despite the intense feelings of manliness some of them derive from such actions, it is they who typically have been seduced. When a woman in therapy has intercourse with her psychiatrist, (a) she is typically an hysteric; (b) she, not he, is manipulating the situation; (c) her action is in the service of resistance to treatment. "How can you confront me with unpleasant things, when you're a man and I'm a woman?" Whatever else one might think of such occurrences, and perhaps they are not so rare as one might hope, they represent poor treatment technique. The therapist has been rendered therapeutically impotent.

The major defensive maneuver of hysterics is said to be *massive repression*, referring, in this instance, to the inability to recall much of early life at the start of treatment. This interference with memory plays a role in the seeming scatter of speech. Once the therapist is convinced the client is neither brain damaged nor psychotic, he be-comes aware of a tendency to skitter from topics that would lead to unwanted insights. Clients may seem illogical, but this, too is in the service of maintaining repression. After all, following certain lines of thought to their ends would lead to conclusions they cannot stand to face. So women may pretend to a little-girlish flightiness.

Two satisfactory methods for avoiding unwanted insight into one's own fantasies are *projection* ("You are trying to seduce me!")

and *somatization* ("What's wrong with me is physical"). Hysterics commonly suffer "pains for which no organic basis can be found" or exaggerate the significance of symptoms which do have ascertainable physical causes. By concentrating on bodily discomforts, hysterical patients successfuly distract themselves from the guilt-laden images which otherwise threaten to break into consciousness. It is partly for the same reason that hysterics so often seem to *court hardship and turmoil* in their lives. The "need to suffer" used to be ascribed to *masochism*, with the implication that the client gained sexual pleasure from pain. However, in my experience, the defensive function of the real-life emergencies they seem to invite for themselves often outweighs the titillation.

Many physicians find it odd that patients known for overconcern about trivial illnesses often prove remarkably brave and reasonable when confronted by a serious physical crisis. This becomes less paradoxical if we remember that the major source of the anxiety is derived from unconscious images, sexual fantasies, and attendant guilt. Having a tangible, conscious danger on which to focus comes as a relief, because they can make active efforts to cope with it externally. There is a corresponding increase in ego strength. We observed, for example, that during World War II the number of mental hospital admissions in Detroit dropped substantially, not just among young men taken into the Army, but for all age groups.

The most characteristic form anger takes is *righteous indignation*. Hysterics are not satisfied to retaliate for hurts suffered, they seem to seek out incidents about which to feel abused. Then they pursue the person they hold responsible with accusations relentlessly stated in a penetrating voice calculated to arouse as much guilt as possible. The burden of the piece is the moral reprehensibility of the other party. Recrimination of this sort is frequently found to add to the other discordant sounds of marital squabbling.

Such outbursts of moral indignation often end by costing the client more than they are worth psychologically. Although feeling unusually well put together in the midst of a tirade, afterwards he arises feeling depleted and guilty from having gone too far. Yet it remains impossible to give up such tantrums, even though they shake the hysteric, disrupt relationships with beloved people and endanger the mental health of children. If a female hysteric has no provocation in her immediate life, she is likely to find herself brooding on more general injustices to humanity or resurrecting hurts from the distant past. However, a factor distinguishing the hysteric from, say, the paranoid character is the extent to which there is some foundation for the accusations.

Why is it so hard to give up this pattern which, among other things, leaves the accuser frequently more shaken than the accused? What are the functions of *righteous indignation?* First, of course, it is a *projective defense.* How satisfyfing it is to escape self-recriminations by saying, in effect, "Compared with you, I'm not evil at all." The high moral tone adopted is the tip-off that guilt and shame are in the mind of the accuser. Second, it is a defense in which *one affect is subtituted for another.* Just as sex is not just sex for the hysteric, so anger is not just anger. The complaint being filed usually has the content, "You don't really love me..." The instinctive reaction to this abandonment is not necessarily anger: a more natural one would be depressiveness and anxiety. However, while busy with anger, the hysteric feels strong and self-assured, rather than crushed and unlovable. Finally, there are a series of other rather obvious functions of the anger: keeping the other person involved in a *hostile-dependent* contact; provocative verbal wrestling with connotations of *sexual foreplay;* the desire to distract oneself from threatening insights by sustained tumult in the environment; and the close tie between righteous indignation and *fantasies of being raped.*

An interesting form of projection involves the *externalization of conflict.* Let us say a woman has an urge to buy a fur coat, but her conscience will not let her squander the family's money, which is needed to pay dental bills for the children. Rather than suffer the conflict within herself, she comes and tells her husband, "I saw just the mink I want to buy." The husband, naturally, hits the ceiling and points out that they cannot afford such an expenditure. His wife quarrels with him about this, ending by saying, "You never let me have anything." At this point, she has converted her guilt into righteous indignation. She finds it more comfortable to convert the conflict from one that lay within her to one between her and another person. Such a person may, before telling her worker of some extramarital flirting, begin with, "I know just what you're going to say." Thereby, she makes the problem of restraining impulses the worker's, not hers.

We have referred to sexual preoccupation, and I have just noted that "sex is not just sex" to the hysteric. It is usually easy to establish that the sexual functions have been invaded by conflict. The man with a "Don Juan complex" seems obviously trying to reassure himself there is nothing wrong with his abilities. The woman accused of nymphomania, or who acts so provocatively, seems bent on hiding from herself her own difficulties in achieving orgasm in a stable, love relationship. Similarly, we would expect defense to be piled upon defense. Thus, the woman who seeks sexual reassurances may try to find them in casual affairs. As a reaction formation against such impulses, she may then become studiously *asexual*—in manner, in dress, and even in body build. One way to secure herself against temptation is to make herself undesirable. Then we end with a large-bellied woman, hastening to her doctor with recurrent gynecological complaints or even what used to be called polysurgical addiction—inviting multiple operations. Meanwhile, she may have become so manipulative in her use of sex with her husband, giving or withholding for extraneous reasons, that she is now unable to achieve orgasm. Or she may have to insist she never feels anything—she has produced three children from a succession of rapes.

There are numerous variations we could list because usually the hysteric is—developmentally speaking—a rather mature sort of person, with correspondingly rich and flexible defenses. The *pseudofeminine* woman, the *pseudomasculine* man, the *neuter*, the *histrionic* homosexual all represent compromises and reaction formations around the fact that normal sexuality has been invaded by conflict. In the treatment of an hysteric, as said before, attention must be given to problems with sex. This layering of defense cannot be skipped in treatment. But, it would be a serious mistake to assume, as we used to, that this layer represents the ultimate source of the difficulty. For among the uses and misuses of sex one finds this: sexual feelings, themselves, may be diverted to the service of defense!

What, then, is being defended against? Given the *exhibitionism* of a woman with many hysterical features, and a penchant for wearing her heart on both sleeves, we are reminded of a wisecrack often used by third year psychiatric residents: "I think there is *less* here than meets the eye." They were referring, of course, to the frequent hollowness of the protestations of love, concern, or even guilt from such people. Actors and actresses in daily life, they seem unable to distinguish the role they play from reality, and like chameleons will shift roles to meet their immediate situation. We may suddenly see the hysteric as an *empty person*, lacking enduring values and even attachments. When I was treating hospitalized women, it dawned on me that many described as hysterics had problems associated with the *schizoid personality* or, as we say, "problems in the schizoid spectrum" (see Chapter 9).

It is natural that our perceptiveness be accompanied by shock and even contempt. But why? Because suddenly we are face-to-face with an emptiness that can afflict any of us! We want to dissociate ourselves from it because it is frightening, which is why we are contemptuous of the hysteric. While our judgmental attitude is understandable, it may prove unfortunate for the hysteric, for we miss a significant insight into what is being most desperately defended against; the sense of emptiness and the accompanying loneliness.

If at times greedy for sex, we see it as an effort to assuage anxiety about being bereft by escaping into pleasure. Even the sort of pleasure is indicative. Mature sexuality consists of an encounter in which there is a progression from interest, to sensuality, to higher and higher peaks of pleasure culminating in orgasm and followed by relaxation and for the time being satiety. The sexuality of immature hysterics, especially, lacks this *orgasmic* quality. It is more like a little girl's gentle stroking of her labia to comfort herself because she misses her mama and can think of nothing else that makes her feel better. The need for stimulation is chronic; there is no latent phase. Similarly, an hysterical man may react against the loss of a loved one, or the threat of rejection by his wife by becoming all the more importunate for intercourse, as if he could re-establish the tie to his loved one by entering her. He tries, figuratively, to suck through his penis.

Because of her fear of loneliness an hysterical young woman may become involved in an affair. What she really wants is to be held and cuddled by a warm and tender mother/daddy, but the man becomes excited, and the result is intercourse. Dependency needs have become sexualized, and this creates reverberations as listed, but the core of the difficulty usually lies more profoundly in the unresolved sense of emptiness. The emptiness also accounts for the *histrionic* and *exhibitionistic* facets of the syndrome. While the overt behavior defiantly says, "Look me over," the covert message is "Don't overlook me." Rather than contemptible, the client now seems appealing, even poignant. But our pity will be misapplied if it distracts us from the necessary psychological surgery. The fact that our hysteric is so often a great "ham," clever in mimicry, skilled in manipulation, and funny need not prevent the treatment so long as one principle holds: if the client cannot distinguish between the drama she has created and her real life, the caseworker or therapist had better not have joined her—at least not in the same script.

I cannot end this section without including for the reader's pleasure another gem from Eliot, which needs no exegesis.

> Grishkin is nice: her Russian eye
> Is underlined for emphasis;
> Uncorseted, her friendly bust
> Gives promise of pneumatic bliss.
>
> The couched Brazilian jaguar
> Compels the scampering marmoset
> With subtle effluence of cat;
> Grishkin has a maisonette;
>
> The sleek Brazilian jaguar
> Does not in its arboreal gloom
> Distil so rank a feline smell
> As Grishkin in a drawing-room.

And there, my friends, is the casework problem.

Mixed Marriage

What happens when an hysterical woman marries an obsessive man? This combination is found rather frequently in marital counseling. The wife is invariably experiencing the greater discomfort and showing the most symptomatic reaction. As she works out of her depressive, martyred stance of "I feel trapped," she may conclude that her husband is going to have to change or she will divorce him. This is not to be taken as an idle threat; often that is exactly what she does. The husand, meanwhile, finds it difficult to take the whole matter seriously. He is embarrassed to be talking about feelings in the first place, and preoccupied with making a living, in the second. He wishes she would just calm down and do a better job balancing their budget.

Such cases are painful to encounter. They often involve a woman in her early thirties, whose chances of a satisfying remarriage are not so great as she likes to think, and a husband in his later thirties, about to be pushed toward bankruptcy. Typically it is a marriage of about ten years' standing, with the fate of several children hanging in the balance. As one husband, less stodgy than many, burst out: "Ten years and three children later — *now* she decides she doesn't love me." What has gone wrong?

Although the wife claims she never really loved her husband, something attracted her to this man originally. As a young woman she was obliquely aware of her emotional lability, her preoccupation with flirting, and the chance that she would get herself into trouble. The husband, let us say, was a man then in his later twenties, single because he was too conservative and shy to have rushed into marriage with a contemporary. To the girl, he seemed successful, mature, solid—just the person to help support her controls against impulsivity. So one basis of her attachment to him was his defensive function and her need for a mother figure in her husband.

The husband's maturity was actually being overestimated. She mistook his stolidity for solidity. It was not that his emotions were so judicious, rather that he feared to express any. At the same time, he was aware of a vicarious sense of freedom and pleasure from watching this girl's vivacity. She added variety and entertainment to his life, even as he felt he had to slow her down at times. And so they were in love, and were married. Such a marriage can work for a time and usually does. If neither partner exhibits too much of the pattern I am describing, they may meet each other's needs for a lifetime. Indeed, they may help each other mature. But there are dangers.

A common danger is that the girl who was fearful of her impulses becomes a woman who, after coping with life for a number of years, is no longer so afraid of them. She wants more excitement and is impatient with a husband who will not give her even a good fight. As she no longer needs a man to support her defenses, she now views him as a wet blanket, a drag, a party pooper. Some of her feelings are realistic, of course, but some are not. It is inevitable that this immature woman will sooner or later grow ambivalent toward anyone she loves. She carries over her sense of emptiness and disappointment in her feelings toward her mother, and punishes her husband for them. She now can project the cause of all her neurotic despair onto her husband. Gullible or unethical marriage counselors and psychiatrists may accept at face value her statement of what is wrong. In that case, there may be a divorce and only afterward will she discover she still has many of the same feelings the divorce was supposed to alleviate.

Such a marriage cannot always be salvaged. Sometimes, when both partners no longer need the defensive functions they served for each other, they find they have no other basis for love. Or, if the parties involved are extremely immature or stubborn, the level of friction in the household may rise to a point too high to risk while one tries to treat the personalities and their marriage. Shooting one's mate has occurred even among apparently successful and sensible people. At a less menacing level, we find that they are making each other worse—that is, as she regresses and acts more hysterical, he withdraws and becomes more anxious and rigidly compulsive. Each would like to think the other is "making me sicker." The truth is they are exacerbating each other's neuroses, but each would still have a neurosis if the other went away.

Fortunately, many such marriages can be treated. Even if the couples exhibit the character structures just described, they often achieve a downward spiraling of tension through ventilation and insight. Then it is possible for each to look at his own contribution to the trouble and think about changing. How much help will be needed of course depends on how extreme the patterns were in the first place.

Although this is not a book about treatment, let us mention that the caseworker's task is to step in and become the "good mama," satisfying dependency needs. By comforting, rewarding, and occasionally admonishing, it is possible gradually to get them to stop acting like two children fighting in the back seat of the family car during a tedious auto trip. When their love of their children and the desire to recover what they once had takes precedence over their spitefulness and bitterness, they will have stopped regressing. At that point, our job is to help them satisfy their dependency needs, needing us the less as they do so, until we make ourselves therapeutically unnecessary. For the sake of their pride, we can call this "re-establishing communication," but we must remember that primitive, violent forces are at work.

The Paranoid Character

Most educated people associate *paranoia* with the serious mental illness *paranoid schizophrenia*. All schizophrenics suffer from thought disorders. They show vagueness in thought and gaps in reasoning and are concrete-minded. They are thought to be psychotic because they have lost the ability to recognize reality in the way others see it *(consensual validation)*. A paranoid schizophrenic suffers from these general symptoms. In addition, he is recognized by extreme *suspiciousness*. He infers maliciousness in the actions of others to an extreme degree. He may have hallucinations and *delusions of persecution*. Typically, too, the paranoid schizophrenic is *grandiose*. He has a great sense of his own importance, his role in history, or the like. It was not uncommon for such patients to think of themselves as Christ, or Napoleon, or Caesar. Today one hears less about such colorful delusional states, perhaps because our psychoses, like the rest of our culture, are growing more sophisticated and less delightfully eccentric. When reality offers the hydrogen bomb, who needs *delusions of omnipotence?*

A *paranoid character,* however, is not psychotic, or not currently psychotic. The term encompasses a person with some of the features just mentioned, greatly modulated and well masked. A paranoid character is not thought to be in the midst of an acute, labile, schizophrenic illness. Rather, as the word *character* reminds us, he is in a relatively stable state. Reality testing is adequate; indeed, it may be hypertrophied in an area of special concern, because of either *suspiciousness* or a tremendous need for *power.* Hence, it is not uncommon to find paranoid characters who are highly successful speculators, on the one hand, or shrewd diagnosticians on the other. There are a great many more paranoid characters, or persons with marked paranoid trends, than the average new practitioner conceives possible.

The paranoid character, like the hysteric, often feels sadly abused. What distinguishes him from the ordinary hysteric, however, is the *rigidity* with which he pursues the person he believes injured him. Many obsessives, as we have noted, are argumentative yes-buters. The paranoid character does not find it necessary to be a yes-buter; he does not accept your point even for heuristic purposes. If you place a fence on what he thinks is four inches his side of the property line, he not only will take you to court but will pursue the case as long as it takes to win. He is *litigious,* and with all his suspiciousness is as much the shyster's friend as the inadequate hysteric is the support of unprincipled physicians. The paranoid character feels friendless without an enemy; as long as he has at least one person with whom he is actively feuding, he is in balance. The paranoid character need not be brave, so it is not uncommon for him to select as his enemy a person over whom he has power and whom he can then prosecute *mercilessly.* If your employer has many of these characteristics, and you find yourself his target for this year, leave. Now. It is seldom possible to mollify such a person, except temporarily; he respects only counterforce. An hysteric can be helped to correct distortions about another person through reasoning and evidence. But the paranoid character "needs" projections and suspicions far more, and this in part accounts for the rigidity. There is something more than stubborn about the way he clings to ideas and persists in intentions. It is as if we were dealing with defenses that are brassy, or somehow brittle, and you get the feeling that if he were to give ground even a little bit he might collapse totally. This is reflected in an *intolerance for criticism*, which may be so strong that it seriously interferes with his ability to learn from mistakes, or from the advice of others.

Where the obsessive is perfectionistic, the paranoid character is *hypercritical* especially about people. There is hardly anyone about whom he does not have serious reservations. This trait may make for an excellent psychodiagnostician; he is preoccupied with smelling out the crannies of others' motivations, anyhow. Many first-rate psychometricians have marked paranoid features. The hypercritical attitude about others often extends to himself, but this he keeps unconscious. Still, he is *pitiless*, and rather than sympathetic is actually *contemptuous of weakness* in himself or others. He is likely to experience attempts at self-examination (casework or psychotherapy, for example), as a series of psychological assaults. He assumes you have the same contempt at remarking his difficulties as he would feel were your roles reversed.

Paranoid characters are not usually very humorous, at least not about their own foibles. They subscribe to the doctrine of personal infallibility. One patient hated to call the railway station to ask when the train left. Not only was she shy, but it turned out that she felt, somehow, she should already know the train schedule; to have to ask for information was an admission that she did not already know it. Actually, this is rather ludicrous, and many patients would be amused to discover their inability to ask directions had such a basis. This young lady, however, was not amused. For her the stakes were too high: to be uninformed was a violation of her defensive *illusion of omniscience*. In plain English, this means being a know-it-all.

Lack of humor in the paranoid characters I have known has seemed to be multiply determined. First, they are unable to enjoy jokes at their own expense, for the stakes are always too high to be taken lightly. They prefer bathroom humor and cruelty jokes—like little boys. Second, much humor involves an element of surprise. We see a sudden juxtaposition of images we had never thought possible, it makes a weird kind of sense, and we laugh. But the professional know-it-all cannot afford to be surprised. Third, he cannot *surrender* to humor; he can tell a joke, but he cannot enjoy one, let us say. He "tops" your story, or he has heard it already. The need to control is even more desperate, even more brassy than in the obsessive. Indeed, some paranoid characters are warding off open psychotic breaks. Others have had temporary psychoses, and the personalities we deal with represent instances of poor healing after such illnesses.

In my experience, the sort of personality we have been describing often rises rapidly in bureaucratic structures—the Army, the university, the mental hospital, even the large social agency. Few of us have the drive toward power which frees the paranoid character to fanatic efficiency in pursuit of status. We may, in fact, be handicapped by concern for our subordinates or pity toward someone with whom we compete. But this sort of person has few such qualms, consciously, and allays such as he has with claims that he does what he does "for the good of the organization."

Moreover, some of the energy others put into love relationship, is, for paranoid characters, drained off into their fascination with *intrigue*. They are expert backbiters and office politicians. As soon as they meet someone new, the question is, "Who will be on top?" Their interpersonal relationships tend to be largely *manipulative*, however superficially warm they may appear. The best-known example is Stalin, but we cannot forget the British double agent Kim Philby, who betrayed his country to the Russians, and John Foster Dulles, who placed our country on nearly the same pedestal of concern as he did his narcissism. It is of passing interest that studies of the Russian national character seem to show that the group that becomes the managerial class has much in common with the personality of the U.S. managerial class—many paranoid elements.

It used to be thought that the crucial dynamic in all paranoid states was *unconscious homosexuality*. So abhorrent was self-recognition of this propensity that the client or patient would project all sorts of evil, accusatory thoughts into the minds of others, thus giving rise to his suspiciousness. Nevertheless, I learned from a patient who was homosexual and recurrently paranoid (and who defeated my attempts to treat him) that the reverse may also be true. That is, it is because the young man is deeply hostile and suspicious that he cannot tolerate any long-term relationship. Certainly he could not endure the commitment and intimacy which, in our culture, go with marriage. Hence the stereotyped homosexual relationship—fleeting, jealousy-ridden, interrupted by side-affairs with casual pickups—was in his case the only refuge against being left completely alone.

The paranoid character utilizes a number of defenses found in both the obsessive compulsive and the hysteric. A major distinguishing feature is the desperateness, the hard, turtle-like exterior, if you will, with which these defenses are organized. This is what we mean when we speak of his *rigidity*. Obviously this character structure represents a developmentally lower stage of maturation, with many anal-stage remnants, whatever his success in manipulating the world. The social caseworker is usually more in the position of recognizing the trends, and dealing with the client realistically (which is *not* to say frankly) in terms of how he is, rather than anticipating much change. The etiological roots of this distressing character formation will become clearer when we discuss the *schizoid* and *paranoid* positions.

The Depressive Character
It has been said that a cynic is a person who, given a choice between two evils, chooses both. A similar comment applies to the depressive person. It is not always clear whether we label him depressive because of the state in which he exists or the talent he has for inducing a sad feeling in us. There is a kind of morose client who is actually so *affect inhibited* he scarcely feels anything. The depressive person does permit himself a modicum of feelings, but they are consistently in one direction. They range from dreadful to "not too bad." It is as well not to ask him how he feels.

Other prominent characteristics include a *self-derogatory* attitude, so that he seldom admits to having done well. If he did so, it was "an accident." There is an *apologetic* manner that accompanies the self-deprecation and says "excuse me for living." Constantly bracing himself to cope with *impending doom*, the depressed person lives by his forebodings. Needless to say, he seldom has, or permits himself, any fun out of life. *Er vergonnt sich nicht.* He does not allow himself the satisfaction.

These attitudes are found in persons experiencing acute depression, usually in response to something that has happened in life—death or illness of a loved one, a major career defeat, loss of caring by a person to whom one has become attached. When we refer to a depressive character, we do not mean an acute state, reactive to some identifiable event, but a chronic one. It is characteristic of the depressive personality that his mood cannot usually be ascribed to any concrete event; rather, it is as if he always finds something to feel depressed about. In short, we are discussing depression as a *modus vivendi*.

Much of what we believe to be true of the dynamics of acute depression also applies to the more chronically depressed person, but with the usual qualifications regarding a symptom that has long endured and become part of character. The technical interpretation of depression is *aggression turned against the self*. The client is angry but unable to express it directly toward the true object of his rage, so, *faute de mieux*, he attacks himself. Why does he not express it openly, "get it off his chest," rather than letting it "eat at him" without even consciously knowing he is mad? The most usual reason is that the adult has too *rigid* a conscience to permit the outburst; we say he has a *primitive superego*. Many people, for example, have been mistaught religiously that to feel hatred is sinful. Obviously such emotions as rage and hate were well-known among those who set down our Bible, and they were taken for granted as part of the nature of man. Rage is an automatic response, something like a reflex, if you will. One cannot decide whether he will be angry; one can decide only whether he will show it or express it destructively. Many clients believe that by some act of will they can feel what they do not feel, or not feel what they do feel. It would not be surprising, then, if their rage were to come out in some other form—like depressiveness.

In my experience, while religious doctrines may contribute to, or exacerbate, the overly strong constraints against expressing anger, they are seldom the primary reason. More typical is the childish association that because one was originally most angry at mama, all later rage is as if one were attacking mama. If one destroys mama (as we mentioned earlier children *do* remark, "I'm going to cut off your head and throw you in the garbage pail"), then one will be left utterly alone. Therefore anger is desperately dangerous. It may also be dangerous if the client or patient is immature in parts other than his conscience. For example, he experiences anger still as the raw, violently colorful explosion of childhood. To a grown man, who may let his thoughts find reality in action, this is frightening. If we ask *why* the ideas of rage are still so primitive, we find a circular process in many cases. Never, since childhood, has he felt free to express such feelings. Therefore, he has had no practice in how to get mad, but to do so in modulated forms, as most of us gradually had to learn through practice and from being punished for uncontrolled expressions. In short, he was held back from the life experiences out of which he could have matured in his handling of anger. Therefore, as an adult he can only alternate between holding it all in, and sudden, violent outbursts which become proper cause for much subsequent guilt.

A frequent concomitant to this set of dynamics is the *passive-aggressive* personality constellation. Literally, this means a person who expresses aggression in passive ways—the husband in the comic strip who frustrates his wife by reading the paper while she nags at him. *Spite* is the form of aggression the weak can dare. Thus, spitefulness is common among passive-aggressive, depressive people. It takes many forms, but the one of greatest interest to caseworkers and counselors is *hostile compliance*. This consists of carrying out a suggestion (experienced as a command) in such a way that it fails. Artful hostile compliance takes the form of overdoing as directed, thereby reducing the prescriber to complete helplessness. The patient does not just peel the potato for her mother: she ends up with a small pebble which she carefully sets in the pot. Slavery produced expertise at this. Northerners discovered that the Southern blacks were being paid thirty or forty cents an hour (while Northern help was getting a dollar) and were often managing to give just about that proportionate amount of effort. The danger with spite is that it can lead to guilt feelings, especially when it is unconscious. And it, too, can be turned against the self, begetting depression. "Cutting off one's nose to spite one's face." The sullen housewife refuses to make herself attractive to her husband, but then she also ends up with no sexual relationship.

Finally, there may be an inability to express aggression directly because the true object is unavailable. We mentioned earlier the lament, "How could you go away and leave me?" But the mourner would be outraged were we to suggest that he was mad at the departed for abandoning him. This would really add to his burden of conflict! So he rends his clothes and covers himself with ashes, while he weeps at his lot.

These formulations of depressiveness and its roots are applicable to many people, in acute as well as chronic states. But they may have become "classical" as interpretations, accepted too glibly. If we routinely *assume* that any depressed person we see is secretly angry, it becomes impossible to verify its truth in any given case. An angry outburst will demonstrate your assumption; failure to get it is interpreted as "covering up." Therefore, I must emphasize strongly that while depression may emerge as a *result* of a defense (i.e. the need to redirect anger), depressiveness may serve as a defense itself.

One defensive function of depressiveness is as a form of *security maneuver*. These are a series of psychological operations carried on with the general intention: play it safe. Among the peasants in Southern and Eastern Europe, there used to be a good deal of fear of the evil eye and the evil spirits. Jews, for example, felt it bad luck to acknowledge pride or satisfaction verbally, as this would call down vengeance from evil spirits. This idea spreads, often, until it seems safer in general not even to think of good fortune lest it be taken away from you. Another familiar version is the effort to *control* the experience of disappointment. If you do not hope for much, indeed if you expect the worst, then you cannot be taken by surprise and are braced to receive bad news. Of course the price one pays for this internal preparation is preoccupation with morbid thoughts.

Another version of controlling by anticipation is the manner of self-abnegation and self-recrimination to which we referred earlier. By blaming oneself aloud, one can get in the punch before it is thrown, at the same time trying to soften the blow by being the person who throws it. Hence, the punitive superego is encouraged to stay immature, for it continues to have a function in the present, to soften criticism. In fact, a skillful practitioner of the art of self-blaming can even select the charges he wants leveled at himself.

These psychological processes tie in with other congeries related to "playing the morality game": maneuvers for attempting to wrest success from defeat by claiming moral victory. When I was at college and our football team never won a game, we would pretend to a massive indifference to the childish sport or else we would say, "Well, our coach is building character again." The defect with such moral victories is that there is no substitute for achievement in the real world. The advantage of setting up life as a series of moral issues—a policy that vastly increases the penetration of the superego into all aspects of living—is that one cannot lose. After all, one can always say, "I could have won, but I would not stoop to such tactics as studying before an exam," or the like. Although the person seems to be taking major chances with his life, he is, actually, "playing it safe." We readily see, therefore, why the depressive person often has a punitive superego. He has reinforced it even in adult life, as a security maneuver. While he wrests defeat from the jaws of victory in the service of his moral superiority, he must suffer from the blows he inflicts on himself in order to keep things under control.

Depressiveness is a symptom and a pattern from which other patterns can be derived. One is the occasional erection of a *manic* defense. Literally, it is as if the ego becomes tired of living down in the sewer and from time to time decides to throw off the whole attitude by a sharp reversal. Unlike the droopy showing that accompanies depression, then, we may suddenly find ourselves with a hyperactive client, who can be—and is—on the go all night. A general sense of euphoria replaces dark, dismal feelings. Absolute certainty and a brassy unwillingness to be crossed or corrected replaces the self-doubting and misgivings. The hint that all is not really so well as the patient likes to pretend to himself comes from the fact that he is now as rigidly optimistic as he was formerly pessimistic. The rigidity in the personality, in other words, continues and is now increased, if anything, by massive denial not only of self-questionings, which may have been unreal, but of reality and its limitations as well.

What is the etiology of this pattern? By what series of life events does one become a depressive personality? Basically, the depressive is chronically dissatisfied. He is dissatisfied, ultimately, because he did not get, or feels he did not get, all he should have from his mother. Therefore, he is demanding of the world about him, constantly trying to make up for what he feels he has missed. The result is that he is *greedy*, and his constant complaint is that life has not given him enough. If a cynic is a secretly disillusioned romantic, a depressive is disappointed because he asks more from life than it gives. Or more than it gives to adults.

If the depressive could express this openly, he might at least come to grips with it, and perhaps even resolve some of it. But it feels insulting to be conscious of these thoughts and emotions. Consequently, he may cover his whining and demandingness completely behind a reaction formation of bravery and self-sacrifice. This cheerfully bitter front has the effect of creating considerable guilt among those close to you. The spouses and youngsters of depressives who become regressed and hospitalized are among the most interested, respectful, and attentive relatives one will find. We must feel admiration for the resolution with which the depressive fights against the feelings that threaten to overwhelm him.

A depressive's extreme *pride* may not let him know how much he yearns to be taken care of and mothered. Pride is certainly a concomitant of this character formation, extending into overconcern about others' opinions, the self-demand for achievement, and so on. This pride, however, also contains a suggestion of the problem's ultimate root. What is the pride of a little boy whose mother leaves him to go to work, or the little girl required, at too young an age, to care for her younger siblings? The pride is a way of saying, "If nobody else loves me, *I* will."

We now see the link between this character type and the obsessive compulsive. Indeed, for those with chronically depressive feelings, constant achievement and activity toward achievement are the only defenses they may know. The ultimate etiology for the depressive person lies in the early mother-child relationship. It is well to remember that no therapy can make up for what has been, and for what may never be. But we can at least seek to dislodge some of the later elaborations on the neurosis which make things worse: the self-demandingness, the dependency on others' opinions for reassurance, the pride and jealousy, the self-hatred, the redirection of reasonable desires for succoring; the denial of needfulness, the tendency to play the morality game and its consequences, the general defensive maintenance of funereal outlooks, the fear of experiencing fun. We may not be able to eliminate all these subsequent developments, but at least they are modifiable in many instances.

It is not necessary to hurt the pride of the depressive person when meeting the needfulness behind his self-sacrificing front. It is not required that one *tell* him that one is being nice, or why one is being giving. If you burlesque his own despairing feelings toward himself by saying, mock-solemnly, "Yes, you are just awful," or, "We might as well bury you now," he gets the concern—and the message.

Borderline Personality

In recent years clinical social workers have increasingly recognized a type of client called *borderline*. There are fads in such matters, alas. Some of the same clients would have been thought of as schizoid a decade ago. At least one influential writer prefers the term *narcissistic* for many of the same people (Kohut, 1971). When the views of experts are compared, it becomes clear that they are unclear about the meaning of the term (Perry and Klerman, 1978). So, I have had to ask myself whether to include this category in this book. I decided to do so because the term helps us understand a set of clients with very puzzling dynamics. These clients are encountered most frequently, perhaps, in the criminal justice system, in protective service, and in mental health settings.

The appearance of some borderline patients became inevitable as soon as Kraepelin developed his descriptive psychiatry. "Psychiatrists soon found themselves presented with patients who failed to adhere to discrete forms of schizophrenia, yet who were not functioning well enough to be diagnosed psychoneurotic" (Williams, 1979, p. 1). Baffled by the mixture of islands of intactness amid seas of weird thought and odd behaviors, psychiatrists took refuge in compound diagnoses. A patient might see one psychiatrist and be diagnosed "pseudo-neurotic schizophrenic," implying he was psychotic but managing to masquerade as otherwise; another, however, would call the same man, "pseudo-schizophrenic neurotic," which implied that his bizarre behaviors were really histrionic gestures, well within the control of the ego.

In the psychoanalytic tradition, Stern (1938) referred to "the borderline group of neuroses." He remarked the narcissism, inordinate sensitivity and cautiousness, rigidity in using defenses, and "psychic bleeding" of these patients. "Instead of a resilient reaction to a painful experience the patient goes down in a heap" (p. 470). Transference reactions tend to involve intense dependency, demanding unconditional love. Various authors, by the way, have commented that whereas neurotic patients produce "transference neuroses" in treatment, borderlines are susceptible to "transference psychoses." This evidently occurred to at least one acquaintance of mine who became psychotic in the course of being analyzed as part of his training.

Young borderline patients at the Austen Riggs Center, where I had my introduction to the conception, were said to have egos that were "decompensating." Decompensation is a medical term describing an overstressed or otherwise damaged organ no longer able to make up for the deficit that is breaking it down. Non-analytically oriented psychiatrists had, at times, spoken of such a young patient as showing "incipient schizophrenia"; I worked for several years with an outpatient who had been diagnosed "incipient paranoid schizophrenic." From the psychoanalytic standpoint, the decompensation of the ego was seen in primary-process thinking invading conscious deliberation, through malapropisms and gross misuse of abstract terms. Defenses were also seen as deteriorating, so that feelings ordinarily repressed (e.g. sexual fantasies toward a parent) were erupting into consciousness. The grasp on reality, the *reality-testing* function of the ego was also seen as collapsing. In other words, we had here a patient thought to be in transition from severe neurosis to psychosis. The ego, like an overinflated inner tube, had started to rupture in places and needed patching. It was also important to relieve the pressure so that with normal processes of self-healing, the ego might have a chance to reconstitute itself. Rather than interpret defenses, one might try to support them (Knight, 1953).

Subsequently, in a series of papers referring to borderline personality organization, Kernberg points out that rather than being transitory, this mode of organization of the personality is fixed in the life of such a patient, a life-long state (1967; 1968; 1972). While the patient may have psychotic episodes—and some do—given the protection and structure a good mental hospital provides, he reverts rapidly to a non-psychotic mode of functioning. Kernberg, like others, has remarked the inability to integrate from deficits in the ego's *synthetic function* among these patients. In this connection, he has described *splitting in the ego* in a way that I, at least, have found helpful. Briefly, Kernberg (1966) reminds us that the very young infant is unable to integrate, to put things together, if it wishes to. However, *splitting* is a process in which the ego turns this earlier inability into an active mode, as it were, becoming deliberately unable to synthesize as a defensive maneuver. Such splitting underlies defenses like denial or projection and is also found in the rigid compartmentalization we see in obsessive compulsives who, having placed their attitudes in separate boxes, are protected against the jar of recognizing their own internal contradictions.

Many social workers of this generation are familiar with the efforts by the Blancks (1974) to apply Mahler's theories to the conception of borderline states. They have written extensively on issues of etiology and treatment (1974). An exhaustive review of the available literature has also been given by E. R. Shapiro (1978).

What, then, is there to say about this client group? The general problem of the borderline patient can be viewed in terms of generally weak ego boundaries. More specifically, one is impressed with the inability to "put it all together," with failures of the synthetic function. As a consequence, we do not see encapsulated sets of symptoms in otherwise intact people, as with neurotics. The symptoms are present, but at least some of the rigidity with which they are held to derives from their being last-ditch efforts to keep on functioning.

All agree that a structured situation, such as an initial interview, often brings out the best in the borderline patient, at least until you cross him or question a defense (Perry and Klerman, 1978). So, the *ability to respond plausibly to structure* is characteristic of this group—a negative positive sign! Hence, the looseness of thought process often present may show itself on projectives like the The-

matic Apperception Test, but not on the well-structured Wechsler
Adult Intelligence Scale. Analogously, borderline patients who,
under stress, have had aggressive outbursts resembling paranoia
may reconstitute very rapidly when removed to a hospital. Many
of us have had the experience of taking risks to have persons who
were acting psychotic committed, only to receive them back in the
community within days seeking vengeance and bearing the label
of "essentially normal" from a state hospital psychiatrist. Borderline people often perform well in military and paramilitary organizations, such as the Army, the police, the post ofice, or as
institutional staff. While they express rebellious wishes and engage
in some acting-out, they may actually be operating better in such a
structure than they ever could without it. Perhaps there was more
than a little insight in the jibe we draftees so frequently directed at
the Regular Army: "You found a home."

The tendency to be *overwhelmed by anxiety* has been frequently
noted in this category of patients. Given a stress situation, they
are—in sports parlance—very likely to "choke." Fear is quickly
succeeded by panic. In short, the resiliency derived from defenses
integrated in depth is simply not there. In addition, one often
becomes aware that the borderline patient's *hostility* exists *relatively
unmodulated*. He feels he is sitting on a powder keg.

The tendency to form chaotic, *inappropriate relationships with the
therapist* was remarked, early on, by Stern. One is either a godlike
figure, or an evil hypercritical devil. Actually, you are likely to be
used as a protective thing, a security blanket rather than a person.
But, after all, the client's self-percepts take equally wild swings; he
sees himself either as impotent and degraded, or as grandly omnipotent, only needing to throw off the beggar's cloak to reveal the
princely garb beneath. A former student, Paul Freeman, has pointed out to me the overweening sense of *entitlement* common among
these patients. Some of their rage is against being treated by the
same rules that apply to everybody since the borderline feels himself someone very special, a privileged character.

From Erikson, I learned that what he terms *identity diffusion* (see
below) is another feature prevalent among borderline cases. Not
only can they often not find a social identity, but they may show
problems in sexual identity as well. To state it carefully: all homosexuals are of course not borderline personalities, but many borderline persons show confusion and indecision, as elsewhere, in
sexual functioning, including bisexuality and polymorphous sexuality (as it used to be called). The confusion about the self is

often complemented, as one might expect, by unrealistic apprais-
als of others, including overestimates of their tolerance for the
demandingness the borderline person imposes with grand una-
wareness. Presented with a request for divorce or evidence of the
loved one's turning elsewhere, the borderline is likely to be as
astonished as hurt.

Obviously, such clients are not in great need of further uncovering of unconscious materials. Indeed, it may be out of order
even to ask about earlier life history, once the diagnostic picture
has been established. Their treatment emphasizes much of what
we in social work call ego-supportive casework—sticking to what
is conscious, discussing practical planning, supporting reality
testing, keeping track of options in order to facilitate the making
of decisions. This treatment style is favored by those who employ
what is termed *psychoanalytically oriented psychotherapy*. For, the analytic movement has a long history of retaining its personality theory
as a general framework, while nevertheless departing from the
classical situation to fit specific cases. This was true of Aichorn
(1935) who was famous for his work with delinquent boys in Vienna;
it certainly was true of Redl and Wineman (1951) in treating ego-
disturbed delinquent boys in this country.

Let me append a few more beliefs about the treatment of these
clients. They are often in need of recognizing their own existence—
that they are, in fact, free-standing human beings. I have found
that the type of treatment which Kaiser has called (see below),
"helping the client stand behind his words," is useful in facilitating
this; indeed, any use of verbalization helps the ego to neutralize
strong affects, and to integrate. The therapist has to fight off joining
the client in the chaos he or she tries to make of the relationship.
One must be neither excessively pleased when flattered nor excessively dismayed when accused. This kind of steadiness, being
comforting while helping the patient gain control of himself or
herself, may begin to make up for some of what was missed in the
course of growing up. The patient also needs to be rewarded for
daring to show autonomy and initiative, in contrast to his early
childhood when such signs of growth were typically greeted with
threats of abandonment (Masterson, 1976). Of course, a major
therapeutic danger is the therapist's angry reaction to feeling
swallowed and absorbed by the borderline—but handling that is
his problem. Despite this ominous picture, borderline persons
often earn one's admiration and respect. Helene Deutsch's formulation to the contrary, these unintegrated personalities are by no

means always "empty." They try to protect those they love, they have beliefs and values regarding the larger society which they strive to uphold. It feels the more poignant when the borderline patient is all too aware of the deficits and handicaps he takes into living and loving. As one said, "It is awful to subject my wife to my outbursts when she's been so great to me. That's why I need to be here." He meant it, too. What clinician would not try to help with such a decent ambition?

CHAPTER 7
A SPEED READER'S GUIDE TO
Development of the Ego

Their close ties to education led academic child psychologists to emphasize the emergence of intellect and cognitive processes. Analysts, more fascinated with emotional growth and failures, presented the psychosexual stages as changing *investments of libido*, pleasure seekings. Thought itself was ancillary to drive expession. A drive that could not be directly satisfied through action produced a conflicted infant. *Detouring* the drive energy into *fantasying* the mother's breast offered partial discharge of oral needs, resolving the conflict.

Then Hartman pointed out that intellectual work may be a direct effort to satisfy drives and their *neutralized* derivatives, with neither conflict nor anxiety involved, hence there were *conflict-free ego spheres*. Child analysts began to study the *maturation* of a wider range of ego functions, but retained a fascination with the fate of instincts and emotions. In studying *hospitalism* and *ana-clitic depression*, Spitz described *deficits in cognitive development* along with potentially lethal emotional reactions.

Erikson proposed several further extensions of analytic theory. Indeed, his *psychosocial* approach needed a series of new concepts. He harnessed conceptions ordinarily devoted to analyzing neurosis toward trying to make sense of whole life courses including those of happy and effective persons. His cultural relativism led to recognizing the role of the social environment in *phase-specific crises* of development. Erikson's synthetic gifts are nowhere more memorable than in his formulation of the *negative identity*.

Mahler's work nicely illustrates an analyst beginning with a clinical preoccupation who is ultimately led to advance general ego theory. From postulating that *autistic children* are symbiotically locked in with their mothers, it occurred to her that both *autism* and *symbiosis* are universal phases of growth. The question, "Why is this child autistic?" became, "How does any child achieve the sense of existing as a free-standing entity?" Delineating the *separation-individuation* process, Mahler's group contributed also to our next topic, object relations.

Development of the Ego

7

A nalysts have entertained images about the epigenesis of the ego that have, naturally, been much affected by the intellectual development of their master, Sigmund Freud. According to David Rapaport, who was in about as good a position to make such judgments as anyone:

> The formative influences in Freud's background were the Jewish tradition, an early developed interest in literature (especially a devotion to Goethe and, through him, to ancient Rome), courses with Brentano of act-psychology fame, the impact of Darwin's theory of evolution, clinical and laboratory research in neurology and neuroanatomy (in the orbit of men from Helmholtz's circle), clinical psychiatric work (with Meynert), clinical work with neuroses (at first with Breuer, Charcot and Bernheim), and self-observation (1960, p. 11).

The evolutionary and historical perspectives make the assumption that aspects of the personality are inborn because they played a selective role in the survival of our species. His years in neurology would have kept alive the recognition that among the inherited characteristics are tendencies to mature, to unfold in a relatively fixed developmental sequence. We have seen these assumptions already, incorporated in the psychosexual stages of development, in Chapter 5. Indeed, the interest in historical perspective is general throughout the theory. "All behavior is part of a genetic series, and through its antecedents, part of the temporal sequences which brought about the present form of the personality (the genetic point of view)" (Rapaport, 1960, p. 43). So the genetic point of view is not limited to the changing focus of pleasure seeking; it also applies to the way that adaptation is developed in the ego.

Psychoanalytic theory has been criticized for its emphasis in the patient's history. Taken naïvely, such an idea of causation deserves to be questioned. It is not literally true that our client is hard on himself because his mother was perfectionistic long ago. As Kurt Lewin put in cogently (1937), only forces that are alive in the here and now can have effects. If the client is hypercritical of others and himself, his experiences of his mother must have left marks on him that endure and are active in the present. For, his mother was of another country, and now she is dead. But an image of her fused with his image of himself continues to speak to the client in the back of his mind.

Often with a complicated adult the nature of the marks left by life is obscured. Knowing the person's history from a simpler time makes the configuration of his scars more visible. Indeed, without knowledge of history, some perspective in time, it is hard to appraise the meaning of a current pattern. Has this woman always been depressive? Or did her mood and behavior shift markedly when she heard her husband was ill? Indeed, experiments on how people read others' emotions from photographs found that agreement is poor unless the subject also knows the event immediately preceding the facial expression shown.

Practitioners face many concrete situations in which we need to employ a time-perspective. The protective service worker visits a home and sees a baby unable to hold her head up. Is this infant three months old or nine months old? On the answer hinges much of the meaning of the observation. Nor does the worker presume that merely by the passage of time, babies become able to hold their heads up. The ability is gained if the baby's maturational processes, the physical changes within her, are proceeding as they do in most babies (so we call them "normal").

The worker also believes that for normal maturation to occur, certain kinds of minimal care by the baby's mother must be provided. A protective services worker has little time for the ideological fermentation that goes around favoring historical or ahistorical (i.e. functional) explanations. So far as the nature/nurture controversy is concerned, life experience makes one an interactionist. We have reason to believe most babies come with readinesses to adjust to care offered. Readiness begins with turning the mouth toward a nipple rubbed on the cheek of a newborn. In rudimentary form, but ready to mature into better, ways of getting along with the world come with the package. Still, babies cannot adjust to any kind of world. The primitive adaptive mechanisms in babies are geared to the kind of care we have reason to anticipate they will find. Hartmann (1956) called this *an average expectable environment*. Given care that departs too far from the standard, babies fail to grow, and may die.

When we talk about the epigenesis of the ego, we are confining our interest to the development of adaptive abilities. Freud eventually developed beyond his early conception of the ego as subservient to the id. Subservience implied in the present context that mechanisms for coping arise at first only because the basic drives find themselves stymied. The idea was that from the effort made to circumvent an obstacle, the finding of a detour, the ego developed thought. Later, however, Freud concluded that the ability to use anxiety as a danger signal, to erect defenses against anxiety (most defenses are surprisingly universal), to think logically, to perceive reality, to relate to other people, and other ego functions must be present in nascent form when the human is born. These ideas were extended and clarified by Hartmann.

How much of the way we adapt to the world and ourselves represents the unfolding of instinctual behaviors? Ecologists tell us that the lives of many mammals, birds and fish are largely dominated by *fixed action patterns* which need only environmental triggering to set them off. The Freudians, like most psychologists, do not think instincts, as such, can take the human very far in life. To those who believe that all but a very few basic responses are learned from one's parents, or from the culture, analysts must seem rank biological chauvinists. Certainly, they retain a healthy respect for the physiological and anatomical side of the person.

The Freudians have had particular difficulty dealing with the aspect of man involved in interpersonal relationships. Partly in the interests of parsimony the view of attachment to others, for example, followed a *drive-reduction* model. The infant needs food and water, his mother is the source of these or, more concretely for a tiny infant, her breast is, so an association is set up linking the fact that the tension of the hunger drive is reduced with contact with the mother. Or, to paraphrase an anthropologist much influenced by psychoanalysis, the infant rises to snip the bait of personal gratification and is caught on the hook of socialization. For followers who became convinced that man is "inherently social," Freud had about the same impatience as for fatuous statements like "Man is inherently good." What does *that* mean? That the speaker is so upset by any rage in himself he has to deny it for the whole human race?

It is also to be borne in mind that Freud, early on, became convinced that neurosis derived from conflict. The typical conflict was between a desire to express a drive and social mores making the patient guilty for having it. He saw man and society as largely in an adversary relationship. A conviction of this sort provided him a sharp scalpel for dissecting the rationalizations and hypocrises in the morals of contemporary middle-class central Europe. Indeed, the Freudian critiques of state-supported religion and other systems for social control of the citizenry make the sociology of knowledge given us by Pareto and Marx seem gentle. But such a cynical stance is of little use in understanding the mutually beneficial and even unselfish things people do for each other.

One result of this stance was the reading out of the Freudian movement of a number of first-rate people. Karen Horney (1937) might easily have led the others in the direction of recognizing the positive contributions of culture to the personality. But she was not the most logical theoretician. Her idea that one can engage in self-analysis, analyze oneself, is in contradiction to the notion that the unconscious contains ideas we cannot bring to consciousness even if we wish to. Not only does the notion of self-analysis violate my sense of scientific logic, it offends the part of me raised by a small town furniture dealer who taught that you rarely get something for nothing. Freud, himself, tried self-analysis and there is considerable question how well he succeeded. Some believe he was depressed during much of his adult life. What Freud said of the socially oriented Adler (1917) to whom, among other things, we owe the recognition of sibling rivalry, has already been recorded. On the periphery was Harry Stack Sullivan (1940), once beloved of American social scientists because he preached that psychiatry is basically applied social psychology. Sullivan produced ideas of such mixed brilliance and gibberish it is impossible to decide, four decades later, how much of his vocabulary students still ought to memorize.

Freud had his own predilections. There was the recurrent question of how efficient the classical technique was as a mode of treatment, but (or so?) he was devoted to it as method for research. Yet to really learn about development of humans, there is nothing for it but to go out and systematically observe large samples of infants and children in their natural settings. Otherwise, your data are adult patients' recollections inevitably affected by what they think you want to hear—among other nuisances. Of course, such data may be supplemented by direct observations made of your own children. But it takes an enormous faith in the uniformity of human growth or in the representativeness of your own offspring to emulate Piaget. The latter built an international reputation on subjects supplied by Mme. Piaget. Fortunately, even with his predilections, Freud was almost always open to evidence. And from a rather early date there were colleagues engaged in child analysis and pedagogy. In the spirit of the Vienna of those times, many of these laborers were women.

The past half-century, then, has witnessed an enormous proliferation of work elaborating the Freudian model of human development. Much has had to do with tracing the emergence of ego functions such as perceiving, thinking, controling impulses and mastering feelings. But since the human infant survives only because of ministrations by parents and other adults, it is nearly impossible to discuss epigenesis without also describing the emergence of the person as a being whose life is dominated by his relationships to others.

Hartmann

Heinz Hartmann was prominent in Viennese psychoanalytic circles before World War II. After migrating to this country to flee the Nazis he continued to practice, to teach, and to write in the New York area. Best known to students is his *Ego Psychology and the Problem of Adaptation* (1958), based on lectures given originally in Vienna. The book has been used in schools of social work as a text—which is madly inappropriate now that my book exists. But it is a profound and influential document which those who remain interested in analytic theory will want to read at some point.

Psychoanalysis is indebted to Hartmann and his collaborators for freeing the movement to consider points of view, and even facts, that had been treated as antithetical to Freud's approach. The early Freudian theory of memory, for example, was almost entirely a conflict theory. You "forgot" because you repressed. The unwary analysand would be left with the impression that, if it were not for repression, everything he had ever experienced could be brought back to view. Only the threatened expense (and, even worse, the threat of Proustian boredom) prevented carrying out such a project. But, of course, not all forgetting is in the service of defense. Some things were originally only thinly "learned"; there is also forgetting due to disuse. So, there were whole areas of ego functioning explored by other psychologists, in part to improve the way pupils are educated, to which Freudians deliberately paid no attention—as a matter of orthodoxy. Into this arena stepped Hartmann.

"I propose that we adopt the provisional term *conflict-free ego sphere* for that ensemble of functions which at any given time exert their effects outside the region of mental conflicts" (1958, p. 8). "We do not need to prove that investigations which are *limited* to this sphere, as those of academic psychology usually are, inevitably overlook basic psychological relationships" (p. 9). He posited that, "The normal human being is free neither of problems nor of conflicts. Conflicts are part of the human condition" (p. 12). Yet, he felt it important to recognize that not all adaptive mechanisms emerge from conflict. Thus, when Anna Freud said (1946, p. 179), "Instinctual danger makes human beings intelligent," she was overstating her point. To describe all intelligent behavior as in the service of defense overlooks the hereditary and other roots of intelligence having little to do with anxiety. This does not, of course, negate the fact that ego spheres like reasoning can become *invaded* by conflict.

It is also important to bear in mind that even if conflict entered into motivating the emergence of an ego function, that does not necessarily remain the function's only value to the person.

> For another example I will chooose fantasy....Anna Freud ...examines the denial of reality in fantasy and shows how the child, refusing to accept a disagreeable bit of reality, can, under certain conditions, deny its existence and replace it by fantasy formations. This is a process within the limits of normal ego development (p. 16).
>
> It is general knowledge that fantasy—not just in the sense of a talent for making new combinations, but also in the sense of symbolic, pictorial thought—can be fruitful even in scientific thinking, supposedly the undisputed domain of rational thought....It is possible and even probable that the relationship to reality is learned by way of *detours* (p. 18).

So the fact that a given ability originally emerged from conflictual necessity may become largely immaterial. Such a sequence is part of normal development. As for the rest of us, Fritz Redl put it succinctly, "It ain't your neurosis; it's how you use it." From this line of thinking, it was a short step to such related ideas as *change of function* of adaptive modes, the *relative autonomy of the ego* (from the id), and the *neutralization* of psychic energy, mentioned much earlier. Hartmann was clear that society needs to have intellectualization fostered in our schools.

"In the conception of Hartmann, Kris and Loewenstein (1946), the ego does not develop from the id but both differentiate from a common matrix: the earliest *undifferentiated phase* of postnatal development" (Rapaport, 1959, p. 12). Their acceptance of the ego's capacity was extended by Kris (1952) in his conception of regression in the *service of the ego*. In this, the person consciously reaches for the more primitive layers of his thinking and feeling to facilitate creativity or, perhaps, to promote empathy. Thus, there is reason to believe that sensitive infant care requires, *inter alia*, an ability by the mother to let herself think and feel as her baby does. The regression is "in the service of the ego," of course, because the mother can turn it off when she has to heat bottles or deal with an emergency. This is quite different from defensive regression, and it reminds us that rigid reaction formations against one own's childishness may make such empathy impossible.

Hartmann also took a stand in favor of the direct observation of very young children as a source of necessary data on epigenesis. It is obvious that with all these heresies he must have been otherwise very acceptable to orthodox Freudians to have remained at the center of the movement as he did. Probably, the general opinion was already changing in the direction he was heading. Like the Catholic Church, the Freudian movement appears more monolithic from outside than from within. Psychoanalytic observations of, and theories about, early child development have been brought together in the first of a fine three-volume collection of original papers on the human life cycle edited by Greenspan and Pollock (1980) for our National Institute of Mental Health.

Erikson on the Life Cycle
One of the tasks of the ego is to perceive reality and facilitate adaptation to it, but not much early Freudian theory dealt with reality. Hartmann's work was a step in this direction. By signifying as kosher for analytic consumption whole realms of psychology, and by signing the ego's declaration of independence from the id, Hartmann opened the door to theorizing about the role of one's current environment in influencing behavior. The writings of Erik Erikson were also geared toward filling these empty spaces in the theory. His concern, however, was primarily with social reality,

with the familial and cultural influences that help shape the child's personality and provide the context for mature living.

Erikson's interest was not unique among psychoanalysts. Kardiner collaborated with Linton, a cultural anthropologist, to devise a theory about the way in which a group's objective economic situation, its system of beliefs about nature and the supernatural, and its values about child-rearing practices interact to produce a typical character structure for that culture, a "model personality" (Kardiner and Linton, 1939). Moreover, a number of prominent anthropologists were applying Freudian theory—as they understood it—to their data. For one thing, our busy ethnographers were drowning in a self-induced flood of observation for which they lacked not only an integrating theory but even a critical question. Analytic theory proved handy if only to provide an hypothesis to be *disproven*. Margaret Mead (1935), for example, surveyed three New Guinean tribes, finding one in which women were more aggressive than men, another in which both were aggressive and indifferent toward children, and a third, the Arapesh, in which both sexes were peaceable and loving. While the credibility of Mead's conclusions was reduced by a subsequent article published by her ex-husband and former co-worker, Reo Fortune, entitled, "Warfare among the Arapesh," she felt she had disproven the Freudian assumption of a natural linkage between biological gender and assertiveness or submissiveness. Her point, of course, could have been readily made by visiting the families in America we knew as social workers (or as children), but we lived in a culture which then evaluated women's assertiveness as deviant.

Erikson brought to his task respect for cultural relativity from some months of participant observation among American Indians in the Southwest. More importantly, he brought years of direct work with young children as a teacher and later as a child analyst. So he was in position to go far beyond such a first approximation as "Look, culture makes a difference!" He could trace the specific mechanisms and dynamics involved. Erikson was also an uncommonly perceptive and persistent craftsman, and he developed a series of new concepts. While the main body of ego psychology has had great trouble finding a way to relate, systematically, to his conceptions, they are clearly important, and he is often taken nowadays as representing the *psychosocial* metatheoretical approach.

Like the psychosexual stages of development, Erikson's image of the human life cycle has by now passed from psychoanalytic auspices into the general literature of psychology and human development. Many students will have encountered his first book, *Childhood and Society* (1950). More advanced are the papers contained in his monograph, *Identity and the Life Cycle* (1959), including one on the growth and crises of the healthy personality. Another is the germinal paper on ego identity.

In Erikson's imagery, the development of the human character can be mapped though the outcome of a series of *phase-specific life crises*. Like the psychosexual stages, the "phases" occur in the same sequence in the lives of nearly all of us; indeed, each of the earlier phases corresponds in time to a psychosexual stage. However, the fact that the bodily zones are highlighted, one after the other, for pleasure seeking was thought to be largely determined by biological maturation. The accompanying life crises, on the other hand, involve an interaction of the biological with the social environment.

Take the oral stage. The infant begins seeking lip and tongue stimulation, apparently erotic needs. There is no crisis. The "crisis" of infancy occurs around the fact that the erotic needs are also coordinated to survival: getting water and food. These survival needs are to be met by the infant's mother. If the mother is competent and empathic, the infant can count on being fed when hungry, well before he feels famished. Some infants, however, have mothers who are irregular in their care. So, says Erikson, the first life crisis can resolve itself by the infant's being given the feeling he can relax and trust the world. Or, the result may be a feeling that the world cannot be counted on. In other words, the infant adopts an attitude of *trust vs. mistrust*. If we think of his life course as laid out like a large map, with the infant beginning at the bottom, about to make his first move northward, his first resolution may be said to determine whether he starts west, toward Basic Trust, or east, toward Basic Mistrust.

The next phase, traditionally, is the anal stage. Anality is very obviously involved in crisis only because of social processes. Left to his own devices, the infant has no great problem about it; the problem arises when his mother takes it on herself to begin toilet training. If the training is clumsy, punitive, or attempted before the child's neuromuscular system is up to it, he will have great trouble maintaining control. On the other hand, if it is paced to his developmental level and done reasonably warmly and skillfully, the infant is left with a feeling that, "I can do it when I want to, and not do it when I don't want to. *I am in control of me.*" This life crisis, says Erikson, deals with the question whether the resulting attitude will be on the side of *autonomy* or *doubt*. So, in this higher latitude, the personality again takes a turning—toward the west, Autonomy, or toward the east, Shame, Doubt.

Note, by the way, that Erikson's polarities are not simple grammatical antonyms. Rather, they are *psychological* opposites. This was itself a shrewd advance over typical academic trait labelings. The latter are usually logical rather than psychological, which can lead to gross error if man is not a rational animal—and there is evidence that he is not. Note also that earlier decisions influence later ones in the development of personality, the epigenetic effect. The child who comes through his early feeding crisis on the side of mistrust is a different one with whom to attempt toilet training than one who feels trusting.

And so Erikson matches his life crises to life phases, labeling each with its applicable polarity. Infancy involves *Basic Trust vs. Basic Mistrust*; Early Childhood, *Autonomy vs. Shame, Doubt*; Play Age, *Initiative vs. Guilt* (about sticking it out in phallic splendor); School Age, or latency, has the polarity *Industry vs. Inferiority*; and Adolescence the issue of *Identity vs. Indentity Diffusion* which we will discuss further below. For the Young Adult, says Erikson, the issue is that of *Intimacy vs. Isolation* (Can you stand getting close to one other?). For the Adult, his polarity is *Generativity vs. Self-Absorption* (Do your days go into getting things done or feeling sorry for you?); and in Mature Age, *Integrity vs. Despair* (Can you stand by what you did, or was it all a vain effort?). The point along each continuum at which each life crisis is resolved depends both on who you are, and in what situation you find yourself. The overall result describes where each of us has arrived at that stage in life. The map offered is not without value connotations; it would be impossible to do therapy without having some ideas about which lifestyles are more likely to pan out in happiness for the person and the betterment of those around him. Clearly, it was better to follow the Trade Winds in a northwesterly direction on our life charts.

What in the character corresponds to each of the polarities? Is each a trait? A cast of mind? An *orienting attitude*? The latter description is, I suppose, as close as we can come to placing Erikson's notions in relation to other theoretical concepts. There was never any question that he meant to depart from the main analytic tradition. He used Freudian concepts continually in his writing and was head of his local psychoanalytic society in San Francisco at the time he began these theoretical extensions. But, one would search in vain for a notion like orienting attitude in the main corpus of analytic theory, or definitions indicating where it ought systematically be fitted in. One can, of course, take one of Erikson's polarities, treat it as a dimension, and abstract it into a trait. I have, myself, done this with *Workmanship*, a term Erikson also employs. Using his ideas, and a few of my own, we developed a scale for this trait that showed good interobserver reliability and validity in predicting from parental personality to level of child care in a comparison of neglectful and non-neglectful families (Polansky, *et al.*, 1981).

Erikson has also given us a schema showing how a polarity, highlighted earlier in life, may nevertheless reappear in other guises later on. Thus, the issue of the phallic stage which he depicts as Initiative vs. Guilt recurs in adolescence as the polarity, Role Experimentation vs. Negative Identity. His thinking here is analogous to the notions described earlier in this book concerning sexual remnants. Even after orality is no longer the main event, erotically, remnants of it survive. But, since they occur later, in the context of a far more mature personality, their expression is naturally far different than it was at first. (Another way of looking at drive derivatives, no?) So, remnants of older orienting attitudes survive into later life, albeit in modified form. One of the person's tasks at adolescence, as we shall see, is to fit all these surviving resolutions into an integrated personality.

Ego Identity

Erikson's concept of *ego identity* was advanced at a time when a great many Americans were having troubles with their own. It made him at the time the most famous psychoanalyst in our land. There is no reason to believe that the average American has resolved this problem, but it is a less popular topic for public discussion nowadays. Nevertheless, the conception survives, for the formulation's value in general theorizing goes far beyond its momentary relevance to popular mood. What, then, is the ego identity?

Students may not be aware that definition, in rigorous scientific theorizing, resembles translation between languages. In *conceptual definition* the aim is to express the new concept in terms of others already in the theory. Beginning with time and distance, we describe velocity as distance travelled per unit of time; acceleration, in turn, is defined as the rate of increase of velocity, again per unit of time. This is parsimonious, and one can even use algebra and calculus to make deductions with these terms. But, what do you do if your theory does not yet have concepts relevant to what you are working on? Erikson was in this position for a couple of reasons. First, he was dealing with issues of social reality, a sphere analysts had previously left mostly to common sense. Further, the relations he wanted to talk about involved thinking in terms of wholes and contexts, fits and harmonies, probably more because of his artistic background than a knowledge of twentieth century physics. Freudian theory was couched in nineteenth century models; it was analytic and additive. What does one do in such a case? One emulates Nicely-Nicely Jones to "do the best you can."

> I can attempt to make the subject matter of identity more explicit only by approaching it from a variety of angles.... At one time, then, it will appear to refer to a conscious *sense of individual identity*; at another to an unconscious striving for a *continuity of personal character*; at a third, as a criterion for the silent doings of *ego synthesis*; and, finally, as a maintenance of an inner *solidarity* with a group's ideals and identity (Erikson, 1959, p. 102).

One generation of Americans referred to "getting your head together." Erikson proposed that the phase in life at which this issue is at the fore is adolescence.

> In puberty and adolescence all sameness and continuities relied on earlier are questioned again because of a rapidity of body growth which equals that of early childhood and because of the entirely new addition of physical genital maturity. The growing, developing young people, faced with this physiological revolution within them, are now primarily concerned with consolidating their social roles. They are sometimes morbidly, often curiously, preoccupied with what they appear to be in the eyes of others as compared with what they feel they are and with the question of how to connect the earlier cultivated roles and skills with the ideal prototypes of the day. In their search for a new sense of continuity and sameness, some adolescents have to refight many of the crises of earlier years. The emerging ego identity, then, bridges the early childhood stages, when the body and the parent images were given their specific meanings, and the later stages, when a variety of social roles becomes available and increasingly coercive (p. 91).

To Erikson, developmental stage is normal, although some of the accompanying turmoil may seem pathological, even among young people who are not, in fact, neurotic or borderline. As some psychiatrist has remarked, "The difficulty with adolescence is its differential diagnosis from schizophrenia!" And, a critical element in finding a workable identity is locating one's social role, one's accepted niche in the social structure of people one cares about.

Others have written extensively about roles from the sociological and social psychological perspectives. (Newcomb, 1950). But when one passes beyond exercises in definition, their key dynamic proposition comes to this: people tend to do what others expect them to do. We know immediately that this is not always true. Erikson has made an enormous gift to social psychology by fleshing out the motivational aspect of roles, that is by describing dynamics that go on *within* the role-occupant in adopting a role and living within his defined position in a group's structure.

In workshops I have used an exercise I call Playing God to dramatize the achievement entailed in putting together one's identity. Imagine you have before you the following young woman: age 18; Black; average height; not homely, not beautiful; physically healthy; ranks second in her high school graduating class of 95 students; loves to write poetry; likes boys and dates when asked; has already acquired ideas about racial equality not talked about in her Georgia town; loves to dress well; is the eldest of five children of a widow living on Aid to Families of Dependent Children; and loves her mother deeply. What could she be doing with her life in ten years so that she would be happy? Also in her class is another person, a white boy aged 18; slight in build; handsome; mild, even "effeminate" in manner, but heterosexual in inclination; loves art and draws well; poor in mathematics; likes children; parents plan to send him to college. What should he be doing? It comes down to "How do you put it all together?" And "What do you have to put together?" As Erikson says,

From a genetic point of view, then, the process of identity formation emerges as an *evolving configuration* ... established by successive ego syntheses and resyntheses throughout childhood; it is a configuration gradually integrating *constitutional givens, idiosyncratic libidinal needs, favored capacities, significant identifications, effective defenses, successful sublimations,* and *consistent roles* (1959, p. 119).

We could rephrase this as your having to find a harmonious way of living with the body and the brains you have; where you happen to get your kicks; what you are good at doing that you like to do; the images of other people that are part of your image of you; how you keep from feeling anxious; how you get your satisfactions without getting into trouble; *and* what others will let you get away with and even pay you to do. The synthesis is a most complicated operation, of course. An adolescent in treatment often fears the therapist is trying to take over his life and tell him whom to be. A look at the complexity of the task is almost always convincing that if anyone is going to work this out for the individual, it is probably going to have to be herself or himself. It seems doubtful anyone else could offer him an acceptable model. When it comes to how he feels, no one is more expert than the client. And no one but the client can make a *commitment* for him.

Now the last term in Erikson's formulation is the one that brings into focus the necessity that the pattern chosen fit an available social role. Many of us who come from "tough" towns had interests in literature or the like but found it prudent to conceal them while young. No boy in my coal-mining town would have confessed a fascination with ballet. If you played the violin, as I did, it was advisable also to lift weights. In short the limited range among available roles in such a town may, itself, interfere with finding an identity. What a relief it is for many to arrive at the state university and find whole cliques of others for whom poetry, music and art are normal, acceptable—even "manly"—interests.

Failure to find an integration may, however, also derive from internal contradictions. I recall one young patient who wanted desperately to emulate his father, a highly competent if distant individual. At the same time he also wanted very much to spite his father, for that was the theme communicated to him by his mother, who resented being neglected by a husband absorbed in his career as a surgeon. So the young man chose an occupation his father disapproved of, traveling as a musician with a rock group. After a couple of years, however, the tawdriness of their day-to-day living and his own disappointment with himself brought that career to an end. Unable to find his way, he became disorganized, depressed and had to be hospitalized. To the inability to put it all together to a degree that you can live with, Erikson has given the name *identity diffusion*. Earlier, I commented that this pattern—or lack of one—is common among patients we think of as *borderline*. The reasons for that comment are now clearer. The general looseness and deficit in synthethic ability of the borderline personality hinder commitment to a role in life.

Identity diffusion is not to be confused with another conception that sounds the opposite of a workable identity but is not. Erikson calls this the *negative identity*. In this pattern, the person has put things together to the extent that there is some degree of wholeness. Typically, the *negative identity* can be seen as organized in the service of *spite*. Spite is the human motivation which in my experience is most often underestimated by young social workers, although it is often the only recourse of the person in a weak position. Thus, as one patient from a prominent family announced, "If I can't be the biggest success, I'll be the biggest failure." A negative identity may describe the plight of the town playboy, the only son of the crafty and industrious president of the bank. Deprived of the courage for initative in the real world, where he might lose, the son plays games of self-destruction. But the negative identity is not always self-destructive. The son of an alcoholic may be addicted to work.

When we encounter a patient showing identity diffusion, we are inclined to say that "the difficulties started in adolescence." But, a bit of thought will demonstrate that this is in error. Adolescence is, after all, a normal developmental phase; everyone passes through it. If most young people resolve their identity crises in this stage, but the patient cannot, we ask, "What was wrong with him that he could not jump this expectable life hurdle?" And we realize that the difficulty with adolescence must have begun *before* it, that it must date to failures in previous developmental stages handicapping the patient from finding a workable identity at a time when most of his age-mates are able to do so. The same logic, of course, applies to identifying the etiology of mishaps in other life periods. It is not hard to presume that the person who shows bitterness and depression when old was not very happy during the prime of life.

Shaking up one's identity is, in my experience, usually accompanied by anxiety, depression and some depersonalization, the feeling that you do not really occupy your own body. Conflicts you thought you had lived down return to plague you; adolescent misgivings about how you look or act are revived. Many clients who have just had a marked change of life-situation, like divorce, report such feelings. Even such planned events as leaving one's job to study for an advanced degree, or proceeding from undergraduate to graduate school may stir similar symptoms. For ego identity is not achieved once and for all in adolescence, even though that is the phase when, as Erikson says, one's identity is "in crisis." Nor are all instances of temporary identity diffusion signs of pathology. Your own growth in skill and assurance may open new unanticipated options. But if the evolution of a workable identity is a major achievement of *synthetic function* of the ego, we should expect a reasonably well functioning ego to be able to repeat its performance.

As a matter of fact, as Erikson once commented to me in conversation, it becomes necessary to surrender one's identity and to back track to other developmental stages every day of our lives. To fall asleep, we gradually give up our social role and the rest of our sense of identity, our industry, our initiative, our autonomy and arrive finally at a state of basic trust. Similar processes of regression in the service of the ego are necessary in order fully to achieve sexual climax. So, a workable identity must also be flexibly gripped.

I have mentioned the difficulty we experience in trying to integrate Erikson's conceptions with the main body of psychoanalytic theory. While his work is rich in insight, there is a question of how fruitful it has been. A fruitful theory stirs other scientists to ideas and elaborations that carry the effort well beyond the work of its originator. Such a theory, let us say, pulls loose some ends of the tangled skein of human psychology which we, less gifted, can tug on, further unravelling the mess. Erikson's concepts are well known, and have been widely used, but often very superficially. They have not been advanced much since he formulated them himself. To change the metaphor, one asks, has he, perhaps left too few ends, but given us some discouragingly well tied bows?

Certainly Erikson did not intend to inhibit others' curiosity while satisfying his own. Among the most gifted and admirable people I have known, he provided us with the vision that one might dare to try to make sense of the whole course of life, and of our clients' repeated efforts to "get it all together." As for our plaint that he has not told us where to take things next, Erikson might point out in a true analytic stance that he has done his best and "the rest is your problem."

Spitz

A large proportion of those contributing to our knowledge of psychogenesis through direct observations of infants have lived and done their work in America, especially after many Jewish and politically liberal analysts fled the Nazis in Germany and Austria and the Fascists in Hungary and other European countries. Such Americans as Margaret Ribble, Edith Jacobson, William Goldfarb, Peter Wolff, and Sibylle Escalona come immediately to mind. I have chosen to single out René Spitz for special mention because his work represented an important historical link from Hartmann's declarations to the substantive work of Mahler and Bowlby, whom we shall cover below. Spitz's discoveries as early as 1945 are notable to social workers, too, because they had a profound impact on the way we provide services to very young children. He is known for the careful studies of emotionally deprived infants which led him to delimit two clinical pictures, *hospitalism* and *anaclitic depression*.

Spitz studied 164 children (1945; 1946), some of whom were foundlings, abandoned or given away by their mothers. Before abortion and other means of dealing with unwanted pregnancies became so widely available, there were thousands of foundlings to be cared for annually. In the Middle Ages secluded convents were known to be merciful to such babies. Mothers placed babies in baskets, pulled a bell rope to alert those inside and fled, leaving their infants to be reared by the nuns. The foundlings in Spitz's study were in a secular institution, very concerned about maintaining a strictly antiseptic nursery. Each baby was picked up by nurses only at feeding time; cribs were separated with sides covered with cloth to prevent the spread of germs. Given little visual or aural stimulation, the infants lay quietly, frequently forming hollows in their little crib mattresses. These infants were contrasted to others in a nursery located in a penal institution for delinquent girls. In this institution each mother took care of her own child, picking the infant up, talking to it, feeding it, and the like. The social backgrounds of the infants in both settings were similar. Also, both places provided good housing, food and general medical care. Spitz and his collaborator, Katherine Wolf, used films of the babies and infant tests to compare developmental patterns in both groups.

The developmental quotient of the infants in the foundling home was half that expectable at the end of the first year of life, and even poorer at the end of the second year. These babies were also susceptible to illness and had a high infant mortality rate despite the effort at antisepsis. "At 18 months to 2½ years of life, the survivors could not eat alone, were not trained for cleanliness, and spoke only a few words. At eight to 12 months in the other institution (nursery) the infants were active, agile and vocal" (Mahler, Furer and Settlage, 1959, p. 817). On further follow-up two years later, the foundling-home children were undersized physically and were retarded in speech, in handling materials, in toilet-training and the like. This vitiated condition of the body and psyche due to confinement in a hospital or other unstimulating, impersonal environment, Spitz termed *hospitalism*. Something very like it is nowadays also called *mirasmus*, and is also found among infants of neglectful families in their own homes.

Many readers will be aware that psychoanalysts were not the only researchers trying to learn more about normal development by pinpointing deficits among children reared in the unstimulating environments that the congregate institutions of the time provided. When I was a new graduate student at the University of Iowa in 1940, I found my teachers in a controversy with Lewis Terman of Stanford. Terman, who had modified Binet's rather crude intelligence test into the more refined Stanford-Binet, was a great American figure in the study of intellectual development. He assumed, and firmly asserted, that the IQ is a constant; you are born with a certain level of intelligence, and if it appears to vary later that is only because those testing it make measurement errors. Yet the group in Iowa had been doing tests and retests among a sample of preschool children being reared in an orphanage and came upon an appalling fact. The children were dropping in IQ, with some falling into the range of mental retardation. Using their expertise at running preschools, the Iowa group instituted a small inexpensive experiment at providing systematic stimulation for orphanage children. The results were startling. Not only were nearly all salvaged toward normal living, but part of the group eventually tested in the superior range of intelligence (Skeels, *et al.*, 1938). A follow-up study by Skeels (1966) a quarter of a century later showed that on the whole, the children retained their gains into adulthood. So, intelligence may be limited by heredity to an extent, but it is clearly also affected by child-rearing experiences. Related work still continues. As a footnote to recent history, I have a reprint of work done in Teheran under the regime of the late Shah, by J. McVicker Hunt of Illinois and Iranian colleagues (Hunt, *et al.*, 1976).

Note, however, that the interest of academic psychologists was traditionally in the intellective, problem-solving aspects of coping; the analytic concern was with emotional development or failure. Still, as Goldfarb (1945) shrewdly pointed out, emotional and cognitive damage prove highly correlated among deprived youngsters. A couple of us have also shown that retarded children being *infantilized* show further losses in IQ (Sharlin and Polansky, 1972).

Deprivation is not the only mishap of early development, even though it is the one that most concerns social workers.

People were busy with various things during World War II, to put the matter tersely, but Spitz's findings hit the field like a bomb-shell shortly afterward. It had been taken for granted that because of their special needs, the initial placement for an infant should be in an agency-run nursery. Following Spitz's work, and related finding by others, most child welfare agencies abolished their nurseries in favor of infant foster homes. Indeed, our field went further, and many marvelous social workers of the late 1940's and early 1950's busied themselves at putting the congregate institutions which they operated out of business—or at least, out of the business of providing basic parenting for young children rather than serving as treatment facilities. But, from a scientific stand-point, Spitz's initial results were too general. What exactly about the interpersonal handling of infants in the delinquent nursery made their development superior to that in the foundling home? The attempt to fill in the details of this process led to further theoretical elabortions, and to the work by Mahler we shall report below.

Spitz also delineated the severe disturbance of infancy called *anaclitic depression*. The syndrome develops in infants with a particular history, namely full care by a mother for the first six to eight months, after which the mother is removed for a period of two to three months. The reaction first shows itself by a sad expression on the infant's face. If an observer approaches him at this time, the infant tends to cling. However, after a longer time, the initial reaction to the stranger is one of apprehension; attempts to make contact lead to crying. Finally after the mother remains away, there is dejection and complete withdrawal, a frozen expression, and a screaming response to attempts to make contact. When their mothers are restored to these infants, there appears to be complete recovery and they become cheerful. But, if the mother is not restored, "there is a picture of stuporous, deteriorated catatonia or agitated idiocy which appears to be irreversible" (Mahler, Furer and Settlage, 1959, p. 817). Of 91 children whose mothers were not restored 34 died over a period of a year following separation. The milder depressions were accompanied by loss of weight, inability to sleep and susceptibility to upper respiratory infection. Parallels to symptoms of depression in adults were patent. Spitz speculated that the infant's version was prototypical of all depression, and that it involved a sadistic superego attacking the ego.

Such a formulation, of course, presumes the infant has internalized an image of the mother as an entity separate from himself. Others in the psychoanalytic tradition whom we shall study—Fairbairn, Bowlby, Klein—make the same assumption. It fell to Mahler, however, to trace in detail the phases by which an awareness of being separated comes into being in the infant and young child. But emphasis on the sixth month or so of life coinciding with "stranger anxiety," and implying the infant distinguishes his mother from other caring people, recurs in the work of a number of students of epigenesis.

As for the meaning of the term "anaclitic," we have this citation from Fenichel,

> Concerning the mechanisms of object choice Freud distinguished between the anaclitic type of choice—in which an object is chosen because it provokes associations about another original object of the past, usually the parent of the opposite sex, sometimes the parent of the same sex, siblings, or other persons from the infantile environment—and the narcissistic type of choice, in which an object is chosen because it represents some characteristic of the person's own personality (1945, pp. 98f.).

Mahler

A child analyst whose work has become familiar in clinical social work in recent years is Margaret Mahler. Another productive refugee from Hitler, she has spent over three decades at treatment, research and teaching in New York. Mahler's efforts are nowadays cited as providing theoretical underpinnings for the understanding and treatment of borderline states. However, her original reputation was made from work with psychotic children, especially those we term *autistic* (Mahler, Furer and Settlage, 1959). Many readers already have encountered the notion of childhood autism. Typically nonverbal such children have few if any meaningful relationships with adults in their environments. What does a conceptualization about such children have to do with borderline adults?

Many years ago, I sat in an analytic seminar in which the discussion concerned the panic of a patient who feared that his life was about to be taken over by his analyst and that he would lose his sense of selfhood in treatment. Others of us had had similar pangs at times, but this man's anxiety was so extreme he was

threatening to break off treatment. How were such feelings interpreted in those days?

There was talk of homosexual fantasies toward the analyst as a
possible source of anxiety. There was talk of oral-aggressive yearnings to gobble up the analyst which, after being projected onto the
therapist, made the patient fear *he* would be absorbed. There was
also talk of feelings related to the Oedipal situation so convoluted
I did not bother to keep them in mind. But, there was really no way
to discuss the source of the terror in the terms the patient was
experiencing it—a fear of losing himself. In effect, he was protesting
that he would cease to exist as a person. What was being lost? What
barely held toehold on selfhood seemed to be crumbling beneath
him? We in the seminar did not realize it at the time since we were
consumers rather than proposers of psychoanalytic theory. But the
fact was that the theory lacked concepts adequate to describe a not
unusual *transference* reaction. Mahler and her colleagues speak of
"old conflicts over separation and separateness" as being stirred
in treatment. Compared with the theory presented thus far, these
new terms seem to aptly encompass the man's complaint.

At the time I first encountered her work in the latter 1950's,
Mahler was pursuing an interesting hypothesis about the autistic
child. Her idea was that the child's deficit arose in large measure
out of an unhealthy symbiotic tie with its mother. The mother
somehow sensed that this child was weak in certain ways and
would have trouble coping. To compensate for its ego weaknesses,
she was lending to it, or substituting for it, from her own efficient
ego. But the mother's intrusive assistance—much of it unconscious
to her—made the child fail to exercise its own capacities for
perceiving, communicating and otherwise managing itself in its
environment. So our committee from the National Institute of
Mental Health recommended support for her project to treat mother/
child pairs jointly. If her hypothesis were correct, joint treatment
seemed essential. For the child's problem lay in itself and in its
mother and in their relationship.

Regardless of her degree of success with these children, Mahler's
interest obviously put her in a position to undertake a lot of direct
observation of very young children. In the course of this work she
came to believe that all schizophrenia-like infantile psychoses were
either autistic or symbiotic in origin. However, if autism and symbiosis are stages beyond which ill children have failed to progress—at which they have been fixated—are they perhaps found
in all children? She was led, by a logic analogous to Freud's in

relating neurosis to psychosexual stages, to her even more general, "Hypothesis of the universality of the symbiotic origin of the human condition, as well as the hypothesis of the obligatory separation-individuation process in normal development" (Mahler, Pine and Bergman, 1975, p. 9). The relevance of a formulation containing "separation-individuation" to the patient who complained of "becoming lost in the other" or "a dominated automaton" or "a melted pool of jelly" was immediately apparent to fellow clinicians.

Mahler's model obviously concerns developmental achievements in two realms, the cognitive and emotional. In other words she does not only deal with how the infant feels toward its mother and the world; there is also the question of what s/he thinks s/he knows about it. Her methods of observation are more clinical and informal than we are generally accustomed to accept in child development studies in this country, with our requirements of representative sampling, indices of interobserver reliability, tests of validity. Hence, as with the models offered by most other analytic researchers, the major criterion for the acceptability of her formulations is pragmatic: Do they help in treatment? Do they advance us in synthesizing what we think is already known?

In developing her theory, Mahler began with Hartmann's postulate that the infant arrives with an "undifferentiated matrix" out of which the various psychic structures (both id and ego) develop. Chances of normal development are best for a child who arrives with adequate inborn equipment into "an average expectable environment." As already pointed out, Hartmann meant the latter phrase to be one geared to meeting basic human needs. In nearly all instances, the mother is the most important single element of that environment. Thus far, Mahler's model sounds in line with the psychogenetic theory we have already covered. However, her work on autism led her to pay close attention to an issue previously underemphasized. We may speak of the person-in-environment, but the human infant certainly does not seem to know, to begin with, that he and the environment are not one. Consequently, leaving aside whether he could stand the vulnerability of being alone, he can have no image of himself as an enduring, free-standing entity. The task of Mahler and her various co-workers has been to trace a series of phases, in painstaking detail, beginning when the infant does not know there is an outside world, through recognizing where he ends and mother begins, and progressing to establishing his own *identity*, as Mahler conceives it, at around age four.

Mahler's formulation recalls an aspect of analytic theory we have remarked on rarely since the beginning of the book, namely that the theory deals largely with ideas and images *in the mind*.

> We use the term *separation* or *separateness* to refer to the *intrapsychic* achievement of a sense of separateness from mother and, through that, from the world at large...Naturally,...real physical separations (routine or otherwise) from mother are important contributors to the child's sense of being a separate person—but it is the sense of being a separate individual, and not the fact of being physically separated from someone that we will be discussing (Mahler, Pine and Bergman, 1975, p. 7).... We use the term *symbiosis*...to refer to an intrapsychic rather than a behavioral condition; it is thus an inferred state. We do not refer, for example, to clinging behavior, but rather to a feature of primitive cognitive-affective life.... We use the term *identity* to refer to the earliest awareness of a sense of being.... It is not a sense of *who* I am but *that* I am (*Ibid.*, p. 8).

As with other theoreticians in the Freudian tradition, it is assumed that, "An old, partially unresolved sense of self-identity and of body boundaries, or old conflicts over separation and separateness, can be reactivated (or can remain peripherally or even centrally active) at any and all stages of life" (*Ibid.*, p. 4). As noted, in line with this assumption the Blancks (1974) and others have sought to draw on Mahler's conceptualization for the diagnosis and treatment of borderline personality organization in adults. Indeed the reader might well follow this summary of Mahler's ideas with a review of the looseness of ego boundaries in borderline personalities depicted at the end of the last chapter, to test their germaneness.

I have been quoting from *The Psychological Birth of the Human Infant* (Mahler, Pine and Bergman, 1975). Its intriguing title represents more than a figure of speech, for these researchers have drawn on Freud's comment that in many ways the inward-turned neonate reminds one of an egg in its shell. Even though outside the mother's body, the bird embryo remains largely cut off from external stimuli; it has its own food supply with it, and so is even able to satisfy its survival needs "autistically." The idea is that the infant passes out of its mother's body but, in a very real sense, is not yet "born" psychologically. The latter is only accomplished en route to achieving an *identity, that* I am. Useful summaries of Mahler's conceptualization are available in Blanck and Blanck (1974) and Shapiro (1978), as mentioned in our discussion of borderline states; there is also a fine *précis* in Lauder (1980). The book from Mahler and colleagues can be read in an evening; my summary is put together from these sources.

Unlike Erikson's critical phases, Mahler's stages have a quite indeterminate relationship to the classical model of psychosexual development. She speaks of two preliminary phases, *autism* and *symbiosis*, followed by four others subsumed under the general rubric of *separation-individuation*.

1. *Autism:* From birth to around the second month. The goal of the infant is homeostasis. He spends most of his day in a half-sleeping, half-waking state—waking when hunger or other stimuli bother him, falling asleep when satisfied. He is primarily responsive to stimuli from within the body. Stimuli requiring organs of perception dealing with more distant stimuli (e.g. light, sound) are relatively unattended to. An analogy to the orientation of a withdrawn psychotic, or a severely physically ill person, for that matter, is apparent.

2. *Normal symbiosis:* From about five weeks to about four months. *Object permanence* begins to develop. The infant is aware of an "it" in the picture, but does not differentiate it from himself. For all practical purposes "infant and 'it' are but one omnipotent system" (Lauder, 1980, p. 19) felt to be capable of accomplishing anything. At this stage, the child's receiving optimal gratification is essential to further development. Rather than speaking simply of loving versus depriving mothers, Mahler considers degree of *match* between the child's nature and the mother's abilities and sensitivities, thus taking into account the frequent observation that infants are born with temperamental differences. Gross *mismatching* at this stage is thought to lead toward regression to autism—back into the shell —and psychosis. Even the memory of good mothering may be lost. Insufficient matching and meeting of needs during symbiosis appears to eventuate in the borderline states. Among other problems is the failure to develop an image of the mother as a constant object, one held in mind when she is not physically present at the moment (Fraiberg, 1969). With insufficient matching, an infant may attempt to develop *premature self-sufficiency,* leaving little room for forming true love relationships later in life and, therefore, limiting availability to therapy. Both the autistic and symbiotic stages have to do with *narcisissm,* as discussed above. Regression to a stage that does not even contain memories of gratifying mothering creates a horrible form of *loneliness.* Hugging the baby face-to-face, talking and singing to him are important at this age.

3. *Separation-individuation:* Begins at five to six months with the following subphases.

a. *Differentiation:* From five or six to seven or eight months of age. The key development here is achievement of further object permanence, so that the image of oneself (the *self-representation*) becomes separated out of the fused self-plus-mother representation characteristic of the symbiotic phase. The discriminant perception rests in part on outcomes of such activities as exploring mother's face and body through touch, or straining the body away from her to look at her. Yet the child retains need for close contact with mother's body, which is enduring, soft, warm, flexible. Choice of a *transitional object* (Winnicott, 1953; Greenacre, 1960) used by a youngster, such as a stuffed animal of doll, or a live animal, is guided by these facets of how mothers feel. Of course, people also serve as transitional objects. We see this in relationships formed "on the rebound" after clients have been jilted; we see it also when the caseworker serves as temporary substitute during the process of treating grief by *restitution*.

b. *Practicing:* From around eight to 18 months. Early practicing is ushered in by the infant's ability to move away physically from the mother by crawling, paddling, climbing up, or moving while holding on. Mahler distinguishes this early phase from the practicing period, proper, which is characterized by upright walking. The child is now able to move away from the mother by volition and to extend his interest to more distant things in ever-widening circles around the mother. S/he cheerfully exploits this freedom of locomotion but comes back repeatedly to the home base mother represents for *emotional refueling.* At such times s/he wants to be picked up and held or may even fall asleep momentarily, only to wriggle free once again with vigor totally restored, leaving the mother fatigued. As the authors say, the "world is the junior toddler's oyster." S/he enjoys spurts of automony of movement, and the ability to learn. Like a bouncing puppy, the baby has "a love affair with the world." These are busy, busy times, and the exhilarated youngster becomes low-keyed only during times when mother is absent from the room. Then, s/he sometimes reverts to thumb sucking in a kind of brown study in which s/he may be bringing her to mind.

c. *Rapprochment:* From about 18 to about 30 months. As compared with the earlier, the refueling approach is now replaced by a more deliberate search for, or avoidance of, intimate contact with the mother. Alternate shadowing of mother and darting away are now seen. This is a difficult time for a child. These authors regard this as the final stage of "hatching" from the psychological egg. Much perceptual development has been taking place, the learning of words, thinking, testing reality, coping with minor obstacles. Yet s/he is evidently troubled about using the increasing abilities to stand alone, even as s/he has given up a belief in the magic of being at one with mother.

There is a struggle on both sides, for the mother must remain emotionally available while giving the baby a gentle push toward independence, as a *sine qua non* of normal individuation. So the "terrible twosies" take on a poignant significance, developmentally. The needful mothers who cling to their offspring present dangers, of course. But so do mothers for whom children lose their usefulness as substitute objects once they are no longer babes in arms. Such mothers may, therefore, push them away once they have achieved mobility. In other words, the mother's own resolution of her separation-conflicts affects the baby's chances of resolving its own. During this stage, for example, we see many problems with leave-taking, with youngsters objecting to their parents' leaving them behind. On the positive side, however, the child can now use language much more to help master such anxieties; s/he can use symbols and transitional objects for working them out.

d. *Achievement of individuality:* From about thirty months. If all goes well, the baby moves onward to a stage in which s/he has an image of mother as a separate individual who has given gratification in the past; s/he can hold on to this image within itself, as a comforting and reassuring piece of itself. In a fashion that brings to mind the work of Melanie Klein (see below) these authors also speak of the *bad object,* an image of the mother the child has which is tinged with the angry or hateful feelings that have passed between them. In order for the maternal image to become stabilized, both "good" and "bad" aspects must be blended into a consolidated representation. And, the child is now ready to have a stable, reasonably consistent self-image.

4. *Identity:* This emerges as the achievement of the work of separation-individuation. Identity here means that you have an image of yourself as something constant, that endures; *that* you exist. Obviously, this is a sense of the term very different from Erikson's conception of the formation of ego identity in adolescence. However, both notions of identity imply having an image of oneself one can dare to face consciously, and as something that can be counted on not to melt away or disappear into another's stronger personality.

The work of Mahler is regarded by many as a milestone in devising a framework linking psychoanalytic learnings about psychogenesis to related work in child development by others such as Jean Piaget. In addition to the detailed observations of infants and young children carried out by her colleagues and herself, Mahler has tried to incorporate the work of various other analytically oriented child psychologists. She has been faithful to the precepts laid down by Heinz Hartmann, discussed earlier in this chapter.

Her model certainly contains much that needs consideration if one wishes to describe ego development. Contrast for example the richness of Mahler's conception with the psychosexual stages of development as summarized in Chapter 5. Yet, though offered by Mahler as a theory of psychogenesis and a contribution to the theory of object relations, there are some surprising omissions. Neither Fairbairn nor Klein (see below) appear in her bibliography, despite obvious allusions to the latter; Bowlby, who has offered us his own synthetic *tour de force*, is hardly mentioned. I believe these omissions were motivated in part by political considerations, by her need to prove orthodoxy to the Viennese-New York axis in psychoanalysis.

Bowing to such nonlogical considerations usually inhibits theoretical creativity. Mahler's is more a descriptive than an integrative vision; her work contains few principles that pull together whole new sets of data in striking fashion. Still she has given us several ideas of extraordinary incisiveness: the infant's awareness that there is an external world that cannot be taken for granted. Recognizing individual existence requires, in part, awareness that there is a non-self. Personal assurance of individual existence emerges only gradually, and then can be obscured or even lost. "Good mothering" is more than a list of desired traits or behaviors, but also involves achieving a match between the baby's needs and abilities with what the mother can offer. Matters such as physical mobility, capacity to think and to reason, perception and memory, and feelings of wonder also enter into the acquisition of autonomy. Conflicts about separateness that are unresolved in early childhood may recur throughout life.

But, unlike some other authors, Mahler does not believe the developmental deficits from a particular stage need be permanent, for she thinks they are often compensated at later stages in the childhood sequence. Surely her work, and that of her colleagues, represents a major step.

In our last chapter, when discussing borderline personalities, we mentioned in passing the possibility that such a patient might respond to the lack of structure in the classical analytic situation by becoming psychotic. Following Mahler, one might say there would be a chance of regressing toward autism. One way the danger has been phrased is that, instead of a transference neurosis, such a patient is liable to a "transference psychosis." What, then, is the transference? What is this powerful, potentially dangerous element in treatment? These questions begin our next chapter.

CHAPTER 8
A SPEED READER'S GUIDE TO
The Theory of Object Relations

The classical analytic situation was designed to minimize the analyst's influence on the patient's free associations. The treatment design, however, intensified *transference elements*. Analysis of *transference neuroses* showed patients bring inner worlds peopled with images of significant personal *objects* to the *reality situation* of the therapy. The first such images form stably enough for *recognition memory* at six months, and permit *evocative* memory of the mother by eighteen months or so. The theory of *object relations* concerns the formation of such images, their influence on behavior and emotion and internal dealings with them.

Melanie Klein, analyzing children, advanced a controversial theory that imputed elaborate transactions to the mental imagery in very young children and emphasized *aggressive instincts* that had been played down in explaining neurosis. By projection and *reintrojection*, she said, the child constructs a *bad-mother* and a *good-mother* image in its mind. To keep the bad mother from blotting out the good, it *splits* the world into good and bad. But, the all-bad mother causes *persecutory anxiety* and other miseries of the *paranoid position*. Loved babies, nonetheless, move on to the *depressive position*. Healthy enough to be capable of guilt, the child turns its anger against itself and tries to make up to the mother, offering *restitution*. Final resolution consists in synthesizing the good and bad images into a stable image of the real mother.

Unfinished business with various early objects leads to a need, later in life, to reenact scenes from childhood some of which may only have been fantasies. The strong impulse to *reenact* such *transactions* was investigated by Eric Berne, founder of Transactional Analysis. Berne's perceptive spotting of *games* widely used in group and individual therapy resulted in a practical contribution; but his theory of personality seems limited and mostly derivative.

The Theory of
Object Relations   8

A funny thing happened on Freud's way into the unconscious. You will recall our presentation of him as a fairly
young medical specialist trying to alleviate hysterical symptoms
with his method of analyzing and interpreting free associations. A
number of his patients were young ladies of good families. Yet, it
was not long before disturbing evidence began to come to light.
Some female patients reported memories from childhood that
involved being sexually aroused by men in their families. Often the
father was implicated. These recollections were highly conflictual
and seemed to Freud to have had significant effects in the patients'
later neuroses. Most readers are also aware that Freud was soon
alerted to the significance of erotic impulses in the psychological
structures underlying symptoms.

Indeed, many think of Freud as having been obsessed about
sex, unaware of the degree to which he was a very proper professional of his time, rather prim by our standards. Taken aback by
what he was discovering, he had the strong conviction that a
scientist ought to follow the truth wherever it led. He believed he
should report his discoveries. In fact he had the bad judgment to
prepare a paper on sexual feelings in the family and read it to an
assembly of fellow physicians. Because of its implication of incest
in middle-class Vienna, his report did not endear him to local
medical circles.

Nevertheless, Freud persisted in each line of inquiry forcing
himself to confront new information that might contradict a previous conclusion. In this instance, becoming suspicious of these
memories, he questioned patients more closely, and ended by
having to saw off the limb he had so vaingloriously climbed onto.

The "memories" he had been hearing were not true reports of events that had actually transpired, but recollections of dreams or fantasies. In fact, some transactions experienced by patients as memories were actually fantasies of rather recent origin. A fantasy that seems like a memory, but really is not, whose function is to hide some other idea is called a *screen memory*.

Freud had to recant his striking "discovery." Little girls may have vaguely lustful thoughts toward their fathers; this does not, of itself, prove their fathers are encouraging them. So, he was wrong. But personal embarrassment can, nevertheless, become grist for one's scientific mill. A dedicated researcher can often salvage new learnings from disaster. If Freud was in error, what was leading him astray? Why were such sexual thoughts likely to come up in his work? Was there something about the treatment situation? Indeed, what was he, himself, repressing to have been so egregiously fooled?

Freud had established the classical analytic situation to facilitate free associations. In order that the analyst would not influence these, he had been at pains to establish an atmosphere of accepting neutrality. The therapist stayed quiet and out of the line of vision. In other words, most of the time the analyst was a *non-participant observer*. But, was he without influence? He was a quiet, kindly person to whom everything one said was of interest, who sympathetically asked for more. The patient was encouraged to discuss fantasies, feelings, motives she had always been ashamed to face. Moreover, the analyst seemed non-judgmental. His own values, his personality, his private life remained pretty mysterious. But he was definitely there.

If the recumbent patient were having erotic fantasies stirred, toward what would they be directed? The couch? The wall hangings? One had to face a fact which Freud found unattractive, namely that he was, himself, most likely to be the target of such impulses. Others, whom he had begun to train in his method, were apparently not so blocked on the issue and were able to help Freud see what was going on. True, there was a puzzle. In the *reality situation*, he was anything but seductive; he was not even particularly warm. Despite his careful neutrality, though, patients were treating him as someone very special. Was he, then, so handsome and charming a fellow? Many a silly man who has followed a similar treatment path has wanted to think himself so. But Freud had already learned to combat this gullibility. It seemed, rather, that the patient was confusing him with someone else, with someone important in her life.

This was now a very different view of the incest fantasies. Still, one cannot help smiling at a fact that has been coming more to light in recent years. Based on what we have been finding out, at least in America, Freud may have been more accurate about the prevalence of incest than he knew—although probably *not* with respect to his own patients. But, what about the patient's confused perception of the analyst? She was *transferring* onto him attitudes toward a figure from her past.

Transference

A succinct, valuable description of the *transference* and related issues is the classic paper by Annette Garrett who taught casework for years at the Smith College School for Social Work.

> It is helpful to distinguish relationships that are based predominantly on unconscious displacements from early life and those that are primarily reactions to the real attitudes and behavior of the present-day person. A relationship of the latter type...is based on the client's conscious appreciation of the worker as he really is, and may be called a reality relationship. It differs in many respects from what has come to be known technically as transference—the unconscious projection onto the caseworker of the client's attitudes toward a potent figure of his early childhood (Garrett, 1958, p. 53).

Speaking of the perceptions involved, we may use the same analogy we did for identification. The patient has an image in her mind of her mother as she knew her in childhood. She also has an image of her current worker. When transference occurs, she slides the two images together, just as one can superimpose one transparency over another. And, having done this, impulses, feelings, attitudes toward the older image are experienced and directed toward the worker.

When the attitude is friendly and loving we speak of a *positive transference. Negative transference,* of course, is hostile, suspicious. Thus, if after doing all one could to help a client, being generally tactful and sympathetic, one is greeted with an aggressive blast, the worker should consider whether he is the target of a negative transference. Since we are all marvelous people, or try to be, we tend to take positive reactions toward ourselves as coming out of the reality relationship. Of course, we could also be the beneficiaries of positive transference in such instances. Again, however, one must guard against guillibility. Most intense relationships from our earliest lives are complicated enough to involve both loving *and* hostile feelings, as we shall see later. Therefore, in any treatment situation we may expect the transference to be *ambivalent*, reflecting both loving and hating. If only friendly attitudes come to light, does it not seem probable that angry ones are being repressed? Or that the conscious positive attitude is a reaction-formation against unconscious anger?

In the sort of work we do, it is seldom appropriate for the caseworker to present an interpretation of negative transference to the client. We also usually allow the positive stance to go unchallenged since it is so useful in our efforts to help. Yet, it is important for the worker to be aware that intense transference feelings are nearly always ambivalent. The relevant defense mechanism, by which we *split off* undesired traits and permit to consciousness only those that we find admirable is called *idealization*. As a mechanism, idealization facilitates falling in love but can be unbearable in people who apply it to themselves. As Oscar Wilde described an English fox-hunt: "The unspeakable in pursuit of the inedible."

Now, the Freudians are not the only psychologists who have noticed that interpersonal perception, the way we see one another, is always a complex combination of what the other person objectively is and what we are ready to see. In other words, the transference is almost never complete. A client would have to be psychotic to confuse her young, blond, slender social worker totally with the elderly, dark grandmother who actually reared her, though they may have enough in common to link them in her unconscious. Both are women and *both are in a life position in which the client is dependent*. Indeed, being in the giving position may be enough to stir unconscious confusion. So that, even with a male worker transference of feelings might occur. Transference, after all, is a matter of degree, not totality. We may speak of a client's feelings toward us as one with "few *transference elements*," for example, or as one in which "many transference elements are present." The degree depends on whether cues from the reality relationship or bubblings from archaic images seem more dominant. Naturally, transference elements may be conscious or unconscious.

Some time ago a client in treatment lied to me about an affair with a woman who was, like him, unmarried. When the facts finally came out, we discussed, Why bother to deceive me, his therapist? "I felt you would disapprove, and try to get me to give

her up." "Why would I do that?" "I don't know. Actually, I suppose you've heard such stories many times, and there's nothing so
wrong in what we're doing, really." "Yet, you're quite sure I disapprove?" "To be truthful, I really am. Even though the belief
does not seem very reasonable." The patient was treating me *as if* I
were his rigid, moralistic father, transferring *his* image of his father's
attitude about sex onto me, though the patient himself shared it.

This leads to the next point. Could he have transferred as readily if he had known my attitudes? Such distortions are easier if the
client has only a vague or *ambiguous* image of the worker's attitudes. Otherwise, reality will disconfirm the perception bubbling
up from within. Suddenly, we become aware of another facet of
the classical situation that encourages transference: the deliberately
vague image of the analyst which Freud maintained in order not
to influence the patient's train of associations.

At a certain point analysts became aware that patients' attitudes
toward them were diagnostic, indicative of characteristic feelings
toward those important to them. If these attitudes were not due to
reality, actually traceable to the analyst through his dealings with
the patient, the odds were great that they reflected chronic feelings
and impulses. The patient's attitude towards his analyst may reveal
baggage carried into the analytic situation from earlier in life.
Analytic passivity and neutrality, then, came to serve a further
purpose. The less real-life knowledge the patient had of the analyst, the surer one might be that angry, suspicious, vengeful,
overhopeful, dependent, childlike—you name it—impulses
expressed in treatment represented carry-over from an old relationship. George Herbert Mead (1934) or Harry Stack Sullivan
(1940) would have called that person a *Significant Other.* On the
other hand, if the therapist had many real-life dealings with the
patient—for example, if the patient was one of his employees—and
if the patient had many bases for judging the therapist, it would
be much harder to decide what was transference, that is which
reactions were responses to the current reality and which were
imported from his past. So, patient/analyst distance was prescribed
"in order not to complicate the transference."

In social work such careful distancing is usually undesirable
and typically not feasible. We see clients face-to-face, sometimes in
the hallway or in their own homes. In the course of offering help,
we have many practical dealings with them and for them. Moreover, they see us in action and, not infrequently, happy or upset.
So the client has many cues differentiating us from an inner image

out of the past. One can list, as Garrett did, factors that increase or decrease transference. In addition to the worker's neutrality, which introduces ambiguity, what else affects the intensity of the transference? Encouraging expression of feelings, Garrett says, intensifies transference; discussion of objective, factual material reduces it. More frequent contact heightens transference. Similarly, *personalizing* feelings, as in "You feel dependent on me," increases the reaction; *universalizing*, as in saying "People often feel dependent," lowers it. In our work, a student must learn to control the intensity of the transference, for the client's sake.

Just as circumstances alter cases, cases alter circumstances. Some clients' character structures make them likely to show strong transference reactions in any helping situation. Often, these are immature people locked into old conflicts with their parents who have a fixed way of relating to everyone. For example, being in a position to give or withhold, the caseworker is seen as an authority figure. Many with defiant childhoods automatically trot out resentment along with the request for help. Similarly, it is disconcerting to be treated with dread and suspiciousness by a person one has never met before who knows nothing about you. In other words, transference reactions may be very general.

Strictly speaking, the term transference applies only to the psychotherapeutic situation. The patient in analysis commonly becomes preoccupied by his or her sessions with the analyst, so conflictual unresolved feelings toward parents and others are likely to reappear. This reappearance of so much childhood emotion, bringing conflicts to consciousness where they can be worked out, often leads to a *transitory regression*. Analysts refer to the *transference neurosis* as an expectable event in intense treatment. In the grip of the "neurosis," a patient may seek to *act out* old feelings. For example, if he felt his father were cold, exploitative and ungenerous, he may now upbraid his analyst. Because the analyst charges for his services, obviously his only interest in his patient is pecuniary. "If you really loved me, you would see me for nothing." Or, a patient might wish to act out a childhood fantasy of sex with a parent.

Our reactions to being treated as a father or mother might well represent *countertransference* (Racker, 1968). That is, if you, like the patient, respond out of feelings to people important to you in the past. Speaking technically then, countertransference in the therapist is a reaction to the patient's transference neurosis. It certainly seems logical for such reactions to arise in the professional involved, under the impact of the raw drives patients verbalize and seek to act out. Accordingly, newcomers are often astonished to learn that there are well-known modes of therapy which do not even acknowledge that the therapist, like the patient, may have unconscious motivations. Any sophisticated therapeutic movement recognizes the potential for countertransference and tries to develop ways for therapists to be on the alert for these phenomena in themselves to protect their patients against possible ill effects.

One fairly common reaction is called *projective identification*. Out of anguish and hostility, the patient may project personal ill-intent, blaming the therapist for lack of progress, or as I have seen in male/female situations, saying that she is "a bitch who likes to watch me suffer." If the therapist accepts this statement—as she accepted her mother's descriptions of her—by the end of the hour she is fighting off the feeling that she is a dreadful person with no business offering to help others. The patient has succeeded in making her apologetic, at least as a first reaction. By the next hour, however, the therapist may have regrouped and be ready to tell the patient off—as she would have liked to have with her mother. She may also find it uncomfortable to deal with this patient, with the feelings he *stirs in her*. So she tells herself, he can either start confronting his own hostility, or he can find himself another therapist. "I'm not his whipping girl." Now the therapist would not have been nearly so uncomfortable if she had not, from her long experience with her mother, had an inclination to join the patient in his assault.

Imagine such processes in the caseworker who must deal with a neglectful and/or abusive mother. Not only is such a mother likely to go on the offensive, which is hard to take, but the worker is involved with her in the first place because the client *is* a mother. Fighting such conflict-laden mostly unconscious feelings, is a major source of *burnout* in child protective service. Yet, the countertransference element in burnout often goes unmentioned (Daly, 1979).

Properly speaking, transference applies only to the therapeutic encounter, though it happens all the time in ordinary living. We *displace* attitudes from old relationships to people who now remind us of them, consciously or unconsciously. It is no accident that men over six feet tall command higher salaries, from the beginning, in executive and sales jobs, for looking up makes the rest of us automatically transfer from the parent-child relationship. Something very like transference goes on constantly in one's marriage. It even dawns on us that each person lives with an inner society, a private world peopled by all those who proved memorable for one reason or another.

We assume that this inner society must be important; the feelings and impulses directed toward older images of humans are critical to treatment. Throughout this book, we have been taking seriously the notion that the ideas and images in the mind are real and have strong effects on behavior and on our bodies.

Libidinal Objects and Mental Representations

We spoke of transference as involving displacement. Perhaps, I should have said *substitution*. In effect, we substitute for a person no longer available, a new person toward whom or against whom we direct older impulses. This implies that both the impulse and the image of the person toward whom it was directed are still alive in one's mind. In the *theory of object relations*, such a personal image is an *object*.

Many years ago a woman who had been abused as a child came to see me. The abuser was a step-mother, who entered her life some months after her real mother died when the client was around three years of age. As described, the step-mother, with two little girls at her mercy all day on an isolated farm, was the sort of child who grew up pulling wings off flies and torturing kittens. Being careful to conceal it from their father she managed to pinch, strike, underfeed, threaten, and otherwise torment the children she had acquired by marriage. Several times, she tried to force one child to stab or shoot the other. The client's dreadful story was nevertheless quite believable; I had no good reason to think she was fabricating or projecting her own hostilities. And how did the unloved, vulnerable little girl react? In part, by *identification with the aggressor*, "I must have deserved this, or nothing at all made any sense."

But she also was kept going by the feeling that somewhere, somehow she was not alone. "I could escape to sitting out on the meadow. In the stillness there, I sensed a presence. I thought it was God." Maybe it was, but there is another possibility, also mercifully provided: the comforting image of the loving, capable mother the girl had had during her first three years. Once during treatment the client had the happy accident (Freud would doubt it was an accident) of finding a box of letters and poems written by her biological mother. The mother's writings and reports of relatives showed her to have been a most unusual person, a particularly intelligent, sensitive and loving woman. The feeling that "Somebody cares about me," was the image of a loving, empathic mother preserved in the child's mind. Mahler believes that having such a stable internal *image* is essential to the child's being able to comfortably accept having his mother leave him, for example, at nursery school (Mahler and LaPerriere, 1965).

Another example is from social work practice. After World War II, Jewish child welfare agencies in America shared the mission of caring for the hundreds of children who survived Hitler's concentration camps, where they had been starved, beaten, tortured, where their parents were killed. The social workers' heart-breaking job was sometimes relieved by the fact that many such children showed a remarkable capacity to recover from the effects of the horror. Ella Zwerdling and Grace Polansky (1949) reviewed a series of cases in Detroit. Many included information on the child's earlier life obtained from relatives and friends who had also survived. The two social workers were struck by the extent to which a child's ability to recover normality in foster care was related to the kind of mothering he seemed to have had. It is easiest to teach about the transference with negative examples, but it is well to bear in mind that an *object* may also be benign, residing in the back of the mind offering reassurance and encouragement.

The theory of object relations is a relatively new aspect of ego psychology. Observations have been made, and several theories advanced. We are now departing the aspects of ego psychology about which I could say, "These formulations are generally accepted." For, there are analysts who scarely use these ideas at all and others still at odds with them.

Let us recommence, therefore, by clarifying some terms. In so doing, I am relying on the writings of another friend from social work, Selma Fraiberg (1969). Initially trained in child welfare, and still closely identified with our field, Fraiberg later became a child analyst and has held professiorial rank in two major medical schools. A number of years ago, a family agency in New Orleans recruited her to devise a program to help children born blind (1971). As compared with sighted children, those born blind have an enormously reduced volume of stimuli reaching them. An important problem, therefore, was how such youngsters form the mental imagery we term *objects*. As a good theoretician, Fraiberg was led from this issue to the more general question of what is known, psychoanalytically, about how *any* child forms stable objects.

What is meant by the term, *object*? The word is used in analytic theory to refer to the *drive object*, the means by which a drive finds satisfaction. When you are thirsty, you do not picture yourself abstractly satisfying thirst; you have an image of yourself drinking water or iced tea. In other words, you associate some thing or person to the act of satisfying the drive which is in a state of tension. For the very young infant, the means may be a part of a person (e.g. the maternal breast); later, drive satisfaction is associated with the whole person. Of course, an object can be a thing. In Orson Welles's classic film, *Citizen Kane,* the dying protagonist yearns for a beloved object from childhood named Rosebud, which proves to be the name of his sled. However, for nearly all infants, the significant early objects are people.

A series of steps must occur in the development of awareness of objects. In the beginning, the baby does not seem to distinguish the object as having independent existence; it is blended into his own activity. "A hill is to climb" as Dr. Seuss remarked. Water is to drink. There is a dawning awareness that objects may have autonomous existence, that the hill will still be there even when you are not climbing it. So, there are discernible stages in the development of what Piaget (1937) has called *object permanence.* He studied this with a series of ingenious small experiments. If you hide a baby's toy under a towel, at what age does he seem to know the toy is still there? If you hide it under a towel and then he can see that you are moving it to a second hiding place, will he look for it under the first towel or the second? To do the latter, the baby needs somewhat more conviction of the toy's independent existence. For example, he no longer responds to the conditioned pleasure of finding it in a certain *place,* but knows the object still exists after having been moved.

Piaget was interested primarily in issues of cognition. He did not concern himself with matters of motivation and emotion which, psychoanalytically, are of far greater interest. Analysts speak, therefore, not of Piaget's object permanence but of *object constancy,* recognizing not only that the person has a separate existence but one invested with powerful feelings. The image of the person associated with pleasure is a *libidinal object.* Another, associated with frustration and rage, is the *object of aggression.* Note in each instance, that the association is to your *own* feelings, *not* those of the object. There is a tendency to perceive those who give us pleasure as well intentioned, but the pleasure is ours, the presumed intention theirs.

In the internalizing of object images, Fraiberg identifies discernible stages. First, the baby achieves *recognition* memory. While not yet able to call to mind the mother's image at will, he knows the person before him either is the mother or unfamiliar. The unpleasant recognition that the person is not mother has been called *stranger anxiety.* Since it occurs in most children between the sixth and the eighth month of life, Fraiberg suggests we consider this the time that *recognition memory* is established. From Piaget's studies, and verification by others, there is reason to believe that true object permanance, the ability to hold an image in mind for more that a few seconds after it is out of sight, is achieved at around eighteen months. Since personal objects, like mothers, have so much emotional significance, one might expect them to become memorized somewhat earlier. So, Fraiberg speculates that *evocative memory* occurs slightly earlier. By evocative memory she suggests the ability to produce a *mental representation* of the object, a "mental image that has relative autonomy from the stimuli of exteroceptive experience and the stimuli of drives and need states" (Fraiberg, 1969, p. 45). Blind infants, by the way, seem to lag behind sighted children in these processes, showing stranger anxiety at eight to ten months, rather than at six to eight.

Understanding the full evolution of evocative memory is obviously necessary when one tries to erect a psychoanalytically grounded psychology of thinking and reasoning (Rapaport, 1950). For those of us in practice, however, I have wanted to mark the fact that experiences of early personal objects may be vague if they date from earliest childhood. Thus, my client in the meadow, feeling a reassuring presence, was probably responding to pleasureable memories of her good mother without reproducing her specific image. Perhaps these memories were from a state too early to have involved evocative memory. The child, under the blow of losing mother, may have split off or repressed the image. The later bad mothering may have obliterated recall of the good.

The parts of the theory of object relations powerfully useful in practice have been couched *as if* the child is already capable of mental representations of mother and other caretakers. These images make up the inner society with which the person lives, thronging with positive or negative, promising or threatening, pleasureable or unpleasureable people. It is possible to formulate the structure of neurosis in terms of these images.

Nevertheless it seems important that the developing very young child have enough stability among the people who care for him, and the places in which he lives, to begin to internalize the loving images that prove reassuring throughout later life. Proposals for employing mothers outside the home, which would gut what is most important from Aid to Families of Dependent Children, must accordingly be looked at with such issues in mind. One recognizes that the social worker in her, as well as the child analyst, led Fraiberg to write her most recent book, *Every child's birthright: In defense of mothering* (1977). She argues strongly for the need to maintain the mother-child pairing by every possible means.

Paranoid and Depressive Positions: Melanie Klein
Mrs. Melanie Klein moved to England in 1925, following analysis with Karl Abraham of Berlin who had encouraged her interest in analysing children's play and fantasies. She became a highly influential figure in Great Britain and South America, where her conceptions have also been studied. In this country she is seldom cited, and there is an implication that she departed the orthodox analytic tradition. I think her ideas are important and useful for social work. Her formulation is a good one with which to begin our study of theories of object relations, for it asks us to adopt a radical reversal in our usual modes of thinking about people with respect to the significance attributed to our imaginary mental world of objects as compared with the "real" people we live with.

Since psychoanalysis traces the origin of the fundamental personality problems back to infancy, it is most appropriate that its further development should be brought about by discoveries made in the analysis of children. Freud opened up the prospect of the analysis of children as early as 1909 in his *Analysis of a Phobia in a Five-year-old Boy.* Adler early developed psychotherapeutic treatment of children on a extensive scale. Not till shortly before 1920, however, was the treatment of children undertaken systematically by psychoanalysts, first by Hug-Hellmuth, and then by Anna Freud and Mrs. Melanie Klein.... Mrs. Klein, by using the child's play in all its forms, games of impersonation, drawing, cutting out, using water, etc. as a substitute for the purely verbal free association of the adult patient, gained direct access to the unconscious of the child as young as 2¾ years. Material from the phantasy life of the pre-verbal period was made accessible... This was a purely psychoanalytical technique (Guntrip, 1961, p. 195).

When I was young, we had an idea about what was required for marriage. Most that failed seemed to involve markedly immature persons. There seemed an obvious inference: only when you have

grown up enough are you ready for marriage. Many years later however, I visited the Tavistock Institute in England and emerged with
quite a different idea: if you stay married long enough, you may
grow up.

To these English caseworkers and Kleinian analysts, most marital
brawls simply reenact childhood conflicts never satisfactorily
resolved (Pincus, 1960). A man might be angry with his wife not
because of something she was doing to him but because of a
pattern that started with his own mother: fighting with the people
with whom he was intensely involved. Did his wife, in fact, attack
him? Indeed she did, for her husband was expert at provoking
her. His pattern required not only that he be in a fighting relationship, but that the other person appear the aggressor. He could
then counterattack with minimal guilt, while the quarrel mounted
toward an unbearable crescendo.

The idea that many people invoke *reenactments* is general among
students of object relations, as we shall see. The conception is more
complicated than transference, for it involves not only the attitude
the patient adopts, but his need to seduce the other person into re-
playing whole scenes with him. Why the need to reenact a playlet
so unsatisfactory in the first place? One reason is the fact that it
ended so unsatisfactorily (see Winnicott, below). Another explanation is that one "needs" these old struggles in the external world
in order to bolster certain (or uncertain) defenses in the inner one.

What would be gained if the husband in question tries to solve
his problems by divorcing his present wife? Would he not be likely
simply to repeat the sorry story with the next one? Certainly,
trying to solve his troubles by doing something so radical with his
life would be ill-advised until he understood his own role in them.
By remaining in the present relationship and trying to understand
it, he has at least a chance that the pattern that drives him to
wreck his love relationships will become fully conscious so that he
can try to change it. In other words, in the effort to salvage the
marriage, each partner may make gains in resolving parts of his
and her personal neurosis.

"A psychodynamic theory is now emerging which takes into
account the fact that man lives in two worlds at the same time,
inner and outer, psychic and material, and has relationships with
two kinds of objects, internal and external" (Guntrip, *ibid.*, p.
194). Klein has greatly enriched our perspective on the inner world.
When she set to work, the dominant theory of neurosis among
analysts stressed the role of the sexual instinct in producing con-

flict. Because of fixations and/or childish consciences, patients' urges made them guilty and anxious. The anxiety led to pathological defenses which, moreover, drained psychic energies. Klein's conception emphasizes *aggression*, the other major instinct, as the source of pathology. When asked why I place so much attention on anger in my own teaching, I reply, "Because so few people are sick on love!" a most Kleinian answer.

In children's fantasies, Klein found oral aggression of the sort celebrated in tales of evil giants who gobble up innocent villagers; she found anal sadism as well. After all, children do say, "I'm going to chop your head off and throw it in the toilet." Even gently reared children, neither neglected nor abused, fill their nightmares with slimy, crawly things who try to kidnap them. They go through periods of terrible imaginings about what will leap upon them in their beds should the magic protection from night-lights e'er be dimmed. Who writes the scripts for such nightmares? Who peoples the dark with evil beings? Children projected hostility long before television offered it form, and even prior to the cheery Brothers Grimm.

Klein offers a complex and controversial conception. Nor is she a clear or succinct presenter of her own theories. Students are apt to profit more from secondary sources like Guntrip, on whom I rely, or Segal. However, it seems well to begin the study of object relations with her formulations because she goes farther than almost anyone toward making us aware of the degree to which *internal transactions* can play a major role in emotional problems. Inner images may overwhelm our view of external reality. Moreover, the mind's busy reworking of its own imagery may elaborate so much on what has been taken in from objective reality—if there is such a thing—as to make it unrecognizable. In a simplified version Klein's contribution may be summarized around two foci, the *paranoid* and the *depressive positions*.

In understanding the *paranoid position*, we commence with the newborn infant, who looks to the mother's breast to meet urgent survival needs—water and food. They are urgent because without water a vulnerable neonate can live only a few days, and without feeding, only a little longer. The breast continues to have special meaning in the unconscious, but it is not long before the infant begins to associate the meeting of this need with the mother as a whole object. Nor are survival needs all. As we learned in our review of the psychosexual stages of development, the nourishing, cherishing mother is also a source of oral pleasure. The mother, in other words, becomes associated with need-meeting and with satisfying the infant's own instinctual capacity for pleasure. She is now the object of libidinal drives. If the urge to satisfy pleasure seeking were projected onto this nourishing person, she would be seen as the *good mother*.

But, another mother arises to coexist with her. Along with primitive libido, the infant also experiences raw aggression seeking discharge. These angry feelings, too, may be projected onto the mother. Looking at the woman in his life, the infant colors her with his own anger. One of my psychotic patients told me his earliest memory of his mother. The image was of a woman with her hair awry, her sweating face twisted in rage. In other words, the infant has another picture of mother, the *bad mother*, who derives from *projecting* his own hostile drives. No wonder the term paranoid came to mind. At this point the infant seems to have taken the most available object in his environment to associate with his own powerfully opposing instincts. There is, of course, only one mother, but the infant invests her with both instincts.

Keeping her as one image proves beyond him. For one thing, we might assume that such a compound image would overtax the synthetic ability of the very young ego; it is easier to image the mother as two contrasting objects, one loved and loving, one hated and hating. There is another reason, however, why the infant might *split* the maternal object into two. If the *good mother* is a relatively weak image there will be trouble when the next episode occurs. In this, the young human begins to *reintroject* the objects, by which we mean he begins to experience them as images in himself and as part of himself. In taking them in, if his mother has failed to reinforce his associations of *good mothering* sufficiently, there is the danger that the image of the *bad mother* will overwhelm and obliterate that of the good. In other words a function of the split is to protect the little bit of good mother imagery that the infant has achieved.

This is a most important dynamic to bear in mind. It may make sense of symptoms we see much later in life that otherwise seem inexplicable. I have in mind such patterns as the need to divide the world into good and bad people or, in the fashion typical of paranoid characters, those who are *for* from those *against* the patient. Of course, if one could get the opposing people from the real world actually to fight each other, the protective internal splitting would be even further reinforced. On the other hand, if one's friends begin to settle their differences with one's enemies, they lose their value in sustaining the inner split. There is at least one person from whom I deliberately broke off when it became clear to me that she constantly fed me information calculated to turn me against others we both knew. Once we accept that splitting the world serves the defensive function of protecting a weak, vulnerable *good mother* image, then some of the desperate machinations of paranoid people and others become more understandable—if *not* more acceptable! Unresolved remnants of the paranoid position get their earliest expression in attempts to manipulate one's parents to fight each other. When a child succeeds in doing this he is pleased, because he is very much in the middle; but he is also frightened, because if he is not stopped it will be the middle of a disintegrated family.

So, the odds are strong that the reintrojected objects will include an *idealized* good mother. All unpleasant aspects of her are psychologically sanitized. The *bad mother*, on the other hand, is all evil, mirroring one's own urge to tear and to destroy. What might a bad mother image feel like inside? Like having a large, nasty woman peering over your shoulder at what you are doing. From time to time, she sneers at all your works in a shrill, penetrating voice—her timbre pierces brick walls. The person is regarded as absolutely merciless; she cannot be placated and is deaf to explanations. Years ago, I had a patient who entered her bedroom one day, and out from under (interestingly enough) the marital bed came, "You're no good; you ain't never goin' to be no good." Here, then, is the source of what Klein calls *persecutory anxiety.* Each of us has a touch of it; perfectionists suffer it cruelly; the world is full of people whose most recurrent dream takes the form, "That which I ought to have done I did not do."

Desperate to rid himself of the carping, merciless inner assault the paranoid finds refuge in projection. "I'm not evil and mean; it is you who want to get me. I'm simply protecting myself." We recall the same mechanism, in less rigid and malicious form, in the self-righteous indignation of hysterics. A related phenomenon is the need of prejudiced people to separate the world into *us and them.* Lest she become aware of her anger toward her parents, the bigot idealizes them. Hostility is then safely directed against persons as unlike the parents as possible. These are the presumed dynamics of the *authoritarian personality* (Adorno, *et al.*, 1950). Outsiders become scapegoats in the literal ancient Jewish meaning of the term, repositories of our sins whom we must destroy to purify us all. It is a sad commentary that so many groups find their closest bonds around a common scapegoat.

Unresolved persecutory anxiety also expresses itself in a *contempt for weakness,* especially in paranoid characters. With the merciless bad mother internalized, to be weak is not only a misfortune; it is evil.

For babies reasonably lucky in their parents, the paranoid position ends at about the fifth month of life, because good mothering is strong enough to prevail. The image of the mother is again integrated into one person, so that the formerly divided powerful feelings are not directed against the same object. Since the infant loves the object, which he also has an urge to destroy, he feels concern for its safety, and a primitive form of guilt. "Love and hatred come closer together in his mind, and this leads to anxiety lest the object, internal and external, be harmed or destroyed" (Guntrip, *ibid.,* p. 239). So the hostility is displaced against the self. Concern for the integrated object ushers in Klein's *depressive position,* said to date from the second half of the first year of life. In this stage, urges to preserve the object appear, along with guilt and strong desires to make *reparations* for the destructive fantasies. In older children these reparative maneuverings are called *rescue fantasies.* They include day-dreams of rushing in to rescue the mother and father from robbers or other threats. The child, having first put his parents into a terrible situation, emerges the hero.

In this country René Spitz (1966) also linked the achievement of a stable, consistent image of the mother (object constancy) to the *fusion* of the libidinal and aggressive drives toward her. Thus, instead of having to alternate the good and bad images of the mother, the child recognizes her as one entity, thereby facilitating the acquisition of a consistent image of her.

To Klein and to those influenced by her formulations, rather than being ominous, the depressive position represents a developmental achievement. Winnicott (1955) reminds us that normal infantile depression indicates the infant is now capable of guilt, and has urges toward making restitution to the injured other person. His superego is developing. The most severely disturbed adults, he believes, never reached this stage, which is helped along by a sensitive mother who operates by "holding the situation in time." (A mystifying way to put it!) Child neglect results in unsatisfying resolution of the depressive position, leaving the victim with unfinished business.

Winnicott suggests further functions of *fixation* and the *repetition compulsion.* The adult with unfinished business dating back to infancy tries in his current life to resurrect an old relationship and live it through again in the hope of *working out a better resolution*. By projecting feelings onto people, and by manipulating them if he can into playing roles in unfinished dramas from the past, the person tries to enact happier endings. Unfortunately, since such unfinished business more often concerns a tragedy than a farce, happy endings are hard to arrange.

The child may, however, emerge from the *depressive position* through consistent good mothering, but this requires that the mother be able to accept the child's aggression without becoming alarmed or punitive, and help him control it. Irving Kaufman (1962) has described clients with lifelong problems from this period as having a *depressive core*. They often fight underlying sadness manfully or womanfully by keeping busy and amused. But as clients have told me, when at rest with little going on, they feel unaccountably sad and anxious. Note however, that in the Kleinian view each of us passes through both the paranoid and depressive positions in the first year of life. Depending on the quality of the resolutions and of the defenses we erect against their traces in the psychic substrata, we emerge "essentially normal," neurotic or even psychotic in later life.

The universality of the dire imaginings Klein describes seems indisputable. Even protected children are capable of composing tales of casual mayhem appalling to sensitive adults. Murder, cannibalism, wanton destruction are found in popular fairy tales. A surprising proportion of adults enjoys the equivalent for their age level, in horror movies and tales of violence. Something from childhood must bubble up in writers who invent such dramas—and in their avid audiences. The pleasure in undergoing such frights must come, at least in part, from being helped to bring our own parallel fantasies to consciousness, so we may try to master them by repetition as children do in recurrent nightmares.

This leads to a rather different view of the impact of the outer world on the inner. What is so destructive about child neglect or abuse? The simple view would be that such treatment teaches the child that this is a nasty, punitive world. The other possibility, however, is that the child already lives with such dreadful imaginings from the inner transactions of the paranoid position. Hence, what is even more sad about the horrors superimposed from the outside is that they do not mitigate—*rather they fail to disconfirm*—an image of the world already reintrojected from instinctual hostilities.

It follows, then, that therapy should encourage the patient to bring this pain and rage closer to the surface, including inevitably hateful feelings toward the therapist. In the presence of a kindly, interested, relatively neutral person, the patient may be helped to understand that such dread impulses are part of man's fate, afflicting the usual person as well as those we think evil. To be dealt with and controlled, one's hostilities need to be brought into the open, faced, and discussed. Certainly, this confrontation would be better than turning rage into self-destruction because of guilt, or against others because of the use of projections to ease the anxiety they cause. All this self-awareness takes time and "working through." I do not know whether it is for this reason, or because of a general English deliberateness and leisureliness, but classical analyses in the Kleinian tradition are famous for their length. I am talking of six years or more in treatment.

Klein's formulations presume very early formation of a mental representation of the mother by the infant. Her ideas on this differ from those of Mahler and Fraiberg. She posits that the child uses these representations in complicated sets of internal transactions. The reader who finds her dating for them incredible will be cheered to know many analytic colleagues of Mrs. Klein have had a similar reaction. Yet whether or not she was correct in the dates she assigned the two *positions* is not crucial to much of her theorizing. Especially for social workers, who see so many people whom life has soundly mistreated and who are steaming cauldrons of rage, her focus on the paranoid and depressive positions, on the "death instinct," and on aggression is very much to the point. And, like other suppositions about the unconscious, Klein deals largely in *constructs*.

Transactional Analysis
It will seem odd to purists for me to refer to Transactional Analysis at length, for TA is often juxtaposed to psychoanalytic theory. Its adherents regard it as a preferred alternative. I include it for a couple of reasons. First, like several other post-Freudian approaches, its roots are in psychoanalysis as Eric Berne (1961), its initiator, freely acknowledges. In practice, many of the conceptions and stances already covered in this book are taken for granted in TA—e.g. the existence of ideas and impulses outside of conscious awareness; the use of defenses; the efforts made by the ego to put things together. This degree of compatibility is itself of interest, for it helps us track ideas which have passed from their original auspices into the realm of those "generally accepted" by all dynamically oriented clinicians.

The second reason for discussing TA is that Berne and his colleagues have proven shrewd, perceptive observers with a knack
for pinpointing interpersonal defenses often encountered in therapy groups and in family interactions. They also have shown a
talent for describing such mechanisms in phrases that hit the
mark with patients. Berne's best known book, *Games People Play*
(1964), is useful reading for all who try to help others by enlisting
and fostering their abilities at self-observation. I am adamantly
opposed to eclecticism in theorizing because it is apt to violate the
rule of parsimony; worse, it puts the theoretician at the mercy of
his own unconscious preferences, perhaps leading him to those
hypotheses that trouble him least. But it is foolish to discard observations by non-Freudians or no-longer-Freudians which might be
parsimoniously incorporated in the theory. Moreover, one may
find on sympathetic reading that, like the work of Piaget on object
permanence, these other formulations do not necessarily contradict
Freudian theory so much as expose gaps and lacunae that need to
be dealt with.

Berne, himself, puts the claim:

> Structural and transactional analysis offer a systematic con-
> sistent theory of personality and social dynamics derived from
> clinical experience, and an actionistic, rational form of therapy
> which is suitable for, easily understood by and naturally adapted
> to the great majority of psychiatric patients (1961, p. 1).

If one compares TA as a theory of personality against the criteria
offered in the first chapter of this book, it comes up short. Its
content largely consists of statements about sources of energy in
the personality. Insofar as it concerns itself with adaptations, its
focus is nearly entirely on adaptation to other people. It has scant
theory about thinking, perceiving the world, learning, or the interaction of psychic and somatic phenomena. Psychoanalysis, on the
other hand, not only offers greater subtlety as a theory of personality; after a century abuilding, it covers much more. One is
understandably reluctant to abandon the whole for the part at this
juncture. Claims for the applicability of TA as a *method of treatment*
have also been very broad and of course should not be discounted
simply on logical grounds. The success of TA with a wide range
of patients is something that has to be established or denied by
clinical trials, not argument.

Eric Berne spent over fifteen years training to become a psychoanalyst at the San Francisco Psychoanalytic Institute. Erik Erikson would have been President of that Institute during at least part of his candidacy, although not at the time Berne was ultimately refused membership in the Institute for reasons never revealed. In any event, he was already a mature man and experienced psychiatrist when he began to pursue and set forth his ideas of therapy, and the model of personality which provided their rationale.

An important event in his development was a patient, a lawyer, who remarked during a session that he was not really a grown man, but in his own mind still a little boy. Berne was struck by this phrasing. All who have done casework or therapy, of course, have had similar experiences, even though the patient does not always articulate the sense of himself that lies beneath them. That is, a woman will come in one day and speak in the manner of a complaining child. Not only are her complaints unrealistic by adult standards; she changes her voice and manner to resemble those of a whining four or five year old. Yet, if you talk with her as one adult to another, the same patient may gradually discard these mannerisms, and end the hour speaking with you as one grownup to another. It is also common for a patient to have a sense of his psychological age very different from his actual years. "I feel as if I shall always be nineteen years old in my own mind."

Such phenomena are easy to account for as instances of regression, or fixation. But Berne was struck by some other clinically familiar aspects: the adoption of a childlike manner—including tone of voice, style of reasoning, facial expression, and body position. Whether or not the client continues to carry on in the same way is, for many, connected to how the worker responds. Berne, of course, was not the first to notice such phenomena. William James and Charles Horton Cooley around the turn of the century both remarked the way social surroundings seem to change the "self" put forth, and even one's self experience.

Berne proposed that we, and the patient, think of these variations as *ego states*. He said that within each of us there are three: the child, the adult, the parent. The functions asigned each in this *structural* analysis, parallel functions grouped in terms of the id, the ego and the superego in traditional psychoanalysis. Berne went further, and noted that in many interchanges between two people, the ego state from which the first is speaking seems to affect the ego state from which the second responds. For example, if you say to me, "You really ought to find a way to condense all this. You are running on, you know." I am apt to reply, "Well, just give me a minute longer. I'm doing the best I can." In short, your Parent state triggers my Child. Transactional Analysis consists in part of helping people become aware of such interactions, especially their fixed and self-defeating patterns. They can then experiment with trying to alter how they relate.

Furthermore, after some introduction to these concepts, most of those in a therapy group can join the treatment. Using the same terminology, the group members can observe each other, make interpretations to each other, try to help each other change. (Not a bad idea, of course, if only because a major problem in any therapy is how to occupy oneself consciously while the cure is happening unconsciously.) So, this *structural analysis* on the individual level becomes *transactional analysis* when the interactions among two or more clients' ego states are tracked.

The aspect of TA in which object relations are most obviously involved are *games*. A psychological game may be seen as an ongoing series of complementary ulterior transactions progressing to a well defined end. The outcome, which becomes predictable, is called the game's *payoff*. A payoff consists of bad feelings for each of the players from having been downgraded or *discounted*. Examples of such bad feelings in a triad might include the sadness of the Victim, the malice and triumph of the Persecutor, the concern of the Rescuer. Even though it may have started smoothly, the game ends with a payoff unpleasant for all involved. The true aims of the game are masked. The invitation to join the game is merely a cover for its real purpose, an invitation termed a *con*. According to TA, a major reason we participate in games is our need to be *stroked*. A stroke is, in effect, recognition by another person. It is assumed we need stroking, emotionally, and that the need is a form of *stimulus hunger*.

The games a person likes to play tend to be repetitive, for reasons similar to those we associate with the repetition compulsion. Long before I had heard of Berne, I sat in staff meetings in which it was said of a patient, "He is still playing the same game with his wife," and so forth. A statement like that implied the patient had a *role* he was motivated to fill. To do so he had to seduce others to join his game and *complement* his role. To the sociologist, a role represents behavior which one's group expects of a person occupying a certain group position; the group tries to get the person to live up to his role. But, clinically, when we speak of a person's role, we usually have in mind the role he wants. He then tries to get the group to fit in with pattern he has in mind. The Victim needs a Persecutor;

the Persecutor, a Victim. We presume the roles people want to play in the real world are heavily influenced by the personal images they carry in their minds. Thus, the patient may people his present therapy group with the mother he used to placate, the authoritarian father against whom he rebelled, the younger brother he protected. If he can induce the other patients he has involved in his conflicts to carry out the roles he has assigned to them, he will be in a position to continue his old self-righteous battle with his family in this new setting.

The games patients like to play can be identified in the here and now. Rather than wait for history, one can observe how the patient treats the caseworker, or others in his therapy group. Indeed, at one point there were group therapists known to the rest of us as Cowboys because they would start "shooting from the hip" after just a few minutes' exposure to a therapy group. Yet, the Cowboy might be fairly accurate in pointing out to a group member what s/he was doing, even on short acquaintance because of having had much experience in groups. There are, after all, roles that come up repeatedly. Doctor's Assistant and the Help-Rejecting Complainer are two roles spotted very early in the practice of analytic group psychotherapy in America.

In the conduct of the therapy the patient is confronted with what he is doing in the here and now. He is not encouraged to take refuge recounting life history. But this practice principle does not mean that the theory behind TA makes no assumptions about the significance of earlier life experiences. In fact, those involved with TA have proposed their own outline of the process of normal development (Woollams, Brown and Huige, 1976).

Games are thought about in a way that is in line with what we have been describing as the theory of object relations. A TA concept that seems even more closely related is that of *script*. A script is the life plan that someone wishes to carry out, or believes he is fated to carry out; it is likely to be largely unconscious. According to the theory, one's script derives from how one interpreted parental attitudes in childhood (for example, that one was reserved to care for the parents in their last years; or that one was the "family idiot"). In Freudian terms, we speak of the patient with a "fate neurosis," such as the woman who believes she will die young, as her mother did, because in some way she "owes" it to her mother. I do not know whether such ideas affected his acceptance as an orthodox analyst, but Berne's conception of scripts is very reminiscent of Alfred Adler's term, life-style. Adler believed that the

concepts used by therapists ought also be accessible to patients, as
does Berne. In any event, much of the work done in the name of
Transactional Analysis is useful to social work. It does not seem to
me that a person holding essentially to a psychoanalytic model of
the personality would find serious difficulties in incorporating the
observations, practical suggestions and some of the theories of
Transactional Analysis into the general theory of object relations.

CHAPTER 9
A SPEED READER'S GUIDE TO
The Pursuit and Dread of Love

The theory of object relations brings us to phenomena of the *schizoid spectrum*, especially the *fear of closeness*. These formulations help explain formerly incomprehensible clients. Schizoid individuals display feelings of *futility*, massive *affect inhibition* leading to feelings of emptiness and cravings for excitement, *negativism* rooted in uncertainty of personal boundaries, and use of a variety of *distance maneuvers*.

To Fairbairn and Guntrip, the *schizoid position* is a universal developmental stage that in some may have a poor resolution. Very deprived children experience intense *oral aggression* that could destroy the loved object. Faced with a *dilemma*—made anxious by closeness but perishing of loneliness—they seek a tolerable *optimal distance* from people. Guntrip proposed that Klein's depressive position represents less deprivation; *love made angry* rather than *love made hungry*. Fairbairn shares Klein's concern with the fate of aggression in early development; Bowlby's, with the need for a good object present at birth, an instinct.

Separation anxiety is a related concept. Bowlby postulated that an *attachment instinct* evolved as protection against *predators*. Separation, then, would be one of a class of situations arousing instinctive alarm. *Security*, feeling that the way back to the attachment object is clear, also comes from internalizing a good object image. Chronic separation anxiety sometimes produces an equally chronic and pervasive *detachment* mechanism causing difficulty with closeness.

In a more limited way, Kaiser also departed the mainstream. The universal fear of *separateness* is denied neurotically through the *delusion of fusion*. Protecting the fusion fantasy, in turn, creates problems for *deciding*, drawing *conclusions*, actively *willing*, and *choosing*. Since the effort to fuse frequently spoils relationships, neurotics need to learn how to achieve closeness through open and direct talk with others.

These formulations are important for clients trying to cope with real personal losses. Lindemann studied grief reactions as responses to loss. At a more refined level, Wallerstein and Kelly showed how children of different ages typically cope with *family break-up due to divorce*, applying ego psychology to a major current problem of practice.

The Pursuit and Dread of Love

9

Ours is a generation of togetherness. In contrast to earlier eras in which social functions were held for such respectable reasons as excluding others, sexual stimulation and cheerful gluttony, we now make elaborate plans to be with, share with, talk with people. Privacy is a valued and expensive commodity in urban living. Nevertheless, we seek each other out.

Such restless searching for human contact bespeaks famine in the Promised Land. Never have so many owed so little to so many. Though constantly tossed together, people feel overwhelmingly alone. Much professional counseling consists in providing prostheses against this void. Group workers encourage group cohesiveness, caseworkers offer support, and "your analyst is the best friend money can buy." What is missing in relationships people already have? Why can these empty people not replenish each other? Most frequently missing is the ability to get close.

Since before 1900, sociologists have been writing about the process of impersonalization as an accompaniment of industrialization and urbanization. Even popular magazines discuss alienation using jargon in about the same way as the American Sociological Review (Seeman, 1959). Philosophers and theologicans have looked up from their preoccupations to notice the estrangement among other men. In a warm, rather naive dissertation, Martin Buber (1958) discussed the "I-Thou" relation, as if he had made a discovery of the distances among people. But, then, perhaps he had. It is not necessary to innovate for the whole culture to have invented for oneself, and each person's uncovering of his own aloneness is, in fact, unique.

Clinicians have encountered the same phenomenon among

their patients. As early as 1942, Deutsch wrote of the "as if" personality. Although these patients appear to behave normally and to have socially expectable responses, she points out that they lack warmth; they are not able to become genuinely attached to others. The *as if* personality employs "a mimicry which results in ostensibly good adaptation to the world of reality despite the absence of object cathexis" (Deutsch, 1942, p. 304). Deutsch saw these patients as members of the group we now term borderline: too well adjusted to be considered psychotic, not intact enough to fit neurotic forms. Indeed, she thought such patients might be moving toward schizophrenia.

The patient's inability to integrate a constant image of himself is a major issue. He is at the mercy of *transient identifications*, in which he adopts, chameleon-like, traits from the people with whom he finds himself. The relationship of Deutsch's observations to the theories of Erikson on the problem of ego identity and of Mahler on individuation is apparent. But, one wonders what she would have had to say about the famous sociologist, Charles Horton Cooley (1902). This inordinately shy man developed the conception of the "looking-glass self," saying that a person's appraisal of his own worth is but a reflection of how he thinks he is seen by those around him. Cooley did not emphasize inner continuities, did he?

Khan began a most important paper by referring to "a new type of patient that has come into prominence in the last two decades" (1960, p. 430). Paraphrasing Fairbairn (see below), Khan remarked further that "a fixation in the early oral phase...promotes the schizoid tendency to treat other persons as less than persons with an inherent value of their own" *(Ibid.)*. The dehumanization of men has been attributed by some to the growth of totalitarianism, by others to population density. In ego psychology, the same sorts of phenomena are thought about as problems in the schizoid spectrum.

Some Relevant Experiences
Anybody who has been involved with persons suffering schizophrenia cannot fail to be impressed with their isolation. At times, they go to the extreme of physical withdrawal by running away, or shutting out stimuli. There is always a feeling of interpersonal coldness and detachment. Psychiatrists used to refer to the characteristic handshake of schizophrenic patients: a fervent salutation, like clasping the tail of a dead fish. Even the schizophrenic with more ability to relate typically prefers a noncommittal stance. We

came upon this in a social psychological study of attitudes among patients in a private psychiatric hospital years ago (Polansky, White and Miller, 1957). If, for example, you use a Likert-type format— asking whether the subject Strongly Agrees, Agrees, Doesn't Care, Disagrees, or Strongly Disagrees with a series of statements—you get an odd statistically significant pattern. Schizophrenics choose the noncommittal alternatives expressing weak agreement or dis- agreement or no opinion. The most severe degrees of withdrawal, of course, involve discounting reality altogether.

At one time, it was thought that one either was or was not schizophrenic. Now, we find it more useful to think of patients as ranged along a continuous dimension we call the *schizoid spectrum*. A person suffering active schizophrenic illness is far out on the spectrum. But a person closer to "normal," who is not psychotic, may be termed a *schizoid personality*. Clinical fashions change, of course, and nowadays it is common to speak of many related problems in terms of *borderline phenomena* and borderline states. However, the earlier formulations about *schizoid elements in the personality* accented the important issues of detachment and fear of closeness so I have chosen to focus on them at the risk of seeming somewhat out of date: clients do not change nearly so quickly as fashions of talking about them.

We come into contact with many schizoid people in daily living. Naturally, they are not so withdrawn as are most schizophrenics. It may require a period of acquaintance to realize how *detached* the schizoid person is, for he often has made strenuous efforts in his early years to compensate for his pattern and mask it from others and himself. The college professor, so engrossed in books and papers that he scarcely notices his surroundings, much less wife and children, may be somewhat schizoid. So is the backslapping politician, salesman or banker who seems warm and friendly until you discover how indiscriminately he distributes his warmth, and how cold his eyes remain. Even the physician who exudes bedside manner may suddenly stand revealed as essentially shy and shrinking from any human contact not ritualized into his profes- sional role.

So, the schizoid individual is frequently odd, self-centered, unfeeling toward you. But then he does not feel much about any- thing. He suffers what we call severe *affect inhibition*. This does not mean he has no feelings but that he blocks out most feelings so that he is literally unable to be consciously aware of them.

Imagine you are a caseworker in an institution for delinquent youngsters. For the past two months you have been having regular interviews with a boy named Pete, struggling to breach his wall of toughness and bravado to involve him in discussing what is wrong with him. During your last interview, you finally had a glimmering of hope. After all the interest and concern he mutters, "Well, you're not a bad guy." You speak hopefully at staff conference this morning about his progress—only to be informed sarcastically by the director of cottage life that Pete absconded from the institution last night. The implication is strong that another gullible young caseworker has been outfoxed by a fourteen year old psychopath. Flashing through your mind is the voice of a psychiatrist who warned you once that any psychopath is like "an asp in your bosom." For the moment you hate this kid and all his kind. Even after you calm down a bit, there remain the questions: Why did he do this to me? And why, now, just when we seemed to be getting somewhere?

Such people pass through our lives as social workers, obviously all somehow related to each other. But how? I believe each represents the presence of schizoid elements in his or her personality. What do we mean by these?

Encounter
When I came out to get him, the young man was lolling in the waiting room, holding a magazine. His response to my greeting was silence — not aggressive, not obviously frightened, just bland, noncommunicative silence. Of course, I already knew something about him. He had a severe upset in college and had to withdraw in his freshman year. Since then, he had been surviving a marginal sort of existence at home, and was neither productive nor happy with his idleness. Pressure from his parents had brought him to our hospital, and to me. About *me*, he knew practically nothing; it would be months before he would admit curiosity if, indeed, he had any.

As he preceded me to the office, I became aware of his gait. Neither deformed nor unsteady, he walked as if afraid of staggering, in a kind of mincing lurch. Gradually I became aware that he was unusually stiff from knee to navel. For a youngster from a well-to-do family, his clothing was also noteworthy, faded blue jeans, a red flannel shirt, a pair of expensive flight boots. His hair was long, but looked neglected rather than deliberately styled that way. His only concession to the raw weather was a nylon windbreaker.

In the office, he stood dumbly waiting to be asked to be seated, took the proffered chair, and finally yielded a passing smile. He began the interview by staring at a spot three feet, two and a third inches beyond my right metatarsal arch. Later, he shifted his gaze to a point four miles and seventy-six yards out the window. He evaded eye contact and, in fact, appeared never to look at me. Yet I soon discovered that he was preternaturally alert to my inflections, expression, general demeanor. Evidently in his darting fashion he was an acute observer of feelings.

I asked him why he had come to our hospital. He took me by surprise. From his pout, I had expected him to say he was here because his folks made him come. Instead, in a slightly shaky voice, he said, "I have problems." There seemed a desire to do something for himself, perhaps a good bit of surviving reasonableness, so I encouraged him, "Care to tell me a little?" He lapsed immediately into silence, and to contemplation of the Bigelow rug on the floor. Was he fearful of beginning? Did all beginnings make him anxious? As the silence lengthened, we were no further along, really, than if he had blamed his presence in the hospital on his parents.

He emitted signals that he was unhappy sitting with me. There were beads of perspiration on his forehead, and he looked glum — did he always? Finally, however, it dawned that he was waiting to see whether I, in my turn, might not become uncomfortable with *him*. He seemed completely capable of letting our time pass without anything much happening on any spoken level. I decided for the moment to overlook his *withdrawal* and *negativism* and try to get a line on another of his possible gambits.

I had no clear evidence as yet, but I knew from bitter experience that, with nearly all schizoid people, any new relationship presents a chief issue: *who will be on top?* As his "doctor," I present a problem. He takes it for granted that I will want to control the situation. After all, it is *my* office. He has to figure out how to let it appear that I do so, while guaranteeing I do not, in any area he really cares about.

He can say the right words, but he has no conviction that two people can become involved in a cooperative venture as independent but still close and equal partners. He believes one must absorb the other, one must dominate. He thinks he fears being absorbed, but his thoughts on this do not involve me. He really wishes to play the helpless infant and is afraid I will let him get away with it, at great cost to his dignity. How rigidly, out of how much desperation he plays this game, I still do not know. At the moment, anyhow, he probably is not even conscious of any need to control the situation, but only a dogged determination that his outline of an identity, scratchy as it is, will not be erased. It is more than likely that what is on his conscious mind is a series of fantasies and experiments he has gotten into about sex. Even though he has the general impressions that this is what therapy is all about, he does not see how he can bring himself to talk about these "problems" right off. But he feels he should. Because therapy, like everything else, is *all-or-none* for him. There are no halfway measures.

He does not know that I agree with him. I do not see how he can expose a lot of intimate details on first acquaintance, and I would find it ominous were he to begin that way. So I decide to offer him a way out. I remark that all we can hope to do today is get acquainted, and perhaps he can begin to fill me in on some basic information about himself. I have read his record, but I need to hear more from him. Where was he living before he came to the hospital?

Although this sounds matter of fact, I am really taking a chance. In truth, all I hope for is to get acquainted and to make some preliminary estimates of his condition. Regardless of how mundane or lurid the tale he unfolds, all it provides at the moment is a way to assess the ego strength of the person sitting with me. This is the first order of business. But the patient may have his own preconceptions about therapy. He may decide that, in offering to ease his way, I have already surrendered to his tactic. He may become contemptuous. I watch his reactions for such signs, as it is a feeling he would not bother to conceal. I will then throw it right back at him. Meanwhile, I ask myself whether he will accept my way as sensible and realistic. If he can, it is a hopeful sign. I have no reason thus far to think him psychotic, although he was described as eccentric. How eccentric and suspicious I will soon know.

My patient accepts the question as reasonable and tells me he has been living at home, with his parents. I begin to ask about the conditions under which he was living, moving gradually toward inquiring about feelings and, before long, about possible symptoms he might have been experiencing. By now we are over our first hurdle, not because of my masterly interviewing skill, but because this fellow is not that odd in his response to a simple indication of interest on my part, and he knows I ought to have a straightforward approach to collecting information. Evidently, along with his peculiarities, he has wide islands of intactness in his personality.

Thus the first five minutes of getting to know each other have passed. The processes of forming a relationship and of diagnosis and evaluation have begun. Eventually I know him nearly as well as he does me, and we get along. I can virtually predict some of the steps in this sequence. For example, after about six sessions we go through a phase in which he obliquely questions my motives, and I remark that he does not seem to trust me. After some hesitation, he agrees. The hesitation is meant to convey polite concern for my feelings, but its true purpose is something else. Addicted to *indirection*, this young man simply hates to say anything directly. At this point, I tell him, again quite honestly, that I am pleased he does not trust me. If he did, on such short acquaintance, it might indicate that he is more childish and less realistic than I had hoped. He does not know quite what to make of my reaction. He would like me to try to prove to him I am trustworthy, as this is a gambit that has worked well in frustrating others in the past. But I decline the ploy in advance commenting merely that trust is something you feel, or you do not feel, and it comes from experience with a person, not from his protestations. For instance, I do not trust him very much, either.

And with good reason. I once treated a man for nearly a year with similar problems. From time to time I expressed concern that he was using up his inherited capital on the long hospitalization and wondered if the benefit to him were worth it. Only after about ten months did he let slip the fact that, while still a youngster, he had invented an electronic device that had been adopted by a large corporation. His monthly royalties alone far exceeded his hospital expenses, leaving aside income from accumulated investments. What he feared we would do if we knew of his wealth, or what labyrinthine satisfaction he gained from letting me make a fool of myself in my overconcern, I never did find out. I can guess, but I lay fewer claims to infallibility after each such incident in treatment!

The Schizoid Personality

The most noteworthy affect of the schizoid personality has been described as a *feeling of futility*. Nothing is worth while, no effort will do any good. It is typified in the remark "Why eat supper? You'll just be hungry before breakfast anyhow." Another patient, author of the classic comment, "Once a slob, always a slob," put it differently: "If at first you don't succeed, the hell with it." Whether the sense of futility be grasped with desperation, or waved about with bravado, the message is always the same: if the milk of life itself is poisoned, why bother?

The feeling of futility would seem to emerge from the defense of *detachment* in the three phases of an infant's handling separation (see Bowlby below). It differs from *depression*, with which it may be confused, clinically. The feeling of futility is a defense against depression, a refusing to care at all. Yet, as so often happens, the cure may be worse than the disease. With the detachment comes a kind of massive blocking of feelings which we have called *affect inhibition*. The patient does his best to literally feel nothing. The price for succeeding may well be terror. For one way we know we are alive, exist, are persons, is that we are filled with feelings. Not to feel and not to care gives rise to enormous *emptiness* and a *numbness* with awesome *connotations of death*. It is a bleak and hopeless state of mind from which, fortunately, not even suicide promises much. The danger, on the other hand, is that it does not threaten much, either.

One would expect futility to be accompanied by a withdrawal from personal relations, and from life, and indeed it typically is. Yet there are persons whose behavior reflects this affective syndrome, with whom we do not immediately make the association. Take the delinquent, for example. The stereotype of a delinquent youngster is of a young man, eyes flashing, face hardened, in motion, aggressively beating someone or driving away recklessly from his latest escapade. These are rare occasions for the truly delinquent personality. More typically, we find him slouched against a wall, eyes half closed, cigarette dangling, flaccid, bored, and boring. His normal stance is an overt demonstration of indifference to the life about him. He has trouble getting pleasure from the milder forms of stimulation most of us enjoy. Among other things, professional criminals are said to be poor lovers, the price paid for psychologically induced anesthesias.

Danger is usually involved in criminal acts, and a punk's face may light up as he tells you how much he enjoyed being chased by the police. Why the love of risks? I was once taught to think about danger as an urge toward self-destruction, but I no longer believe this the most parsimonious explanation. There is *indifference* to self-destruction, to be sure, founded on an illusory omnipotence. But the driving force is a *craving for excitement*. Only at moments of crisis, pain, intense pleasure does the delinquent feel fully alive.

The craving for excitement, with its ugly and frightening consequences, must be seen as itself a defense against massive affect inhibition and its emptiness, echoing death. Were he able to enjoy smaller pleasures, the typical delinquent would not need such heroic forms of entertainment. Similar logic applies of course, to the sexual sprints and gymnastics of other persons, *including hysterics with marked schizoid features.*

The schizoid youngster, like the detached infant, wards off feelings in order not to be overcome by his anger and despair. The cost of this defense, alas, is the desolation and emptiness which, in turn, demand another layering of defenses in order to overcome them. I have also alluded to the *stubbornness* and *negativism* so frequently prominent in this character. Stubbornness has many roots, but one of them may well be the sense of emptiness. The client feels that if he permits himself to be influenced, something will have been taken away from him, and he already has too little to work with in any case.

The *negativism* has a closely connected source. For a person who feels himself a vacuum, a nothing, to stand *against* something provides a sense of being. His firm grasp on *futility*, with its claim that no goal is worth the effort and no good can come of striving, affords him the luxury of avoiding failure and defeat. He can even surround the feeling with elaborations of superiority, telling himself that he is onto a secret other mortals have not penetrated. But again, the feeling of futility cannot be so successfully maintained if the youngster admits something matters to him, and takes a positive stance. The only way he can integrate himself into a person is through negativism. Paraphrasing Descartes, he says, "I oppose, therefore I am."

Let us face it. Whatever his admirable qualities, the schizoid individual is typically an odd, gawky personality, rigid when yielding might be graceful, un-with-it. He knows this; he has known it since early childhood when he already had thoughts that he was not like other children. Indeed, he was not, for he had already suffered from a childhood neurosis. Such self-recognition is of course frightening to a child. Many of these patients reacted in the only way that must have seemed possible to their young minds. They hoped that by *acting* like other people, they would *become* like them.

It is important to bear in mind that this struggle to break through his self-imposed barrier of detachment is no trivial matter in the life of such a child. Not to be like other people is to be less than human, an object in terror for his very existence because he is *unlovable*. No wonder, then, that the business of *appearing to be human* should be gone at with such dead seriousness, such solemn self-preoccupation and self-consciousness, such strained and rigid role-enactment. For this reason the schizoid adult seems teetering and odd in his mannerisms when he tries to be warm and spontaneous.

Given any new role, each of us is likely to overplay it at first. This patient may well overplay being a person. Perhaps because of this I have so often found, in dealing with such a patient, that it may clear the air if both of us recognize sooner rather than later that much of how he acts with me is *phony*. It seems to help him to know that I know. And it helps me to like him in spite of his spuriousness—although he prefers to think he is engaged in an act he can turn off at will, I know better. I recall a patient who liked to think he was escaping unpleasantness at home by feigning being crazier than he was. In poignant truth, he was sicker than he pretended.

We can list a number of other characteristics of this fascinating syndrome. Without training or therapy, such a youngster often exhibits and articulates an unexpected *insight* into others' dynamics. Repressive mechanisms normally to be anticipated simply do not exist in him, and their absence contributes to an *excruciating sensitivity* in limited spheres. The same absence may make him the more masterful *manipulator*, and it is not uncommon to find that the patient has been tyrannizing his whole family despite his own difficulties. In fact, when in the first interview you find a patient with no previous treatment already explicating his own dynamics with reasonable accuracy, it is likely he is fairly far out on the schizoid spectrum. Often this represents an overvaluation on his part of the contents of his own thoughts as compared with a remaining open to the world about him. Like the Jews confined to European ghettos, he knows much about motives and feelings because that is all he has had to preoccupy his mind. He is Proust sans pen.

All these features of the schizoid personality are a woefully incomplete description if we leave out his characteristic inability to form warm human relationships.

Distance Maneuvers

We have already described at length the early experiences leading to alienation among persons with markedly schizoid features. To help us understand the schizoid's *fear of closeness*, let us add a characteristic of mental functioning discussed earlier, *looseness of ego boundaries*. When he begins to form a tie to another person, the schizoid youngster tends to "go all the way." It is not enough to approach each other as two loving but independent beings. Out of greed founded in his deep sense of emptiness, and indefiniteness of the outline of himself in his own mind, he has a tendency not so much to relate as to want to *absorb* the other person into himself, or to *lose himself* in the other.

For many such persons, talking is simply not enough: there must also be physical contact, cuddling, caressing, often sex relations. Because of such needs, the schizoid youngster may mistake his therapist's interest in him as a homosexual pass. Adding to the projection of his own desires into the relationship is his feeling of unworthiness: "What could possibly make me of interest to you unless it is my body?" Similar feelings exist in the pseudo-hysteric nymphets one encounters in high schools. One cannot help also but remark the emphasis in hippie cults on total fusion between two people—intellectually, but also preverbally, physically, and erotically regardless of the sex. In such a subculture, the desire to fuse physically with the other is permitted full expression. For most schizoid youngsters, however, the childlike needfulness and desire to be cuddled which they experience on coming close are embarrassing and disconcering. They are also dimly aware of the ravenous orality that makes them wish to devour the people to whom they are attached. Hence, such a youngster signals, more in kindness than in anger. "Stay away, or I will hurt you." There follow from these dynamics a group of mechanisms calculated to keep other people at arm's length. We call these, graphically, *distance maneuvers*.

Distance manuevers make up one of the most interesting collections of psychological operations identified and associated with ego psychology, and we have had frequent reference to them already throughout this book. Now we shall bring them together into a more compressed outline.

1. *Flight:* An obvious way to prevent others from coming too close is literally to flee them physically. There are various way of doing this, some more obvious than others, some offering evidence of severe disturbance. Boy runs wildly into the woods and disappears out of fear of his growing dependence on his therapist. The chronic "loners," hermits of the lakes and seas, and forest cruisers. Professors comfortable only in their studies; teachers who

hate to teach. Youngsters who cross the street rather than greet a person. The girls who shrink from touch. All are physical forms of withdrawal.

Psychological withdrawal is more subtle, of course, but it can usually be easily sensed. I have commented on the "schizophrenic handshake" in which the schizoid person goes through the motions of sociability while shuddering from relating. The most frequent withdrawal, however, is found in the person who, in the midst of his family or other company, simply is not there. He is said to be absent minded, and there is no doubt he is absent, in thought and spirit.

2. *Fight:* Bion, who brought some of these formulations into the area of group therapy, described phases through which a group might pass as "fight, flight, and work" (1951). "Fight and flight" are highly visible in the schizoid pattern of operating, and the fighting serves some of the same purposes as fleeing. Not all aggression, of course, is in the service of running away: far from it! But squabbling and battling can facilitate taking distance.

I have seen a number of patients who, after involving themselves in a reciprocal love relation, nearly always provoke the person they love. The *usual* reason for this goes back to the basic ambivalence we often feel toward those on whom we are most dependent. We form a love/hate relationship, and as we love, we also begin to get somewhat hostile. This is but part of the explanation in cases where the pattern is fixed; to label it a *hostile-dependent relationship* may obscure its full meaning. There is the person who, having become attached, becomes frightened. If he is unable to leave the one he loves, he provokes the other to take the initiative of breaking off. The fight is a distance maneuver.

Others fight as their peculiar way of resolving the schizoid dilemma. They want to be in contact, but they cannot tolerate the open expression of affection and caring. So they camouflage their loving behind a good deal of bickering, thus keeping their feelings at just that state of ambivalence which makes affection possible for them. Nagging, querulousness, teasing, or even good-humored kidding suffice to dilute the degree of warmth they are feeling. Others require so strong a camouflage against open recognition of their tenderness that the resulting battles may become physically dangerous. Wilde said, "You always hurt the one you love." Yes, if you are Oscar Wilde.

3. *Emotional Coldness:* A socially acceptable form of withdrawal is contact without feeling. I have mentioned the intellectualized col-

lege professor; I also mentioned the doctor, or other professional, who can tolerate impinging on fellow humans so long as he is relating from within a professional role. Quite a few schizoid individuals, by the way, resolve the dilemma between the Scylla of being engulfed and the Charybdis of loneliness by finding positions in which they too can "meet the public" without getting too involved. This group includes waitresses, sales personnel, clergy, hospital attendants, secretaries. You do not have to have a doctorate to barricade yourself behind occupational status while maintaining fleeting and stereotyped contacts with your clientele. Who else but a doctor can absent himself from wife and family during all but minimal time for sleeping and eating, while seeing people and serving humanity at the same time?

In such desiccated relationships, money need not always change hands. The friendly, impersonal prostitute can use her occupation to earn an emotional living in the same way as does the reservations clerk. In my observation, many schizoid young men are needlessly concerned about whether they will be sexually capable. Often, so long as the relationship is primarily erotic, sex without affection, they are quite adequate at achieving satisfaction.

It is much easier for the schizoid adolescent to rail against his parent than to confess the rest, which is that he loves him very much. Once for instance we needed to measure openness of communication of children in an institution for the treatment of the emotionally disturbed. Ratings of the children's *hostility* proved relatively meaningless. Angry expressions toward adults in the institution were common and even more or less encouraged by the theraputic atmosphere. Hence, the readiness to express hostility did not discriminate among our subjects. A measurement based on willingness to verbalize liking or affection, on the other hand, proved much more valid as an index of *verbal accessibility* (see below), since it came harder and reflected individual differences. The open expression of *tenderness* is most devastating; such admission may be accompanied by tears and genuine sadness.

4. *Noncommitment:* The schizoid individual finds it very hard to become *committed* to another person. When the tie becomes closer than he can bear, he finds ways of breaking loose, for example, by precipitating a fight and being ejected. As he feels himself being committed, his discomfort increases. It is her schizoid element which ofttimes leads the thirty year old mother of two, so apparently hysterical in other ways, to come for marital counseling with the annoucement, "I am trapped." There are other variations on

this theme. One of the more interesting, and amusing, is the *verbal denial of commitment*. At the same time as the patient is arriving early for his appointment, and otherwise showing his attachment to you, he will have to take time out to let you know that all this means very little in his life and he has been thinking about quitting treatment. He needs words discrepant from his actions. These are the same sort of men who must soon announce to their girl friends, "I am not ready to get involved, so I hope you will not take all this seriously." Such a young man may be terribly chagrined should the girl take him at his word and begin to date others.

The fear of commitment afflicts men who in other respects seem rather intact personalities. Many stories are told about reluctant swains. One is of the maid, Mathilda, who had been dating Jasper for fifteen years. Finally, one night she said, "Jasper, don't you think it's about time you and me was marrying up." Jasper reflected for five or ten minutes before replying, "Tillie, I believe you're right. But at our age, who'd have us?"

Commitment to another person is dangerous because it makes the schizoid patient aware of his extreme vulnerability. *Who loves has given hostages to fate*. The schizoid person, therefore, feels lonesome at times, but he also has a smug feeling that he will keep secret even in therapy. Making a virtue of necessity, he believes, "Nothing ventured, nothing lost." While the young caseworker tires himself encouraging him to find outside interests and companions, he barely conceals his conviction that he is much smarter, he knows a better way.

Because of their fear of closeness which, in turn, involves tremendous infantile separation anxiety, schizoid persons, as we have reiterated, keep their distance. For persons with schizoid elements in otherwise intact personalities, we see a related mechanism. To play it safe, and avoid becoming vunerable, they must remain in control of the relationship. To love and feel love is to risk becoming unloved, because of something over which you may have no control. This they cannot stand. Consequently they are preoccupied, at the beginning of a relationship, about the circumstances of its termination. Just as it is easier to take leave on the train than stand on the platform and wave good-bye, so they much prefer any rupture to occur at *their* initiative. Therefore they repeatedly play out the scene, "You can't fire *me*; I quit!"

By controlling the timing of the ending, the schizoid feels at least somewhat more the master of his fate. By meeting the rupture actively, the weakened ego is somewhat better able to tolerate the anxiety. All this has a logic and a purposiveness. What is not purposeful, unfortunately, is the repeated tendency to break off ties at the least threat. In this way friendships are broken needlessly by a person who yearns for friends. The same mechanism, of course, can easily invade the treatment, spoiling the patient's chance of getting help because of just the thing for which the help is needed! And I have alluded to the jockeying for position from the beginning of therapy.

The difficulty of commitment is most visible in relation to personal objects, but it typically pervades the personality. There may be fear of becoming tied to a place or to a job: hence, a drifting existence. During World War II, I worked in an Army Disciplinary Barracks. We saw many soldiers charged with AWOL or desertion. A fair proportion of them had no civilian record. They were now in legal difficulties because, for the first time in their adult lives, they were required to remain in one place, among one group of people, and this they found intolerable. When we received our first shipment of General Prisoners at the disciplinary barracks, we were still (unknown to them) desperately closing gaps in its barbed-wire wall, on a distant side of the compound. While we sweated in the midday sun, we heard our blithe, former comrades caroling, "Don't Fence Me In" as armed GI's herded them into our care.

There is usually an associated noncommitment in attitudes and beliefs, with the exception of a few rigidly held for defensive purposes. The schizoid man or woman professes no opinion on so many aspects of living. This includes religion, which otherwise might have been a considerable solace against self-imposed isolation. Naturally, one will find many evidences of what Erikson (1959) has so marvelously described as *identity diffusion*. Along with other problems, the schizoid young woman may have avoided deciding which sex she really wants to claim as her own. Homosexuality and bisexuality often occur. Even more frequent, however, is the sexual neuter, the person permanently poised in preadolescence—the man who feels he somehow is not yet mature enough to take command among other men, or the lady golfing champion.

5. *Selfishness:* Alienation, isolation, detachment, preoccupation are some of the words we have used to describe this syndrome. To these I must add another: A striking feature of the constellation is *selfishness*, in just about the meaning we attach to it in everyday speech. The ability to love others has been shunted backward: the

love is turned toward the self in a combination of *primary* and *secondary narcissism*. Primary narcissism refers to the infant not even aware there is anyone worth attending to but himself; secondary, to the infant who has started to be attached to his mother but who, out of disappointment, has made the defensive switch, "If no one else loves me, then I will."

The selfishness became markedly visible to me in hospital work. Whatever the parents' defects, and they were manifold, they had tried to provide their daughter with treatment and to help with the treatment as they could. The patient, on the other hand, patently could not care less about the expense, or their feelings, or their fate. Indeed, it is a mark of success in treatment when one notices a letup in selfishness and a developing considerateness for others. Some withdrawal, for instance, is within the patient's control; that is, he can make an effort to pay attention to his wife and children if he will bother, rather than be so obsessed with "work" whose main aim is to increase his status in his own eyes. Even though he may need to withdraw, he can fight against it rather than yield to the symptom without a struggle. His wife's complaint, that he simply does not care, may have more justification than she dares to know.

Similarly, if you are the caseworker or therapist for such a person, you may be concerned for him, even go out of your way to see him. Do not be surprised if he repays you, for a very long time, by scarcely noticing your existence beyond the times he needs you. He is truly incurious about your life except as it impinges on his. He can transfer from one therapist to another with equanimity. Whereas an adult depressive whom you saw briefly and helped with little effort will write you at Christmas time for years afterward, the schizoid adolescent whom you labored and fought for two years to drag back from the brink of psychosis often sends no word until there is something he wants. In seducing the schizoid personality into treatment, the path to follow is the same as for any other extremely narcissistic person. There is no point in appealing to his love for his family or his duty to some higher ethic. His interest in change derives from the questions: "What is there in it for me? Now?"

Should the schizoid personality succeed completely with his distance maneuvers, he will have failed. For the price of freedom from the threat of separation and from the more current anxieties of intimacy is utter loneliness. Thinking to play it safe, he wants to "quit before I'm fired." By seeking to gain absolute security though refusing to take a chance on losing, he only guarantees his loss. After all, the person who has never loved, nor ever dared to seek to be loved, is as much alone as if he had been loved and then abandoned. Indeed, most of us would think him worse off. His life, too, passes just as inexorably as if he had lived it with pleasure.

The Schizoid Position

I have tried to concretize and illustrate with trait names an image of the schizoid personality formed from experiences in practice. We may say that the schizoid individual personifies the pursuit and the dread of love. But, how shall we explain such a personality? We turn for insight to the theories of the Scottish psychoanalyst, W. Ronald D. Fairbairn (1952), and to the brilliant exegeses of his theories and others' by Harry Guntrip (1961; 1969) who, analysed by Fairbairn, has contributed two fine books on the theory of object relations.

Which characteristics of the schizoid personality need explaining? Several come to mind which were not covered by previous theory. We think of the schizoid's typical *unrelatedness*, his *fleeing of closeness* and treating of other people as *less than persons*; we think of his *flatness of affect*, in which he neither shows nor seems to experience much emotion; indeed, the most prominent feeling expressed or implied is *futility*, "What good will that do?"; and we think of the *emptiness* of which such patients complain. Fairbairn hypothesized a process that accounted parsimoniously for these phenomena. While his theory is not without major faults, I have found it extraordinarily helpful for dealing with these patients.

Fairbairn began as a quite orthodox analyst. Initially, he followed the standard formulations about neuroses, which explained them mostly in terms of the vicissitudes of the sexual or libidinal drives. However, his own patients, and his acquaintance with the ideas of Melanie Klein, led him to differ from traditional theory in several important ways.

Fairbairn placed great emphasis on the role of aggression. Not only does one find evidence of this instinct throughout the analyses of adult patients, it is patently accessible in the behavior of young children. Although the Death Instinct, aggression, had long been recognized in analytic theory, its vicissitudes had not received the attention Fairbairn proposed. To him, it appeared that directing, sublimating and controling aggression is the chief problem a young child faces in achieving emotional development. Yet, nothing in the literature on the vicissitudes of aggression matched the model

of psychosexual development proposed for the libido. I found
Fairbairn's focus on the fate of aggression enormously fruitful for
understanding patients ill enough to require hospital treatment.
Older theorizing about sexual impulses did not match it.

Take *spite*, for instance, one of the few outlets for aggression
available to people in weak positions. One can make a botch of
one's own life to get even with one's parents through a negative
identity. We see spite all the time in our work with clients and
patients, though it was never mentioned in my original training.

The other fundamental on which Fairbairn carved out his own
line had to do with the need for a "good object." A "good object"
would be an image of someone you love and who loves you; such
an image, would be in the back of your mind saying, "You are a
lovable person; you are going to be all right." Now, previous analytic theory, which was heavily biological, assumed that the infant
begins with eroticism, the drive to achieve pleasure. If the mother's
breast gave oral gratification, then it—and eventually the mother—
became associated with reducing tension of this drive (*drive reduction*). Hence, one's fondness for mother derived from associating
her with drive discharge. Fairbairn on the other hand saw the
relationship the other way around: *"The ultimate goal of the libido
is the object"* (Guntrip, 1961, p. 288). In other words, the baby
wants the mother for a good object, and then channels his pleasure seeking in her direction.

Commenting on a case, Guntrip wrote, "So basic is the object-
relations need that a human being can die in consequence of the
complete frustration of the primary libidinal need for a basic
parental good-object relationship during the developmental period"
(1961, p. 254). The reader will recall the related work of Spitz,
cited earlier. Many of us have noted that some "hysterical" women,
for example, protested their sexual involvements were coincidental;
they had really wanted to be held and cuddled and were surprised
when their male friends pushed for intercourse. Even if the sexual
urge was denied, an interest in being comforted might well also
have been present. Indeed, sex itself may be used as bait to achieve
this more basic goal. In short, the patient's conscious version of
the events was partially accurate.

But, if there is a need to be loved and loving, why do some
people dread closeness? The answer, for Fairbairn, stems from
the infant's helplessness and enormous need of the mother as
primary caretaker. She is the source of all goodness: from her
comes water, from her comes food. The mother is also the natural

person to whom to look as "good object." Yet this woman who loves you and keeps you alive is also inevitably frustrating. No mother can be so perfect as to anticipate every infantile need. By the time the mother gets the signal that the baby is hungry, he is already crying and demanding food. Even then, she may be delayed by having to care for others in the household, or her own urgencies. So each of us without exception experiences deprivations in infancy. Everyone has angry feelings toward mother, mixed in with the loving.

Some infants, however, undergo far more deprivation than most of us. Extended deprivation, however, is more than angering; it is frightening. For, the gaping void portends death by desiccation or starvation. The emptiness the adult schizoid complains of, "I feel all empty inside; I feel dead," perhaps derives *in part* from these very real early experiences. The emptiness also seems to me to derive from massive *affect inhibition* (see below).

Even more destructive from Fairbairn's standpoint, is the fact that the depriving mother does not make her child feel loved for his own sake, as a *person in his own right*. Such a mother may be preoccupied with her own needs. We have described the infantile person who openly talks about having babies because they make *her* feel so good nursing them. Or the mother may in fact dislike having the baby. Such rejection is usually repressed, of course, and may show itself as a reaction formation, which Levy (1943) called maternal overprotection. The mother's harsh, penetrating tone of voice, clumsy touch, her obliviousness to the real needs of her squirming infant all contribute to a baby's anger and fear. Still, to Fairbairn, the fact that one does not feel loved as a person for one's own sake predominates over these other life mishaps.

Certainly patients often complain bitterly of such feelings. "My playing the piano so well gave her something to brag about; she did not notice what I got out of it. Finally, I didn't care whether I ever played again." Note the *disappointment* of this good little girl's best efforts to be loved for herself. Given her mother's limitations as a person, her attempts all proved *futile*. One would not require Fairbairn's insight to remark, as we sometimes did, "But, you're sucking on a dry tit!" Patients, by the way, prefer to see the parent as *unwilling* to meet their needs, rather than *unable*. For, if one's father is *unwilling* to love one, one might be able to change his mind. But if he is a man with nothing to give, where are you then? It feels better to be angry at him than to be "understanding." The latter implies that you have given up hope.

So, the massively deprived infant is disappointed in the search for a good object. And is likely also to be severely frustrated in oral needs very early in life, so much so that besides being angry, s/he feels empty and downright frightened. Such gaping hunger when fused with aggression gives rise to a ravenous, oral aggressive (oral-sadistic) impulse toward the mother. Guntrip has aptly termed this state, "Love made hungry." This stance presents the patient with an insoluble dilemma. *"Love made hungry is the schizoid problem* ... the fear that one's loving has become so devouring and incorporative that love itself has become destructive" (Guntrip, 1969, p. 24). If you gobble up the mother, you will not have her any more; you will be alone. So, you take distance, let us say, and urge her to "Keep away lest I destroy you, for both our sakes." You will in fact, now perish of loneliness.

These are powerful and frightening conflicts for the severely deprived child. Fairbairn postulates that under their impact the infant "splits." By this he means that the infant tries to wall off all these feelings in his mind, and keep them rigidly out of consciousness. There is a terrible price for such splitting, however, because— in addition to the oral aggression—many other feelings like love and joy are also walled off. Splitting may result in *massive affect inhibition,* a *self-induced numbness* to one's own emotions which comes across in interviews as *flatness of affect.* It is not, of course, that such a person has no feelings; s/he is not conscious of her feeling. No wonder s/he complains of being "all dead inside." How does one know s/he is alive except from inner emotions? From this numbing, I believe, comes the *craving for excitement* found in at least some hysterical men and women, the same numbing found rather widely among delinquents, most of whom idealize their mothers. Also, many schizoid patients have body-images lacking depth. As one told me, "I picture myself as a silhouette."

The proclivity of severely deprived youngsters to commit crimes against persons when they are teen-agers and older derives, in part, from their distancing; they treat others as nonpersons as they often do themselves. But, the massive affect inhibition also contributes, since it limits their ability to empathize with another's pain (Polansky, *et al.* 1981).

Fairbairn's powerful set of formulations explains most of the schizoid syndrome. By a line of reasoning with which we already are familiar, he went further. The unfortunate may emerge with a schizoid stance toward life, it is true, but each of us passes through a developmental phase when schizoid issues are in crisis. Occurring in the first six months of life, this phase is labelled the *schizoid position*. It parallels Klein's *paranoid position* and, indeed, she began later to speak of a *paranoid-schizoid* position. Most children, fortunately, resolve this life crisis happily and end with a few or no schizoid elements. But just as remnants of the various psychosexual phases may be discerned in many of us, so unresolved remnants of the schizoid phase are also present.

For example, most of us are capable of feeling futile. We do not feel that way much of the time, but the feeling *can* be brought to the surface—for example by contact with another person in whom it is conscious and manifest. We have written elsewhere about women who neglect their children. Many neglectful mothers show the Apathy-Futility Syndrome, as we have called it. One of its features is that protective services workers find the futility contagious; after some time in the presence of such a mother, you begin to wonder not only whether it is worthwhile to keep trying to reach her, but whether anything is worth doing. A feeling like that obviously cannot be suddenly injected in you by the client. The feeling must be present but well defended. The client's pattern, and skill, brings it to our conscious awareness (Polansky, Borgman and DeSaix, 1972, pp. 54ff).

From dealings with patients, Guntrip (1962) has aptly sketched what he calls the *schizoid dilemma*. Should the schizoid person begin to feel involved with another, powerful feeling are stirred in him. Some make him feel childishly needful and ashamed; others, aggressively demanding and frightening. So he tries to evade the anxiety by fleeing to aloof isolation. There, he is overtaken by devastating loneliness. Torn between Scylla and Charybdis, the patient desperately tries to strike a bargain among the forces competing within him, and works out the *schizoid compromise*. The compromise consists in finding the *optimal distance* between perishing of loneliness, or of coming too close. Just as people tend to get involved with others of the same psychosexual stage as themselves, I have noticed that in quite a few couples, regardless of surface differences in sociability, there is a likelihood to have picked each other out to maintain the mutual distance each finds optimal.

The schizoid compromise reminds us that taking distance is a particular kind of defense, a *security maneuver*. A therapist actively encouraging a patient's involvement with others out of pity for the isolated life is met with polite disbelief. "I've got a secret" is the attitude. The therapist may be urging, in effect, "Nothing ventured, nothing gained"; the patient is smugly paraphrasing "Nothing ventured, nothing lost," and feeling superior while doing so. Alas, the confidence is mistaken. Thinking that by keeping distance one can avoid turmoil that goes with closeness, the possibility of ending up all alone, patients reduce the risk by remaining aloof. In so doing, the gamble is limited—such patients *guarantee* that they will be alone.

For schizoid persons to break out of their shells requires, among other things, that there be an admission of fondness for, or commitment to, another person. It is easy for such clients to bawl you out; it is very hard for them to say, "I like you." For expressions of affection create vulnerability and sadness by reminding clients of early yearnings and disappointments. Such an expression may be accompanied by an urge to cry. In my experience, unless sad tears occur in treatment in discussing feeling toward the therapist or toward others in the client's life—not once, but repeatedly—the schizoid individual is likely to remain immured behind the brittle battlements we have described. How one gets such a person to risk is not well understood. Success has as much to do with the client's stance as with our skills, at this stage of our knowledge.

Guntrip has also attempted a kind of synthesis of the theories of Fairbairn and Klein showing the relationships between the schizoid and depressive stances. The schizoid stance reflects major early deprivation—love made hungry, in Guntrip's telling phrase. The depressive stance reflects a much less severe deprivation, and leads to *love made angry*. Here, the urge is to attack an object perceived as actively refusing to meet one's needs, a rejecting, *bad object*. "It leads into *depression* for it rouses the fear that one's hate will destroy the very person one needs and loves, a fear that grows into guilt" (Guntrip, 1969, p. 24). Guntrip in effect identifies two kinds of bad objects, one you want to devour, the other you want simply to attack. Clinically, one has the impression that the schizoid stance is more pervasive, earlier in origin, more ominous than the depressive. Depressives are usually related to people; their anger is against a *particular object* that may have been lost, for example. But, other than this, I am not sure whether Guntrip's distinction clarifies our understanding very much.

Fairbairn's interesting ideas have not had the popularity in England that Klein's enjoyed. Serving to integrate new information, his formulations create major problems of theoretical parsimony. If you alter emphasis as he did, it becomes incumbent on you to show its effects elsewhere in the theory. Otherwise, your colleagues may discount your ideas and go on as before. The situation is analogous to Erikson's, an engaging, almost tantalizing set of ideas from a master clinician, enormously important to some but seldom mentioned in the more general literature.

There is a second reason for reluctance in adopting Fairbairn's and Guntrip's ideas. The citations from adults they use to illustrate their points are well taken and credible. But as with Klein, one is hard put to think of a way of testing, through the direct observation of tiny infants, whether the imagery presupposed is anywhere near what goes on in those developing minds. Now, as a tiny house-fly can elude swatting for twenty minutes on end, the fragile human neonate is surely capable of sensing its survival needs and the danger of death it faces from being uncared for. What greater danger does the human infant face, really, than being "unlovable?" No wonder we fear it thoughout life! But how much of the rest of the theory applies? Fraiberg (see Chapter 8) and her colleagues would find it rather hard to believe it all happens in the first year. So again, we are in the position of observing psychoanalytic theory in the process of becoming, but not yet achieving final synthesis. Meanwhile, as sources of insights into the dynamics of clients with very severe anxiety about human intimacy and commitment, the writings of Guntrip are unsurpassed.

Attachment—and Detachment

All who aspire to create a basic science of human behaviors must be impressed by a man like John Bowlby. Consider his professional biography. A youngish English child psychiatrist became widely known after World War II for a study done under the auspices of the World Health Organization, a branch of the brand new United Nations. The study concerned the effects on very young children of being torn loose from their mothers by Hitler's armies, and had to do with deprivation of maternal care (Bowlby, 1951). From this, the author was led to ponder the general issue of children's reactions to such separation and noted that anxiety was a universal concomitant (Bowlby, 1960a). But, *separation anxiety* had an ambiguous position in analytic theory. After reviewing the literature on anxiety, Bowlby decided that to propose that "separation leads to anger leads to guilt leads to guilt anxiety" was clumsy and forced. Why not just accept separation anxiety as an instinctual reaction to loss of the object (Bowlby, 1961)? But, if this form of anxiety is instinctual and rather specific, the tie being ruptured must also represent something instinctual. Bowlby then began to study *attachment behavior* (1960b).

Humans are not the only animals who show attachment behavior, and so Bowlby, while remaining active in clinical work at the Tavistock Institute in London and closely identified with psychoanalysis by preference and training, began to delve also into the relatively new field of ethology. From this perspective he saw that a number of reactions found in humans parallel attachment behaviors and responses to ruptured attachments in other animals, such as dogs, wolves, bears, even chickens. Bowlby has since spent years exploring clinical manifestations of attachment and its loss and trying to draw implications that would make clinical practice more efficient (1969). There are not many examples of such theoretical breadth coupled with coherence and tenacity of purpose. The work of Bowlby is, of course, taught very widely in psychology courses and does not require detailed explication here, though in fact, his ideas are not generally accepted within psychoanalysis (Dinnage, 1980). Still, how can one discuss the pursuit and dread of love without reference to Bowlby's work?

Separation anxiety can be typified by this scene. Imagine a small child, helpless, easily damaged, being held to the mother's breast. Should the mother suddenly let go, the child would find itself wrenched from security, falling alone through space—as many of us did in desolating nightmares in childhood. Or in adult life, try to magnify the sensation you have when the floor of a high speed elevator drops beneath you—again, the terror of falling through space. To Bowlby, this terror is the *primordial form of all anxiety.* That is, the various other meanings such as *guilt anxiety,* or the fear of internalized punishment by the superego, and *ego anxiety,* the sense of being overwhelmed by stimuli, all derive ultimately from basic separation anxiety.

Bowlby became interested in the reactions of infants old enough to be attached to their mothers (more than six months old) when the mother left. He found a regular sequence of events. First, the infant looks uncomfortable, and thrashes around. Next, if she does not return, he becomes angry, and *protests.* If his wailing does not bring about the mother's return, the infant lapses into *despair* in which he looks and acts depressed. Eventually, this too seems to pass, and the infant seems resigned to his fate. He comes to terms, but sullenly and without joy. To Bowlby, the infant is now *detached.*

The phases following separation from the attachment object are *protest,* which has to do with anger; *despair,* which has to do with depression; and *detachment,* which is a defense. That this detachment represents repression rather than a final resolution is readily demonstrable. Imagine a woman you once loved, whom you have not consciously thought of in years. Should you suddenly confront her, you are swept by unexpectedly powerful emotions. As one of my students suggested, detachment is a reaction formation against attachment; it represses separation anxiety, anger and depression.

Now, detachment is a wonderful, merciful mechanism. Without it we could hardly bear the deaths, the partings, the disappearances from life of all those we have loved but lost. But, like many useful coping mechanisms, it may become pathological and symptomatic. Children who have had to use it over and over in life, beginning very early, seem to become *addicted to detachment*. Almost before a bond with someone has started to form, the adult who was a disappointed child begins to pull away. One reason we social workers are so concerned about children with undependable parenting, or who have to be placed and replaced constantly in early childhood, is fear that they will emerge as detached adults unable to form close ties with anyone. My generation saw a lot of this in youngsters from large, congregate child-caring institutions, and spoke of *institutionalism* as a kind of personal pathology.

Let me now briefly summarize Bowlby's theorizing, from various sources. From the standpoint of ethology, there are three common responses to fear: withdrawal from the situation; freezing into immobility, like a startled rabbit or deer; *retreating to the attachment object*. Young primates, as soon as they can move, physically cling to their mothers when in fear, and try to reach them if they are not already close. This impulse to find someone to cling to in the face of danger is innate. It is readily visible in the reaction of green troops to artillery fire, for example. Why has it been bred into the species? Because the trait had survival value in our long evolution. Fleeing to the shielding mother gave the young animal protection from other predatory animals who wanted to catch him alone and eat him. The evolutionary function of attachment behavior is protection from predators.

The danger of predators is seen, as a matter of fact, in a number of other situations leading to fear responses, although none of these is dangerous, in and of itself. These situations include darkness, sudden large changes of stimulus level (sudden noise, sudden quiet, flash of light), strange people, strange places, sudden movements, looming objects. Each of these frighten most young children, at least at first; each situation can be readily associated to a position where something very large might pounce on you. Separation, then, is but one of a class of situations experienced instinctively as dangerous.

Why, then, do some children emerge relatively secure and able to leave their parents while others continue anxious clinging? What happens when a youngster is taken to nursery school for the first time? At first, s/he stays close to mother, clutching tightly to her skirt or blue jeans. S/he looks fearfully out at the other children, and finally moves to join them. But from time to time she comes back to mother. After a while, s/he has assured herself that the way back to the attachment object is clear. At this point, s/he can comfortably leave the mother for longer periods. Indeed, within a short time, usually several days at the most, s/he becomes, (a) attached to a substitute object, one of the adults in the nursery school and (b) confident that the mother will reappear and take her home after a few hours. Over a period of time, Bowlby believes, all fortunate children develop confidence that the attachment object will be accessible when needed. They also internalize an image of a *good object*. This mental image has the enormous advantage of being portable. In effect, one is now able to offer one's own psychological source of security derived from the internalized good object. Children who have experienced separation or threats of separation from their parents do not develop this kind of confidence, according to Bowlby. They show *anxious attachment*, clinging behavior. No wonder it is the neglected or abused child that makes such a fuss about being removed from a home in which, objectively, so little care was being given!

Bowlby's theorizing has much in common with that of Klein, Fairbairn, and Winnicott, but differs in a couple of critical respects. First, he places much less emphasis on internal transactions within the ego but thinks that a child's degree of confidence is a "tolerably good reflection" of actual life experiences. Second, Bowlby does not think that the processes he describes leave fixed effects in the first three or four years of life, but that the period during which these "representational models," these favorable or unfavorable expectations, are being built goes on until around pubescence.

In terms of clinical practice Bowlby asserts that attachment processes represent a class of behavior independent of — but as significant as—such other instinctual drives as sex or feeding. Therefore, each patient's experiences around attachment need to be explored. Difficulties with relating to the therapist may well reflect expectations of disappointment, and a defensive detachment. The job of the therapist is also to interpret the model the patient seems to follow, calling attention to inappropriate clinging, or his detaching himself from those to whom he might want to become close. As do other therapies in the analytic tradition Bowlby's aims to free the patient from archaic responses that cripple him in his present reality.

In terms of this chapter theme, what may we derive from Bowlby's work? If there is indeed an attachment instinct—that is if it is parsimonious to postulate it in listing sources of energy—the instinct certainly accounts for much of what we mean by "the pursuit of love." Bowlby's theory implies that a person unable to form attachments does not intrinsically lack such a need but that it has been blunted. In effect, the attachment process is *invaded by conflict*. What of those who remain studiously detached? It is as if, in the act of becoming involved, they already anticipate the pain of abandonment which, to them, is how things inevitably work out. They keep their distance to avoid the pain.

If you go on a trip and leave your dog in the kennel for several days, he will probably jump all over you with delight when you return. Should you leave him for several months, when you come back he will act as if he does not really recall who you are. He will stare away from you, and act indifferent. It takes several days before he lets himself dare to enjoy being near you once again. Something like this is found in the complaints of parents whose emotionally disturbed child must be taken for in-patient treatment. "It's nice to have her home, but things are just not the same." This does not necessarily mean they are less neurotic; it may mean they are becoming *detached*. Parents of children in placement, including those who have madly fought their removal, sometimes visit less and less often and, after a matter of months, act as if the children no longer were theirs. We are learning to observe these phenomena to understand them better in our practice: we owe much to Bowlby's insights into attachment and detachment.

The attachment need seems operative in most reasonably normal people. In our university, freshmen are placed more or less at random in huge, impersonal dormitories. Nevertheless, they carve the mass into people-sized units. How are groups formed? Primarily, on the basis of sheer contiguity—"the fellows on the south end of the fifth floor." Before individual transportation became so matter of course in the United States, studies of marital choices used to find, touchingly (no pun intended!), that propinquity of residence was a major factor. I believe it was Mark Twain who remarked, "Familiarity breeds children."

The Fusion Fantasy

We have covered a number of theoreticians who have in individual ways remarked on the intense loneliness found among the emotionally ill. Spitz, Mahler, Fairbairn, Guntrip and Bowlby. Each with very diverse conceptual preoccupations. Yet, regardless of viewpoint, the encountering of yearning isolation demanded clinical attention and understanding. Of course personal qualities and the *Zeitgeist* affect individual sensitivity. Guntrip, for example, remarked that if Freud had not had such a schizoid cast to his own personality, he might have paid more attention to such feelings in patients.

> Freud said he employed the couch technique because he could not stand being looked at by his patients for eight hours a day.... He showed fairly clear signs of a resistance against the 'human closeness' involved in the kind of work for which at the same time he had such extraordinary gifts (Guntrip, 1961, p. 250).

None has focused the issue more forcibly than Hellmuth Kaiser. The Nazis gutted the middle years of his professional life, so Kaiser has left only a few posthumous writings (Fierman, 1965). He fled Germany to Majorca, was driven out by local Fascists, and went to France where he lived for many months under the Pétain regime, without papers and supporting himself by teaching figure-skating when he could. Having failed to gain refuge in England, he eventually escaped to Israel where, unable to acquire fluency in Hebrew, he made his living as a woodcarver. One wonders how much need there was for another psychoanalyst in that young, impoverished embattled country! After World War II, David Rapaport was sent on a mission to Israel to recruit Jewish refugees who were analysts to join the staff of the Menninger Foundation, in Kansas. The Foundation had received governmental support to train a large number of young physicians in psychiatry. Kaiser was one of those recruited. Most of the refugees had been living hand to mouth in Israel, but after some years in Topeka, they realized how cheaply they had been hired by American standards: most left for other settings. Kaiser, whose doctorate was in philosophy and mathematics, came to Hartford, Connecticut, where I saw him for analysis. Already an older man suffering from angina, he eventually moved to the warmth of the Los Angeles area where he died.

Kaiser was apparently always something of a loner, an original and critical thinker. Trained in psychoanalysis in Berlin before World II, he had not been long in practice as an analyst when he began to wonder what was "therapeutic" about what he was doing for patients. Conferences with senior colleagues were not reassuring, for he found they did not agree among themselves about which aspects of the complex analytic encounter were actually specifically geared to curing patients. The usual explanation, of course, had been that the cure depended on *insight*. When the patient was able to recognize consciously why he was doing what he was doing, he would lose the desire to do it. Yet, as Kaiser reasoned, to be capable of having an insight means the patient can now stand to be conscious of an idea or impulse that he could not tolerate before. This means that in order to have an insight, one must already be somewhat better, "a little bit cured," shall we say? Hence, Kaiser had a major question: Is insight the cause of cure, or one of its effects—a reflection of the fact that the patient is already somewhat better? And, if encouraging insight is not *the* specific in treatment, what is?

Having arrived at such questions while still in practice in Berlin, Kaiser continued to mull them over during his long years of exile from the work. As a person, he was tough, bright, engaged. The most helpful thing I found about treatment with him was that I had, this time, full permission to speak freely all I really thought, including my ideas critical of the treatment and the theory behind it. Rightly or wrongly, many of us in classical analytic treatment had the impression that if you did not "believe," you could never get well. Of course, this was nonsense since believing is not something you choose or refuse; you believe or you do not, just as you trust or you do not. With Kaiser, all such reservations were up front and if you were too polite to raise them, they came out anyhow. For one thing, disbelieving the whole theory can be an elementary intellectual form of resistance. What, then, did Kaiser finally distill?

Patients are lonely persons...even those who move in a circle of friends...are at least alone with their neurotic problems....
However painstakingly the patient may describe his symptoms to his wife or his friend, he will never feel completely understood; for good reasons: He cannot tell what makes it all so hopelessly complicated because he does not know himself. What drives him into the office of the psychiatrist is not so

much the realistic hope of getting cured as the wish to step out of his isolation. . . .

As long as the patient's interest in the therapist is not too intense, the patient can behave in an approximately adult fashion. When his interest increases beyond a certain limit, the adult relationship becomes intolerable for the patient. Closeness, as it is accessible for an adult, illuminates more than anything else could the unbridgeable gap between the two individuals and underlines the fact that nobody can get rid of the full responsibility for his own words and actions. . . . The patient tends to form with the therapist what one could call "a fusion relationship." . . . It is characteristic for transference behavior (or, in my terminology, for an attempt at a fusion relationship) that the patient is not really interested in communication (sharing of thought, feelings, experiences) but has to do things which create in him the illusion that there is some subterranean connection between him and the therapist (Fierman, 1965, pp. xix f).

Kaiser does not attempt a theory of personality, nor anything like one. What he offers is a rationale for his therapy, a theory covering just those aspects of mental functioning which seemed most crucial for effective treatment. Fierman has abstracted Kaiser's formulation about people with psychological disorders as follows:

The universal triad consists of the *universal psychopathology,* the *universal symptom* and the *universal therapy.* The universal psychopathology is the attempt to create in real life the illusion of the universal fantasy of fusion. The universal symptom is duplicity in communication. The universal therapy is the communicative intimacy offered by the therapist (p. 207).

Kaiser's work is memorable because he has traced out a series of defensive operations patients use to deal with existential loneliness. One might say, he starts with an "awareness of separateness" anxiety and then considers some neurotic ways of handling it which worsen one's existential condition. Each of us is, after all, an isolable biological unit. Each is born alone and will die alone. This truth is hard for most people to face, but for persons with certain types of emotional problems it is unbearable.

Detailing his observation on psychopathology, Kaiser sees a conflict ("the universal conflict") between recognizing one's aloneness and the need to deny it. "The struggle against seeing oneself as an individual is the core of every neurosis" (Fierman, 1965, p. 135). "Being 'an individual' entails a complete, a fundamental, an eternal and insurmountable isolation" *(Ibid.,* p. 126). What brings one's essential aloneness most forcibly to attention?

> Three mental activities—very ordinary activities, indeed—seem especially conducive to producing this fateful inner experience: first, and perhaps foremost, is making a decision; second, in reaching a conviction by thinking; and third, in wanting something.... Whenever the patient comes close to having it driven home to him that it is *he, himself* who is going to make a decision...a piece of delusional ideology rolls like a fog over the mental scenery, softening or even obscuring the lines of the picture.... Of course, what is necessary to make the inner experience of deciding, thinking or wanting so potent that it needs obscuring is not a routine decision expected and approved by the patient's environment" *(Ibid.,* p. 133 f).

The "universal" defense to which Kaiser points is what he terms the "delusion of fusion," the mental game that you and another are somehow connected—two bodies with a single mind. A lady in your office has been complaining about her husband's inattentiveness. "I love the movies, but he never offers to take me." Without thinking, you ask, "Well, have you asked him?" "No, of course not. If I have to ask him, that will spoil it." What would be spoiled: the fantasy that, "Since he loves me, we are as one, and he *knows* what is in my mind."

In writing about the obsessive-compulsive personality, I mentioned the need to feel forced, giving the example of the man who *"Has to* go to the great sale and buy a new suit." Why the *need to feel forced* by something bigger than, or outside oneself? In terms of Kaiser's theory, the feeling serves to help you obscure that recognition that *you* are choosing. And, in the long run, everyone does this all the time. Indeed, *not to act* is also a decision! Even inmates in concentration camps exercised choice: some chose death as the punishment for a quick act of defiance. Feeling forced also gives the person the feeling he is not alone. Someone, somewhere cares enough to look over his shoulder at what he is doing, and this is better than feeling totally on one's own.

The "universal symptom" is duplicity in communication—appearing to be involved in sharing ideas and facts, but actually being preoccupied with maintaining connection to your hearer. A whole chapter will follow illustrating how this mechanism appears clinically. But, the effect of duplicitous communication is usually to increase, rather than reduce, one's isolation. If, for example, it becomes terribly important to you that the other person completely adopts your opinion—so you can feel at one with him—you may argue so long that he never wants to see you again. Preoccupation with the impression you are making, quite as much as what you are honestly thinking, certainly does not make for lively, attractive conversation.

And yet, human speech may be the channel by which the greatest amount of closeness between adults can be achieved. No wonder we get the complaint, "The sex is fine; but, she never *talks* to me." (Not only women file this grievance.) To Kaiser the *universal therapy* consists in *helping the client stand behind his words*. In part, this emerges naturally from the therapist's example in making possible a relationship in which the equality and the autonomy (one's being in charge of oneself) of the patient are respected. In part, of course, it emerges from refusing to go along with the patient's fusion-fantasy as expressed in the interview. As in other analytically derived psychotherapy, one may from time to time use *clarification* and even *interpretation*—"You seem to mean you do not agree with me, but you are putting it in the form of a question."

Kaiser's method of doing treatment may be easily condensed, but not so easily described. There is a critical shrewdness in his approach worth remarking. After all, what behavior by a patient is most directly observable and most directly at stake in any talking treatment? The patient's use of the speech function. One can hear, in person, how it has been invaded by conflict and neurotic defenses. Treating the ego function of speech gives us a point of leverage by which to treat the whole neurotic structure. And as we have noted earlier, those able to talk directly and meaningfully put themselves in a position to achieve the degree of closeness realistically possible among adults. Such closeness may not promise as much fantasy of fusion, but it will not be as utimately disappointing, either. We cannot really fuse ourselves with others, but can comfort each other with talk against the darkness and the void.

In my experience, Kaiser's approach is an effective style of talking treatment for patients diagnosed as having many schizoid or borderline elements. Though a severely limited theory of personality, it has been used successfully in treating neglectful mothers with problems in these realms. Kaiser has made a signal contribution in at least one sphere. Freud said that the denial of one's mortality was universal in man. The denial of one's ultimate aloneness must be nearly as ubiquitous. Kaiser has given us the most complete statement of the various situations we find ourselves in—deciding, taking responsibility—that exacerbate the loneliness and awareness of separateness anxiety. And he has provided the most complete analysis of the various defenses people use to allay loneliness. Some of these make it worse (Polansky, 1980).

Kaiser's formulation refers to that "eternal and insurmountable isolation" which is Everyman's fate. Given that the reality is universal, one may expect to find at least some traces of the fusion fantasy in almost anyone. For example, the intolerance that cohesive groups show toward persons holding opinions that break the consensus may be traced to a need to sustain the unconscious idea that all are mentally connected, and as one (see Chapter 13). Yet, only a minority of people are obsessively involved in fusion-fantasy maneuvers. Why do they suffer more awareness-of-separateness anxiety than others? Kaiser was silent on this issue. He had some interest in characterology, but very little in historical causation.

The Lonely Children of Divorce
While Kaiser has given us a creative understanding of defenses against existential loneliness, a longer list can be made of the various ways people go about coping with loneliness in general. A rich lode of insights is to be mined from the writings of Judith Wallerstein and Joan Kelly on the children of divorce (1980). Wallerstein was trained initially in social work and later in child analysis; Kelly, in clinical psychology. They studied 131 children ranging from 2½ to 18 years of age from 60 families in Marin County which had recently been, or were in process of being, broken by divorce. Marin County is an upper-income San Francisco suburb, predominantly white with one of the highest divorce rates in the world.

The project had several aims. One was, "The teasing out of the intricate patterning of defensive, restitutive, and coping mechanisms employed successfully or unsuccessfully in response to the parental separation and the postdivorce family structure" (Wallerstein and Kelly, 1975, p. 601). Referred by lawyers, pediatricians and teachers, the children and their parents were seen individually for five or six individual clinical interviews in a preventively oriented planning service for divorcing families. All were followed up about one year later. Children determined to have had previous contact with a psychiatrist or psychologist were excluded from the study.

"Since 1962 there has been a 135% increase in the number of divorces. The steady rise in the divorce rate, from 2.2 per 1000 population in 1962 to 4.6 per 1000 population in 1974 is a national trend that shows no sign of diminishing" (Kelly and Wallerstein, 1976, p. 20). As a study of typical responses to be found among a segment of the community at large confronted by the same life disaster, the study by Wallerstein and Kelly is strongly reminiscent of Lindemann's (1944) classic paper on grief (see Chapter 4). These authors point out, however, that although reactions by children to divorce have often been treated in terms of object loss and mourning, more is involved. The missing parent—usually the father—is typically still in touch with the the child; divorce also induces other major life changes. Many mothers must resume full-time employment, for example, and the same menage must be run with one less pair of adult hands.

Wallerstein and Kelly were especially interested in how children respond at differing developmental stages. In their youngest sample, 2½ to 3¼ years, all nine children reacted with

> Significant behavioral changes, which included acute regressions in toilet training...increased irritability, whining, crying, general fearfulness, acute separation anxieties, various sleep problems, cognitive confusion, increased autoerotic activities, return to transitional objects, escalation in aggressive behavior, and tantrums...In the main, these children possessed very few mechanisms for relieving their suffering (Wallerstein and Kelly, 1975, p. 602).

So, despite the continuing presence of the mother, this group shows the full impact of the object disruption. Pain is very great because it is unbuffered by the ego. Yet, even at this age there are efforts at restitution, that is, replacing what has been lost through transitional objects and autoeroticism.

I have preferred to cut across the various reports of differential response in order to abstract the ego mechanisms that seem to have most to do with handling loneliness. Here then is a partial listing of the coping mechanisms identified, commencing with defenses commonly employed (see Chapter 3).

DENIAL

Denial may distort the actuality of, or the degree of the disruption. Very typically, it involves renunciation and splitting-off of the feeling involved "I don't mind; it's just as well."

REACTION-FORMATION

Sadness may be overlaid by a kind of manic, brittle cheerfulness. "Everything is just great." Tendencies toward immobilization and regressive disorganization may be countered by becoming galvanized into busyness and involvement in projects and structured extra-curricular activities. Through such participation, even fairly young children were seen to "provide themselves with needed supports and, in effect, construct their own support systems" (Wallerstein, 1977, p. 287).

RESTITUTION

The impulse to reinvest an object may be expressed as a regressive *neediness*, so that the child clings to relative strangers. I have observed that even generalized *negativism*, seen in patients whose impluse is to "Yes, but" every statement is another kind of clinging, for the loved person is kept actively in mind as a standard to oppose. Urges toward restitution also came out in fantasies (e.g. "My Daddy sleeps in my bed every night"). Some youngsters made efforts at reconciling their parents, all the more pathetic when the adults in the case were glad to be rid of each other. One workable form of restitution occurs in instances in which the departed father actually has a better, more loving relationship with his child after leaving the home. The father who unconsciously resented his child for tieing him into a frustrating relationship may change his feeling after divorce. And we have noted above that many children achieve some restitution by forming important relationships outside the family. From my sister, Adele Polansky, I have learned that many, many teachers are sensitive to the needs of the children and burdened mothers involved in a divorce, and make extra efforts to reach out helpfully toward them. So, realistic restitution depends in part on the readiness of the child to form new ties; it also depends on how lucky she is in her surroundings.

DETACHMENT

Adolescents were interesting in the way they used detachment to heal the pain of loss. It is the developmental stage where they begin to detach from their parents; but the divorce process actually speeded the developmental work for many and stimulated a surge toward growth and maturity (Wallerstein and Kelly, 1974). *De-idealization* of the parent is part of the expectable maturational process and it too may be hastened because divorce encourages the child to individuate his parents. So, the process may advance the adolescent's phase-specific effort to achieve a workable identity. One suspects, however, that whether detachment becomes addictive (because it works so well) and therefore generalizes to hinder attachments to new persons, or proves, instead, to encourage growth largely depends on how much anxiety is in the picture. As with *defensive progression*, detachment too far out of phase with development can prove crippling. That was how it seemed to us in the personalities of neglectful parents (Polansky, *et al.*, 1981).

MASTERY THROUGH REPETITION

The urge to repeat an anxiety-laden experience in order to "wear out" the anxiety will be remembered as an explanation for the recurring nightmares of childhood—and adulthood, for that matter. Children of divorcing couples may need to re-enact situations in which they became helpless and vulnerable, and this can become an additional impulse toward regression. At a later stage in life, the person who repeatedly makes but breaks relationships may also be in the grip of the repetition compulsion.

MASTERY THROUGH CONVERTING FATE INTO ACTIVITY

Closely related is the other generalized coping mechanism, described by Rapaport (1967b). Self-blaming by the child and taking responsibility for the divorce was often noted. Wallerstein and Kelly see its role just as we depicted it in relation to grief. "This loss could not have just happened to me; I must have had some control over what took place." Thus, the little girl or boy achieves a bit of mastery, but at the cost of creating a new source of guilt. "I had control but I let it happen." The ego's search for mastery also seems present in efforts made by some children to find a principle by which to explain to themselves what must otherwise seem an arbitrary disaster. Small children adopt a querulous, confused questioning: "Why? What goes with what?"

COGNITIVE RESTRUCTURING

Some youngsters on the other hand were able even in preschool to develop a fairly good understanding of the divorce-induced changes in their lives, and this seemed to help. Not only did this lend to the experience, a *meaning* which Frankl (1963) has elevated to the status of an ego need (see Chapter 14); it must also have provided a map from which predictions could be made, which also added to feelings of mastery. While the ability to verbalize feelings of sadness and longing is ordinarily regarded as useful for advancing one's realistic restructuring of his map of the world, Wallerstein and Kelly did *not* find that the preschool child's ability to verbalize necessarily prognosticated better adjustment a year later.

WITHDRAWAL

As with the defenses in general, the distinction between coping and defense mechanism is partly a matter of how avidly and rigidly the maneuver is pursued, and partly of the purpose served. Withdrawal in the younger preschool children usually seemed pathological. But, a number of adolescent children simply distanced themselves from their parents' struggles in a way that, at least for the moment, seemed to alleviate pain and forward growth. Similarly, the ability to "take distance"—which we have seen as essential to accurate self-observation—also proved useful for children in their attempts to get a realistic handle on what they were facing in their parents.

As always, it is hard to determine whether the happy choice of a mechanism protects health, or healthy people are more likely to use the coping mechanisms available to the ego in effective ways. In any event those engaged in family counseling will obviously want to read and reread the work of Wallerstein and Kelly in the original. Their study has been drawn upon here to illustrate the point made by Kaiser, from another vantage point. Life repeatedly injects loneliness into our lives unbidden; but more chronic loneliness is self-imposed. The persistence of efforts at adaptation into later life stages where they do not really fit may interfere with the effort to remain involved with people, and to cure loneliness after it has been visited on one by the ill luck of the draw. These are persistent mechanisms which, in fact, subserve the "dread of love."

Motivations for Keeping One's Distance

By way of a quick review, let us now put together what various theoreticians have told us about the reasons behind clients' taking distance, fleeing closeness. At least, my phrasing of their contributions. In each case, I will present what the patient seems to be saying from the viewpoint of particular theoreticians:

Mahler: "As we get close, I lose track of where you end and I begin; I cease to exist. Let me out of here."

Klein: "As I get closer, I get angrier at you. So, let's not get involved and end in a tangled mess." Also, "As I get close, I fear you will hurt me."

Fairbairn and Guntrip: "If I come close, I will devour you. Please stay away from me for both our sakes."

Bowlby: "As soon as I start to love you, I can already foresee how bad I'll feel when we break up. So, leave us not get started."

Kaiser: "I'd rather have the delusion that we are as one, which cheats me, than to give it up for the limits of a real relationship."

A Note on Theory

We have now reviewed a series of theories of object relations. I included them all because, in my opinion, each offered insights somewhat different from the others. Klein and the Fairbairn-Guntrip pair teach us about the instinct of aggression and its vicissitudes; Mahler, Bowlby and Kaiser, about separation-individuation, about separation anxiety, about the dread of separateness. It is fair to wonder whether these various conceptions could not somehow be synthesized into one unified theory.

The task is not easy. Take, for example, the matter of depression following loss of the object. Bowlby suggests that the depression is one of a series of instinctual reactions following loss of the object, along with anger and anxiety. Spitz, who encountered the same issue in the 1940's and identified *anaclitic depression* followed the classical formulation in explaining it: orality, incorporation of the object, loss of the object, oral aggression directed at the object, guilt anxiety, anger turned against the subject (the self). Bowlby's formulation of an instinctual response seems much more simple and direct. Why not simply adopt it? Well, consider which is actually more parsimonious. Other problems to be explained require we assume an instinct of aggression; many observations make us aware that there is guilt involved in most depressions. If one assumes, with Spitz, that even a young infant is capable of guilt, one can get by with just these concepts adding nothing to the theory to explain anaclitic depression. But if one adopts Bowlby's idea, one adds to the theory another form of anxiety, and another instinctive response. This is not what we mean by parsimony!

Why then have I assumed two forms of anxiety thus far? Consider the possibilities. A type of anxiety often mentioned has to do with situations like this: the young man is sensitive about being short, and erects defenses against realizing it. What is the nature of the anxiety? It is hard to find guilt in this picture; no one is being injured and therefore likely to retaliate, symbolically or otherwise. It is more credible to presume he is anxious about being *unlovable* which, to the human infant, portends death. We can think of this as *separation anxiety*. A further idea occurs. Is not being *rejected the ultimate punishment?* In other words, does not guilt anxiety come down to separation anxiety? A case can be made, as Bowlby makes, for presuming the latter form of anxiety is the *primordial* form of all anxiety. We can confront this now. But if I had begun with this more complicated notion in the second chapter, the person new to Freudian theory would have had a nearly impossible time understanding the conflict theory of defense, and the conflict theory of neurosis as they were being presented at that point. Freudians assume that there is one form of anxiety, that it *signals danger*, and that is has something to do with being overwhelmed. But they do not follow Bowlby's reasoning, cogent as it is.

In short, whoever attempts to integrate the theories of object relations with the main corpus and biologically oriented sides of psychoanalysis faces an extremely difficult task. There are those who have attempted it, but the efforts I have read thus far have been marked more by obsessive rumination than elegance in formulation. So, we shall have to live this way, for the time being, lacking a more satisfying synthesis. Freud never promised us a rose garden.

CHAPTER 10
A SPEED READER'S GUIDE TO
On Duplicity in the Interview

Having covered the major conceptions of ego psychology, we now make theory explicit by showing how it applies and illuminates events in practice.

Duplicitous communications in the interview, the saying of one thing while meaning another, may have utility to clients. Forms of duplicitous communication may be divided into maneuvers to *evade responsibility* and maneuvers to *maintain control* of the conversation. Both are in the service of the *fusion fantasy*. Penetrating these *neurotic invasions* of speech also exposes the need for fusion. But, in so doing, the worker offers the solace of an honest, caring relationship.

"Helping the patient stand behind his words," Kaiser's pithy guide to talking treatment, sometimes involves a complicated process. It helps to know about the rest of ego psychology in order to carry out Kaiser's prescription.

On Duplicity in the Interview

10

Our major means of professional helping, the face-to face interview is the most important arena for skill in treatment. Adept interviewing is the *sine qua non* of expert casework and psychotherapy. Accordingly, one would expect a very large number of books and articles on its theory and technique, but actually the literature remains limited. It is hard to write about interview tactics. Its skills and guiding principles are probably best imparted and learned in relation to concrete experiences. Broad generalizations about "how to interview" are often ludicrous, teetering on the knife-edge that divides the high- from the simple-minded. After some years in practice, it is discouraging to reread an essay touted to the pious as a classic admonition in our field. How profound was the advice to the earnest young student, "Start where the client is!" Is there a choice?

Most of what any worker has learned over the years is property owned jointy with his age-mates. So another reason for hesitation about writing on interviewing is the opinion of one's friends. Who, then, has the *chutzpah*, the temerity to synthesize joint knowledge for us all? I am encouraged to set down some of my own observations in the hope that they may stimulate further dialogue with others.

The theoretical context for the present chapter was given above, in the discussion of Hellmuth Kaiser's formulations about the origins, expressions and preferred treatment of neurosis. In Chapter 12 we will pursue related theory, showing that *verbal accessibility* is a character trait, reflecting and causing effective ego-functioning. In this chapter we will look at verbal *in*accessibility and client efforts to communicate and mask communication at one and the same time. In other words, we shall illustrate partially blocked communication, and lay bare some of the motivations lying behind such efforts. Following Kaiser (Fierman, 1965, pp. 54ff), we characterize such speech as representing "duplicity" in the interview.

Duplicitous speech, however, is not the same as silence. The latter represents, obviously, an extreme form of blocking and may conceal thoughts and impulses that are hostile to a psychotic degree. Silence in the interview is of less concern to caseworkers than it is to psychoanalysts (Zeligs, 1961). For one thing, we are not often in relationships that will survive massive resentments. In fact, it may not be advisable to attempt casework treatment that seems so powerfully threatening and anxiety provoking as to precipitate a stubborn refusal to talk. Such a frozen response is almost certainly out of all proportion to any realistic threat, and so it may well sound an ominous warning of a deep depression or a psychosis thinly covered by the client's unresponsiveness.

Duplicity in the Interview
Kaiser does not explicitly define duplicity. He prefers to illustrate what he has in mind through examples, parables, the device of the dialogue. This form of European *Gemütlichkeit* may be the only way to convey a conception rich in apperceptive mass, but some American professionals find the style discombobulating (Higgins, 1966). Therefore, I submit my own definition.

There are two related features of verbal communications that we call duplicity. First, the same words are made to serve two purposes, even as they are being spoken—purposes, often at right angles to each other, or even directly contradictory. Thus, the client's overt intention is to describe his situation to the caseworker. But the clarity is substantially dissipated by the need to evoke a particular feeling response, even as he gives "facts."

The second aspect of duplicity derives from Kaiser's comment that the speaker does not appear to "stand behind his words." The speaker does not seem all of a piece. A psychiatrically naive client once commented that he felt "fragmented," and this was certainly reflected in the convolutions of his speech. Often, after one points out the manner in which a client has presented himself, he will say, more in relief than rancor, "I have long felt myself a phony."

I am very well aware that some of the examples of duplicity I shall give have usually been put in other contexts. Speaking in an illogical or seemingly irrational manner may be ascribed to a structual defect, such as "looseness" or "scatter"—which can represent organic damage, among other things. It is by no means my intention to imply that such interpretations are always incorrect. However, I have often found a mode of speaking that seemed at first to reflect the esssential thought disturbance was *actually within the control of the ego* and being used defensively.

Two main defensive functions are likely to be subserved by duplicity in communication. They may be labeled *maneuvers to evade responsibility* and *maneuvers to retain control.*

Maneuvers to Evade Responsibility

The overt task of the client in the casework situation is to contribute his share to a purposive conversation. Any leading themes in his motivations or defensive needs are likely to become noteworthy in the way he goes about speaking. I am indebted to the paper by Enelow (1960) for recognizing that the client's problem in assuming responsibility will show itself as a desire to evade responsibility *for his own words!* But why should he wish to do this?

Enelow summarizes concisely the stakes for the client. In order to "stand behind his words," the person must have evolved an image of himself as an independent entity, expressing what *he believes.* But the assumption of an explicit identity implies that acceptance of his *aloneness,* a basic experience for everyone which continues to frighten some of us throughout life. To cope with this awareness-of-separateness anxiety, Kaiser postulated that neurotics entertain a *delusion of fusion.* The client who cannot bear his separateness will maneuver to create this illusion in real life. In the interview, this will come through as an attempt to create a situation as if the client, and the worker, were somehow blended into a larger whole. He will imply that he is moved not by his own motivations but somehow as an extension of the caseworker or someone else. Indeed, so strong may be the fusion fantasy that the client may prefer to see himself as "forced," so long as this means someone else is taking responsibility, even if his response to this, in turn, is to feel put upon, and therefore indignant! Below are some illustrations of how this duplicity is visible in action; several were drawn from Enelow, the rest are from my observations in interviewing.

1. Creating a situation in which one is *asked to speak.* The client begins an account of some happening presumably relevant to what he is doing with the caseworker. Unaccountably, he trails off

into silence in the middle of the tale, until the worker says "So?" or "You were saying?"

2. Being *unable to speak first.* The client is silent, needing the worker to "Make it easier" for him to talk. Easing his way usually consists simply in the worker's saying something, thereby taking responsibility for the conversation's beginning. Related to this decision reluctance is inability to choose a topic—e.g. "Tell me what I should talk about."

3. Offering *conversational bait.* This consists in beginning a story, proceeding to a critical point, and then asking, "Guess what happened?" Beyond the dramatics, the aim also is to get the worker to say "Tell me."

4. *Surfing on someone else's conversational wave.* The same client who at first finds it difficult to choose a topic on his own may yet finish the worker's sentences, from the middle.

5. Administering a *conversational* Rorschach. The prime example is the client who mumbles in a inaudible voice. He appears to be speaking, but does not wish to commit himself by enunciating clearly. It is as if he were saying, "I offer you some clues. Interpret them as you will, and then respond to what you think I said."

6. Skulking behind the *declamatory question.* "So he made me mad. Wouldn't anyone be angry?" In this claim to universality, the client announces that he does not want his reaction questioned or discussed. Why does he not simply say so?

7. The *optional pass play.* This client demonstrates a kind of verbal doing and undoing such as the worker last encountered in the writings of classical philosophers—except that our offices seem not quite the place for Kant. He uses the device mentioned earlier, "I'm a man of firm convictions, one on each side of the issue." Greedily retaining all options through his indecisiveness, he plays it safe. The worker is then enticed either to clarify for the client or at least to be the one to insist that he clarify where he stands.

8. Coming on *pilgrimage to the oracle.* The client watches the worker's face with an expectancy that hovers between the worship of a Beatle fan and the deathwatch of a hopeful heir. He has an intense desire to find agreement or support for what he is saying; indeed, he will cheerfully reverse the *words* he is using to achieve this. But of course he will not ask for this outright. "If you really loved me, you would know what I need."

9. Putting *one's foot in another's mouth.* The client offers a selected quote from uncollected thoughts. "My husband said you're not fit to sleep with pigs, but I pled your case." By adroit tactlessness,

the client lets the worker have the bad news, while simultaneously setting up friction with a third party.

10. Taking the *loyalty oath*. This client, evidently without any sense of doing something unusual, consistently refers his opinions to some outsider. "My father always said...." "My husband told me...." More sophisticated, somehow, is the version, "I was brought up to believe...," which leaves open the question of who now does the believing for the speaker. Manly, and felt as suitable, but completely analogous is the statement, "Where I come from, they say...."

I have described these operations as if they were consciously thought out and devised as traps for the unwary caseworker. In my experience the client who employs these devices usually is selectively inattentive to them and quite unaware that they play a role in his interview behavior. Not only the intent but even the style of the maneuver may be unconscious.

Maneuvers to Retain Control

We are all familiar with the client who has to take over the interview process, lest we fumble it. Yet, when one asks colleagues why clients do this, ideas about it are rather vague. The client is said to be a "controlling" person, or he expresses an infantile will to power, as if these were fundamental givens in the personality, with further analysis unnecessary. The strong desire to control the interview also serves defensive purposes, in most instances. What are some typical dynamics?

One reason a client may constantly have to structure every relationship into a power hierarchy, with constant jockeying for position, is the associations he has to the issue, "Who is the stronger?" After some help, it may become evident to client and worker that the former is *contemptuous* of weakness, in a rigid, merciless way which derives, I imagine, from the scrupulous distinction he makes between the "good mother/bad mother" images. But recognizing his contempt may come easier for him than registering his *fear* of being weak. For to be weak is to be vulnerable, according to the formula, "If you are the stronger, you will be able to walk away and leave me." Hence, there may be a need to dominate (as to infantilize) those in his environment, in order to escape the ultimate catastrophe of being left alone.

Another reason he struggles to control the interview is that in his way of living, he is constantly *comparing*—himself with others, others with others. With this client, one will sooner or later come to a recognition of a deep sense of inadequacy not to be mistaken for the core of the disturbance. The question is why the client has not come to terms with what he has to work with, in himself, so that he can go about the business of getting what he can out of life. To tell such a person he has to "love yourself before you can love others" is to talk nonsense, for he is already quite adequately engrossed with himself. Rather than saying he is in love with himself, it would be more accurate to say that he is in love with an *image for* himself. Indeed, he is addicted to polishing the image.

In many such persons, we find a history of having felt *detached*, as a result of the mother-child relationship. The child, perplexed by this, feels somehow odd, not as others, even not quite human. Therefore he takes the only way out he can think of: if he acts like others, he gradually should become one with them. Although this home remedy is understandable, as life works out it is ill-advised, for the problem of detachment persists. In the struggle to be human, rather than a piece of waste, a "nothing," there is an intense intolerance of criticism, along with other symptoms, such as pre-occupation with matters of *shame* and *blame*. This concern with "Have I dirtied myself?" is occasionally confused with guilt by younger workers. The client will welcome such mislabeling of his preconscious feelings for defensive reasons, even though he has not internalized others' standards to a degree that would make guilt meaningful in his case. But with fear lest something unexpected come out—which he hopes for, but dreads—the need to maintain contol of the situation is of course heightened.

These dynamics will usually be found in constellations, over-determining the inability of the client to conceive of a relationship between equals, and one in which neither is in danger of being absorbed by the other. The attention and motivated cunning he devotes to one-upmanship in the interview signals the concealed anxiety.

With this as general background regarding the impulse to control, let us turn next to some typical, by no means mutually exclusive, examples of how this pattern may play out in the interview.

1. *Circumstantiality:* This hardly needs discussion as a method by which clients succeed in dominating the interview. Talking at length, with tedious attention to emotionally neutral details of the environment or events, the client keeps the conversation in his own mouth. He avoids having to face questions he would not like to consider, effectively shuts off comments he would not like to hear, and so forth. A frequently cited characteristic of the voluble

client is that he engulfs the hearer, surrounding him with amoeba-like pseudopodia. The connection with living out the fusion fantasy is obvious.

2. *Planned adolescence:* Sometimes related to compulsive talking is a flightiness that makes it hard for us to catch what the client is trying to get at. If the worker feels confused, it is always possible that this was the client's intention, and the main thing to be understood from his talk. Perhaps the client cannot afford to be too logical; if he were to think in a straight line, he would find himself drawing conclusions he would rather not face. Similar comments apply to the related tactic of presenting oneself as a "good little girl or boy" but incapable of sustained thought.

3. *Speaking in pronouncements:* Another maneuver, similar to circumstantiality but less markedly controlling, is for the client to conduct his side of the conversation as if the worker were an audience. Although presumably having come for help, even after a few interviews the client still almost never asks a question! A typical reason for not asking is that the client is not sure s/he will like the answer. Hence s/he may go as far as to comment, "Now I know what you'd say...." With others, the avoidance of questions is related to the obsession with perfection. There is fear (unconscious of course), or hating to have to ask, for this is an admission there is something one does not already know. I frequently have found that this pattern was already established during the school years, and partly accounted for the client's unwillingness to raise his hand in class.

4. *Turning in homework:* The lecture to the caseworker may go better if the speaker has his notes in hand. Many clients think about what they want to discuss (or talk about?) in advance of their next appointment, some to the extent of preparing written memoranda. This step presents problems because the carryover into life outside the office hour is a desired indication of the penetration of the casework. However, we must bear very much in mind that preliminary work usually includes preparation for what is *not* to be said as well. Because I believe in the importance of helping the client express himself directly, I am most reluctant to deal with written communications. The practice (to save time!) of having the client *write* his autobiography is potentially destructive.

5. *Escape into love:* This maneuver does not require much commentary, except to emphasize that "transference" does not begin to describe the way such feelings can be used. The extreme form, in which a client actually seduces a therapist (the latter usually

thinks it was his idea!) is typified by: "How can you ask me to talk about all this unpleasantness in myself, when you're a boy and I'm a girl?'" Another version, less sexualized is: "I did not tell you, because I did not want to hurt you." Escape into love is used for defensive control as well as to cover the hostile phase of the transference.

6. *Escape into hate:* This gambit has been reported less often than escape into love, but it certainly is used. With great difficulty, for instance, we get the client—who has been dropping pretty broad hints—to say, "I guess I don't really like you." As we indicated in Chapter 8, there are a variety of reasons for this feeling which, I must emphasize, is experienced as quite real. In the present connection, however, I want merely to point to its use as a lever. The implication is that the caseworker should now watch his step and try to get into the client's good graces. This is similar to the schizoid adolescent's remark: "I don't trust you." It is not possible to meet the demand for a guarantee of course, nor is it conducive to the youngster's reality testing to imply that trust is gained from discussing it intellectually. So long as we are being as straightforward and dependable as we can be, we should guard against giving up our own independence of action To do this will destroy "trust" on a deeper level, for the client will recognize it as either weakness or a cheap attempt to seduce him for obscure purposes. With a bit of exploration, it usually comes out, anyway, that such a youngster feels unable to trust anybody—and this is the real problem.

7. *Invidious comparisons with one's predecessor:* There are a number of functions served by discussing one's relation to a previous worker. The one I want to emphasize is the use of such a description as an indirect way of prescribing one's own treatment. In telling us what he did and did not like about the former treatment, the client also lets us know what he prefers. Of course he may have a point when he obliquely criticizes us in this way, but why not bring it out openly?

8. *Passive resistance:* In addition to the desire to evade responsibility, the use of passive control is another good reason to employ the "tell me what to talk about..." routine.

9. *Coercive tears:* Some tears are sad, and some are mad; and the fundamental mission of anger is to move the environment into line with one's needs. It is sometimes terribly hard to tell what lies behind a client's tears, but there is no doubt they often interrupt a painful line of thought, distract both worker and client, make us feel unaccountably guilty, and so forth.

10. *The hard sell:* This familiar mode of relating is the client at his most dramatic and convincing moments. Except that a little voice within us complains, "Methinks thou doth protest too much." Super-salesmanship is identified with the ill defined group we call hysterical personalities (of both sexes). However, as in escape into love, it is easy to overlook the defensive controllingness that lies behind the dramatics as behind the sexiness.

11. *The great debate:* Litigiousness is pervasive in many people who will argue whether this is really true of their behavior. The function it serves, for some at least is to counteract the sense of emptiness and nothingness; in "standing against" they feel suddenly more sure of themselves, more of a piece. A person with such needs will manipulate the caseworker by arguing, to argue.

12. *Mea culpa:* The extreme form of this self-recrimination is often found in an agitated depression that has reached hospitalizable proportions. My caricature of the sequence is: The client acts as prosecutor and files a list of complaints; he sits as a judge at the trial, ruling on admissibility of evidence; as jury, he hears the case in hostile silence; finally, as defendant, he pleads guilty—to the wrong charge! Nothing bossy about all this; nobody mad at being crossed by life.

13. *Self-derogation:* We could devote an entire chapter to the various functions of "running oneself into the ground." The client may be making himself a mess, to spite one of his parents, or both; indeed, he may be caricaturing one of them, as in male homosexual "camping." "Look what a ridiculous thing you are, and have produced." He may be warding off demands for achievement (which he exaggerates). "From whom little has been given, little can be expected." Frequently he is wincing against expected bad news about himself by keeping the process of breaking it in his own hands. Or he may exaggerate his defects because he does not want clarity or self-definition. The non-committed outline he maintains (for he does not believe the bad things he says of himself) is, in turn, useful for two other purposes: he can maintain a secretly vaunted opinion of what he would be like if he ever *tried*; and the indefiniteness of his self-image facilitates the process of losing himself in some other—the fantasy of fusion. Obviously, the last thing the worker can afford is to be provoked into reassurance, in the face of all this complexity!

14. *The structured use of time:* I am convinced that long before the Rankians decided to use the time dimension in structuring casework treatment, clients did (Taft, 1933). Think how the end of the

hour can be used. Painful material may be delayed until then so that not much can come of it. Important decisions, which the client wants to make a gesture of having "discussed," but does not really want to, will be introduced with the remark, "I did mean to ask you today what you think I ought to do about...." The other possibility, of course, is that his "material" is offered as an enticement to delay the ending of the hour, which the patient finds painful, as he does any separation experience. Out of the same concern, by the way, he may break off the hour prematurely, unable to stand having separation imposed; "You can't fire me, I quit!" This type of reaction is noteworthy, as it may well signal the way the client precipitates other endings in his life. This familiar dynamic reflects itself in the interview.

All clinicians probably can make a list similar to this one. The patterns are labeled "maneuvers." At this point, it does not yet matter which we see the more frequently. We are still at the stage of specimen collecting in which to be able to say that a given pattern *did* occur, and to begin to ascribe its function, is quite enough. Quantitative issues may be relevant later. Hardly any of the maneuvers cited will be found to be used *only* in the service of a defensive need to control. But our task was to select those patterns for which this is at least one of the motivations. Finally, there is the obvious question whether the list would not profit by further grouping, or extending, in terms of a deeper grasp of ego functions involved. I believe this will prove true, but at this stage of work we should be wary of a premature lumping to conclusions.

Handling

We have seen a variety of ways in which duplicity is displayed. At one time or other, each of us undoubtedly uses one or more of these maneuvers, for reasons similar to our clients. The dread of loneliness is a universal anxiety, and the delusion of fusion a position to which any of us might fall back, more or less persistently. The question that naturally follows, therefore, is: What should the worker do when faced with these maneuvers in an interview?

We have to judge whether, after unveiling the fears being concealed, a less crippling way of dealing with them is likely to be found. How necessary is this defense to the client, at this point? Will our relationship bear the strain? While one might routinely note the peculiar forms of duplicity being employed, as part of continuing diagnosis in all contacts with clients, in a good many instances noting them may be all we can do. Nevertheless, our theory encourages an activist stance. For a client, or anyone else, to cling to an illusion of one-ness is a poor substitute for true closeness to fellow humans on a more mature basis. It neither heals nor satisfies. Kaiser postulated that whatever helps the client talk more directly and honestly in the interview is a step toward better emotional functioning, and this is certainly true in my experience. Rather than recounting the contraindications to intervention, I list some situations in which a caseworker might find it worthwhile to try to penetrate duplicity.

The most obvious is when the client has come for help with a problem he sees as in his own functioning, or with an important interpersonal relationship marred by how he operates as a person. The worker may have to try to dissolve such patterns in seeking to establish, or reestablish, communication within a family. Distortions or blocks in communication are frequently stepped around in contacts concerned mainly with "environmental manipulation." Yet, from work with prison inmates and transient men, for example, many of us have long concluded it is all the more important to get down "to tacks" as quickly as possible in such cases. So long as the client is keeping us, and himself, in the dark about his real wishes, and his chances, our conversations toward joint planning will be farcical. Often, until we can get the other person to stop his double-talk, at least momentarily, it is well nigh impossible to get any case history on a relative. We must also confront the fact that there are instances in which the caseworker's willingness to accept the client's indirection is a potentially noxious side effect of his "tact." Even in routine calls on recipients of AFDC, for example, acceptance of evasion in place of honest talk can only contribute to an image of weakness and insincerity. At some point, collusion in an evasive conversation becomes corrupting.

Assuming, then, that we want to do something about breaking through the duplicity, what do we do? Kaiser gives us only a very general picture of the principles he found useful, and I do not believe they are a quite accurate image of his own *modus operandi* (Fierman, 1965, pp. 158f). Here are my own general principles and some specific techniques.

1. Because much duplicity reflects the client's fear of experiencing his own separate identity, anything that helps the resolution of the confusion or noncommitment will be a step toward greater verbal accessibility. The obverse is also true: one can treat *identity diffusion* in part by trying to help the client commit himself about what he means.

2. The worker should try to watch for *duplicity* in his own talk with clients. While we may not find it strategic to verbalize everything we happen to be thinking, we should try to be sure we can stand behind what we do say. This kind of behavior by the worker offers the client a role model out of which he may incorporate greater directness of speech. There also appears to be what Jourard and Landsman (1960) termed a *dyadic effect*. It is harder to maintain duplicity with someone who does not play this game (e.g. a literal ten-year old).

3. Insofar as possible, the caseworker should aim for plain English, regardless of the social and intellectual status of his client, and expect it in return. This means the clichés of the slums are quite as open to the comment "I don't get you" as is the argot of the professions. While it is not really necessary, as Heywood Broun once commented, to "call a spade a dirty, lousy spade," verbal shock is not routinely to be avoided, despite it dangers.

4. In common with Enelow (1960), I have found that an easy way to get through several forms of duplicity in clinical interviews is simply to ask the client to fill you in with concrete details and specific facts, especially when these seem to be evaded.

5. Requesting clarification works very well with perhaps a voting majority of clients, and often leads to greater commitment on the part of the client. For example, I do not believe it useful to say to the client who makes opposing statements about the same thing, "I see you feel two ways about. . . ." Rather, one might recall with him the statements, ask him which one he means—or does he mean both? For the worker to label his ambivalence for him provides no challenge to the client's synthesizing ability. By the way, I find very few instances in which a client will lie outright to me, and in pushing for clarification, it is sometimes helpful to say openly that this is not what one has in mind.

6. In a large number of cases, the inability of the client to be verbally accessible derives from his intolerance of imperfection in himself. If he misrepresents his feelings, it may be hard for him to "take it back"; instead, he wastes effort repairing the old statement. There are many rigid persons who *over*value the spoken word, for they see it as a product of themselves. They may feel it necessary to act upon whatever they have found themselves saying even if it was only part of what they felt. (This represents a danger in the technique we are describing.) Hence, the issue of being able to admit error is often worth reviewing. It seems quite appropriate for the worker to comment at times that what he has said does not

fit what he meant to say—something that will come hard to the know-it-alls of our mental health professions.

I am aware that these remarks sound as if I do not believe that slips often—perhaps, usually—directly reflect the unconscious. I do, of course. Once again, however, I would urge that there may be other motivations in addition to the one revealed in a slip, and that to "stand behind one's words" one must take them *all* into account. To assume routinely that the "slip always represents the true feeling" is both oversimplified and pedantic.

7. The need to aim for precision of expression has been mentioned. How can it be implemented? A client often deals with an issue that is chronic and repetitive. If the worker has to keep pointing out the same thing, he must try to do so in a different way in successive interviews. The aim is to avoid getting trapped in one's own word-ruts, whose sounds gradually lose impact for client *and* worker. A second device is to substitute figures of speech for abstractions. The best example which comes to my mind is to contrast the color of the direct translation from the Hebrew of a pastoral people, with the generalities in the sermon of a recent divinity school product. "The Lord is my rock..." vs. "Are we dedicating our lives to the eternal verities?"—which means that some people in this congregation will steal from the poor. Interpretation by parable also works well, but requires ingenuity.

Finally, there is the question of using examples from one's own life. Here the dangers are that one will either imply that "to do as I do is to be normal, healthy and virtuous" or reveal too intimate facts that will deeply color the relationship. I often find it useful to comment on how I am feeling *at the moment*, in the interview, as a way of "reflecting back" effects of the client's behavior on me. Occasionally vignettes from one's own outside life may be useful, but they have to be used with discretion. However, freedom to reveal one's feelings *in the present interaction* may serve a role-model function for the client, as it does for the group in group therapy. Obviously I take a dim view of trying to exploit the "dyadic effect" (Jourard and Landsman, 1960) by talking much about oneself in casework treatment. The dangers from one's own exhibitionism far outweigh the presumed gains: as I see it the whole maneuver is clinically too sloppy.

8. Euphemisms are frequently as revealing, and filled with duplicity, as are clichés. "I have this little problem with weight" may mean, "I'm a greedy slob." Depending on the timing in the relationship, and whether the client has *yet* shown visible signs of

a sense of humor (most do, as they improve), the self-serving function of wood-pussy language often can be depicted simply by echoing it, with a slightly questioning tone. To join the client in euphemisms is not helpful. Worse, it can prove unnerving, since the client (who has some sense of what he is doing) may wonder how dangerous or disgusting the symptom is if the worker, too, must circumvent it.

I could add to this list, but it grows long. Besides, the more criteria one lays down about how to be verbally accessible, the more impossible it becomes to say anything at all. After all, an obsession with being "honest" such as adolescent clients proudly wave at us, can become as inhibiting of freedom of speech as it is of assembly. I like to say that the older I get, the more I will settle for at least a decent hypocrisy in my fellow man. Does not our hypocrisy have a right to spontaneous expression, too?

This chapter has dealt with a single aspect of client behavior as experienced in the casework interview. A form of blocked, or partially defended, communication has been identified which, following Kaiser, we have termed *duplicity*. In the present context duplicity is a pattern, which is ultimately a defense against the fear of experiencing aloneness. Two categories of maneuvers have evolved—maneuvers to escape responsibility and maneuvers to retain control—and examples of each were given. Finally, some suggestions were made regarding modes of operation by the caseworker that may prove useful in helping the client overcome his tendency to use these defenses, momentarily or as part of a more pervasive life pattern.

We offer this as a contribution to the conceptual formalization of casework technique, on the molecular level of skill in the interview. It relies heavily on the insights of Hellmuth Kaiser in psychotherapy, but seeks to specify them and relate them to the casework process. In so doing we have tried to make vivid for the reader an arena in which the various concepts of ego psychology find intensive and fruitful application.

CHAPTER 11
A SPEED READER'S GUIDE TO
Ego Functions in Psychodrama

Moreno's psychodrama presented an attractive treatment modality supported by *ad hoc* theorizing. How might one conceptualize the processes involved in the terms of ego psychology?

In line with the *repetition compulsion*, patients show a need to reenact conflictual relationships from the past in current living. However, the recapitulation is usually unconscious. *Psychodrama* provides a setting, at once real and unreal, in which remembered scenes can be acted out and contribute to insight and clarification of present patterns. The therapist and fellow patients also try to help the patient *resolve unfinished business* with key objects by dramatizing happier endings.

Action may enrich communication in therapy by promoting both *ventilation* and *insight*. *Transitory regressions* occur; *unwanted identifications* are exposed and sometimes ejected; childish remnants may finally be integrated into the more mature personality. Hence, this modality is helpful to a good proportion of patients a fair proportion of the time, which is all that can be said for any of the psychotherapies.

Ego Functions in Psychodrama

11

Nearly all trainees in case work or psychotherapy can typically tolerate receptivity for only so long. Sooner, rather than later, they break in with "This is all well and good, but what do I do?" At that point, I tell them what I was told in my time. "In order to do, one must first understand. If you fully understand, the question of what to do is easy." Of course that is not completely true, and they know it, and I know it. The jump from analysis of what is wrong to deductions about how to repair it does not happen automatically. Besides, the learner can understand only so much at any one sitting before he feels the urge to try it out on somebody, if only to retaliate against the instructor for telling him hard to swallow things about himself. Perhaps it is as well that this is true of those destined to be practitioners rather than simply knowers in our fields. If their defenses were so organized as to permit endless immobility and analysis, it might not be safe for their clients and patients. Art is long, and science is eternal but, as Lord Keynes reminded us, "In the long run, we shall all be dead." Certainly, it is important to move as rapidly as possible from knowing to doing. The question, is "How rapidly?"

This is not a "how-to" book. Nevertheless, despite deliberate limits on applications, it has seemed useful to mention treatment techniques, as regarding the management of duplicity. Techniques serve to illustrate how the ego operates; much of what I know originally came from my own attempts at treatment. For these reasons I think it appropriate to introduce a few examples of ways to apply what we know about the ego.

The last chapter offered an application of ego psychology to the process of the interview. It would be profitable, next, to show how the theory works in some form of group treatment. Our topic will be psychodrama and the ego mechanisms and functions that become most visible when treating emotionally ill people. We shall see again the varied ways in which *communication*—verbal and nonverbal—can take place, how it may be used in the service of defense, or harnessed to the service of therapy. We shall also comment on the *self-observing functions of the ego*, varieties of *identification* including some which are unwanted, and deliberately *induced regressions* whose aim is the furtherance of treatment. The material in this chapter has been revised from a paper written with Elizabeth B. Harkins.

Psychodrama is a powerful modality in the psychotherapies which has not had the widespread application its potentialities warrant. Few prestigious psychiatric facilities maintain ongoing programs. Although many mental health professionals have had at least some exposure to the technique, it is treated as if it were expected to be a passing interest. One is embarrassed in some circles to confess to a fascination with psychodrama extending over a period of years.

One seldom finds psychodrama approached with the combination of hopeful curiosity and scientific skepticism that has served to develop social casework and psychotherapy to their present stages. Our view is that the method is neither a panacea nor a nullity. It is a mode of treatment that can be helpful to a good proportion of patients a fair proportion of the time—which is about all one can say about any of the psychotherapies.

We arrived at this appraisal despite considerable initial dubiousness. There are, understandably, a number of reasons why the method has not gained more popularity. Most of us prefer a method of treatment grounded on a well developed general theory of personality, such as the psychoanalytic. As a movement psychodrama seems fixated at a curious professional phase: a promising technique has yielded new insights into human personality; its enthusiasts are trying to erect a whole theoretical metropolis along these few avenues of vision. "Psychodrama's scientific roots are buried deep in Moreno's philosophies of spontaneity, creativity, the moment, and theories of role and interaction" (Yablonsky and Enneis, 1956, p. 149). It is not necessary to accept all of Moreno's metatheory to avail one's patients of the benefits of the technique which he and his co-workers have done so much to develop.

Other factors have inhibited the spread of psychodrama. For one thing, its demands are incompatible with the character defenses of many individual therapists, thus violating their preferences even more than group therapy. It requires interpersonal energy, moment-to-moment inventiveness, and occasional controlled flamboyance in a measure not all of us have. Because of the spontaneity necessarily involved, the therapists are open to intensive group scrutiny. Even the intensity of nonverbal communication released in the group is uncomfortable for therapists who like to hide behind abstractions.

The psychodrama situation involves a focal patient (the *protagonist)* embedded in a group situation. At its best, it is lively and complex. Only a megalomaniac would presume to have all strands of the individual and group process under observation, much less precise control. It is necessary to take calculated risks again and again. Finally, psychodrama is a technique that can drain the worker; he grows tired and resistant to conducting sessions after six or more months of continual working, especially with hospitalized psychotics and character disorders.

Despite these drawbacks, we persisted with this mode of treatment, trying to improve our skills in its use and to better understand its rationale. We were mature practitioners at the time, more impressed by new results than new formulations. Our persistence came from the knowledge that from time to time exciting results were achieved with some patients who were left untouched by interview treatment.

An example occurred early in our experience. I had in inpatient treatment a twenty-year-old young man who had been admitted after having been found in the basement of his home in a confused state, with blood streaming from his forehead, which he had lacerated by beating his head against the basement wall. In the hospital, the confusion cleared rapidly, but he settled into an extremely passive, superficially amenable young fellow with a firm, schizoid grasp on futility and no recollection of the events preceding his admission. He described his mother as extremely hostile and verbally hypercritical; her indifference toward him and her general self-centeredness were also evidenced amply during his stay. A marked characteristic was his massive affect inhibition. He was taken into psychodrama with the hope that this would stir something in him, but here, as elsewhere, he continued his plan of sitting life out.

One day we proposed he enact a scene. He suggested nothing specific, of course, but accepted the idea that it might be useful to show how he related to his mother. He told the group about her verbal temper tantrums and assaults, and proudly announced that he had developed a method of simply not hearing her. Mrs. Harkins assumed the role of the mother, and began a tirade, to which the patient showed no reaction, at first, but he finally admitted unease. We continued, nevertheless, and I fell into the role of "doubling" (i.e. speaking out what I imagined might be the patient's thoughts) from behind him. Because his individual therapist was speaking, the meaning to the patient was all the stronger. As the scene continued, it suddenly occurred to me that the picture of stubborn resentment of the mother which had been expressed repeatedly in individual treatment did not fully account for the patient's anxiety. Still *verbalizing for the patient*, I asked, "How can you be so mean to me when I love you so much?"

The impact on the patient was startling to all of us. He pitched forward from his chair, sobbing like a small child in a blend of anger and despair, and *beating his forehead against the floor!* Concerned lest he harm himself, it was all I could do to wrest his glasses from his face, and then gradually hold him and quiet him, reminding him that he *was* in a hospital, I was there, and no harm would come to him.

Naturally the group was upset, and several other patients were also crying, but we resisted our impulse to isolate the protagonist at this point. Taking him away would be even more frightening to the group. Then and there, we had a brief discussion when he felt better. For the first time he recalled that: (a) he had severe temper tantrums throughout his early childhood; (b) there was a favorite place on the dining room baseboard where he had butted his head at such times; (c) he would sob to the point that he had "asthmatic attacks." None of this had come out in the history given by the patient or by his parents. Neither had he been willing to know that what made his hatred of his mother so upsetting was the fact that he also loved her. Of course the episode he had just enacted was a replica of the scene with his mother which led to his hospitalization in the first place.

This excerpt from a long treatment process illustrates what can possibly occur in psychodrama: communication at the level of action and imagery; massive ventilation but also clarification for both therapist and patient; regression in the service of the ego for therapeutic change; and ultimately, rather sudden emergence of repressed images and feelings. We were impressed by the continuity of psychodrama with other forms of analytically oriented psychotherapy—as is apparent in the varied therapeutic functions performed as well as in the common conceptual formulations applicable.

The peculiar features of this modality which we emphasize are: (1) If one views communication on a developmental continuum moving more or less from action, through concrete imagery, to abstract symbols, psychodrama is characterized by the unusually broad spectrum it can employ in the course of a single session. (2) Psychodrama makes possible communication in rich detail; this facilitates maximum reintegration of ideas and affects by the focal patient as well as the emergence of new clarifications and insights not otherwise reached. From this detail and breadth—including the primitiveness—of its communication the special advantages and dangers in the use of this method flow.

In carrying out our intent, we first note a similarity of psychodrama to the other psychotherapies. Provided one has talent for it, psychodrama is easier doing than teaching; and it is easier to teach than to analyze.

Structure of Psychodrama in Our Hospital

At the time of these observations, Highland Hospital was a private, general psychiatric hospital of about 120 beds. The professional staff consisted of eight psychiatrists, one clinical psychologist, and seven social workers. Our hospital had a tradition of a strong activities department, which made it suitable for patients requiring longer stays and for young patients. Median length of stay fluctuated around four months.

Historically, psychodrama was initiated in 1962 at the behest of the former Clinical Director, Dr. John D. Patton. The program was conducted over the years almost entirely by members of the Social Service Department, although this has been more a matter of interest than an exclusive policy.

Most of those in psychodrama were inpatients. However, we did have a number who, following discharge, continued to attend sessions as outpatients. We never established any strict criteria about which patients to include, other than the opinion of the individual's psychiatrist that he was likely to "get something out of it," and was currently in reasonable contact. We accepted patients with a highly experimental attitude about selection. It would be fair to consider the treatment population a typical inpatient group not currently severely disturbed.

The format of our conduct of a session followed rather closely that described in the fundamental papers by Moreno (1958) and Yablonsky and Enneis (1956). To quote the latter, "Psychodramatic therapy has five essential components: the group, the subject or *protagonist*, the psychodramatist or *director*, his therapeutic aides or *auxiliary egos*, and a system of methods and techniques adaptable to the requirements of the situation" (p. 150). We did not feel committed to their structure from the start. Rather, we found no good reason for major shifts from their design. We always operated in ordinary large rooms, with the patients seated either in a half-circle or in the round. Props were adapted from the objects in the room—with card tables, folding chairs, ashtrays, and a couch perhaps offering the greatest flexibility. From experience, we believe we would be uncomfortable using a raised "stage." As to specific techniques used, we either followed methods cited in the literature or created new ones, sometimes out of ignorance of others' work. However, several features in our situation appeared to differ from the main trends in published reports.

First, we did not believe that psychodrama can, by itself, effect a "cure" of a seriously neurotic or disturbed patient. All our patients were simultaneously in individual psychotherapy. We tried to have events in the psychodrama coordinate with and feed back into the individual work, where they could be dealt with more intensively under circumstances of greater therapeutic precision and control. Second, our patients were simultaneously receiving a variety of other treatment, including group therapy, the protection of the hospital environment, participation in organized activities to promote resocialization, and often chemotherapy. Therefore, we thought it desirable to be specific about what we wanted to do in psychodrama to add something different from the other therapies.

One consequence of this appraisal of the technique as frankly *ancillary* was our view of verbalization. We did not favor providing the focal patient, or protagonist, with still another setting in which just to *talk* about his problems. Rather, psychodrama was seen as the place one begins by *externalizing* one's feeling and images, with acting and in action. We made practically no use of the device Moreno called the "soliloquy," in which the protagonist stands before the audience and holds forth about his feelings. Even during the "warm-up" phase of a session, we were constantly on the alert against the patient who seems to want to "talk the thing to death." This is despite the fact that we *do* accept as a major goal in psychodrama as in other psychotherapies helping patients switch to more verbal-conceptual modes of expession.

> One highly intelligent (and exceedingly verbal) woman had managed to "talk herself out of treatment" with her individ-ual therapist for several months. Naturally she tried the same method in psychodrama which had worked so well for her in other settings. We learned, almost by accident, that if we could stop the flood of words and return to the thought she had mentioned *first*, before she began to "undo" it by her usual flooding, the episode that was portrayed in psycho-drama was meaningful for her and was then available for her use with her individual therapist.

The tendency to talk in abstractions rather than to come to grips with one's feelings is a facet of what is often called *intellectualizing* in treatment. It is of interest, therefore, that intellectuals seem to take so well to psychodrama, perhaps because of the phenome-non pinpointed by Malcolm Muggeridge: "As Cervantes showed so splendidly centuries ago, the intellectual longs for the excite-ment of action as eunuchs do for the excitement of sex" (1969, p. 76). In any case, we did not typically have much difficulty explaining the usefulness of the technique to patients who were, otherwise, verbal and intelligent people.

Particularly with younger patients who made a fetish of their pervasively doubting attitude, we proffered the program in pro-saic, nonevangelistic terms. Frank discussion of how psychodrama works can be helpful in "loosening" the group and focusing their interest. We did this when new members were assigned; the repe-tition also served as a review for ongoing members. We often acknowledged with the group that a particular episode or scene seemed to have accomplished nothing more for the protagonist than that he tried to do something before a group. We reminded them that this is indeed *drama*, and we must take a half *play*ful attitude toward it. Such a reminder lightens the mood of the group and helps free them to experiment.

We preferred to have about twenty patients assigned to a group, expecting to average fifteen attending any one meeting. From expe-rience, we dreaded situations in which one staff person must try to handle the entire situation, because of the need to observe significant clues to "audience" responses and the possibility of an upset. On the other hand, a group can be weighed down with too much staff. If active, they reduce the likelihood that patients will have an opportunity to participate. If passive, they encourage patients to stay on the sidelines, by their example. We preferred three staff members present.

Nor were *auxiliary egos* drawn only from staff. Being asked to play the role of another patient's mother or father was often as useful to the helping patient as to the protagonist. This is the more possible with groups that operate continually and over longer periods of time. There is then always a cadre of patients with experience who can, should, and do step into auxiliary ego roles. Our groups met weekly, for sessions of one and one-half hours each.

The Aim in Each Session

Insight is not seen as the major goal of psychodrama, but rather the ability to become spontaneous, that is, to make new perceptions of old situations, or at least to reorganize old cognitive patterns in such a manner that new and more adequate responses are facilitated (Yablonsky and Enneis, 1956, p. 159).

This seems to us one possible goal of psychodrama. Quite a number are possible with this extremely versatile modality. The goal in each session is a step to the ultimate goal: therapeutic change. What one aims for in a given session may depend on how intact the protagonist is, for example, how ambitious one may be in reaching for true insight, verbalization, or merely role play and communication through gesture. In the remainder of this chapter we will discuss some of the uses to which psychodrama may be put, each desirable with certain patients at an appropriate phase in treatment.

Psychodrama has something else in common with the other psychotherapies. Each is essentially a beneficent structure in which change has an opportunity to occur. The expertise in therapy consists, then, in exploiting the most promising targets, of opportunity which the patients and the group present.

Psychodrama for Affect Discharge

We noticed early in successful sessions the depth and intensity of feelings expressed by the protagonist and others. The discharge involved exceeds what we are able to elicit in the office interview, in both rawness of affect and primitive gestural communication.

A somewhat paranoid young mother sat frozen and silent through a number of sessions. Invited to participate, she finally decided to demonstrate to us what a weak, contemptible person her husband was, and why she could not bear the thought of returning to her marriage with him.

She chose to illustrate his mealy-mouthedness by showing how he acted at a family gathering. This finally came down to a particular incident at dinner at her family's house. From experience, we believe that the impact is likely to be the greater if we help the patient recreate the situation in as real a way as possible. Therefore, I asked a number of questions about who would sit where, at table, how each family member behaved toward her, and the like. The patient portrayed her father as a dictatorial, pompous, self-made man, who ordered his construction workers around in a roaring voice, and carried this over to his home life.

Although the episode was to have shown her husband's style, the patient instead became engrossed in a verbal battle with her father, which became so intense she seized a knife as if to stab him—an actual gesture she had not recalled until that moment. From observations, it appeared that this family battle was partly engendered by rivalrous feelings toward a sister who knew better how to handle the father, and was favored by him.

The episode became so unruly that the patient "left" amidst tears and recriminations, which she then turned against her husband in the car driving home, because he "did not come to my rescue." However, after all this discharge, the patient seemed less rigid, if more openly anxious. She was softer in manner and more open to discussion.

In the subsequent group discussion, three themes were stressed: that she equated hardheadedness and bellicosity with "strength"; that she felt more secure and integrated in the midst of such an outburst than at most other times; and that she was contemptuous of the man she had chosen, originally, to be different from the unreasonable father—whom she actually tried to emulate. Of course, we do not know that the real man, her father, was the same as the way she had us depict him, but seeing herself as trying to be like that image left her shaken but elated. Two weeks later, she told the group of a satisfying weekend with the husband she had wanted to divorce because he would not give her a decent fight!

This vignette can be used to demonstrate a number of principles. We point first to a few things that seem to *augment the primitivism of the affect* likely to be elicited. First, it is most important to be sensitive to details in the scene the patient envisages. Such elaborate re-creation makes it all the more vivid to the protagonist; it also makes it more possible for the auxiliary egos, staff and patients to warm up to the situation. Second, the affect discharge frequently is the result of relaxing usual inhibitions. The latter is unquestionably facilitated by a process of *behavioral contagion* from auxiliary egos, who demonstrate less conflict and fear expressing strong feelings before the group than the patient would have felt appropriate. We exploit the dynamics of behavioral contagion, as described by Redl (1949b) and Grosser, Polansky, and Lippitt (1951). Finally, expression in action increases reintegration for the patient of the more primitive affects.

So impressive were such episodes that we began to think of psychodrama as perhaps *the* specific for treating affect inhibition. Yet, as in other psychotherapy, one recognizes sheer ventilation is not enough, and that feelings expressed strongly are themselves often defensive maneuvers. We also noticed the discharge that occurs most unequivocally and "honestly" overemphasizes one range of feelings—the hostile, spiteful, or embittered ones. For a long time we wondered whether this was due to something in us that was being communicated, or to our sampling of patients. After all, severely neurotic people are not sick on love. More recently, however, we came across a passage by Anna Freud which suggests that the limitation in range of affect may be due partly to the treatment situation we create. Discussing the analytic treatment of children she notes:

> While free association seems to liberate in the first instance the sexual fantasies of the patient, free action—even if only comparatively free—acts in a parallel way on the aggressive trends. What children overwhelmingly act out in the transference are therefore their aggressions, or the aggressive side of their pregenitality... (1965, p. 30).

Miss Freud does not offer an explanation of why there is a differential impact on content from freedom of speech versus free action, and of course she is contrasting children in play therapy with adult therapy. Nevertheless, it is stimulating to have so related an observation from a person who has been working with a markedly different patient population. Time will demonstrate whether she has suggested the nucleus of a more general law.

There is a group of patients for whom the use of psychodrama as an arena in which to ventilate primarily bitter and angry feelings is most in evidence—the young men and women with personality disorders and problems in the schizoid spectrum.

One appealing sixteen year old had to be hospitalized after developing severe symptoms involving phobias, withdrawal, and a loss of reality testing. Even after she had settled to a point where she was attending classes once more, she continued to be extremely negative toward her parents, hating to visit with them. She finally asked to enact a scene with them, and did so, decanting a little of the rage and disappointment which poisoned her attitude toward them. Here, as elsewhere, we looked for what was obviously not being expressed, since this could be at least as meaningful as what was. It became apparent that if she only despised her parents, as she claimed, it would be hard to understand the discomfort she felt about them. We surmised that she must also love them.

To this the patient agreed, with relief. However, what now came out was that she was unable to enact even a fabricated scene in which she expressed any warmth toward them. No wonder they seemed rejecting! Then we learned that the problem was more general—she could not let a boy know she liked him, either, which *was* a problem; she could not even say "Thank you" without feeling hypocritical.

This syndrome was familiar to us from individual treatment of such youngsters. In this setting we handled it by engaging her curiosity and desire for help. We set up a short series of playful vignettes; in each, she was to say something warm to an auxiliary ego, while her fellows in the audience gave her immediate feedback on how she sounded, using role reversal, mirroring, and group discussion. The protagonist alternated between being deadly serious and, fortunately, amused. At the end, I teased her a little, but then sympathized with how hard it must be to fear closeness while starving for it. I complimented her on how far she had been able to move against her pattern in one session. Later, as I was getting into my car, she dashed up to me with a determined look on her face and whispered, "I like you." All I could think to say was,

"I like you, too," before she was off like a frightened doe. It was one of those unforgettable interchanges which keep us alive as caseworkers and therapists.

We see enacted here the schizoid dilemma about closeness with some resolution occurring. Adolescents often beautifully illustrate that when one exploits the psychodramatic situation to bring about *ventilation*, the feelings put forward are but the beginning of the unveiling process. Resistances operate here as in all the other psychotherapies. Generally, ventilation is not enough, in part because the feelings being expressed with the least equivocation are still at some distance from what is troubling the protagonist most.

Especially because of the phenomenon noted by Anna Freud, we must recognize that the expression of hostility may be *overdetermined*. It may be a response to the potentialities of action freedom, and a favored defense, in which one substitutes anger for the deep sense of loneliness and despair that accompanies admitting one needs others. Conversely, psychodrama has worked well in our experience with constricted, overly moralistic, middle-aged patients who must deny their all too apparent anger because it is not "Christian" or "polite" to acknowledge such feelings. Even when such a patient cannot allow his anger to be examined, there is frequent evidence of "spill over" as he plays an ancillary role or simply as he takes vicarious pleasure in the protagonist's free expression of his anger.

The experienced therapist becomes aware of a number of dangers in the use of psychodrama, just because it *can* be so powerful a tool. Obviously, when one encourages ventilation the cautions against premature uncovering that apply in other therapies are also relevant. I have already commented on the tendency of rigid people to premature closure in their thinking, once they have blurted something out. "If I said it, that must be what I think." The idea of standing behind one's words is not that literal! Because sessions involving ventilation seem so vivid and genuine to all concerned, staff must be especially on guard against accepting what is *currently conscious* as the whole story. Further exploration of what gets expessed is in order. Protagonist and group may have to be reminded of the need for discussion with their individual therapists of ideas that come out in psychodrama.

One is advisedly cautious with the patient still shaky after a severe breakdown. The most important protection for the fragile patient is his ability to prevent himself and the others from hitting on the things most troubling to him. But at times the staff may have to guard his defenses against too rapid interpretation from the other members of the group.

On the positive side, the use of psychodrama for affect discharge appears to have the following advantages: (a) It affords the patient an experience of self-disclosure in an accepting, noncriticizing environment; (b) the availability of action-channels helps some patients make a gradual switch to verbal-conceptual expression, meanwhile heightening their verbal accessibility; (c) there is frequently a reduction of tension, during which phase the protagonist is more accessible to clarifications and interpretations; and (d) an episode concentrating primarily on catharsis or ventilation may provide an opportunity to move into new integrations, and uncovering of the unconscious.

Clarification and Insight

In common with other analytically oriented practitioners, we use the terms *clarification* and *interpretation* with specific meanings. By *clarification* we refer to the process wherein content that is conscious or readily available to consciousness is brought into a new configuration for him. This may involve relating previously isolated elements, or it may require giving more emphasis to a fact than the patient or client prefers to give it. *Interpretation*, on the other hand, refers to proffering to the patient something we believe to be unconscious. In the office, nearly all interpretation is necessarily verbal-conceptual; in psychodrama the possibilities are extended. The client or patient may be said to have an *insight* when something previously repressed becomes conscious.

The goal of psychodrama cited from Yablonsky and Enneis is certainly that of facilitating clarification. And it fits comfortably with a background in social casework, as this is the level at which caseworkers are accustomed to operate. It is not that their clients do not have insights, but rather that they do not make interpretations to try to hasten them. Nearly all experienced psychotherapists expect insights to emerge from a steadfast process of clarification at the conscious level as a matter of skillful technique.

In Highland Hospital, brief leaves at home were a frequently used therapeutic measure. Many patients anticipated how such leaves would be through preliving them in psychodrama. A once regressed schizophrenic girl who had shown marked improvement was anticipating a ten-day visit at home. Her relationship with her parents had been manipulative, but when they fell into her trap she panicked. In projecting her arrival at home (in three different ways) she found herself trying her same old tricks, and again experiencing the familiar feelings of anger and panic. When her simulated parents remained firm she felt more comfortable. Discussion after these scenes brought out the fact that in all probability her parents would not be firm, as they had had no help in this area. She then decided that if she wished to avoid the old feelings *she* would have to be the one to change her tactics.

Much of the literature of psychodrama deals with various techniques involved in bringing about clarification for the patients involved. It would be redundant to add to it, beyond confirming that we too find the method valuable for this purpose. What we should like to do, however, is mention a few observations we have not found elsewhere.

As must be visible in the vignettes already given, there seems to be a fairly regular sequence in a large proportion of those psychodramatic episodes in which the protagonist has really "caught on." Although the protagonist may say he wants to understand a situation, it is not unusual for him to launch into the scene on a wave of *catharsis*. If we ride along with him, more and more facets of his problems are revealed as he seeks *tension discharge through re-enactment*. During subsequent group discussion there often follows a phase of considerable clarification. Sometimes this is hammered home for the protagonist by another patient's redoing the scene, while he watches from the audience; at other times the protagonist accepts the group's verbal appraisal of what he has been doing. Although he might have sought to avoid knowing what he knows quite well, it is rare that what is discussed up to this point has actually been repressed and is truly unconscious. The session may end at this point, with an attempt either by the focal patient or the psychodramatist to pull things together. Or it may continue into questions of *why* the patient behaves as he does. It is not at all unusual, then, for the process of clarification to be capped with a true insight.

This is a familiar sequence, as we noted, and we have learned something about how to try to bring it about. At the same time, remember that clarification is not the only way in which insight can occur. Very often it issues out of an intensive emotional experience in the course of which some defenses are no longer sustained, or become unnecessary. No interpretation may be involved in the usual sense, but the auxiliary egos may have pushed through intuitively to a preconscious or an unconscious level—just as I did in telling the mother, "I love you," in the first illustration.

An extremely important aspect of the process of clarification is helping the staff obtain a fresh and vivid view of the patient's psychodynamics in a way that may alter a case formulation previously taken for granted. This seems to follow from the greater richness of detail and the concentration made possible by re-evoking a scene and giving full play to the spontaneity of the participants.

> The protagonist was a twenty eight year old woman, married, the mother of four children. She had been hospitalized after a long siege of ill defined somatic complaints, followed by a period of withdrawal, loss of interest in herself and the children. Her difficulties seemed to revolve around her demanding, childish husband. Her inability to deal with him, in turn, derived from her childhood fear of her father. So she decided to show us how things were "when daddy came home...." The idea was for the father to come storming into the house, while her long suffering mother and the children cowered and hid to avoid his wrath. As we often did, however, we asked her to show where each sat, what her siblings' reactions were like, what her mother said, and other remembered details.
>
> The first thing to emerge was that *she* was not actually frightened, for somehow her father never picked at her. He reserved his outbursts for her brother. Although she felt guilty, she also felt relieved, and "special" that the latter should bear the brunt of the old man's irritability. The second clarification came when the person playing her mother asked how she was to act. "Oh, you hear him coming in the drive, and you tell us all to be quiet and come into the back room where he won't see us." It became evident that the mother, who had always seemed somewhere between a victim and a nonentity in the patient's descriptions, actually played a significant, manipulative role in the family. She effectually shut the father out of the family circle, making him feel a stranger in his own home. It seemed now more understandable that he should flaunt the mistress for whom he finally left the mother, and leave home every evening, even though he faithfully supported them all!

When the second facet was brought out—in this instance by the Director—the patient offered a third, related clarification. "This is what *I* often do with my own children, when my husband comes home, although he loves the kids, and certainly never abuses them." Neither the *need to be special* nor the extent to which she seemed determined to relive her mother's life tragedy had ever before become so visible to me as in the first ten minutes of this playlet.

It was possible that this drastically revised vision of events would eventually have emerged in her individual therapy. Our point is that in this instance the psychodramatic situation brought about cognitive restructuring for the therapist rapidly and convincingly, and was a major contribution to the individual work.

Dealing with Unintegrated Internalized Objects

A protagonist in psychodrama frequently becomes aware he has been emulating a person he thought he despised. Psychodrama, in common with the other therapies, can be used to facilitate normal integration and release the patient toward achieving a workable sense of *identity*. This is especially desirable among hospitalized patients, many of whom have markedly schizoid features and represent *borderline personality organization*.

Sometimes this lack of awareness that they have been modeling themselves after a person they claim to dislike seems to reflect *splitting*. Kernberg formulates this as a primitive operation in which the original inability of the infantile ego to synthesize has in later life become rigidly active in the service of defense (1966). When splitting is involved, the acceptability to the protagonist of the other person may vacillate wildly from session to session. In one session mama was all good and daddy was all bad; in the next, mama was the bad one.

A somewhat more mature patient reveals another mechanism behind the contradictory behavior in which he acts like someone while declaring that he always wanted to be diametrically different from that person. Complexities have occurred in the processes of introjection and identification. By *introjection* we mean the taking in of an idea or image so that it becomes part of one's self. *Identification* refers to a more elaborate process. Speaking generally, it refers to the sequence in which some personal object, to whom we have been exposed, is made part of our image of ourselves. We seldom completely model ourselves after *all* of the other person—as tiny Sam Shubert is said to have done with the admired actor, David Belasco. Typically, we have *partial identifications*, in which we take on one, or several, facets of the object's personality and make them part of our own.

For example, the late Gordon Allport was my tutor at Harvard, and I regard him, still, as more or less my intellectual "father." I should have liked to emulate his humaneness, scholarship, and breadth—together with the position he so long occupied in our field. But I came to reject his self-proclaimed eclecticism because I have never met a man who was not fanatic about his theory who ever came up with a striking idea. And, of course, the preciousness of Allport's speech at the interval of his life when I was exposed to him now appears to me ludicrous, as eventually it did to him. Which is not to say that I did not, for a long time, lay claim to vestiges of a Harvard accent.

I give this bit of autobiography to illustrate both the degree to which identifications may be piecemeal and the extent to which unwanted fragments of the other person may become part of ourselves along with those we cheerfully choose in our youth and continue to like—in ourselves—in our maturity. The most familiar example of this kind of self-rejected identification in my experience was from mothers who came for help about their children's difficulties. Often a mother would tell me how much she had hated her own mother's controllingness and had determined "to treat my children different." I recall one such mother I saw as a young caseworker. Interspersed among her remarks about how important she felt it was to give a child leeway were angry shouts at her son to stop what he was doing, smile at the the nice man, and so forth.

Most cases are not that obvious; unconscious identification with mothers is often masked. The woman determined not to be rigid and controlling may be nondirective with her child. So far does she lean over backwards not to discipline the child, or tell him what to do, that we cannot escape the conclusion she is fighting tremendous impulses to be a managerial, smothering woman. Her misreading of Spock is actually a reaction formation. Otherwise, why be so rigid about it? Why not leave the child alone, at times, and discipline him at other times, depending on the realistic needs of the moment?

The awareness that she is acting the mother she had so much *not* wanted to be comes as a blow to such a woman. We must point out that her mother was, in fact, the only model she had, when she was a baby, of what it is to be a woman. Her copying took place when she was so young she could neither be aware she was doing it nor pass mature judgment upon the person she would later choose to be.

In psychodrama we sometimes discover that *unwanted identifications* not only have occurred but also have become *idealized*. A mother's querulousness and petulance are more than picked up: they are invested with the value that that is how women *ought* to be; they are admired; they become ego-syntonic.

Because life's vicissitudes mix in fragments we want to keep with fragments which, as adults, we no longer can accept, we may have *unintegrated internalized objects*. One's *bête noire* may be unmasked playing privy councillor to a self-ideal. Psychodrama is peculiarly apt for the exploration of such object relationships. All episodes involve images of significant others in the patient's mind. "The dreamer dreams the dream": all these representations are part of the patient. In this sense it may not be too important to know—as we shall never know—whether the father and mother were as they are described. The essential fact is that the idea the patient has of each is, itself, real, even if it may later change.

A middle-aged female patient recalled her mother with abhorrence. Unable fully to communicate why, she finally asked to enact a scene in which she proposed to show us the sort of person her mother was, by taking her role. As the scene progressed, she entered in with great gusto, presumably caricaturing the attitudes and mannerisms in her mother which she found so distasteful. When she had finished, however, a group of women with whom she lived in the hospital burst out with one voice, albeit not unkindly, "But, X, that is you!" The patient had already noticed it.

It is usually not possible within the psychodramatic situation alone to puzzle out the origins of introjections or *why* the patient appears "to struggle against identification" in the particular instance that may have come to light (Greenson, 1954). The aptness of psychodrama, rather, extends primarily to bringing the identification to consciousness through evidence difficult to re-repress. More precise exploration of the leads turned up becomes the task of individual therapy.

We have found two techniques that work well to help in the clarification of such problems. Frequently, while the patient earnestly searches his case history for reasons for his lack of success, the answer lies in patterns and mannerisms right at the surface, of which he is aware but does not want to look at too directly. Hence, we can use direct confrontation or *mirroring* of his mannerisms. It is seldom possible in individual casework or psychotherapy to bring his presenting defenses so vividly to the attention of the patient. Preferably, of course, this should be done in an accepting atmosphere and with a light touch.

The other technique we call "exploiting the ripple effect." The term is from Kounin and Gump (1958) who studied the effect, on other children in a class, of witnessing the teacher's manner in disciplining one of their members. A psychodramatic episode necessarily evolves around the imagery of the protagonist, as our case examples illustrate. However, we regard it as extremely poor technique to permit the postepisode discussion to degenerate into a one-to-one "treatment encounter in the presence of a group." Optimally, the episode portrayed should be discussed generally, first by those directly involved as auxiliary egos, and then by as many others as wish to join in. The psychodrama serves as backdrop for a fruitful group therapy session.

An episode's impact on the audience is of major concern. One or more patients in the audience will have identified with the protagonist. Sometimes they volunteer, "This is what happened to me"; more often, a staff member becomes aware of their strong response and draws them into discussion. Their empathy will have shown itself unconsciously mimicking the focal patient's facial expression; it may also come through in evidence of discomfort. Signs of strong identification with the action often indicate that a patient who has never paticipated is now ripe; these are clues to timing.

Despite their individualities, patients have much in common. Thus it is often possible to involve several in a single session, each of whom is trying to show us how he experienced his parents, or something that happened in his life which came to mind during the previous episode. When we are lucky, one scene builds upon the previous one, as patients teach each other—and us—dynamics.

It is not unusual to find patients who have a need to "perform" and be on stage center but who are also so well defended that no matter what they do or how hard the therapist may work with them, they always succeed in defeating any real action. One patient managed to frustrate us all, in scenes she had asked to try, by her constant interruption of them and her insistence that we were not playing the scene as it should be done. This she did in spite of her inability or unwillingness to give her fellow actors any real clues about their roles. If any suggestion was made as to the significance of a given scene, her stock answer was "Yes, but—." This pattern continued for several months. Then she observed another patient engaged in the same kind of maneuvers. She became irritated with him and suddenly realized she was reacting to her own behavior. She talked about this freely and expressed eagerness to try another scene, herself, to determine whether she could avoid a repetition of her old pattern.

Because patients want to participate for diverse motivations, a proportion of the volunteering simply communicates, "You have been in the center of the stage long enough. Now it's my turn."

One hysterical adolescent greeted a variety of scenes with quiet but somehow ostentatious tears. If staff became too engrossed in the protagonist to pick up on these immediately, she was apt to ask to be excused from the audience. Otherwise, she succeeded in becoming immediately the center of attention in the group, pulling the rug out from under the patient we were presently trying to focus on.

Even if the motivations for vicarious involvement are mixed, useful results come from the ripple effect. A thrilling experience with this technique is a session in which waves of clarification seem to spread outward from the protagonist and auxiliary ego until all but the most obtuse patients somehow have found new integrations from being present in the group. Not all the responses, by the way, involve identification. Sometimes it is recognizing role complementarity. Thus, following a scene in which a younger patient showed his disappointment with his parents, a middle-aged woman burst out, "I wonder if that is how my son feels about me?" After years spent in coddling her character neurosis, even this much recognition of her son's needs represented progress. The dynamics involved in the ripple effect are the same in group therapy as in psychodrama. The advantage of psychodrama lies in part in its not being so confined to symbolic communication, but being able to use childlike levels.

Transitory Regressions

Often during an episode the worker has the impression that what the protagonist has been evoking is but one of a series in his life, in accordance with the *repetition compulsion*. Consequently, the psychodramatist may follow by saying, "I believe that what you have just portrayed was not the first time something like this happened to you. Does something similar come to mind from when you were younger?" A fair proportion of the patients will indeed recall an earlier scene whose relevance may not at first be so apparent. Thus, defiance toward mother in the teens recalls the battle of the table as a preschooler. But when the patient tries to demonstrate the earlier event, she finds herself unable, often because of an inability to unbend. They fear that if they permit themselves childlike behavior, they will not find the strength to give it up. Given the tenuous hold many have on maturity, their wariness is understandable. Yet, do they really have so much to lose? Their rigidity derives from the fact that they are really *pseudo-mature*. We feel it might be helpful to regress a bit, in a momentary and localized fashion, in order to move forward on a sounder basis.

We arrived at this conviction about attempting therapeutic *transitory regressions* from experiences in psychodrama, but the idea is of course familiar among writers representing various schools of thought. Moreno has always recognized this process as a key element in psychodramatic therapy. "The persons play themselves... as they did once out of necessity in self-conscious deceit, the same life again...they re-experience it, they are master..." (1946, p. 28).

Heinz Werner, a developmental psychologist, points out that "an organism, having attained highly stabilized structures and operations may or may not progress further but if it does, this will be accomplished through partial return to a genetically earlier, less stable level. One has to regress in order to progress" (1957, p. 138).

Winnicott presents a more complete, highly provocative rationale for the analyst's participation in regressions for therapeutic reasons. He makes a number of cogent distinctions with respect to the types of regression encountered in clinical work and between types of fixation.

> One has to include in one's theory of the development of a human being the idea that it is normal and healthy for the individual to be able to defend the self against specific environmental failure by a *freezing of the failure situation*. Along with this goes an unconscious assumption (which can become a conscious hope) that opportunity will occur at a later date for a renewed experience in which the failure situation will be able to be unfrozen and re-experienced, with the individual

in a regressed state, in an environment that is making adequate adaptation possible (Winnicott, 1954-55, p. 18).

Winnicott's referent is, of course, the psychoanalytic setting. In our experience there are several specific reasons for the deliberate provocation of transitory regression in psychodrama. A more thorough *abreaction of childhood trauma* is one. We may also wish to help the patient undercut a current character symptom by reverting to an earlier way of relating. A rigid, inhibited person may have to discover that he can engage in playfulness without falling apart or being shamed by his associates. And *any experience of controlled regression helps us to integrate the childish remnants in ourselves which otherwise we struggle to hide and isolate at great expense in psychic energy.* This explains the healing power of "spontaneity."

The technical problems, then, are: (1) How to help the patient achieve regression; under (2) conditions which are experienced as within his control—*regression in the service of the ego;* and (3) make it momentary and localized in its impact.

Thus far we have found two useful methods in psychodrama. The first is the successive process to which we have alluded in which the patient, while "tracing the affect back," associates an earlier to a present conflict, and then enacts it. The second maneuver referred to by Redl (1949),involves exploiting one of the dynamics in behavioral contagion, the *dominance of the unconflicted personality constellation over the conflicted.* The psychodramatist may get down on the floor, forsaking his present group prestige to abandon himself fully to the role of the patient's childhood playmate or sibling. In doing this, he also demonstrates his own freedom from fear of consequences or ridicule.

As with all other techniques, precautions must be observed. A patient only recently reconstituted from an outright psychotic break hardly wants loosening up. A substantial number of infantile patients unfortunately require no outside assistance to act childish; for them the aim of psychodramatic intervention must be in the opposite direction. For a large proportion of patients, *deliberately evoked regression* under the conditions cited is the treatment of choice. This technique emphasizes the range of possibilities within the psychodramatic situation. Whereas clarification and insight treatment utilize the *secondary process* in therapy, evoked regression may put its emphasis more at the level of the *primary process,* although of course not all regression is to this level.

* * *

We have described a program of psychodramatic treatment utilized at one hospital for more than five years. Although we began with a skeptical and experimental attitude, we soon acquired general acceptance and conviction regarding its potentialities. Our program differed from a number of others in that the method was seen as frankly adjunctive to individual psychotherapy and embedded in a situation where other therapies were being used simultaneously with the same patient. We also have the impression that the continuity and sheer time in psychodramatic treatment (ranging up to two years or more, for some) were somewhat unusual.

Working totally independently of Moreno's groups, we nevertheless had occasion to confirm the usefulness of a number of techniques he and his followers created, despite our having operated consistently in the framework of an analytically oriented psychotherapy they do not share. Our conclusion is that the psychodramatic situation may be exploited to bring powerful intrapsychic forces into play that, when harnessed may achieve striking results. Psychodrama is not univocal, but rather, especially characterized by its versatility and range of communication possiblities. A spectrum of psychotherapeutic aims can be pursued, depending on patient readiness and staff competence.

This chapter has illustrated the use of psychodrama in bringing about affect discharge, in the service of clarification and insight therapy, in the exposure of unwanted identifications, and in therapeutic regression. Each of these proximate aims of a psychodramatic session may lead to the ultimate one of *enhancing the verbal accessibility* of the protagonist—and, indeed, that of the other patients involved. For some patients with massive affect inhibition, the expression of feelings through gesture and facial expression may be a required prelude to expression in words. For others, who misuse words defensively, the requirement to act out their feelings psychodramatically while speaking of them may heal splits between words and affects.

Albert Camus wrote of the Nazis, "When one has no character, one *has* to apply a method" (1956). Its inherent flamboyance and the manner of its proliferation have at times restricted psychodrama to practitioners with little method and no coherent personality theory. Its responsible use requires both. Our intention has been to move toward integrating this treatment technique into the theoretical corpus of the other analytically oriented psychotherapies.

CHAPTER 12
A SPEED READER'S GUIDE TO
The Healing Powers of Speech

The bulk of our work with clients and patients involves talking, verbal communication. What can we derive from analytic theory and research regarding this medium of practice?

The client's degree of *verbal accessibility* is a *character trait*. Consistent in various settings, reasonably stable over time, like other traits it is condictable from other knowledge of the person. Studies indicate that the verbally accessible client shows other evidences of *ego strength* and is likely to respond to talking treatment. Inaccessibility implies less favorable prognosis.

A high level of verbal accessibility reflects good *synthetic functioning* and indicates relatively few areas of *conflict* or massive *repression*. Further, the capacity to use speech strengthens the ego: it facilitates *need-meeting* functions, promotes *problem-solving, binds raw impulses*, supports clarification and *integration* by combatting *repression* and providing *abstractions*, and transmits *meaning*. Directness in expression promotes closeness with others and thereby *combats loneliness*.

Like any other important adaptive function, speech may be *invaded by conflicts* and neurosis. It may have been poorly developed because of deficits in the client's early environment. It is sometimes necessary to *promote* the client's *verbal accessibility* to lay the groundwork for talking treatment; suggestions are offered as to how this may be done.

The Healing
Powers of Speech

12

"O ne man's Mede is another man's Persian" said the late
Charles MacArthur, playwright and humorist. In social
work, which draws on so many other disciplines for theory and
information, we find that one field's gossip is another field's
datum. A good case in point is the way in which we view, or
overlook, the client's freedom of speech.

By and large, we used to take the client's verbal style for granted.
For one thing, diagnostic vision has always been blurred by social
work's reluctance to judge clients. Respect for individual dignity
is always admirable, albeit sometimes misplaced, so there was a
disinclination to scrutinize the way the client talked. At most,
speaking style seemed either a help or a hindrance to getting at
some other personal characteristic regarded as "deeper," more
meaningful. The woman who was both frank and articulate in the
first interview was a great convenience, giving relevant history
useful for an initial diagnosis. If on the other hand she proved
sullen and nonverbal, it was the caseworker's job to use his
interviewing skill to help her communicate more easily. Little attention was paid to the probability that a client who finds it hard to
talk freely with a caring caseworker is similarly constricted in most
other relationships, and that this limitation may be as significant
to making a diagnosis and planning her treatment as are other
much harder to come by observations.

More than any other theoretician Hellmuth Kaiser emphasized
the ultimate existential anxiety: each man is, in fact, biologically
cut off, at sea in a potentially meaningless universe. The delusion
of fusion is a neurotic attempt to deny one's aloneness. But its
manifestations may make one's position worse. What are the more

realistic ways by which we can try to get close? It is uniquely human that one is best able to achieve intimacy through the power of the spoken word; it is also human that one's power of speech is subject to distortion and neurotic invasion, like any other ego function. Duplicitous speech does not bring others closer; it only adds to alienation and eventual despair.

Through Kaiser's influence and my concern with why people have so much trouble healing each other's loneliness, I became fascinated with the concept of *verbal accessibility: the readiness of the client to communicate his most important attitudes through speech, and to permit others to communicate with him about them.* The conception does not take sheer volume of talk as an indication of accessibility. As we saw in Chapter Ten, circumlocution may be used to evade the expression of true feelings. In effect, we are concerned with the kind of talk in which one "stands behind his words."

This chapter will present what I have learned about verbal accessibility (VA) as a characteristic of client speech. As a character trait interdependent with other enduring personality features it affects treatability. We will also examine situational influences affecting the level of VA. And, through this conception, we will discuss the role of verbalization—a social caseworkers' main medium—in normal maturation and in healing.

Clients' Verbal Accessibility in Initial Interviews

An experience with family agencies twenty-five years ago brought me to study verbal accessibility. In those years, family agencies under private auspices occupied a central position in all social work services, as they had since the founding of Charity Organization Societies in the 1860's. Those working in them were very likely to have had graduate training and to be highly skilled. We looked to them for advances in the practice of casework. Yet, studies of family agency statistics revealed a troubling fact. A substantial proportion of all clients who came to them were seen for one interview only (Blenkner, 1954; Kogan, 1957). Of course, some clients had come to the wrong agency for what they wanted; others' needs could be met in a single conference. Still, a large number—thirty to forty percent—recognizably in need of social treatment over a period of time nevertheless did not return. In effect, their workers were not succeeding in holding them in treatment. Why not?

One can, of course, analyze clients' limitations and motivations— or their lack (Ripple, Alexander and Polemis, 1964). But I was impressed that each client had come far enough to present himself with a request for service, but then gave up the idea. It is not useful to conclude simply that most were "not ready for treatment" and let matters rest. A current joke inquires "How many social workers does it take to change a light bulb? Two, but the bulb must want to change." A person already oriented toward autoplastic solutions with an ego capable of accurate self-observation is in rather good repair; he might well go all the way and cure himself. Thus our job is to deal with the client's marginal motivation. We may not be able to overcome limited motivation. This event, a misfortune for the client, would be the professional's failure, as I learned from Kaiser. Therefore, my hope was that we could do research to develop principles that would improve workers' success in establishing initial bonds in helping relationships.

The question was: What must a worker do or act like in an initial interview to give the client the feeling his needs are going to be met? To study this, we arranged a series of research interviews with 150 clients. Each had just had an initial interview at one of a variety of social work or other treatment agencies in Detroit. From these research "post-interview interviews," Jacob Kounin and I were able to assess the client satisfaction with the interview and the aspects of it that were associated with any satisfactions reported.

Our data indicated two separate forms of client satisfaction were repeatedly mentioned: experiences leading toward solution of problems (problem-centered satisfactions); and experiences of pleasure or disappointment in the current relationship (relationship-centered satisfactions). Anticipating that the two forms of satisfaction would correlate, we found that they were relatively independent of each other in clients' judgments (Polansky and Kounin, 1956). One might feel helped, but not particularly warmed, by contact with a particular doctor; and the obverse might also be true. Not only did clients make such assessments independently of each other, the things that determined relationship-centered satisfaction were demonstrably different from those having to do with solving problems. Twenty years later, Tessler (1975) did an experimental study in Wisconsin which confirmed these generalizations. We also found that the perception of worker motivation was judged quite separately from worker competence. One prefers one's surgeon be highly motivated but hopes, above all, for competence!

One experience correlated with all the other major indices of satisfaction: the client's expressed *freedom to communicate feelings*. It was the only client rating which appeared in both the relationship-

and problem-centered rating clusters. Its significant place in the client's experience had not been predicted by us, though I remembered Kaiser's emphasis on helping the patient "stand behind his words." Incidentally, I picked up these ideas in sessions with him as an analysand; his own book appeared posthumously more than a decade later.

But, *why* should the judgment that one felt free to talk about feelings prove so central to overall satisfaction with an initial interview? One could assume the reasons derived from two sorts of factors: how the worker handled the client and what kind of person the client was. In short, we can separate the *situational* from the *characterological* determinants of clients' verbal accessibility. Since we play a large role in making "the situation" what it is for the client, we certainly would like to know how to help him be as verbally accessible as possible at the time he is seeing us. I will later summarize what we have learned about how to foster another's verbal accessibility; first, let us look at the trait.

Verbal Accessibility as a Trait

We can readily believe that whether or not a client is being open at a first interview relates to how well you handle him. Could his degree of verbal accessibility also reflect a *trait*, something enduring about him relatively independent of you? Well, how do we decide any piece of behavior represents a trait? We expect a trait to be stable over time and through changing circumstances. As the personality functions pretty much as a *gestalt*, all of a piece, we expect a piece of behavior that reflects a trait to be related to other traits, and to be *condictable*, perhaps, from knowing other things about the person. The logic is the same as we reviewed in the rationale for studying characterology.

Does VA remain stable over time? Using a scale of self-reported *social accessibility,* Rickers-Ovsiankina and Kusmin (1958) found test-retest correlations of .52 for one group of college women retested after four years, and .69 for another sample retested after eighteen months.

My colleagues and I have, by now, collected considerable evidence of the stability of VA under alterations in circumstances. The evidence comes from studies often done for other reasons, and so is extremely varied. For example, in a Cleveland institution (Bellefaire) emotionally disturbed children lived in small cottages, each staffed by four adults. The staff of each cottage was asked to rank order their children on Verbal Accessibility with regard to five different kinds of things they might talk about. Each staff member's independent rankings showed very substantial agreement. Moreover, each child's average ranking correlated with scales of his openness to casework in a different treatment setting (Polansky, Weiss and Blum, 1961). The same phenomena were confirmed in a replication by Appelberg (1961). In an experimental analogue, done at Case Western Reserve University at about the same time, Nooney and Polansky (1962) found that the subjects maintained similar levels of VA of communication across changed circumstances. More recently, we had a rather large-scale study of 125 low-income white families in Philadelphia, aimed at discerning the causes of child neglect. Each parent was seen by a research social worker, usually in the home; each was also seen by a psychologist, in the office. The correlations of ratings of parental VA between the two professionals were: for mothers $r = .54$; for fathers $r = .33$ ($P < .001$) (Polansky, et al., 1981).

It seems fair to conclude that while readiness to talk fluctuates somewhat, depending on whom we are with, and under what conditions, each of us also has a typical level. There are colleagues you feel you know rather well after a week; others seem "closed" enigmatic people. Even after several years, you may be surprised to discover you have no idea of their earlier lives or major attitudes. We have found the same to be true of clients in our studies. We may, then, think of verbal accessibility as reflecting something characterological.

If verbal accessibility is a character trait, what are its functional connections with other traits? For patients who do not approach *pathological frankness* (like patients who celebrate their therapeutic release by wanting to tell everybody everything) our observation is that the higher the VA, the greater the ego strength. VA is a sign of how well a person adapts generally. We shall deal with why this is true later; for the moment, let us mention some of the evidence for the conclusion.

In the children's treatment institution, we found that while youngsters lower in IQ are not necessarily verbally inaccessible, those with high-average or superior intelligence rated high on the trait (Polansky and Weiss, 1959). Ganter conducted a study of children seen for four sessions in diagnostic groups as part of a work-up for child guidance treatment. Subsequently, a number were seen for individual therapy. The child's *organizational unity* and his *capacity for self-observation* proved predictive of subsequent VA in individual therapy (Ganter and Polansky, 1964). When the causal direction of this relationship was subsequently tested clinically, youngsters formerly regarded untreatable as outpatients survived in that treatment after being offered an *intermediary group treatment program* that concentrated on improving the two personality dimensions identified in the first study (Ganter, Yeakel and Polansky, 1967).

A study of preadolescents in Ohio found that delinquent or predelinquent boys were lower on VA than their classmates (Jaffee and Polansky, 1962). Boys in residential treatment scored lower than a control sample drawn from the same Jewish community (Appelberg, 1961). In a study of low-income mothers in Southern Appalachia, we constructed for each an index combining educational achievement, dating experience and occupational adjustment in adolescence. This E-D-O score, based on history, correlated with the mother's VA as rated by her current research social worker (Polansky, Borgman and DeSaix, 1972).

Haring (1965) compared the VA of children under treatment in a Cleveland social agency with that of their mothers, who were also being seen. She found a low but significant association between the VA of mother and child. In our Appalachian research, we had a rating of the VA of a child from each family, obtained from the staff of his day-care center. These ratings correlated significantly with those done by research social workers on the mothers. The same issue was studied in our replication in Philadelphia (Polansky et al., 1981). Once again, there was a low but significant association between the verbal accessibility of mother and child, but no correlation with that of the father. In both family studies, the mother's VA correlated with the quality of child care as measured by our *Childhood Level of Living Scale*. We concluded that the child's relatedness, as evidenced by his VA rating, reflected both identification with the mother's pattern and the caring atmosphere of the home. Like other important character traits, verbal accessibility is *con*dictable from other current knowledge of the person, and *pre*dictible from background information.

Moreover, the same personal feature seems fruitful for making predictions. Jourard (1961) reported a correlation of .79 between self-disclosure scores of sophomores in a nursing school and their grade point averages at graduation. Arthur Blum and I also found in one small study that social work students with extremely low VA scores at the beginning of training were at risk of poor performance in field work, and of being dropped from the program.

As Kounin and I discovered, clients who reported themselves feeling freer to communicate feelings were more generally satisfied with initial interviews. Florence Hollis (1966) pursued the issue of who was likely to continue in treatment. Contrary to expectation, women who devoted the greater part of the first contact to describing their situations and *ventilating* about them were more likely to continue in treatment. Weber (1963), of our group in Cleveland, found that the child who rated higher on VA during his first three months of residential treatment was generally better adapted and fulfilled age-expectable roles at the end of treatment two or three years later.

The evidence is persuasive. VA consistently associates with overall ego efficiency; in the lack of other evidence it may, indeed, be a rather good index of it: a surprising discovery about a facet of the client typically observable within the first thirty minutes of contact, which we regarded primarily as an indicator of how well *we* were conducting the interview. Why does the person's verbal accessibility play so unexpected a role in character? How do our results relate to general ego theory?

Adaptive Functions of Speech

To term some communications *duplicitous*, as we did in Chapter 10, implies speech has been invaded by conflict. In effect, this marvelous human capacity seems to have been subverted from its "proper" intentions into defensive maneuverings. Speech is not unique in this respect. As we have remarked repeatedly, any ego function may be enlisted in the service of defense. What, then, are conflict-free uses of speech? What human aims has it been designed by nature to serve?

The psychoanalytic writings relevant to this topic yield a mixed impression. Despite the overwhelmingly verbal nature of free-association, there is ambivalence about being so dependent on the spoken word. Some authors seem dismayed to be encumbered by a treatment that clients from culturally deprived backgrounds often are unprepared to use. Some papers glamorize *non*verbal communication. Their authors suggest that gestures, grimaces, and grunts possess magical depths of communication unobtainable in English. Such confidence flies in the face of the fact that the decoding of nonverbal signals has a far higher rate of error than penetrating the worst abstractions. No sensible clinician should discount nonverbal cues to a client's feelings and wants, but getting him also to talk about them is preferable. The capacity to communicate so well so rapidly through symbols is, on this planet, unique to humans. It is safe to assume it has given us a leg up in evolutionary competition.

Social workers and other clinicians have long recognized that facilitating the client's talking is helpful in therapy. Gradually switching aggressive children from action to verbal channels of expression is taken to signify growing impulse control. Redl and Wineman (1952) list "Increased ability to use verbal modes of communication" high in priority among the gains at their Pioneer House. The connection between speech and anxiety tolerance was identified through the lack of both among severely neglectful mothers. "The problems in verbal communication at the affective level not only involve a lack of experience in talking or having the requisite vocabulary, but also are the result of an incapacity to tolerate anxiety. Therefore, anxiety is discharged in a range of activities" (Sullivan, Spasser and Penner, 1977, p. 103).

What is it we hope to get from speech? Loewenstein has summarized his view of the significance of the patient's talking in psychoanalysis:

> Speech in the analytic process serves as a means of discharge and binding of affects; it adds to thoughts and memories a degree of perceptual and social reality; it leads to an objectification of inner processes; it permits the differentiation of past and present, the testing of psychic realities, and makes psychoanalytic insight possible. It promotes the integrative processes to which we ascribe the major part of the therapeutic effectiveness of psychoanalysis (1961, pp. 4f).

From Rapaport, we have these related comments:

> (1) Communication enriches the store of experiences and thereby enriches psychic life; (2) Psychic life is not a one-way avenue in which defenses limit communications; communications may also combat the deleterious effects of defenses. ... (6) It provides new percepts and resuscitates old ones; thus it also makes for an integration of isolated experiences and further integration into broader or new units...Communication enhances the "synthetic function of the ego" (1951, pp. 727f).

Katan commented that verbalization of feelings by the younger child leads to an increase of ego mastery. Writing of the nonverbal child, she notes, "If the child could verbalize his feelings, he would learn to delay actions, but if the delaying function is lacking...the situation may have pathological consequences" (1961, p. 186). Anna Freud put the same idea more elegantly,

> The ego of the young child has the developmental task to master on the one hand orientation in the external world and on the other hand the chaotic emotional states which exist within himself. It gains its victories and advances whenever such impressions are grasped and put into thoughts or words, and submitted to the secondary process... (1965, p. 32).

In this country we have been accustomed to associate an unstimulating environment with intellectual deficiencies among children reared there. Writing of his investigations in England, Bernstein (1962) posited that social class differences in "linguistic codes" affect the availability of abstract words and the complexity of sentence stuctures. An impoverished, simplified linguistic code limits the nature of thought capable of being sustained by persons from such a culture. A. Freud and Katan, however, have reminded us that such deficits also extend into the systems for controlling and modulating drive-discharge. Miss Freud quoted a passage written by her father in 1893, "The man who first flung a word of abuse at his enemy instead of a spear was the founder of civilization."

Aims of Speech

Our survey of related writings has thus far emphasized how verbalizing strengthens other ego functions. However, strengthening the ego is not one's usual motive for talking. For most of us and for our clients, the good that happens *for* the ego is generally coincidental to the immediate motives for speech. If the client tells you all about an episode with her boy friend last weekend, she may end with a more objective view of her own role in the events. However, that would not have been her reason for telling her story. She wanted to discuss what a sad spectacle he made of himself, perhaps, or to tell you how hard her life has been lately, or to enjoy a laugh at her own expense. Objectification, even ventilation, are usually side-effects. So, there is another question about the functions of speech which can be phrased: What *motivates* talk?

One of the earliest child psychologists, William Stern (1914) considered what he called the roots of speech. He posited three:

the expressive, the social, and the intentional, which is talk for the communication of meanings. The first two aims, he thought, are found also in sounds emitted by other animals, including dogs, horses, birds, and so forth. Only intentional communication seems singular to humans. The Russian psychologist, Vygotsky (1962) has picked up from Stern and given us a brilliant way of relating speech to thinking and problem solving. Children, he believes, use speech initially to discharge affect or for such "social" reasons as trying to get needs met or to approach others. However, when they make early attempts to solve puzzles at play, they talk to themselves, carrying on a dialogue that actually assists them in what they are doing. For the child's running commentary often leads to word-associations that provide new ideas or relate the present problem to another one already solved. At about age seven the dialogue becomes purely internal; it is now "silent speech" directed to oneself. Vygotsky believes the silent dialogue is the way we harness our knowledge of language and grammar into logical thought. These notions were more vaguely stated, of course, by Rapaport and Anna Freud in the quotations above, but the insight is related.

Indeed, when we comment on a person's uncritical style of drawing conclusions or his superficial thinking, are we not pointing to the absence of any silent debate? I must say I have not found many colleagues whose silence and inarticulateness reflected profound thinking. To the contrary, a number of highly verbal people prove suprisingly well informed and reflective. Franklin Roosevelt and Hubert Humphrey come to mind as widely known examples. There may be something to the jest "I really won't know what I think until I've heard me say it." It is very helpful to casework if the client has previously come to the conviction that talking a problem over with someone is a good way to help yourself find new solutions.

Just as talking is always motivated and, indeed, usually overdetermined by several purposes at once, so is *silence*. One use of not-talking is to shut the other person out. Do we not interpret silence toward ourselves as snubbing? In the analytic hour silence may reflect the preference not to be there at all; it has been interpreted as a wish that the analyst were dead or that the patient himself were (Weisman, 1955; Zeligs, 1961). Some silent clients are loaded with hostility, so much so that they dare not open up at all. They fear that as they speak, their anger will first leak into words and then explode, a fear frequently based on having experienced this sequence in the past. And, of course, silence as an expression of anal-sadistic withholding is familiar to all who have encountered it.

Well, then, why do people talk? Meerloo (1952) has made a list of the desires that energize verbalizations: to express emotions and moods; to make sounds; to make contact; to inform, state facts; to formulate ideas; to take a position opposite the world; to establish one's individuality; to control things; to control others; to be controlled by others; to express sexual desire; to use words as part of a defense; to express unconscious motives; to refuse contact (pp. 84ff).

Like all behavior, feeling, and ideation, speech is found in the service of both drives and defenses: it is usually overdetermined. Some of the drives seem primitive; others, derivative and neutralized. Some are conscious and preconscious; other impulses to speech are quite unconscious. In each case, however, talking is used to fulfill a need, conflicted or not, and to this degree articulate speech obviously serves manifold adaptive functions. No wonder Kaiser was led to conclude that helping a person straighten out his talking would, itself, be in the direction of cure!

Let me, now, summarize in my own fashion, the various conscious and unconscious purposes subserved by verbal communication. All are interrelated, but we can put them under the following headings:

1. *Speech is used to achieve drive satisfactions.* We employ speech to influence others, starting with infantile vocalizations meant to signal needs to one's mother. From the beginning, the needs satisfied include survival needs; they may also include libidinal needs which are oral at first but eventually primarily genital. Speech is also used in the service of aggression. We may seek to inflict harm by manipulating the person at whom we are angry, by influencing someone else to inflict harm on him, or by a direct, verbal assault. For, clearly, talking involves a *blending of ideation with action* as a channel for partial discharge of drive energies.

Talking is also used to satisfy a variety of needs of the kind considered in the theory of object relations. Verbalizaton is employed in order to come closer to others. When we comment on the weather, after all, we are not setting ourselves up as meteorologists; we are merely touching, or brushing against the other person with words. Talk is used to combat loneliness and isolation, and at various levels. Women pinned down in their homes by the care of small babies escape into adult company by having telephone conversations. Very interesting, in this connection, is the need couples often feel, when falling in love, to tell each other all about themselves, their dreams, their likes, fragments of life history. Why? As Fritz Redl pointed out to me years ago, the motive is *as if* they were saying, "As you know me, I become part of you." Using Klein's phrase one might say that by such means lovers seek *projective identification*.

2. *Speech binds affects and impulses by offering a detour to action.* We mentioned ideation as one of the channels whereby drives are discharged: we have also remarked that speech contains an element of action. Hence, speaking of an impulse to someone else seems to reduce drive tension more effectively than simply thinking about it does. How much more satisfying it is to tell a friend about a grievance than to suffer, and ponder, it in silence! Such talk is called *ventilation;* we noted it particularly with respect to the treatment of depression where it drained rage into verbal channels. So, talk provides a substitution for action. Having described what you would like to do to someone you hate, you have less need to do it. The availability of a verbal detour helps *bind*, or control, strong impulses; it facilitates neutralization and sublimation.

However, the *substitution value* of speech is not limited to ventilating rage and relieving terrifying experiences by describing them in detail (called *abreaction)* in order to master them. Old men love to discuss business victories and successes in attracting women that they are no longer capable of. We all have marvelous times talking about exciting trips with old friends; the best such conversations are with others who were with us. Since we are not telling each other things we do not already know, wherein is the pleasure? In reviving old memories, we re-experience the feelings that went with them. In recounting past glories, we *re-pleasure* ourselves.

As we shall note later, speech helps combat repression. In an even more general way, we may say that it helps to resuscitate— that is, breathe new life into—old memories of all kinds. Rapaport, quoted to this effect a few pages back, liked to recite the Iliad in the ancient Greek version he had been taught when growing up in Hungary. It was his way of keeping the poem available to recall and of enjoying the pleasure he took in his phenomenal memory. Speech offers a detour that supports the ego in coping with unacceptable drives; speech also provides a channel for combating repression and preventing the simple forgetting of conflict-free memories because of disuse.

Yet, one cannot help note, again, that there seems to be no coping mechanism that cannot be invaded by conflict and become symptomatic. The substitution value of speech makes a fine example of this. Whole movements are made of up people who believe they have changed the world once they have announced their beliefs. A former colleague, Stuart Miller, used to say, after one of our lengthy committee meetings, "Everything that needs to be done has been said." (Miller is also the source of another memorable remark, "This is something up with which I would not put.")

As one would expect, the wordy professions are especially prone to tedious conferences expensive to their employers. Psychoanalytically oriented therapists are, in my experience, worse even than social workers, but academicians top them all. Clients and patients may also try to use talk as a substitute for action in ways not helpful to themselves. Endless planning that eventuates in remaining fixed is one example. Others, like alcoholics, become adept at offering confessions of guilt as if they were sufficient reparation, thereby leaving themselves free to go away and sin again. I have not been in touch with Alcoholics Anonymous in years, but my recollection is that those in it were sophisticated about this mechanism. Members were supposed to *do* something to repair the damage they had done to others; confessions and apologies were not enough.

3. *Speech facilitates thought and problem solving.* The reader is by now familiar with the Freudian idea that the young child first detours into producing an idea of mother because she is not immediately present to offer satisfaction. Recall too that Hartmann said detouring into thought is not always defensive, or the accepting of a poor substitute for the real thing. Which would one prefer? To try out each conceivable way of going to a new restaurant, or to sit for a moment and *think* about alternative routes across town? Exploiting ones' capacity for ideation, in words or images, saves physical energy in everything—from choosing a football play to adding a line to a poem.

Verbal abstractions summarize more concrete ideas. Hence, they make it far easier to store observations about the world in the form of generalizations. In science, we call these generalizations theories; however, poker players who win usually follow formulated or borrowed principles. Studies of people from cultures that lack written language suggest they, too, often use general principles to guide planning. In solving any concrete problem, then, it helps to have an assortment of stored principles to draw on.

Words make it far easier to borrow from others' wisdom and to store it. Persons with active minds often do this even when they have no use for the information at the moment. So talking things over with another adds his wisdom to our own. Moreover, the new combinations stirred by such dialogue often provide solutions neither had thought about before. Groupthink has been accused of stifling creativity; that is neither its inevitable nor its usual effect. Stifled creativity is a pathology of joint thinking that comes from too much need to achieve fusion. Most normal people benefit from talking over a decision.

Yet, some subcultures in this country share a disbelief in the efficacy of conversation. In a small town in Southern Appalachia I once watched two mechanics struggle with a balky carburetor. Although they talked to each other constantly, neither ever referred to the motor they were working on, or puzzled about it. Their behavior fitted a general observation we had made, that men of their background recognize the social functions of speech but have no confidence in its usefulness for solving problems. Such a mechanic would have to teach his son about motors entirely by letting the boy watch him and help him. Neither would be a good prospect for psychotherapy.

4. *Speech supports the synthetic function of the ego.* The usefulness of words for storing general principles and thereby integrating thinking is fairly obvious. Less obvious, perhaps, is the way the same ego function can support the synthetic function of the ego, in general, and help resolve conflicts.

As Rapaport said, *communication combats repression.* Once you have said something, it is experienced as more "out there," more an objective thing. It is harder to repress something you would like to forget once you have spoken of it to another. For example, we often have thoughts only marginally conscious. They have been described as *in statu nascendi,* in "the state of being born." When such an idea is blurted out immediately, it is more likely to remain fixed in consciousness. Writers employ the principle in keeping notepads by their bedsides to record ideas that have come to them while dozing. But the principle cuts both ways. If an idea is something you would prefer not to deal with, consciously, you have good reason to remain silent about it.

Hence, silence may be used in the service of denial. I have a vivid recollection of sitting in an isolated cabin in the mountains with a young woman eight months pregnant who was applying for AFDC. Her pregnancy was illegitimate; she was dreadfully troubled about her fate, and awfully lonely. I asked whom she had had to talk with, and it became clear she had no one. "How about your mother. Don't you two talk about it?" "Neither of us has ever mentioned that I'm pregnant."

Earlier in the book we discussed various methods of *uncovering* that a caseworker might use to evoke *insight*. One of these was labelled *clarification*. Through relating already preconscious ideas to each other, something previously unconscious may become unrepressed. Words, the symbols of all these ideas, have an obvious use in clarification; words also help to preserve an insight against immediate re-repression.

What does all this have to do with ego synthesis? Often, we may live with a contradiction but not know it was there because one of the discrepant impulses was unconscious. A function of clarification in the interview is to force us into confronting our conflicts and, perhaps, resolving them. The patient may have to try to choose, consciously, whether she wants to have a certain image of herself as a person, or continue to have sexual affairs which are, actually, casual and meaningless to her. By her own testimony, she cannot have matters both ways. In a general way, we may assume that any important impulse which, nevertheless, remains unconscious strongly implies unresolved conflict. To come to a synthesis, one must either give up the superego inhibition or weaken the impulse to the point that one can admit it to conscious awareness.

Speech also facilitates conflict resolution through another familiar mechanism. Why does the client come in and announce, "I have had it; I am not going to go on getting fat on beer every night in the week." Intuitively, you feel that if he were sure of the decision, he might have kept it to himself. Why the pronouncement? Actually, he is trying to use a public statement to bolster his private resolve. Announcing the decision digs him further into his decision.

5. *Verbal communication transmits meanings.* We begin to use speech, let us say, to express feelings and to influence our mothers and fathers to meet our needs. We learn to use it, later, for other purposes, including problem solving and the relief of loneliness. At some point, however, transmitting meanings seems to acquire autonomous motivation of its own. We tell our friends things about painting, boat-building, car repair, mortgage shopping perhaps for some of the reasons already listed. We may also tell them about these topics to review and try to bring order into our own minds about things we know a lot about; this is one of the more acceptable

selfish motives for teaching. But, we also tell them about things we know because the desire to transmit information has itself become a drive derivative powered by *neutralized* energy whose ultimate source is immaterial. At least some of the talk that goes on in therapy has this kind of motivation. While it may not serve the goals of therapy very well, who is to say that mutual enrichment of each other's view of the world has no value as growth experience?

Talk for mutual informing and enlarging one's view of the world is one of the joys of civilized conversation. At its best, such talk is also entertaining. And, where is it written, really, that enlarging the capacities of the ego cannot be accompanied by pleasure?

Some Life Experiences that Limit Speech

If talking holds such potential benefits for the ego, it is natural to ask ourselves why we meet so many clients in whom this capacity seems poorly developed. What sorts of things deter the development of verbal accessibility as a personality trait?

Obviously, any facet of child rearing that limits, or *fails to encourage*, the development of speech will lower verbal accessibility. Nonverbal mothers, especially, are important deterrents. It is possible to survive on an astonishingly small vocabulary in this country, and children often have achieved fully half their eventual working vocabularies by the age of three. To be from a subcultural group that uses an extremely limited daily vocabulary, say one of five hundred words or so, may also mean you have no way of *expressing* feelings, even if you want to, when older. This has further effects, in what general systems theory calls a *spiral of causation*. An educated person has a range of ways to file a complaint—"You are being annoying"; "Is this something you really mean to be doing?"; "How about stopping it for now, eh?" But, if the only way you know to express a complaint will put you in the middle of a knife fight, you either say nothing, or wait until you explode. In other words, the danger imposed by one's speech limitations makes one keep silent, which further exacerbates one's limitations. All Army recruits were taught, "Keep your bowels open and your mouth shut." This wisdom is not applicable to middle class American living!

There are subcultures which, I believe, devalue speech because it threatens a defensive use of the delusion of fusion (Polansky and Brown, 1967). Articulate speech, after all, makes it more apparent to each of us that we are *not* the same in what we feel or think. So, speech patterns precise enough to express small differences are dangerous to this defense. Many popular songs' universality of appeal lies in the limited vocabularies that permit hearers to project many meanings into them. No great rock group could possibly unify audiences, otherwise. Music, which I love, is said to be the universal language, and have charms to soothe the savage beast, but except for blatant imitations of songbirds, or simple matters of speed and rhythm, listeners have wildly differing verbal associations to the same concerto. Hence, speaking in a vague jargon— including those of the professions—or communicating by music may be motivated by the mechanism Kaiser so shrewdly identified, the need for a delusion of fusion. Children from defensively nonverbal subcultures learn to conceal the more sophisticated speech they acquire in school, reverting to the local jargon at home. Otherwise, they may be attacked as being "uppity"—another unacceptable form of difference!

On the other hand one also encounters the formidably articulate family whose children are not. Sometimes, the lack of verbal skill is feigned; the child masquerades as nonverbal in defiance or as part of a negative identity. Other children from such backgrounds depreciate speech, telling you it serves no useful purpose. Sometimes the depreciation is part of a stance that *all* efforts to touch each other are foolish; in other words, the silence expresses schizoid feelings of futility. But, I have also known young people who became cynical about speech because their highly verbal parents used it to dominate them. They were constantly being invited to "Sit down and let's talk this over" sessions which led to the child being in the wrong, or having to give up some wish. In other words the young client distrusts verbal communication with grownups because to him free talk is just another means for parental manipulation and control. T. S. Eliot wrote of an "Argument of insidious intent leading to an overwhelming question." Eliot expressed what your nonverbal middle class youngster too often expects of a treatment interview.

But these are just notes on matters that have particularly struck me over the years. The more general source of deterrence to verbal accessibility was strongly implied in the researches cited earlier. To be able to "stand behind one's words," after all, implies that major motivations are pretty much conscious; it also implies that the person's synthetic function is sufficiently strong and operative so that he can compromise among competing motivations in himself, or resolve contradictions and conflicts, and arrive at where he stands. Further, as Kaiser told us, to be able to make up one's mind requires that one not be terrified of discovering his aloneness. It takes only a quick review of such basic principles to conclude that to speak "responsibly" implies being a rather well integrated person.

We add other observations having to do with how one relates to others. If you are chronically hostile, but your rage strikes you, yourself, as inappropriate, you are not going to be able to speak freely; analogously, if you have strong needs to cling, so strong that you fear you will lose yourself in the other, or engulf her, or act in a way that is embarrassingly childish, you will also with-hold free expression. All in all, as Kaiser generalized, and as our research has shown, the ability to articulate important attitudes and the readiness to do so in an appropriate situation like case-work, are hopeful signs that the client is free of crippling emotional disorder.

Fostering Verbal Accessibility

We began our concern with verbal accessibility because a study showed that clients who felt freer to talk about important feelings were more satisfied with initial interviews than those unable to speak freely. Next, it was found that a major determinant of the client's verbal accessibility lay in himself, in the pattern that he brought with him. So, we have been discussing the ways verbal accessibility correlates with and, indeed, supports other adaptive mechanisms of the personality. But, focus on character does not imply that how the client is treated makes no difference. Adroit and sympathetic handling will help a usually shy and inarticulate person become more expressive; contrariwise, a brusque manner silences everyone. So, besides the characterological determinants of verbal accessibility, there are forces in the momentary interaction the patient finds himself in. In speaking of such situational influences, we have in mind stimuli to which "almost anyone" would respond in similar ways. Paraphrasing the psychoanalytic conception of an *average expectable environment*, when we talk of situational forces, we are thinking of their effects on an *average expectable person*.

In group dynamics, we have had many investigations of the conditions under which people will or will not communicate, and to whom they will direct their communications. Having low status in one's group is associated with being less likely to speak up. So much is this taken for granted that when low-status group members assert themselves even a little, others in their group are apt to overestimate how much they have talked (Hurwitz, Zander and Hymovitch, 1953). Low status seems to dampen behavioral spontaneity nonverbally as well as verbally (Lippitt, Polansky and Rosen, 1952). Low status means occupying a lesser position in the group's power hierarchy. Such a position exacerbates feelings of *vulnerability*, so it is all the more necessary to be sensitive to the feelings of clients who feel powerless. Many upper middle-class clients on the other hand carry social assurance with them into the office, so it requires less skill to put them at ease.

Communications in groups are more likely to be directed toward those in high power positions. The average group member acts as if knowing a prestigeful person "to talk to" allows one to partake symbolically of her position (Kelley, 1951). As one would expect, people are more apt to pass information on to friends, chosen partly for sheer geographical propinquity (Festinger, Schachter and Back, 1950). And, as also seems reasonable, the information communicated is selected in terms of whether they think it is something you would need to know about, or that has relevance to you.

Unless it is bad news. Tesser and Rosen (1975) have conducted a series of experiments explicating the circumstances under which people will, and will not, bring themselves to bear evil tidings. Shared fate is one factor. That is, if you and another woman are both waiting for the results of biopsies to see if you have cancer, and you find out that you are in the clear but she is not, you will be extremely reluctant to tell her. If you think the other person would not be able to cope with bad news, you will not want to share it. Important, for clinicians, is the finding that if the subject thinks *he* would be unable to cope with such news, he is also very unlikely to transmit it. Workers sometimes project their own squeamishness onto clients; clients also withhold unpleasant information that they feel their worker would find shocking or anxiety producing.

We have found that if you think another person has the same values you do, you will find her a more attractive person than someone dissimilar. "Birds of a feather flock together" expresses a verifiable phenomenon (Polansky, White and Miller, 1957). Does it not seem likely, then, that you would also be more verbally accessible to someone you thought more like yourself? After all, he should accept your values and your defensive attitudes because he shares them. Yet, in a series of studies, we have not found the predicted relationship to hold. In fact rigid people seem more open to those who challenge their attitudes (Nooney and Polansky, 1962; Tucker, 1961). The failure to verify what seemed to us an obvious prediction remains a paradox in interviewing (Tessler and Polansky, 1975).

Drawing on the literature and clinical experience, what principles can we set down about how to help those we talk with be as verbally accessible as is possible for each? (Polansky, et al., 1971). We have set some of these down, over the years, in other writings, so I will just give highlights here.

To begin with, one must ask *why* the client would want to tell personal things to his caseworker. The person who comes for counseling or psychotherapy has an obvious reason for talking. To have one's problem understood, it is necessary to inform the person trying to help you. But social workers see other clients too, under conditions in which no standard motive for talking can be presumed. Abusive parents think of us as adversaries. Often the parent believes it is to his interest to reveal as little as possible, so it becomes part of the task to advance a reason the parent might profit from talking: "It will help us form a better judgment if you will tell me how all this seems to you."

In some social work missions, at first glance no reasonable case can be made that discovering more about the client's basic attitudes is our business. Take, for instance, a woman who has just been deserted who is applying for Aid to Families with Dependent Children. Officially, we are there simply to determine that the breadwinner has in fact left and the family has no other resources to count on. At a certain point, it is necessary that the mother file charges of abandonment against the husband. Although her children are in need, she finds it hard to carry out this requirement. At this point her feelings and underlying motives *are* our business since we are concerned about the children and her. So we say, "You are are having a hard time taking this step, and that could mean trouble about your getting support. Do you want to talk about what is going on with you?" Social work, after all, is rather unique in recognizing that both external and *internal* influences affect people's use of resources. In that extended sense, the mother's conflicting feelings of anger and yearning toward the missing man are as much our concern as her bank account. I like to say that we in social work are dedicated to minding others' business, and it is good we are here to do it in many of these situations. For beyond the practical matter, that if the mother does not resolve her conflict and take action her children will go hungry, is the sad probability that she has no one else with whom to talk over the issues. Perhaps the chance to ventilate and to share her worries with someone sympathetic for even twenty minutes or so will help her get a more objective view, clear the air, and pull herself together to do what she has to. Even if she cannot take the needed actions, as we tried to show earlier in this chapter, the effort to talk over her decision should have an integrating effect; another reason her feelings are our business.

But, I mention the issue of *why* the client should talk for good reason. To be able to do penetrating interviewing is so valued in our profession that there is an impulse to strive for revelations even when they are inappropriate. Such misplaced skill is the mark of amateur night at casework burlesque. To become privy to feelings a client has never been able to bring herself to share or even recognize is a privilege, perhaps, but it also lays a burden on an ethical worker. What are you to do with the mother who says, after a research interview has turned up ghosts of her earliest sufferings, "No one ever bothered to hear my story before." Do you thank her for her time and walk away? Or, do you take the extra hours that might be required for a decent human ending and, perhaps, a referral? In our own research, we felt we had to take the time (Polansky, et al., 1981).

Given good reason to encourage verbal accessibility, what further leads can we provide? A series of these has to do with reducing restraints or inhibitions against revealing oneself. And, many of these are related to problems with feeling *vulnerable*.

Vulnerability, for us, includes the chain of associations: rejection leads to loneliness, which portends death by starvation or desiccation. This is no trivial anxiety; it is a powerful deterrent against self-revelation. How can anxiety about being found unworthy or weird be reduced? Concrete experiences in the interview may reassure the client he is liked and accepted. I was impressed that a senior analyst like Erikson was far more likely to help a visiting colleague on with his coat than most of his juniors. Concern about your immediate comfort tells you the professional you are with likes you as a person.

It is taken for granted that maintaining a *nonjudgmental attitude* reduces vulnerability feelings. This idea merits elaboration. The desired attitude is not the same as approval; it does not require the worker to congratulate the man who tells you he has just accomplished adultery and proved "I am quite a man!" You might choose to say nothing; you might comment that you are glad he has been able to tell you about it; but there is no need to reinforce behavior which, in fact, may be destructive to him and hurtful to his wife. I have come upon the recommendation that we owe those we want to help "unconditional positive regard," or some such quasi-religious injunction. There is no such thing as unconditional love between *mature* adults. That is why we miss our mothers. The world is full of men and women who can tell you how the actions of a partner eventually killed feelings of love. I imagine that those professionals who prescribe the attitude expect to be paid regularly by those they serve.

To pretend an oceanic acceptance of every motivation you hear expressed is unrealistic, or else the caseworker himself may have a poorly put-together superego. So, as many have pointed out, you may accept the person *as a person*, while deploring his behavior, or you may just hear it out without comment. Two things seem relevant to bear in mind: do not add to the burden of persecutory anxiety the client may be carrying as a remnant of poor resolution of the paranoid position; and do not add unnecessarily to his separation anxiety.

Of course, it helps if you really are rather accepting toward things clients do that are more symptomatic than sinful. You cannot, however, will yourself to be that way. Life experience fosters the development of tolerance. After some time in practice, confrontations with the things people get into which at first were shocking seem to be mastered by the ego, according to the principle of the *repetition compulsion;* the worker simply is not made anxious by tales of such actions any more. With experience, healthy workers also develop a sense of their own firm boundaries. You are, naturally, more shocked by behavior when that voice within you says, "I can easily imagine myself doing that, too." While this transaction may aid empathy, overidentification could on the other hand make you deny the feeling and become more obtuse. After some years, the statement changes to, "I can imagine a person doing that, all right; but I did not do it—he did." Oddly, the awareness of your separateness may make it easier for you to maintain closeness, since you are now less likely to confuse the patient's weaknesses and sins with your own.

It goes without saying that workers who radiate their own vulnerabilities discourage client admissions. Clients feel they "could not take it," and they read a worker's *premature reassurance* for what it signifies—the worker is feeling anxious about what has been said. So instead of saying, "Well, I can see why you had to do that" in response to a guilt-laden confession, it would be better to recognize the client's real feelings, "That is a hard memory to live with. Do you want to talk more about how it feels? Is there more?" All who have taken chances in life have things they are guilty about, or ought to be.

The perception of the worker as caring and strong becomes most relevant when what needs to be talked about is the client's unreasonable rage directed against the worker. It is human to respond to anger with anxiety and with urges to retaliate. So, bracing oneself against expressions of dislike is a problem for all who do this work. The only promise I offer the newcomer to the field is that this anxiety too diminishes after repeated experiences of being attacked. Responding to rage with laughter is occasionally a useful tactic—but only occasionally. Laughter helps the worker because it fits in with the defense of *minimization:* one makes a threat symbolically smaller by ridiculing it. But, the danger is that laughing off the client's rage is a put down. How would you like to give someone your best shot, and have them laugh it off? The put down is similar to that experienced by professionals who tell you that what you have been worried about for a week is not all that important. Premature reassurance, once again, may reflect the worker's anxiety at what he is hearing, rather than the client's. It is best to assume the client is really not an idiot, so that if he is magnifying a worry in his own mind, he has an unconscious reason for doing so.

I have mentioned that chronic feelings of powerlessness add to a client's vulnerability. So, we carefully avoid maneuvers that might be experienced as demeaning, which we would want to do anyhow. Various efforts go into encouraging the sense of equality in the interview situation. "There are things I have in mind that are too hard to talk about. Must I talk about them?" "Well, *you* are in charge of what you say. I imagine you'll talk about them if something changes, and when you feel more ready." About half the time, after such an exchange, the client follows through immediately by bringing out anxiety-laden content. Is this because the worker has declined to be teased? More likely, it is because the client is made to feel stronger by being reminded of his autonomy. Equality is also communicated by offering the client the right to decide, whenever realistically feasible. Decisions may even be about details of the treatment, like choosing appointment times if there are alternatives in one's schedule.

Concern with respecting equality brings into focus the fact that some clients cannot conceive of being in such a relationship. We have remarked the schizoid person's using status differential as a distance maneuver. To him, no simple closeness between equals is possible. One member of a pair has to be on top. As part of easing feelings of vulnerability, one may have to interpret for the client the fact that s/he scrupulously treats you as if you were his superior— and he is the defiant underdog.

Much can be said about how one's manner and style affect vulnerability. A modulated voice, one that can even be caressing at times of pain, makes most clients feel more secure. So does speech that, without dragging, is not very rapid. For reasons probably connected to their being laid down when we are very young, central feelings and attitudes tend to be phrased internally in simple words and short sentences. So, part of the style that encourages client accessibility is the ability to talk of feelings in simple, straightforward English.

Clients often use the worker as a model for behavior in the interview. A very shy and constricted worker may inhibit clients. Being verbally accessible, yourself, does not require that you burden those you are charged with helping with intimate details of your own history or personal life. Readiness to communicate can be demonstrated on the spot with comments like, "When you talk that way, I feel you are trying to pull a curtain down between us." In any event, it is essential to the conduct of casework or psychotherapy that the worker be articulate. People who have trouble putting their own thoughts clearly into words may have to get professional help if they want to be useful to others by offering talking treatment.

Helping an essentially nonverbal person talk about anything is a step in the right direction. Talk about recipes or football is not wasted time with such a client, if it is envisaged as on the road to helping in the eventual verbalization of more central attitudes. Many clients from backgrounds with restricted vocabularies may even lack words for expressing feelings, as noted earlier. A phase in their treatment might include teaching them such a language.

Now, client-centered therapy, in which one mostly echoes back to the client what he has been saying, is seldom appropriate for the people we deal with. Slavishly adhered to, it is a technique primarily useful for middle-class adolescents with minor maladjustments who require only an audience while they cure themselves. However, echoing back can be used well in phases of the interview in which one wants to "trace the affect back." For example: "Then I thought about my father, and what he'd have to say about buying that rotten car." "You were reminded of your father's rubbing in what a fool you were?" "Yes, to him it was sinful to make a dumb mistake." "Not only are you in car trouble, but you are also a bad, bad boy?" With uneducated clients, or those unaccustomed to talk about their personal lives, the same interview strategies may become a tactful way to feed a vocabulary they will want to make use of. "You were embarrassed?" "You were annoyed?" "You felt upset?"

Timing is an important element in facilitating verbalizations. A client may be silent because she is searching for a way to phrase what she wants to express; and one must wait until she has found it. Analysts used to think that a silent patient was probably using silence to control the interview, so one should simply wait her out. In my experience, however, adherence to this tactic is easily overdone in casework. The person who says, "I wish you would ask me some questions" is, perhaps, playing it safe, but is also telling you of a need for help in structuring how to get started. It can be in order simply to ask a question relevant to the reason for coming. If you believe you should remain silent, you might explain the reason: that you want to know what is on the client's mind and do not want your thoughts to be an influence. One risk with the client who remains caught in an impoverished silence too long is fostering even greater feelings of inadequacy and worthlessness than before. Or of boredom.

Clients need us to be honest in our communications. The need for honesty sounds like a moral imperative but is not meant to be. If we could invent a systematic deception through which people are cured, I would have no reluctance at all about using it—if only because so many have cheerfully deceived me in order to stay ill. However, most who do this kind of work will agree that the client's own confusions and self-delusions create a complicated enough morass without our adding to them. As one unknown American has put it, "If you tell the truth, you don't have to remember the details."

So telling white lies is ruled out; so is maintaining the myth that therapists never make mistakes or misstatements. The attempt to be honest—and all we can do with our own defensiveness is struggle against it—is essential to the adult level of closeness we offer. Which does not imply we say everything we are thinking. You may have to remain quiet about hunches that are still too vague to communicate, or an insight you have that would add to the patient's anxiety before it can be handled. What honesty should mean is that the worker is, indeed, able to stand behind what is said, and to keep silent when not prepared to stand behind one's own words. So honesty in talking is not recommended simply as a moral issue. As Kaiser suggested, it provides a model for the client and is a great convenience for the worker.

An example of what I have in mind comes from my own training. After a time, I realized that I had been asking open-ended questions in interviews as I had been taught to do. I was being a good little boy, following the forms taught me. The awareness dawned on a day when I finally knew enough about dynamics and differential diagnosis to ask questions for a new reason: I was truly curious about how they would be answered because the responses would tell me something I wanted to know.

Drawing on Learning Theory

This book does not attempt coverage of *behavior modification* nor of *learning theory,* which provides its scientific base (Skinner, 1969). Our mission is in another direction, and there are a number of fine texts in that field available to the student by authors who have devoted chunks of their lives to mastering that content (e.g. Wodarski and Bagarozzi, 1979). Freud's original theory was heavily associationistic, so the two theoretical approaches share some common roots. Moreover, all modern personality theories accept Thorndike's (1898) law of effect, which stated that "pleasure stamps in; pain stamps out." Still, psychoanalysts have not pursued the same intricacies of these propositions in ways that laboratory experiments make possible. It is not possible, for example, to derive from ego psychology the proposition that a conditioned response established by random, intermittent reinforcement is extremely resistant to extinction. A Freudian might well utilize some facets of *desensitization;* few would avail themselves of the *aversive* conditioning also found in the work of Wolpe (1973), a simple example of which is giving the patient antabuse so that alcohol becomes unpleasant. In the analytic tradition, there is great concern about treating only symptoms, rather than underlying causes, lest the underlying anxiety simply lead to replacing one symptom by another, maybe more crippling than the first. But there is another issue: the analyst would be unlikely to know Wolpe's rationale in any depth.

In trying to encourage a client's greater verbal accessibility, one may well use maneuvers associated with behavior modification.

The tactics would supplement, rather than substitute for, techniques described above. Thus, statements of strong feelings which seem genuine may be *positively reinforced*. "I'm fed up with being the one who worries about the bills." "Good for you. Better to say it out loud than to go around the house in a full-time pout." Remarks that seem evasive, or unduly constricted, may be reacted to in a way that encourages extinction of the pattern they express, such as ignoring them or even offering mild reproof. "Why are you calling him a wood-pussy? You seem to mean he's a skunk." One can even reinforce selectively while encouraging a certain degree of realistically controlled reaction. "It's not necessary to resign in a huff from a job you very much need. But, I'm glad you are now able to express your feelings here, in the privacy of this room. Maybe we can now start to find out just what is stirring you up."

In general, a style of treatment that makes for clarification and insight is preferable. Only if the client becomes aware of the things s/he is doing that lead to difficulties can the client's intelligence be brought into play, the next time, to try to avoid repeat performances. Still, there are other aspects of psychotherapy and casework that do not involve understanding but are, nevertheless, important to the whole process. What better reassurance against feelings of being unlovable, with all the archaic terror they imply, than experiencing the steadfast and highly personal interest of one's caseworker? At least a part of what used to be called a *corrective emotional experience* involved *unlearning* noxious attitudes toward oneself and acquiring new ones.

*   *   *

Even after forty years, it remains to me something of a miracle that happenings as tangible as a depression, an anxiety attack, a physical symptom are treatable by something as intangible as talking together, exchanging ideas, expressing attitudes. Yet, the miracle occurs all the time, perhaps because talk is, in fact, so basic to our comforting each other against the existential void and the loneliness which is our fate. Among civilized adults, the greatest intimacies we are able to achieve come through verbal communication. Of all the other functions that speech serves, which is as important?

CHAPTER 13
A SPEED READER'S GUIDE TO
Group Psychology

Ego psychology deals with how the individual relates to others and should apply to understanding group processes. However, analytic theory is primarily about ideas and images in the mind, so one cannot reduce *group dynamics* to ego psychology. As illustrated, the two compatible lines of theory often complement each other.

Having the same person as *ego-ideal* and/or object of love drives, gives followers "similar content in the ego"; it provides a bond among them. *Central persons*, around whom groups form, often support other ego functions, for example, resolving conflicts. The repressed character of such common elements may account for the aura of mystery surrounding *charismatic leadership*. A bond is provided by joining to defeat the group therapist through acting out regressive group fantasies which Bion called *basic assumptions*, for example, *dependency*. Indeed, individual and collaborative *resistance* is always a basis for group cohesiveness in milieu therapy and other group situations.

To understand *behavioral contagion* requires theory about both group and individual dynamics. Acquiring a high position in the *prestige structure* is itself a goal. Thus, modeling a high status person becomes a way of incorporating his position. Contagion also occurs without reference to group structure. Redl said the *trigger function* of the *initiatory act* often derives from its resolving conflict through *guilt assuagement*.

Research has confirmed Freud's postulate that "common content in the ego," perceived similarity, is one basis for group formation. Cohesive groups press for *uniformity* of opinions among their members: *deviants* are apt to be excluded. The need for uniformity derives from seeking *consensual validation* from our peers to reassure us about what is "real." Also, deviant opinions threaten a common delusion of fusion. Like behavioral contagion, pressure toward uniformity is value netural. Such group processes may strengthen individual resistance to therapeutic change. But, they may also operate to favor movement, for example, by making previously accepted symptoms *ego-dystonic*.

Group
Psychology

13

The aspect of the personality engrossed in group processes is the ego. To the convinced Freudian, therefore, group psychology is simply applied ego psychology. Of course, it is more than that. We knew this 30 years ago while I was taking my doctorate in social psychology among the followers of Kurt Lewin (1951), the founder of the field called *group dynamics* (Cartwright and Zander, 1953). One cannot simply reduce all group regularities to the principles encountered in ego psychology.

Students of group dynamics have discovered laws governing the action of small face-to-face groups at several levels of analysis. One set has to do with the transaction between groups; in these, the group is the unit of analysis. For example, if two groups are consistently in competition with each other, the members of each are apt to become progressively more hostile toward each other. Yet, a pair of adversary groups may put aside their differences when confronted by a common danger and join to meet the emergency. A superordinate goal transcends the issues which have divided them. Sherif showed this in a field experiment in a boys' camp. Two fiercely competing teams nevertheless joined forces when the whole camp's water supply was cut off (Sherif, 1966).

Another set of laws covers ways in which groups' internal processes function relatively independently of the individuals involved. Stalin used the opportunity provided by being pivotal to internal communications of the Russian Communist Party (i.e. General Secretary) to first become widely connected, eventually all powerful. Following the laws of group process, one can recast the operations of work units in order to coordinate their work more smoothly (Lippitt, 1940). Typical treatments of group processes are clarifying role definitions and work assignments. The outcome may be that the group now carries out its mission more efficiently and works with less friction among group members. But, the people making up the work force will not have changed or, at most, changed only in superficial attitudes. Group principles at this level of analysis fascinate students of management. As a matter of fact they interest clinicians, if only because, as my friend Charles Brink used to say, "Life has a way of leading you on." Today's therapist may prove to be tomorrow's team leader or hospital superintendent.

Efforts to achieve group homeostasis often involve the imposition or reinforcement of individual pathology. We have all too often witnessed a mental hospital staff whose high morale and cohesiveness rested on its unwillingness to grapple with the fact that many patients were stagnating in treatment. We have also known the home that buys its freedom from familial conflict by assigning one child the job of being *schlemeihl*, the inadequate who unifies the others by deserving their contemptuous protection. These phenomena are, of course, related to ego psychology, but it is one thing to explain regularities once they have been discovered; it is quite another to have a theory that predicted them. In short, significant laws of group equilibrium and change, powerful enough to defeat our work, have been discovered independently of ego psychology.

My intention in this chapter is not to offer an ego psychology of group dynamics, rather to trace connections between the two fields of discourse illustrating compatible lines of theory, and how they may supplement each other. In tracing these connections, I will choose examples that have interested me over the years and about which I have some expertise.

Charisma

Most of us think of *charisma* as a mysterious inner force in leaders which attracts others and makes them susceptible to influence. It is as if people with charisma glow in the dark—which must be disconcerting to their spouses and lovers. Nor are we moderns alone in this impression. Medieval painters routinely showed saints and other religious figures aglow with nimbuses and halos.

While the conception of charisma is very old in theology, its use in modern social science dates from the writing of Max Weber, the German man of letters, who is one of the great figures in the history of sociological thought. Weber writes first of one kind of leadership related to the patriarchal postion in a family, and of another based in holding a top position in a bureaucracy.

The provisioning of all demands that go beyond those of everyday routine has had, in principle, an entirely heterogeneous, namely, a *charismatic* foundation. . . . . The "natural leaders"— in times of psychic, physical, economic, ethical, religious, political distress—have been neither officeholders nor incumbents of an "occupation" . . . that is, men who have acquired expert knowledge and who serve for remuneration. The natural leaders in times of distress have been holders of specific gifts of body and spirit; and these gifts have been believed to be supernatural, not accessible to everybody. The concept of "charisma" is here used in a completely "value-neutral" sense (Gerth and Mills, 1946, p. 245.)

In contrast to any kind of bureaucratic organization of offices, the charismatic structure knows nothing of a form of, or of an ordered procedure of, appointment or dismissal. It knows of no regulated "career," "advancement," "salary," or regulated and expert training of the holder of charisma or of his aids. . . . Charisma knows only inner determination and inner restraint. The holder of charisma seizes the task that is adequate for him and demands obedience and a following by virtue of his mission (p. 246).

Weber was writing about a kind of leadership apt to emerge during great social unrest, when usual societal structures have broken down. Leadership depends on qualities of energy, attractiveness, and certainty of purpose emanating from the leader. If such gifts are supernaturally endowed, they are of course beyond the province of this book. For in matters supernatural Freudians surely are not expert. But, if the feeling that the charisma endowed so mysteriously represents largely unconscious processes, analytic theory may offer insights. Let us begin with the principle that to understand leadership, one must study followership; the ability to lead rests, in the last analysis, on how the leader fits into the motivational lives of those who follow him.

Very shortly after World War I, Sigmund Freud wrote a slim book which appeared in English as *Group Psychology and the Analysis of the Ego* (1922). He took as his starting point a book by Gustave LeBon, *The Crowd* (1903), which sought to explain mob behavior during periods like the French Revolution. Freud accepted LeBon's observation of the homogeneity of opinion that seems to form at such times, so that there even seems to be something in a mob analogous to a "group mind." He also accepted that there is an intensification of emotion in mobs, with each group member inciting the others. Freud also agreed that those in a mob are highly suggestible to each other and that the common thought processes are at a childlike, regressed level. Of course, nothing we know of Freud's personality encourages the idea that he would have chosen any group as the place to think a problem through. But, he doubted LeBon had satisfactorily explained the importance of the mob leader's prestige, and he undertook to theorize about this facet of what sociologists call *collective behavior*.

To Freud, "The essence of a group lies in the libidinal ties existing in it" (S. Freud, 1922, p. 45). Hence, one of the causes of panic is the disappearance of emotional ties holding the group together. This interesting comment by the master foreshadowed later writings in the theory of object relations which emphasized the need for a "good object." How do libidinal ties among members emerge? In ongoing formal groups like the Church or the Army, each person is connected, first, by libidinal cathexes to the awesome leader, that is, ties to Christ or to the Commander in Chief. The church communicant identifies with the head of his religion, using him as an *ego ideal*. The ego ideal is an image of what each person would like to become; it is not the same as the superego. The identification object, however, also becomes an object you want to absorb into yourself, so the ego ideal shifts to being, also, an object of drives. For example, Freud says, in falling in love, "The object has taken the place of the ego ideal" (p. 75). The head of the large organization becomes both ego ideal and drive-object for each member. Since all in the group have the same object imagery, it is a bond among them.

Of the ties among mob members, or people in situations without permanent structure (e.g. audiences of rock groups; spectators of sports events), Freud said, "A primary group of this kind is a number of individuals who have substituted one and the same object for their ego ideal and *have consequently identified themselves with one another in their egos*" (p. 80, italics added). It is as if they were saying to each other, "I see you trying to make yourself resemble the same figure I would like to be; so we are connected with each other."

How then is the *group ideal* selected in unorganized crowd situations? Selection derives from how well he fits the unconscious needs of his followers.

He need only possess the typical qualities of the individuals concerned in a particularly clearly marked and pure form, and need only give an impression of greater force and of more freedom of libido; and in that case, the need for a strong chief will often meet him half-way and invest him with a predominance to which he would otherwise perhaps have made no claim (p. 102).

The charismatic leader, then, typifies widespread group wishes which the group dare not express, or about which it feels conflicted. He, however, is unconflicted about pursuing the pleasure-seeking they all emulate. The person with *charisma*, moreover, is partly an invention of his followers. Their need for a "strong chief" leads them to see in him vigor he does not necessarily possess. A striking example was the adulation given Dwight Eisenhower during his presidency. Elderly, often ill, an indifferent president, he was invested by the public with qualities of energy and kindliness that did not accord with the impressions of those closest to him. By maintaining a carefully ambiguous public image, Eisenhower nurtured a mass transference as everybody's good-mother.

Where Freud left off, the modern student of group dynamics recognizes him as a brilliant, perceptive man with a gift for theorizing —who obviously did not know very much about group psychology. His later followers, on the other hand, having sometimes spent years of clinical work in and through multiperson helping settings, know a good deal more than he did. One such is Fritz Redl, whose germinal work with ego-disturbed children we alluded to earlier.

Freud attributed the formation of mobs to two dynamics: the leader's emergence as a common ego ideal; his becoming the common object of love/hate drives. In a classic paper, Redl (1942) extended the conception, specifying eight other ego functions which such a *central person* can serve, so that a group collects around him. First, as an object of *identification*. When the identification is on the *basis of love*, that is, fear of loss of the love object, it may lead to incorporating the leader figure into one's conscience. An example of this is the attachment of a group of adolescent girls to their well loved Sunday School teacher. Or, the leader might be incorporated into each individual's ego-ideal, as a boy's basketball team may do with a coach, still active in the game, who dresses well and owns a sports car. Not mentioned by Freud, however, was a group's jelling because of a shared identification based on fear, *identification with the aggressor*. All those who suffered together through Mr. Pythagorus's terrifying class in intermediate algebra salute each other, forever after, in the high school halls.

A central person may be the object of love drives, as is the figure of Christ in Christianity. But groups also form around having someone to hate. In a neighborhood common antagonism toward one developer may be the strongest bond among the residents. Sad to say, a common *scapegoat*, or projective repository for sins, is one of the most reliable bases for group formation. All propagandists know this, as if they had each been schooled by Melanie Klein on the universality of *persecutory anxiety*.

Redl also reminds us that a central person often holds the group together through generally *ego-supportive* functions. The youngster who bubbles with ideas for fun and games may attract a clique, by finding acceptable *means for drive satisfactions*. As a matter of fact, a material possession others can enjoy may also make one central. Many people maintain yachts or swimming pools with some such ambition in mind; sexual availability has been similarly used. Besides the facilitation of others' drive-discharge, Redl pinpointed another major form of ego support the central person sometimes provides. S/he helps *resolve conflicts* between urges to express sex and/or aggression and restraints stemming from feelings of guilt and anxiety about the impulse. How does the resolution take place? One way is from what Redl calls "the technique of the initiatory act." You want to steal a nibble from a chocolate cake, but it is supposed to be saved for tonight's dinner party. However, you sister nabs a little piece, so you follow right behind her. If your mother catches you at it, you protest, "But Adele did it first!' From his work with delinquent youngsters, Redl learned that this rationale for projection of blame is very widely ego-acceptable among delinquent youngsters and, indeed, among many others as well. If on the other hand your sister says, "Well, we ought to let the cake alone," she may also resolve your conflict. Her example augments *drive defense;* your controls are strengthened; and so the impulse is repressed. We shall return to the *trigger function* of the initiatory act later in this chapter, in discussing our research on *behavioral contagion*.

Now, the trigger function of the act affects your controls in a guilt-anxiety conflict, as does the manner in which the central person acts. Redl speaks of the "infectiousness of the unconflicted personality constellation over the conflicted one." If your sister nips off some cake, but seems scared and hesitant as she does so, her act is far less inviting than if she commits her crime boisterously and obviously without fear of sin. As a matter of fact, the infectiousness of demonstrating guilt-free drive expression is one basis of all seduction. After all, seduction generally involves helping another person do what he already wants to do anyhow. Seduction always makes people think of sex, but that is too limiting a view of its dynamics. In Germany, the Nazis followed Hitler in smashing the weak. In this country seduction's primary function is to induce the public to spend money by showing the happiness of those who have already purchased a car, a TV set, a grandfather clock, or a pair of hand-hewn oak andirons. And, of course, the *dominance of the unconflicted personality constellation* may operate in the direction of withholding drive expression—as anyone who has been reared by a stingy parent can tell. After a certain age, there are things you simply see no point in owning. So another ego-supportive function of the central person derives from apparent decisiveness. Freud, it will be recalled, referred to the leader's "freedom of libido."

Ego psychology, then, can complement Weber's sociological depiction of *charisma*. The source of the charismatic leader's emanations is mysterious because it is repressed or unconscious: at least part of the process is at first unacceptable to the follower, such as surrendering an existing ego ideal for a new one. Indeed, the source of charismatic authority is not univocal. The emergent leader when normal social structures have collapsed most likely fulfills several functions simultaneously in the lives of those who follow him.

It is usually not apparent how much of the image projected by the leader of a great movement, like Gandhi or Tito, was deliberately planned, and how much is simply the leader's being himself. Nearly all such successful figures know they must retain some mystery in order to inspire awe. But even if they did not trouble to do so, numerous followers would presume the wonder for them, projecting on them depths not really there. Many of the old Bolsheviks systematically jailed and destroyed by Josef Stalin in his paranoid rampage through Russia refused to believe that he was personally aware of their fates. For such a victim to admit he had given his whole life to a party that could reduce his nation to the absolute rule of a beast would have been completely unbearable. The victim preferred to believe he was being used for some great purpose by the Party, or else that he would be rescued at once if only he could get word out to Stalin (Koestler, 1941). What a grand illusion!

Perceived Similarity and Interpersonal Attraction

We have been tracing the role a charismatic leader or central person may play in the psychic economy of the individual group member. Freud believed that ties to the leader instilled ties among group members, based on having common "contents in their egos." Of course, Freud's formulation about incorporation into the ego ideal would be extremely difficult to subject to empirical test through experiment or scientific study. But some of us who have been associated with the Research Center for Group Dynamics at one time or another have conducted studies that either support his hypothesis or are compatible with it. The convergence of the two schools of thought is the more interesting because those of us doing social psychological research were following our own leads, not reading and rereading Freud. His heavy reliance on constructs in formulating theory and vagueness about operational definitions had already made analytic hypotheses notoriously difficult to test.

The relevant hypothesis is fairly simple, highly credible. Someone you perceive as similar in values and so forth will be more attractive than another who is dissimilar. From a series of studies in children's camps, Rosen, Levinger and Lippitt (1960) analyzed sociometric test data showing the children rated those cabin mates judged more similar to themselves as more likeable. Which was cause, which effect? If you find someone else attractive, do you make the benign projection of similar attitudes? Or is it that, having found similiarity, you now begin to like? The answer could come only from experimenting with perceived similarity, manipulated between pairs of strangers with no relationship. One could find out whether they like each other. Such a study, by Nooney and Polansky (1962), had two findings. First, it was shown that if a subject is given the impression he resembles another on a series of attitudes, he will *generalize* the perceived similarity, and judge the other more similar on a number of additional personality traits. The generalization of perceived similarity from musical preferences to other values was further demonstrated by Stotland, Zander and Natsoulas (1961). Second, those perceived as similar to oneself are definitely given more positive evaluations than those perceived as dissimilar. Incidentally, Freud's differentiation about the ego ideal one carries into a new group, and the group ideal which may evolve, was also encountered by those studying group dynamics (Zander, Stotland and Wolfe, 1960).

This benign projection of similarity to oneself, likely when one is fond of another person, is only one of many distortions made by people in groups to make themselves feel good about things. In a very early German experiment an investigator measured the relative popularity of boys in the gymnasium class. The class was then put though a series of floor exercises—tumbling, using the horse, etc.—and each youngster's performance was rated by the others. Several of the popular boys had been privately coached to make certain obvious mistakes. Yet in rating each other, the boys attributed mistakes to the boys who had low status. Good performance accords best with the image of being a good person. Class perceptions were distorted in order to maintain that balance. Years later, Fritz Heider (1958), a colleague of Lewin's from Germany, organized these phenomena into a more general theory of perceptual balance or harmony in interpersonal perceptions. Freudians, of course, would subsume all such processes under the synthetic function of the ego but, as I noted earlier, this does not mean they would have been able to specify and predict the various relationships shown.

Now, much of the projection that goes on in groups revolves around the group leader and is often unconscious. Shortly after World War II, a series of papers by the English analyst, Wilfred Bion, began to appear in the journal, *Human Relations.* Named sequentially "Experiences in groups: I...II..." and so forth, the papers eventually appeared as an intriguing, stimulating book (1959), too close to free association to make intelligible reading. One is, therefore, grateful for the summation Rioch (1970) subsequently provided, derived from her direct contacts with their author.

Bion's argument was that when one listens closely to the doings of a group organized for psychoanalytically oriented group psychotherapy, one gets an odd impression. There is the Work group: ten people who seem to know what the group is about and who undertake various activities to help it do what it is supposed to be doing. And at the same time there are ten people present, visually the same, who nevertheless are not a Work group at all. Rather, they behave *as if* their expectations had very little to do with the group's realistic tasks, but were quite otherwise. They act *as if* they were following a quite different Basic Assumption about the group's nature, as if they were on quite other business. Bion was clearly, or unclearly, talking about the same sorts of differences in level of operation which, speaking of the individual person, Eric Berne called ego states. One wishes Bion had called them group states too.

Bion identified three Basic Assumption groups into which the Work group may regressively abandon itself. The *dependency group,* calling for all involved to act as if totally helpless, ill, and unable to help themselves, turns submissively but hopefully to the great doctor to cure them. Of course they will be disappointed with him, eventually. Then they will turn from him in anger to some group member, who assumes the mantle at his own risk of ending up discredited. The *fight-flight group* acts *as if* all had come together to preserve the group against some awful danger. They need a leader to mobilize them to fight, or else to guide their fleeing. Naturally, they have no time for self-examination nor anything like it. Finally, the *pairing group* has come together to witness a union of two in their midst who will bring forth a savior. This savior, or messiah, will work magic for them so that, without effort, all will be well. A group operating *as if* this myth were true is given to brittle cheeriness and fatuous hope. "We'll all feel better when the Spring comes." Despite a perhaps tasteless analogy between these figures of speech and widely held religious beliefs, any group therapist who has survived extended platitudes will recall the nausea induced by so much Pollyanna-like sweetness and light.

Bion identified states into which therapy groups drift which certainly represent *regressions* from the Work session. Nearly always these are *regressions in the service of resistance*. Group members, being asked to face something unconscious which they are anxious about, take refuge in the modes of dependency, fight-flight, pairing and the like. Each Basic Assumption group requires that the therapist's role be recast to fit the image of him that the group needs at the moment. And, all three Basic Assumption groups are useful at blocking the therapist's attempts at *uncovering*. Each also sets the therapist up in a role he cannot fulfill; the stage is set for the therapist to disappoint the group. Disarmed and dismounted, he then no longer threatens to bring about insights.

Group Resistance

Resistance is a familiar phenomena in individual treatment. To avoid unwelcome insights, patients "play stupid," or "act out," or even physically flee treatment. Likewise, in life-encompassing treatment settings such as psychiatric hospitals, a motive as nearly universal as resistance shows up in the clique formations and other dynamics of social living. In places devoted entirely to treating alcohol addiction, it is common to find pairs of patients or small cliques supporting each other's *denial* that their drinking is at all dangerous. In defiance of the staff's emphasis on the need to stay sober, thereby giving up the defense to confront one's underlying self-destructive impulses, pairs of patients go to town on sprees. While the term *acting-out* is applied in many inpatient facilities to all instances of rule-breaking or rebelliousness, we also see it in its more technical meaning, dispelling the *uncovering* process in treatment.

We encountered an intriguing example of clique formation in the service of resistance in a small, private psychiatric hospital in New England many years ago. While studying ways that the milieu might be marshalled to complement individual psychoanalytically oriented psychotherapy, we administered sociometeric tests and a small series of attitude questions to all patients in residence (Polansky, White and Miller, 1957). We found the patient's informal group life was dominated by a "core clique," whose members, a minority of the total patient body, were relatively young, attractive, and in good social contact. They operated as a prestigious clique of insiders does in a high school class. It became evident that they had picked each other out for their potential for fun, and also for their readiness to let each other alone with his or her character disorder. In addition to a common unwillingness to take one's treatment very seriously, it appeared those in the clique used many of the same defenses, repeatedly. As Robert White put it, their rallying cry was, "Don't you step on my neurosis and I won't step on yours."

Now, if one operates a hospital like a concentration camp, one denies the patients chances for mutual support and socializing that might combat feelings of being alone and unloveable. But, if one frees the patients for spontaneous informal association, the phenomena of resistance become expectable group pathology. There is no treatment without its side-effects; some are potentially noxious. Patient-group values have little meaning unless formed largely from within the patient group. But is it not expectable that these values will sometimes favor, and sometimes oppose, what the staff is tying to do? Or, there may be a resolution of forces. At one point, for example, the staff tried very hard to encourage greater involvement by patients in activities that approached real work. We were concerned that the long-term hospital stay was feeding into passivity and withdrawal among patients. A few amenable middle-aged folks actually began to busy themselves constructing a patient's kitchen. Not the core clique. They neither joined us, nor did they completely disregard us. They started to compete at giving more and more elaborate cocktail parties before dinner. Maybe they were telling us what their real work was, outside the hospital. Certainly, a future in carpentry was not in the cards for these children of wealth.

One young woman left this memorable plaint:
All day I sit at the God-damned loom
Making God knows what to give to God knows whom.

Redl undertook to identify some of the expressions of resistance that he and his staff were encountering in attempting group treatment of delinquent children in Detroit. "Whole groups may, if their group code and outlook on life is threatened, develop one or another form of group resistance under all sorts of disguises" (1948, p. 313). The forms of group resistance included:

Escape into love: "All they have to do to avoid the necessity for real change is to lure the group leader into a continuous 'love' relationship, and they are safe" (p. 309).

Protective provocation: When the children feel in danger of softening up toward the group leader, they try another way out. They try to provoke the leader in order to put him "into any one of the categories of their traumatic life history, so as to get rid of this dangerous enemy of their delinquent fun" (p. 310).

Guilt escape through displaced conflict: If the children have reached a point where they no longer act out in the treatment group because they are now capable of guilt toward the leader, "They seem to develop an uncanny skill and frequency of getting themselves in trouble with the world outside" (p. 311). They are resisting the total surrender of a delinquent fun exempt from guilt by displacing it elsewhere.

Escape into virtue: Many a delinquent gang will, after a short time in treatment, show an amazing responsiveness. This is a smokescreen. By this maneuver, they can have a vacation with the treatment personnel, enjoy them and be liked by them—and reserve their delinquency for when they get home.

The forms of resistance Redl lists derive from his efforts in the group setting and reflect his genius at bringing psychoanalytic abstractions down to the operational level at which social workers live. The temptation is great, when thinking about delinquents, to presume that any psychological mechanism used is dedicated primarily to manipulating adults. In true Freudian tradition, however, Redl reminds us that the child's need for a *defense* has another basis. The resistances the children were showing were directed mainly against changes in themselves that might have laid them open to experiencing their guilt anxieties consciously.

Behavioral Contagion

One problem to be expected from bringing patients together in a residential setting is the danger that they will form counter-therapeutic alliances. There are other possible side-effects. For example, emotionally ill people may augment their illnesses by taking on symptoms from each other. This is not only cause for concern to parents who fear their loved ones will be spoiled from being confined with "those awful other children." We worry, too. In deciding whether to offer treatment to an adolescent with a record of unsavory sexual practices, a natural issue is whether impressionable younger boys might be tempted to emulate his patterns.

Redl (1949b) called *contagion* the process whereby one person unconsciously picks up another's pattern even though there has been no overt effort to get him to do so. Although Redl described emotional contagion in his original writings, when a group of us joined him in research on the phenomenon, we limited ourselves to *behavioral contagion*, acts which could be directly observed and verified. Our interest was in applying social science to the clinical setting, but we found hardly any earlier research on related phenomena. Most of the previous writing on the topic was speculative and anecdotal (Tarde 1903), so our clinical interest also required us to undertake basic social psychological research.

We first studied the proposition that a group member's behavior will be "contaged" (i.e. picked up) by others in his group depending on his prestige in that group. Using field studies in camps for emotionally disturbed children, we measured prestige by interviews with the children, asking them to rank all children in the cabin as to perceived power positions. Behavioral contagion was assessed by following camp groups around to record incidents of contagion—whose behavior was being picked up by whom—on precategorized data recording sheets (Polansky, Lippitt and Redl, 1950; Lippitt, Polansky and Rosen, 1952).

The results showed that by the end of the first week of camp, children's treatment groups usually have rather clearly defined and generally agreed upon power hierachies. There may be some uncertainty about middle ranks, but who is on top and who has the lowest status are recognized. Those with power are inclined to use it consciously in direct attempts to influence others. In addition, even when not asking to be imitated, their behavior is much more likely to be picked up spontaneously. Our hypothesis associating initiation of contagious behavior with prestige was verified.

We asked why it seemed that there were strong needs to occupy the higher power positions. Acting like the person with high prestige became a *substitution* for having his position, as well as an expression of *identification* with him. "I'm acting like you, I become you." A previous generation of sociology and social psychology students of these phenomena, drawing on the psychology of their day, referred to the "suggestibility of the crowd man." But, of course, this conception could not account for why children emulated those with higher prestige.

Were the children contaging from those with the higher prestige because they *admired personalities* who had acquired status, or because of their *position in the group*? In other words, is group position itself something valued and striven for, by conscious and unconscious mechanisms? One could not separate out these two components of prestige in the summer camp study, but some years later I had the opportunity to stimulate a doctoral student in psychology, William Warner, to undertake a laboratory experiment in which the subjects were strangers to each other, but one of each pair was in the more prestigeful positon. He also found that the low prestige person was much more likely to "contage" behavior from the higher than vice versa (Warner 1960). In Lewinian psychology one would say that taking on the behavior of the person in a high position has *substitute value* and partially satisfies the need to occupy that position. From the theory of object relations, we would see the roots of the need to be bigger and more powerful arising in early parent-child relationships.

For practical purposes, the implication from our research is that admitting a severely character-disordered child to the group is not likely to introduce a focus of infection in the patient body unless s/he can become highly prestigeful. An out of control youngster may well be viewed by the others as weird or odd, someone whose judgment and doings they would not take seriously. Such behavior would be unlikely to be picked up by the rest. Low prestige should serve most of the time to insulate the group from emulation.

There is, however, one type of dynamic situation in which the presence of an impulse-ridden individual poses a real danger for contagious loss of control by the whole group. Suppose the group is in a fairly intense state of conflict. They have an impulse to do something—let us say, steal cigarettes from the camp store—and they also feel they really ought not, or dare not. The conflict is familiar to us by now, involving (id) impulse opposed by (superego) restraint, and it exists in nearly everyone in the group. At this juncture, we confront what Redl called the *trigger function of the initiatory act*. A highly impulsive child, *not* usually followed in nonconflictual situations, who moves first to break into the store, facilitates the shifting of balances within the others, and may result in an episode of stealing by the whole group.

The trigger function then, is fairly independent of the person committing the act. That "he did it first" permits others in the group to assuage, or evade their own guilt-feelings. So the restraints are weakened, and the group episode follows. (We see similar processes in lynchings and gang rapes, too, that make a camp break-in seem, literally, child's play.) The trigger-function was also demonstrated experimentally, by Grosser, Polansky and Lippitt (1951).

The weakening of a defense does not always end in the carrying out of a forbidden impulse. For, when a defense is threatened, the anxiety that motorizes it is apt to become conscious. Further, in an effort to re-repress the impulse, the ego may take refuge in new symptoms. Recognizing this, Redl spoke of the "shock effect" in treatment settings in the same paper in which he described contagion (1949b). For example, a fairly tough youngster concerned with projecting his *macho* indifference to camp rules and proprieties is introduced into a group of emotionally disturbed youngsters, some predelinquent, others rather withdrawn. One bedtime, when the counselors have left, he stands in the middle of the cabin floor and masturbates. Of the other boys, a couple emulate him, a couple act disgusted. One boy says nothing, but later when the counselors return, they find that after he fell asleep he reverted to a symptom he had not shown in years, enuresis.

Shock effect, then, is a hazard especially for the youngster who has a fairly strong set of values but worries about his controls. Those whose averison to public masturbation was very firm probably reacted little to what they saw; those who had little guilt about it, simply joined in though, of course, they might show signs of anxiety later. But the boy with enuresis responded with heightened conflict and anxiety. Redl made us aware that shock effect is dynamically on the same continuum with contagion, a kind of *anti-contagion* response.

A not unusual expression of shock is to attack the person whose behavior is stirring up feelings. The person who feels unconsciously tempted works to *externalize* his own conflict by converting it into a battle between his evil impulse, now projected onto the instigator, and his righteous good side, that is, himself. Therefore, when an official moves to outlaw practices he disapproves of, which is sometimes understandable, but does so with a vindictive indignation that seems out of proportion, we may well be witnessing shock effect. At one time, for example, there were detectives whose job it was to frequent public lavatories to attract approaches from cruising homosexuals. Not only did the detective arrest his accoster; he would routinely beat him in the squad car that was taking them both to the station house so that the homosexual could be "booked." Fortunately, not all these detectives behaved this way.

We ought not close this discussion of behavioral contagion with the implication that it is always, or even usually, something to be dreaded by a group worker. Many instances of contagion are welcomed by social workers responsible for groups—the building up of excitement and pleasure at a birthday party, so that even ordinarily withdrawn youngsters are carried along; the spontaneous spread of a movement toward citizen participation in what were known in Cleveland as Block Clubs (Turner, 1959). The reader may recall our exploiting contagion, in psychodrama, to encourage temporary regressions which advanced the therapeutic impact of that modality. So, as a group dynamic contagion is value-neutral.

As always, we discover the natural laws of individual and group psychology; but we do not get to vote on them. A scientifically based practice takes such laws into account. At times we have to try to counter them, but more often we try to exploit the natural laws of group dynamics for the welfare of our members. In the long run, all we can do is cooperate with the potentially healing processes of nature. Nowhere is this more evident than with respect to group pressures toward uniformity.

Uniformity in Groups
Like many another scientific innovator, Freud was not much of a joiner. He was little given to membership in organizations that he did not dominate. The only exception that comes readily to mind was his regular card playing with his cronies in the local B'nai B'rith, but that was all that expressed the remnants of devotion to the Jewish tradition he had been reared in. Freud was given to describing his followers as if they were an intrepid band of scientific buccaneers carrying out hit-and-run raids, ravaging the settled terrain of the self-satisfied establishment in psychiatry. Applied to so sedentary a group of quiet intellectuals as the early analysts, the conceit was ludicrous. But Freud enjoyed his renegade role.

More importantly from our standpoint, he owed much of his success in penetrating the unconscious to a willingness to espouse unpopular opinions.

One can readily imagine, therefore, the satisfaction with which he must have read LeBon's descriptions of the suggestibility that sweeps across unruly crowds, and the unthinking unanimity that emerges in primitive mobs. Most rational men feel something like contempt for those swept up by movements. In Freud's case, the distaste would have been overdetermined by his years spent as something of a medical outcast. The distaste, however, is not reasonable. Pressure toward uniformity of opinion and action is widespread, of course, in groups of all kinds and not just in disorganized mobs. Freud's movement developed its own orthodoxy. In a quick review of one line of research into group dynamics and its connections to ego psychology, I will discuss the work of Leon Festinger, an old friend, and some other elderly colleagues who were once his students.

It had long been surmised, with considerable evidence, that people use the groups they belong to or which they retain as mental images as *frames of reference*. In judging whether something we have done is acceptable, we "refer" it to our internal audience and imagine what our family and those we were reared with would think of it. Both Freudian and social psychology agree that part of the superego is based in such *reference groups*. In deciding whether we, ourselves, are acceptable/loveable or not, we use a similar standard. Take the question of ability. Are you a good golfer? You do not compare yourself against Tom Watson, or the venerable Sammy Snead. Your standard is from your own foursome, or "the guys at my club." Festinger (1954) integrated many of these principles into a general "theory of social comparison processes."

Even your view of what is "real" is based in large measure on the reassurance that others you regard as sane agree they see what you see. This has been called *consensual validation* and we all rely on it especially in forming judgments of reality when the data otherwise available are somewhat ambiguous. Asch (1956) did a series of studies which showed that, confronted with a unanimous majority of others in the group, a subject may well change views of what is "real" to conform to their report, even if it differs from the evidence of one's own senses.

These social psychological phenomena are familiar to all students of that discipline. Psychoanalytically, they would be thought events in the domain of ego psychology. These laws, based on responses of "average expectable" subjects, are part of "normal" psychology. However, in my experience these laws are rather universal, affecting patients as well as persons not receiving treatment. And they need to be taken into account in appraising clients' reactions in treatment groups. Individuals' reactions may be based nearly entirely on what is going on within them, but may also derive from something more general sweeping the group. I have learned from experience that if one person on staff seems particularly depressed and anxious, it may be a matter of personal neurosis. But if everyone on the staff is suddenly "neurotic"—one has a backache, the other gets tearful in midafternoon, the third has taken to missing work—we have a general problem of group morale, and the problem may well be Polansky. Analytically oriented personnel sometimes do not see this; they often have a trained incapacity to take in the obvious.

In any event, it was known that people use groups as frames of reference in various ways, when Festinger began his work in a couple of projects for housing married students outside Boston shortly after World War II (Festinger, Schachter and Back, 1950). The Jewish organization sponsoring the research had a justified dread of authoritarianism, and therefore a willingness to sponsor behavioral science research into processes of participatory democracy. Accordingly, Festinger's group undertook to try to instigate a tenant's organization in the student housing. A corps of social science researchers was assigned to follow the process of the effort and—naturally—one lone social worker was sent out to be the *change agent.*

It was important to the research that the social worker not be identified as management, so she appeared on the scene without official connections. Lurking around at various places where children played and women sunned their babies, she tried to involve people in discussions of the desirability of forming a tenant's organization. The researchers, meanwhile, prepared for a series of "interview sweeps" of the entire communities involved in which one member of each couple would be interviewed regarding attitudes toward the tenants' organization, at periodic intervals.

Since the lone social worker had no visible sponsorship, one early reaction among the tenants was that she must be some kind of Communist, a rumor that nearly undid the whole field experiment. (The researchers responded with true opportunism and published their results under the title, "A study of a rumor: its origin and spread.") Meanwhile, the social worker managed to survive and, over a period of time, succeeded in making the question of forming or not forming a tenants' organization something of an issue. Since nearly all the couples included one veteran coping with readjustment to civilian life, earning a degree, and earning a living, and with everybody involved in starting new families and beating off older attachments, the tenants' group cannot have loomed as large in their lives as it did in those doing the study. But, it was an issue and somewhat talked about.

At this time the researchers performed one of their periodic sweeps, asking a variety of questions. A few had to do specifically with the tenants' organization; one question asked simply who the couple's current friends were and where they resided. Now, the data with respect to whether or not the residents favored having a representative organization were not of much enduring interest. Something else was, the question of *uniformity of opinion*, pro or con, in each housing court or apartment building. The courts varied from near unanimity to hardly any agreement at all. Theories about reference groups and their influences presumed near unanimity within them, but this is not the way things happen in life. What seemed to determine how much agreement there was in a given group?

Festinger, Schachter and Back found that they could rank order the courts with regard to degree of uniformity of opinion. They could also rank order them on another aspect of group life—relative cohesiveness. The index of cohesiveness were the results of their questioning about whom each couple named as friends. The more those named as friends lived in the same court, the higher the cohesiveness score given that court. When the two rank-orders, degree of uniformity and of cohesiveness, were correlated, the association was substantial and statistically significant. Festinger and his colleagues broke through theoretically. They took us from speaking of groups as if all represented the same degree of homogeneity of opinion, to recognizing their variation on this, and to locating a feature that might explain the differences.

Why the association between cohesiveness and degree of agreement within the group? It was found that the couple whose opinion was *deviant* from the majority view in its courts was likely also to be isolated from the court group socially: they were not named as friends by the others. Did this mean they had withdrawn, or been rejected? From a field study, with only correlations to work with, one could not tell. But in a subsequent experiment Schachter (1951) demonstrated that persons who hold deviant opinions in highly cohesive groups undergo a rather typcial process. At first, the others argue with the deviant and try to bring him into line. But if he persists, they stop talking to him and simply reject him. One explanation might be that the group achieves equilibrium by redefining its boundaries to exclude the deviant. But why is it so hard on a group to let its deviant be? And why is it especially hard for a cohesive group?

The other hypothesis was a bit more mysterious. It stated simply that in a cohesive group there emerge "spontaneous pressures toward uniformity"; the more cohesive the group, the stronger the pressures. This hypothesis tested in an ingenious experiment conducted by Back (1951) was also verified. But why the "spontaneous pressure"? Festinger's psychology left the explanation at that level.

To the student of ego psychology Kaiser's fusion-fantasy hypothesis comes immediately to mind. Holding the same attitude about matters important to the group supports the fusion fantasy. Loss of group consensus threatens each member with feeling lonely and abandoned, so they eject the non-fitting group member. But, why is the anxiety especially pronounced in highly cohesive groups? The temptation to rely on this defense must be heightened when people feel otherwise close and intimate. A somewhat rigid older man, for instance, able to maintain *pro forma* tolerance toward acquaintances with different standards, will be incensed to find that one of his children opposes him. In a general way, these experiments reinforce an impression we might have gained from the earlier chapters. The sense of oneself as separate and free-standing, born in difficulty but eventually achieved with relief and satisfaction, conflicts in adulthood with remnants of contradictory urges to obliterate the separations we know are there.

For, it is both exhilarating *and* frightening to find oneself out on a limb. One justifiably fears group exclusion. Schachter, for example, arranged to redo his experiment in six or seven other Western nations; in nearly all of them deviants were likely to be rejected. In Asch's studies of the effects of unanimous majorities, the subject was included in a group said to be fellow subjects and proceeded with an exercise in judging which of two lines flashed on a screen was longer. After a series in which all went believably, where the subject saw what everyone else saw, the subject was suddenly confronted with unanimous reports contrary to what the subject was seeing. About a third of the time, under these conditions, the subject will "yield," and join the unanimous majority. But what is not mentioned in the published reports may occur when one tries to replicate the study. The naive subject may become confused and very anxious, and you may have to suspend the experiment. Why the anxiety? There seem to be two bases. One is the fear of "losing my mind," since one becomes accustomed to getting consensual validation of one's view of reality. The other source? The subject cannot verbalize it, but following Kaiser we may infer a sudden coming face to face with a lonely void.

So one of the experiences common in groups is pressure toward uniformity. The nature of the pressure is not fully understood but obviously has a number of meanings as illustrated above. As with the other phenomena examined, group pressures are value-neutral in the sense that they may be noxious in their effects, or they may be harnessed to therapeutic ends when we are skillful and lucky. I mention luck because a group leader can influence but cannot really prescribe the predominant attitude of the group. We *hope* to have a group for alcoholics dedicated to offering each other emotional support, and to penetrating the massive denial so common in alcoholics, treated individually. We may *get* a group that offers support, all right, but the only person whose defenses are put under scrutiny is the leader.

When I was working near him a quarter century ago, Erik Erikson once commented in passing that he felt most really serious neuroses were developed in one-to-one relationships and so, ultimately, would have to be treated in such a relationship. Erikson's awareness of the importance of early experience with the mother is by now very familiar to the reader of this volume and it seems to me likely to be true. What, then, may we expect of group treatment? I think of several things. The pressure on attitudes a group may exert, particulary in defining what is experienced as "real," may not reverse the whole course of neurosis; it can change symptoms from being *ego-syntonic* to *ego-dystonic*. "Staying the way I am" becomes no longer acceptable to the rest of one's whole ego, and while this is not the same as change, it is an essential beginning toward psychotherapy.

For better or worse, therapy groups are usually led by professional helpers, but they are always dominated by amateurs. Your fellow patient may not have his counter-transference reactions under adequate control but, on the other hand, he offers some advantages. If he seems to like you, that is a very real experience: he is not trained and paid to feel that way. It does not go through your mind, "Your analyst is the best friend money can buy." Patients from therapy groups may *act out*, even forming pairs or liaisons outside the group. They are anything but immune to the urge to repeat old, unsatisfying relationships. But the spontaneous love/hate relationships that come up are just as real as the rest of life, and some of them are healing. Being loved right now at least conflicts with feeling unloveable! So, this provides a further advantage. The therapy group becomes a *protected reality* in which to try to practice newer ways of dealing with other people. The group setting is not real life, in the sense that even if you make a miscue, you remain a member of the group to work it out and try again, whereas in the outside world an acquaintanceship would probably already have ruptured. But, the reactions you beget are real, and the feedback given, franker and more explicit than in most life situations. Probably, most critical for many patients is the discovery that they can achieve closeness with a range of others, with nothing bad happening. On this cautiously hopeful sound I shall close this chapter.

CHAPTER 14

A SPEED READER'S GUIDE TO
Will, Choice and Responsibility

Western religion, philosophy, and psychology have long assumed that people exercise choice and are responsible for their acts and omissions. The belief that each must impose personal meaning on life was, if anything, strengthened by the events surrounding World War II. Yet, because of its roots in nineteenth century determinism, psychoanalysis has dealt ambivalently with the issues of *will*, *choice* and *responsibility*. The patient who disclaims choosing is said to be denying or minimizing; the explanation of his maneuver allows him no choice. Something is missing in the theory.

Two theoreticians offered explanations for why willing is denied. Kaiser related recognition of choosing to realizing you are separate and alone; hence the need to deny volition. Erikson traced similar anxieties to developmental failures with respect to achieving autonomy and initiative. Neither offered a systematic position for the will as a cause of behavior and not just a feeling about behavior. Shapiro attempted to treat the will as cause, but his conception postulated two kinds of motivations.

I have proposed that willing cannot occur in violation of the necessary internal conditions for behavior. Given that these exist, an organization within the ego may or may not choose to impose the final, sufficient condition that synthesizes motivations by choosing and assuming responsibility. Willing and a sense of purpose also presume behavior is influenced by a perspective of possible futures, Lewin's future time-perspective. The capacity to imagine the future seems an ego function deserving inclusion in the main body of theory; it is nearly as important as memory.

Maslow's postulate of a *self-actualizing* tendency at the apex of the *hierarchy of needs* presumes also that the ego has the ability to project alternative visions of the person one might become. Oriented more to doing than to being, Frankl believes that each of us has a life task which lends direction and purpose to our days. A *noogenic neurosis*, then, would consist in denying or otherwise repressing recognition of one's task, frustrating one's *will to meaning*. Again, the conception is that behavior is not just pushed by drives; it is also pulled by purpose.

For ego psychology to incorporate ideas from creative psychologists like Maslow and Frankl, it must continue to grow and to update its assumptions. While the rule of parsimony requires that theoretical change be careful, even grudging, a response to valid new observations may be expected.

Will, Choice and Responsibility   14

Accordng to tradition, a group of European rabbis assembled during one of the waves of Jewish persecution and asked: If the Lord is good and all powerful, why has he permitted so much evil in His world? Their answer was that the Almighty allowed both good and evil in order that Man might choose between, following His injunction, "Therefore seek ye the good." Similar notions are found in other creeds. The belief is widespread that people do have choices—between good and evil, wisdom and foolishness, pleasure and pain. Yet, major systems of psychological theory have trouble incorporating choice and finding places in their logic for terms like will and responsibility.

B. F. Skinner (1971), who has done fundamental work on *operant conditioning*, has vigorously challenged the view that people exercise free will. Since behavior, like other natural events, is subject to strict cause/effect relationships, there is no place for the operation of choice. What then of the subjective feeling that one is choosing? To Skinner, this signifies only that the subject has been conditioned to think of himself as doing so. Once one acccepts the scientific tenet that natural events are strictly determined, the concept of will is an appendage, or epiphenomenon. The behavior of pigeons can be accounted for without such imputation. Why embellish human behavior by saying it has been "willed?"

Despite their many divergences in approach from Skinner's, Freudians have a very similar problem with the idea of free will. As David Shapiro has written, "Psychoanalysis acknowledges choice or volition only as subjective experience—that is, sensation or belief—and it attempts to understand them only as subjective experiences" (1970, p. 329).

Analysts shared a commitment to laws precisely linking effects to causes. After all, devotion to this kind of explanation has brought physics a long way since Galileo and Newton. Closer to the couch, the assumption that there are no "accidents" in nature paid off handsomely in laying bare unconscious impulses. If the scenes in your dreams are not just happenstance, can we not infer that the same aggression that fills them with plots of murder and mayhem explains the anxiety of your waking hours? And your inability to talk openly of your rage is traceable to your identifying with a passive father. Analysts had good reason to share the behaviorists' zeal for strict determinism. Indeed, they stood together on this issue against the theologians and romantics whose claims to intuitive knowledge of the human psyche they hoped to displace with scientific method.

Yet, there is ambivalence. One theorizes about patients' behavior as if they are at the mercy of cause/effect. But, one treats them as if they have free will. Consider this conversation.

"The next thing I knew, there I was, waking up in her apartment."

"That's awful. Somebody drugged you and carried you over there?"

"Well, not quite. I called Beckie up and we talked and she finally said why didn't I come on over."

"You called Beckie up?"

"Well, yes. I was feeling low with Jean out of town and all, so I decided I had to call up somebody. Beckie's always been a good old girl."

"You said, earlier, that you wonder how you always get into things. Like waking up in Beckie's apartment and having to worry whether Jean called home. Do you feel you had nothing to do with setting all this up?"

"Doc, I guess my unconscious meant to get me out on the town all along."

"Nice of him to take you along." Both grin, but with different satisfactions.

Exchanges like this one could be taken out of the process of casework oriented to personal change and most modes of psychotherapy, including the psychoanalytically oriented. The client has thrown out a playfully evasive tactic, and the therapist has responded with an obvious counter. What is being evaded? And why bother to make an issue of it? The patient is not really *denying* what he did. He recalls the sequence of events clearly and brings the whole episode into treatment. So, what was missing? He was *minimizing* his own *responsibility*—another of those words like choice and will.

It would not be helpful to let this aspect of his report go unre-
marked. Minimizing his own responsibility for the miseries in
which he gets involved is not just a detail; it is the gist of the tale.
How will he become an integrated person, all of a piece, so long as
he pretends that he has no control over the scrapes he gets himself
into? Skinner says that feeling one has chosen is a conditioned
response, an effect, not a cause. But the worker in this instance
sees the denial that the client has chosen as, itself, in the service
of defense, a way of slipping a fast one past his superego. Is this
not paradoxical? Following the principle of strict determination,
the worker presumes the evasion of responsibility is caused by the
need to avoid anxiety. But, the worker is dubious about letting the
client lay claim to the same principle, namely that what happened
was due to unconscious forces over which he had no control.

As one might expect, the events of the evening in question were
foredestined in a manner of speaking.

"Tell me. Did your unconscious give you any warning this might
happen to the rest of you?"

"Sure, I guess so. When I heard Jean was going to be gone
overnight it went through my mind it would be fun to raise a little
hell, but I said to myself, 'Don't make an ass of yourself.' Did it
anyway, didn't I?" Now, there is a question best left as rhetorical.

So here is the quandary. In confronting the client, the worker
tries to help him see clearly that the escapade was deliberate.
Willing is treated as a cause of the incident. Indeed, the client's
minimizing the act of choosing is treated as a partial denial of what
really happened: that the client chose to flirt with trouble. A
litigious client, however, could convert the worker's effort into
quite a debate for there is inconsistency here. Either the convictions
that emerge in our treatment tactics are remnants of a prescientific
approach to helping people, or the theory underlying the tactics
has gaps in it.

The latter certainly seems to be the case. Analytic theory remains
incomplete now, as it has been in the past. Repeatedly, conceptions
have had to be altered to take new phenomena into account. While
it is *parsimonious* to only add theory grudgingly, it is feckless to
refuse to alter it at all. A number of other psychologies have
emerged in the past several decades that deal with willing, intend-
ing, choosing and responsibility. It would be unwise for practitioners to abandon analytic theory in favor of one of these newer
approaches, if only because each is severely limited as to how much
of the personality it seeks to cover. On the other hand, it would be

helpful to clients to find a way to incorporate into the rest of our thinking the contributions of certain non-Freudian writers.

In this last chapter, let us look at ideas that seem important for practice, but which have not yet made their way into ego psychology. These ideas include notions such as these: that the personality may be viewed synthetically as well as analytically; that behavior is often pulled by conscious intention as well as impelled by blind drive; that for many people the requirement that life have meaning is really a quasi-need not to be dismissed as intellectualization. Part of our quandary about freedom of the will derives from an outdated image of causation, so I will deal with that matter, too.

Humanistic Psychology
A number of those who seem to offer potential contributions to our work with people in serious trouble are called humanists, and their approach *humanistic psychology*. I undertake a critical review of their field with trepidation. To become truly conversant with a new theory of personality it helps to have gone through a phase of falling in love with it so that one reads it with absorptive passion. As with other love affairs, even after the passion cools one is left with a vast store of intimate knowledge. Alas, I have never had such feelings for the writings of Carl Rogers or Rollo May or Eric Fromm or Fritz Perls or R. D. Laing; even the admired Jean Paul Sartre struck me most as an obsessive scrivener. Having already survived affairs with Gordon Allport, Kurt Lewin and latterly, the Freudians, I was no longer so impressionable. Novelty is especially hard to find. So, in place of the intimacy of naive infatuation, I have had to make do with the perspective provided by sophistication. How might an experienced clinician look at humanistic psychology?

One might say that psychoanalysis is psychology in a depressive mood. What does that mean? Well, suppose you are with a group of good friends who are a little tipsy and getting joyous. They laugh, they talk largely, they make big plans. This afternoon, alas, you cannot join in; you are just not in the mood. As you listen, you think: "How juvenile! How silly. He'll never in a million years pull that deal off. If there were any market for that widget, IBM would have already moved in." And, in so saying, you sit back, sad but wise. Since you cannot have fun, at least you enjoy having superior knowledge. No rose-colored glasses confuse your view. You see the world sere and clear as it really is. Small comfort, but something salvaged from feeling flat and out of things. And of course your little maneuver works. Probably, your skeptical view of the world is the more accurate one. But it costs. You can see what is wrong with your friend's scheme, but no alternative idea occurs to you.

Humanistic psychology presents a more expansive mood. Rather than drawing exclusively on observation of people in difficulties, it is unafraid to look at personalities that have proven highly successful. As a matter of fact, humanistic psychology often presumes to aid those already coping rather well, suggesting they might raise their expectations of what life has to offer. Marie Baldwin, a psychiatrist of our acquaintance, once remarked to my wife, Nancy, "Life is so daily." Maslow (1971) would ask, "Then why put up with the way it is?" A reasonable question, but the line between "giving up teaching and going to preaching" is sometimes sketchy among humanists. It is tempting to skip from "Man can be more" to "Why aren't you?" So that exhortation is one general problem with their writings.

Whereas analysis was historically rooted among, and lives in daily practice with, the psychically lame, halt and blind, these psychologies are directed more at those who have a chance but are about to blow it if they do not bestir themselves. For, most humanistic psychology deals with a limited range of psychic functioning—primarily in the realms of motivation and emotion. Their presuppositions rarely apply to the retarded, the autistic, the psychotic, the profoundly anti-social, the chronically inadequate or the physically damaged, among whom many practitioners spend their working lives. Indeed, appraised as theories of personality, the humanistic psychologies are ill-equipped to deal with such client deficits. Only a few issues in perception are covered; they offer no explicit theory of learning or of memory; no attempt is made to separate logical from paralogical thought, like that represented by the primary process. Wide lacunae in theory would be acceptable if it were true, as has been asserted, that "You really don't need to know all that stuff." But, when the chronic deficits in the executive spheres of clients' egos so often fall within the realm of matters not dealt with, one is reminded of the old YMCA slogan: "If you can keep your head when all about are losing theirs, perhaps you don't understand the situation."

The aspect of humanism in psychology that would profit practice theory is the systematic relating of motivation to a perspective on the future. For ego psychology to incorporate this perspective requires clarification in the implied image of causation. Let us turn next to that.

Images of Cause/Effect Relations

It is not necessary that a theoretical model resemble nature in its form. As my friend, Leon Festinger, once remarked to me, "If I could invent a game of chess that would correctly predict human behavior, I would adopt that as my theoretical model." This seems a nice way to make a point that is very widely accepted among modern theoreticians. For example, there is no resemblance between a hunk of metal falling through the air and algebraic jottings on a sheet of paper that predict how long it will take to fall from a height of 300 feet according to the formula $S = \frac{1}{2} gt^2$. But, it is necessary that the prediction that *emerges* from following the rules of induction fit what is being observed.

The aspect of a theoretical model that governs the logical rules by which inferences may be drawn from it is of course not the content of the theory. The rules of inference play the same role in stating a theory as time and key signatures do in musical notation: they do not tell you the tune, that is in the notes, but you cannot reproduce the tune accurately without them. Rules of inference built into theories are sometimes implicit. An older generation of sociologists, like Pareto, reasoned in syllogisms. Ordnance engineers predict the flight of bullets with analytic geometry and the calculus. We have remarked that Freud, at one time, thought of the libido as if it were in a hydraulic system.

The nineteenth century image of causation was mechanistic. A weight pushed down on the long end of a lever and the short end projecting beyond the fulcrum raised your car out of the ditch. Or, the cue ball hit the six ball and rolled it two inches right of the pocket. One cause connected to one effect. Very neat, and refreshing at a time when the behavioral sciences were bogged down in verbal play and imprecision.

The one cause/one effect model, however, did not prove apt for a situation where the same effect has multiple causes. Freud's principle of *overdetermination*, for example, recognizes that the same action—or thought or affect—may express more than one motivation. When the symptom also becomes a source of pleasure, we speak of "secondary gain through illness." Likewise, the same cause may have more than one effect, depending on other variables. The urge to destroy someone may result in kicking him, or saying something cutting, or having fantasies of hurts he will suffer (from which you may even be rescuing him), or doing nothing but feeing low in spirits. We do not ever assume the hostile impulse has no effect, but in predicting the direction in which one will act, we add the phrase, "Depending on...." In multivariate statistics, the same kind of qualification is called an *interaction*. A more complicated view of cause/effect seems much better coordinated to predictions made in the study of personality.

Yet, there are situations in practice that give us problems with this mental model, too. How about the times that we introduce a cause that *seems* to have no effect? In Chapter 13 we described the effort the mental hospital staff made to get its group of patients more engaged and active about dealing with their real world. They proved refractory to suggestions they undertake projects, but they did react with a series of elaborate cocktail parties. So, the cause introduced had some effect. There are misguided interventions whose effects are hard to trace because they do not do what we intend; they may even make the patient sicker. The difficulty then, alas, is not with the rules of inference. There are also interventions that induce psychological forces so weak that the effect, if in the right direction, is so minor it is indiscernible. Once again, however, the problem is not with the mental model of cause/effect. But, let us take a further complication.

Giving Aid to Families with Dependent Children to certain families has not altered the fact that the children are neglected. Does the money make no difference? That is hard to believe. Try deleting the grant from the family finances, and it seems likely that the children's nourishment will drop from abysmal to nothing. As elsewhere in our field, the issue is the difference between *necessary* and *sufficient* conditions for successful treatment. We are often boxed in by the fact that we dare not withdraw the conditions necessary to survival but are unable to introduce the conditions sufficient to produce real change. As a former Governor of Georgia reportedly remarked in a speech on the subject, "What our prison system needs is a higher type inmate."

A conditional mode of thinking about causation has been identified and formalized by those who work on the philosophy of science. According to Ackoff (1977):

> The idea was first systematically developed here at the University of Pennsylvania by Professor-of-Philosophy Edgar Arthur Singer, Jr. He formulated an alternative to the deterministic cause-effect relationship and called it producer-product.... Whereas the classical cause was both necessary and sufficient for its effect, the Singerian producer was only necessary, not sufficient, for its product.

Singer's thought model is apt for predicting various catastrophes. Conditions may be ripe for a tornado but nothing happens until the final ingredient falls in place. Events in treatment often follow the model. Without continuous contact and an atmosphere of trust, casework toward personal change is often impossible, so effort to maintain the relationship is not wasted. However, we know that for movement to occur, the worker needs further skills and must apply them at the right time. Indeed, having done our utmost to supply the necessary conditions for improvement, we often have the feeling that the final sufficient condition is beyond our control.

Singer's producer-product relationship offers a model for thinking about the operation of choice or willing in the personality. An active center within the sphere of the ego achieves a resolution among varied and competing drives, drive derivatives, defensive needs and superego injunctions. This active center, which might as well be called the *will* assigns priorities so that the forces become organized and one direction of motivation sways the whole. The outcome is experienced as having been chosen. One suspects that the need to achieve such a synthesis and keep it intact must have psychic energy at its disposal. Like other synthetic functions of the ego, for example, the concentration of attention, the energy available for willing seems to vary among people, and to wax and wane within the same person. "I'm too tired to make that decision tonight. Let's face it again in the morning."

The proposed model of an active, integrating center does not admit absolutely free will the way some would like to believe in it. A disappointed child who is now an adult may like to think that if only his father wanted to, he could give the love he always needed from him. The father's neurotic constrictedness is left out of the picture. It must be very rare in the course of synthesizing motives that there is an outright reversal of motivations typically in evidence. Limitations and powerful attitudes and drives within the person set the necessary conditions within which the active will can make its choice. The choice becomes the sufficient condition for organized action. But an absolutely free will is a myth.

Willing
As long as the act of willing is treated as a dependent variable, the effect of other forces that really move the personality, its systemic position in analytic theory presents no problem. Often the idea that one is exercising choice is simply a defense. Machiavelli for

one recognized that once a region is conquered by force, it can be held by pretensions to legitimacy. People ashamed to admit they are cowed are also terrified of being killed during a revolt. It is a relief to be able to say, "This, after all, is the government we are supposed to live under." The subjective feeling of choosing is in the service of rationalization.

The theories of Hellmuth Kaiser (1955) present much more of an issue. According to Kaiser, we are deciding and choosing all the time. To *decline* to take responsibility for having chosen is a distortion of reality. The client who avoids thinking of himself as willing is seen as subverting his thoughts to the *delusion of fusion*. To choose, or to make up one's mind reminds one of essential aloneness which stirs anxiety. So, to Kaiser, the exercise of will is real; denial of willing is the defense. Kaiser had analogous thoughts about responsibility by the way. It was fairly common in the old days to hear younger psychiatrists complain about a patient's being "resistant" or "unmotivated." In effect, the patient was held responsible for the fact that treatment did not progress. Kaiser, on the other hand, points out that the therapist is responsible for treatment, not the patient. If the present state of the art is such that a person lacking certain motivations cannot be helped, the patient loses but it is the therapist who fails. How are we to make a place for such ideas in a field in which analysts believe the patient's behavior is determined by forces he is largely unaware of (Knight, 1954)? Kaiser simply dropped out.

Shapiro (1970) was influenced by Kaiser, and has sought to "place" the will in modern analytic theory. In a refined throwback to a European tradition stemming from Brentano (Boring, 1950), Shapiro suggests reexamining the "psychology of the act," as it was called. Psychoanalysis, he believes, has dropped the role of volition, reducing it to a need/drive action based in primitive drives that really afford no choices. Shapiro argues that as the ego develops and matures, it diverts increasingly large segments of psychic energy to its own disposal. We then arrive at conscious motives. "Conscious motives are generated by the experience of needs in a mind that is aware of the possibilities of action" (Shapiro, 1970, p. 335). Two levels of motivation are proposed to explain action: need driven and consciously volitional. Freud's emphasis on the intentionality of our actions, even when the purposes are unconscious, was partly derived from Brentano's influence. Shapiro's argument is that intention in a mature person should be seen as very different from that in an infant. The capacity to make choices would be one of the products of ego maturation that go along with the elaboration of controls, neutralization of drive energy, and a fuller awareness of what is possible in the world around one. I agree with Shapiro that what we call the will must, like other ego functions, be something that gradually evolves into the form we think mature, and this enters into my idea of conceiving willing as an active, synthesizing center. But, I am troubled by his notion of a two-tiered system of motivation, for good theories contain few qualitative discontinuities.

The active synthetic center I would call the will, moreover, does not just "mature." We have some ideas about how its maturation may be encouraged or discouraged. Parents who intrude their "controllingness" into every cranny of a child's life are apt to produce an adult whose inability to make up his mind drives them up the wall. Children may also be reared in a fashion that seems to yield responsible adults, soberly unafraid of responsibility and capable of decisions. Of such matters, we do not really know as much as child rearing textbooks claim. Some children of dominating parents emerge equally bossy, rather than squashed; many children given very wide areas for decision-making in childhood seem unable to choose what they want from life in late adolescence. But we know something.

Erikson (1964) has written latterly of the "virtues" he associates with ego strength, selecting aspects of functioning that may be used as criteria to decide whether a patient has benefited from treatment. They are marks of health in any mature personality. Among the virtues that have their beginnings in childhood are *Will* and *Purpose*. Erikson elides the general issue of how these concepts fit into the general corpus of analytic theory, for he does not gladly accommodate to boundaries at the cost of discarding insights.

> *To will* does not mean to be willful, but rather to gain gradually the power of increased judgment and decision in the application of drive.... Here, no doubt, is the genetic origin of the elusive question of Free Will, which man, ever again, attempts to master logically and theologically. The fact is that no person can live, no ego remain intact without hope and will. Even the philosophical man who feels motivated to challenge the very ground he stands on, questioning both will and hope as illusory, feels more real for having willed such heroic inquiry... (Erikson, 1964, p. 118).

The rudiments of will are formed in infancy, and the training of the eliminative sphincters is the focus of the struggle experienced. "A sense of defeat (from too little or too much training) can lead to *shame* and a compulsive *doubt* whether one ever really willed what one did, or really did what one willed" (*Op. cit.*, p. 119).

Yet, in healthy people, it is important to feel one has taken an active part "in the chain of the inevitable." For, paradoxically, it is important to believe you have decided even though you know that what happens is largely predetermined by things over which you have no ultimate control. *"Will, therefore, is the unbroken determination to exercise free choice as well as self-restraint, in spite of the unavoidable experience of shame and doubt in infancy"* (*Op. cit.*, p. 119, italics in original). So, to Erikson, the Will is treated as an identifiable aspect of ego strength. It has its rudimentary beginnings, he believes, in the childhood stage at which the personality is first engrossed in achieving some muscular (including sphincteral) control. The signs of pathology in development of the Will are to be found in behavior that clusters at either extreme of a compulsive/impulsive dimension (1964, p. 186). Whether the Will enters the causal chain of drive expression was not directly addressed by Erikson, but the implication is that it does. At least, one infers that wanting to exercise choice is an important impulse, and has effects.

Acting from a sense of Purpose is, to me, a related idea. For Erikson, the rudiments of this feeling are laid down during the resolution of the life-crisis we associate with the phallic phase (i.e. Initiative vs. Guilt). As the fear of willing reflects Shame and Doubt, so reticence of Purpose implies an overweaning Guilt. "Who am I to *project* into the future how events should turn out?" Kaiser, then, has given us a formulation which accounts for a reluctance to think of oneself as making decisions and acting from purpose in terms of current defensive functions threatened by such feelings. Erikson, from his side, has complemented Kaiser's analysis by tracing the hesitancy to its psychogenetic roots.

Analytic theory also lacks concepts for describing what happens *cognitively* when behavior is directed with a future end in mind. Lewin (1936) has supplied conceptions which might be fruitfully incorporated. He wrote of the person having a mental image that includes a view of the future, a *future time-perspective*, further differentiated into levels of reality and unreality. The future at the level of reality is what you truly expect will come to pass; at the level of unreality is a future you also imagine, but which you recognize is a hope—or a fear—and not all that probable. Without some way of conceptualizing a sense of the future, there is no way of speaking rigorously about *purposive behavior* either. Despite the fact that having a *perspective on time* is certainly one of the criteria for assessing ego strength—and that we note constriction of time-perspective in infantile and depressed persons—the issue is not systematically covered by psychoanalytic ego psychology, either. The field would do well, therefore, to review the work of Lewin and his students on this topic.

Self Actualization

Erikson taught us that a sense of continuity with one's past is a significant ingredient in the formation of a workable *ego identity*. That a vision of continuity into the future also significantly influences present functioning has been emphasized by two others whom I think of as humanists, Maslow and Frankl. Although neither is (or was) a Freudian, both freely acknowledge the value of the psychoanalytic contribution to an understanding of the personality. Each has advanced ideas that seem particularly relevant to clinical practice. So it seems appropriate to end this volume with extracts from the work of these men.

Abraham Maslow, who until 1943 had been going about the business usual for a comparative psychologist, then published a paper, "A theory of human motivation," in which he introduced his notion that people are moved in terms of *hierarchy of needs*. The arrangement he proposed may be set down as follows:

Self-actualization; self-esteem; social esteem; social affiliation; interpersonal safety; material safety; physiological (needs).

The saliency of the need, its priority for the organism is inverse to the order given here. In other words, not until the need lower in the order is reasonably well satisfied can the person move onward to try to satisfy the one higher in the hierarchy. Applying Singer's idea of *teleological causation*, one might say that meeting the more basic need is a necessary condition for the person to turn his attention to another higher on the scale. In social work, where we so often encounter people in desperate circumstances, we have long believed that such a priority must exist among motives. Charlotte Towle (1945) wrote a book to this effect. Her book, which I can still visualize, paperbound, in my mind's eye, was titled *Common Human Needs*. We know that when people are starving (physiological needs) they will risk being shot (material safety) to steal food. The primacy of survival needs came up in the theory of object relations, how pressing it is to the human infant *not* to be left alone.

So, Maslow's well-known listing has self-evident appeal. Still, evidence is mixed whether motivation works quite as indicated. Soldiers routinely risk death for the sake of their units (social affiliation); narcissistic characters put self-esteem ahead of being accepted by others (social esteem).

The part of Maslow's listings that has aroused most interest is his notion of self-actualization, the ultimate need.

We have, all of us, an impulse to improve ourselves, an impulse toward actualizing more of our potentialities, toward self-actualization, or full humanness or human fulfillment, or whatever term you like. Granted this, then what holds us up? What blocks us (Maslow, 1971, p. 35)?

What blocks us, he thinks, is the Jonah Complex. "We fear our best as well as our worst, even though in different ways" (p. 34). "It is partly a justified fear of being torn apart, of losing control, of being shattered and disintegrated, even of being killed by the experience" (p. 38). During those rare moments when one is operating at full capacity, useful and competent and knowing it, we have an exhilarating joy which Maslow calls a *peak experience*. But, one cannot live always at the peak; it would be like trying to maintain a sexual climax, on and on. So, "It must give way to non-esthetic serenity, calmer happiness" (p. 38). Some people, however, never achieve peak experience, and do not strive toward self-actualization. It is as if the fear that they may be carried away stirs an anxiety too strong to bear. One thinks of the terror of "losing one's boundaries" that blocks constricted borderline patients from intimate relationships. To Maslow, the inability to reach for self-actualization *is* neurosis. Those unable to bestir themselves in that direction should seek professional help, he says, from someone versed in depth psychology.

This is not all of Maslow's contribution, but the gist I want to deal with here. The notion of self-actualization is, perhaps surprisingly, very traditional in social work practice. While always aware of realistic limits to people's lives, especially among the poor and disadvantaged, social workers have always asked themselves, "Survival for what?" The offer of casework, in addition to financial assistance, in our family agencies expressed the thought. Not only was there the hope that people could change enough so that they would not fall repeatedly into financial need, but there was the feeling that even if they were eating and had a roof over their heads, there was much else in life that they were missing. Settlement houses, of all unlikely places, offered courses on poetry, taught music, had drama groups from which famous actors like Paul Muni, Edward G. Robinson and others emerged. Joe Louis fought his first bouts as a boy in a Detroit settlement. Homes for the aging, under social work auspices, have always sought to maintain independence and activity—to prolong life, of course, but also to enrich it. Although a book like this has been necessarily slanted toward understanding pain, social work is very much oriented also toward pleasure. We *know* the Viennese street-saying, "Man lebt nur einmal." You only live once.

So, there is no problem with the principle of self-actualization. Practice, at times, is something else, and this principle—or preaching—can also be diverted to the service of defense, produce noxious side-effects. How is striving for self-actualization to be distinguished from other narcissistic endeavor? If being yourself requires that you take off for a year or two knocking around the Caribbean, who will care for your children? Who, indeed, will deal with the depression and loss your departure visits on them? Who is to say when staying in place and carrying out your commitments, is or is not self-actualization? At the same time, we all have in our memories long lists of people we have tried to help whose willingness to settle for so much less than what life can offer wore us out. So we think that Maslow may have something. What he has is, perhaps, the germ of an important idea in need of refinements.

"Before his death, Rabbi Zusya said, 'In the coming world, they will not ask me: "Why were you not Moses?" They will ask me: "Why were you not Zusya'"(Quoted by Secrest, 1979, p. ix)?

Will to Meaning
In the Preface to Viktor Frankl's wonderful book, *Man's Search for Meaning* (1963), Gordon Allport wrote:

> But these moments of comfort do not establish the will to live unless they help the prisoner make larger sense out of his apparently senseless suffering. It is here that we encounter the central theme of existentialism: to live is to suffer, to survive is to find meaning in the suffering. If there is a purpose in life at all, there must be a purpose in dying. But no man can tell another what this purpose is. Each must find out for himself, and must accept the responsibility that his

answer prescribes....Frankl is fond of quoting Nietzsche, "He who has a *why* to live can bear with almost any *how*" (1963, pp. x-xi).

Surely, these are profound and moving sentiments. Are we to accept them as rhetoric or poesy, but disregard them as irrelevant to the hard business of helping people?

Our clients' lives have often been filled with pain and our own are not easy. The least we can hope to wring from one of life's disasters is some new learning, a more ultimate truth. Out of the rotten mess that existed in Europe from the 1930's until well after World War II, and out of the troubles we, ourselves, lived through in the same period, there was ample opportunity to observe both the depths of the human spirit and the heights of coping some achieved. Both occurred in response to incredibly grim realities. Frankl's invocation of a *will to meaning* was inspired by the tortured and dying of a concentration camp. Analytic theory has never had an adequate way of conceptualizing "external" [sic!] reality (Erikson, 1964). So, we are attracted by the writings of a Frankl who, if he does not conceptualize reality either, certainly takes it fully into account.

His illustrations are from his life in a concentration camp and the efforts he made to help his fellow inmates want to stay alive, and himself to stay alive by retaining even there his professional role as healer. To the man who lost hope, who wanted simply to "turn his face to the wall" and die, Frankl brought this message. For each person, there is something he must do, a purpose, and only he can do it. Each has a mission, larger than himself, which requires that he go on trying to live and carry it out. No one else can tell him his mission; he has to *let* himself be aware of it. But, it is there waiting for him to recognize it and pursue it. Thoughts like this go through a practitioner's mind in talks with a depressed, potentially suicidal client. "Only you can be Mother to your children, no one else can play that role." "What of those who need you, what do you propose for them?" Are we treating them or curing ourselves, or both?

The loss of meaning, Frankl calls the *noogenic neuroses*. There are other types of neurosis, and he recognizes these as based in other drives and appropriate for other treatments. But he believes noogenic neuroses are more widespread than has been recognized and they require another treatment.

According to logotherapy, the striving to find a meaning in

one's life is the primary motivational force in man. That is why I speak of a *will to meaning* (Frankl, 1963, p. 154).

...The truly neurotic individual does try to escape the full awareness of his life task. And to make him aware of this task, to awaken him to a fuller consciousness of it, can contribute much to his ability to overcome his neurosis (p. 153).

Hence, as contrasted with analytically oriented psychotherapy, *logotherapy* is less introspective and less retrospective. It focuses on the future and the world, on the assignments and meanings the patient has to fulfill. To a man who described psychoanalysis thus: "The patient must lie down on a couch and tell you things that sometimes are very disagreeable to tell," Frankl replied, "Now, in logotherapy the patient may remain sitting erect, but he must hear things that are sometimes very disagreeable to hear" (p. 152). Yet, he denies that his method involves preaching or exhortation, since the aim is insistent that the *patient* find the life-task he has been avoiding. Nor has he much patience for notions like self-actualization as a life goal. To Frankl, a true life-task is far less introvertive, inturned; it is directed toward doing things with the real world. For, the Personality is only actualized when, there is peak experience only when, the self is lost from view. "'Tis well said" replied Candide, "but we must cultivate our gardens" (Voltaire, 1930; p. 144).

References

Abraham, Karl, 1927. *Selected papers*. London: Hogarth Press.

Ackoff, Russell L., 1977. The aging of a young profession: Operations research Philadelphia: University of Pennsylvania Presidents's Lectures, 1975-76.

Adler, Alfred, 1917. A *study of organ inferiority and its psychical compensation*. New York: Nervous and Mental Diseases Monograph Series, No. 24.

Adler, Alfred, 1924. *The practice and theory of individual psychology*. New York: Harcourt, Brace.

Adorno, Theodore W., Frenkel-Brunswik, Else, Levinson, Daniel J. and Sanford, R. Nevitt, 1950. *The authoritarian personality*. New York: Harper & Bros.

Aichorn, August, 1935. *Wayward youth*. New York: Viking Press.

Alexander, Leslie B., 1972. Social work's Freudian deluge: Myth or reality? *Social Service Review* 46: 517-38.

Allport, Gordon W., 1937. *Personality: A psychological interpretation*. New York: Henry Holt and Co.

Allport, Gordon W., 1942. *The use of personal documents in psychological science*. New York: Social Science Research Council.

Allport, Gordon W., 1963. Preface, in Frankl, Viktor E. *Man's search for meaning*. New York: Pocket Books.

American Psychiatric Association, 1969. *A psychiatric glossary*. Washington, D.C.: The Association.

American Psychiatric Association, 1975. *A psychiatric glossary*. Washington, D.C.: The Association.

Appelberg, Esther, 1961. Verbal accessibility of adolescents. Unpublished DSW dissertation. School of Applied Social Sciences, Case Western Reserve University.

Asch, Solomon E., 1956. Studies of independence and conformity: A minority of one against a unanimous majority. *Psychological Monographs* 70, No. 9 (Whole No. 416).

Back, Kurt, 1951. Influence through social communication. *Journal of Abnormal and Social Psychology* 46: 9-23.

Berne, Eric, 1961. *Transactional analysis in psychotherapy*. New York: Grove Press.

Berne, Eric, 1964. *Games people play*. New York: Grove Press.

Bernstein, Basil, 1962. Social class, linguistic codes and grammatical elements. *Language and Speech* 5: 221-40.

Bettelheim, Bruno, 1943. Individual and mass behavior in extreme situations. *Journal of Abnormal and Social Psychology* 38: 417-32.

Bibring, Edward, 1953. The mechanism of depression, in Greenacre, Phyllis, ed. *Affective disorders*. New York: International Universities Press.

Bibring, Edward, 1954. Psychoanalysis and the dynamic psychotherapies. *Journal of the American Psychoanalytic Association* 2: 745-70.

Bion, Wilfred R., 1951. Experiences in groups: VII. *Human Relations* 4: 221-27.

Bion, Wilfred R. 1959. *Experiences in groups*, New York: Basic Books.

Blanck, Gertrude and Blanck, Rubin, 1974. *Ego psychology: Theory and practice*. New York: Columbia University Press.

Blanck, Gertrude and Blanck, Rubin, 1978. Psychoanalytic developmental diagnosis, treatment and some casework antecedents. Northampton, Mass.: Smith College School for Social Work Lydia Rapaport Lecture Series, Number Four.

Blenkner, Margaret, 1954. Predictive factors in the initial interview in family casework. *Social Service Review* 28: 65-73.

Boring, Edwin G., 1950. *A history of experimental psychology 2d Edition*. New York: Appleton-Century-Crofts.

Bowlby, John, 1951. *Maternal care and mental health*. Geneva: World Health Organization Monograph Series, No. 2.

Bowlby, John, 1960a. Separation anxiety. *International Journal of Psycho-Analysis* 41: 89-113.

Bowlby, John, 1960b. Grief and mourning in infancy and early childhood, in *The Psychoanalytic Study of the Child Vol. 15*. New York: International Universities Press.

Bowlby, John, 1961. Separation anxiety: A critical review of the literature. *Journal of Child Psychology and Psychiatry* 1: 251-69.

Bowlby, John, 1969. *Attachment and Loss: Vol. I. Attachment*. New York: Basic Books.

Bowlby, John, 1974. Attachment theory, separation anxiety and mourning, in Hamburg, David A. and Brodie, Harold K. eds *The American Handbook of Psychiatry Vol. VI*. New York: Basic Books.

Brown, George W. and Harris, Tirril, 1978. *Social origins of depression*. New York: Free Press.

Buber, Martin, 1958. *I and thou 2d Ed*. New York: Charles Scribner's Sons.

Camus, Albert, 1956. *The fall*. New York: Alfred A. Knopf.

Cannon, Walter B., 1932. *The wisdom of the body*. New York: W. W. Norton.

Cartwright, Dorwin and Zander, Alvin eds., 1953. *Group dynamics: Research and theory*. Evanston, Ill.: Row, Peterson and Co.

Cooley, Charles H., 1902. *Human nature and the social order*. New York: Charles Scribner's Sons.

Daly, Michael R., 1979. "Burnout": Smoldering problem in protective services. *Social Work* 24: 375-79.

Deutsch, Helene, 1942. Some forms of emotional disturbance and their relationship to schizophrenia. *Psychoanalytic Quarterly* 11: 301-21.

Dinnage, Rosemary, 1980. Understanding loss: The Bowlby canon. *Psychology Today* 13: 56-60.

Eliot, T. S., 1963. *Collected poems, 1909-1962*. New York: Harcourt, Brace and World.

Enelow, Alan J., 1960. The silent patient. *Psychiatry* 23: 153-58.

Erikson, Erik H., 1950. *Childhood and society*. New York: W. W. Norton.

Erikson, Erik H., 1956. The problem of ego identity. *Journal of the American Psychoanalytic Association* 4: 56-121.

Erikson, Erik H., 1959. *Identity and the life cycle*. (Psychological Issues Monograph 1) New York: International Universities Press.

Erikson, Erik H., 1964. *Insight and responsibility*. New York: Norton.

Fairbairn, W. Ronald D. 1952. *An object relations theory of the personality*. New York: Basic Books.

Fenichel, Otto, 1945. *The psychoanalytic theory of neurosis*. New York: W. W. Norton.

Festinger, Leon, 1954. A theory of social comparison processes. *Human Relations* 7: 117-40.

Festinger, Leon, 1964. *Conflict, decision and dissonance*. Palo Alto, Calif.: Stanford University Press.

Festinger, Leon, Schachter, Stanley S. and Back, Kurt, 1950. *Social pressures in informal groups: A study of human factors in housing*. New York: Harper.

Fierman, Louis B. ed., 1965. *Effective psychotherapy: The contribution of Hellmuth Kaiser*. New York: Free Press.

Fraiberg, Selma H., 1950. On the sleep disturbances of early childhood, in *The Psychoanalytic Study of the Child Vol. 5*. New York: International Universities Press.

Fraiberg, Selma H., 1959. *The magic years*. New York: Charles Scribner's Sons.

Fraiberg, Selma H., 1969. Libidinal object constancy and mental representation, in *The Psychoanalytic Study of the Child Vol. 24*. New York: International Universities Press.

Fraiberg, Selma H., 1971. Intervention in infancy: A program for blind infants. *Journal of the American Academy of Child Psychiatry* 10: 381-404.

Fraiberg, Selma H., 1977. *Every child's birthright: In defense of mothering*. New York: Basic Books.

Frankl, Viktor E., 1963. *Man's search for meaning: An introduction to logotherapy*. New York: Pocket Books.

Freud, Anna, 1946. *The ego and the mechanisms of defense*. New York: International Universities Press.

Freud, Anna, 1965. *Normality and pathology in childhood*. New York: International Universities Press.

Freud, Sigmund, 1922. *Group psychology and the analysis of the ego*. London: Hogarth Press.

Ganter, Grace and Polansky, Norman A., 1964. Predicting a child's accessibility to individual treatment from diagnostic groups. *Social Work* 9: 56-63.

Ganter, Grace, Yeakel, Margaret and Polansky, Norman A., 1967. *Retrieval from limbo*. New York: Child Welfare League of America.

Garrett, Annette, 1958. The worker-client relationship, in Parad, Howard J. ed. *Ego psychology and dynamic casework*. New York: Family Service Association of America.

Gerth, Hans H. and Mills, C. Wright, eds., 1946. *From Max Weber: Essays in Sociology*. New York: Oxford University Press.

Goldfarb, William, 1945. Psychological privation in infancy and subsequent adjustment. *American Journal of Orthopsychiatry* 15: 247-55.

Greenacre, Phyllis, 1960. Considerations regarding the parent-infant relationship, in *Emotional growth Vol. I*. New York: International Universities Press.

Greenson, Ralph R., 1954. The struggle against identification. *Journal of the American Psychoanalytic Association* 2: 200-17.

Greenspan, Stanley I. and Pollock, George H. eds., 1980. *The course of life: Psychoanalytic contributions toward understanding personality development. Vol. I. Infancy and early childhood*. Washington, D.C.: Government Printing Office (Stock #017-024-01026-0).

Grosser, Daniel, Polansky, Norman and Lippitt, Ronald, 1951. A laboratory study of behavioral contagion. *Human Relations* 4: 115-42.

Guntrip, Harry, 1961. *Personality structure and human interaction: The developing synthesis of psychodynamic theory*. New York: International Universities Press.

Guntrip, Harry, 1962. The schizoid compromise and psychotherapeutic stalemate. *British Journal of Medical Psychology* 35: 273-87.

Guntrip, Harry, 1969. *Schizoid phenomena, object relations and the self*. New York: International Universities Press.

Hamilton, Gordon, 1958. A theory of personality: Freud's contribution to social work, in Parad, Howard J. and Miller, Roger R. eds. *Ego psychology and dynamic casework*. New York: Family Service Association of America.

Haring, Jean. Freedom of communication between parents and adolescents with problems. Unpublished DSW dissertation. Western Reserve University, 1965.

Hartmann, Heinz, 1956. The development of the ego concept in Freud's work. *International Journal of Psychoanalysis* 37: 425-38.

Hartmann, Heinz, 1958. *Ego psychology and the problem of adaptation*. New York: International Universities Press.

Hartmann, Heinz, Kris, Ernst and Loewenstein, Rudolf M., 1946. Comments on the formation of psychic structure. *The Psychoanalytic Study of the Child Vol. 1*. New York: International Universities Press.

Heider, Fritz, 1958. *The psychology of interpersonal relations*. New York: Wiley.

Higgins, Joseph W., 1966. Review of Fierman. *American Journal of Psychiatry* 122: 1194.

Hill, Lewis B., 1952. Infantile personalities. *American Journal of Psychiatry* 109: 429-32.

Hoch, Paul and Polatin, Philip, 1949. Pseudo-neurotic forms of schizophrenia. *Psychiatric Quarterly* 23: 248-76.

Hollis, Florence, 1972. *Casework: A psychosocial therapy. 2d Ed*. New York: Random House.

Hollis, Florence, 1966. Development of a casework typology. New York: Columbia University School of Social Work. Mimeographed.

Horney, Karen, 1937. *The neurotic personality of our time*. New York: W. W. Norton.

Hume, David, 1890. *Treatise of human nature*. London: Longmans, Green.

Hunt, J. McVicker, Mohandessi, Khossrow, Ghodssi, Mehri and Akiyama, Michiko, 1976. The psychological development of orphanage-reared infants: Interventions with outcomes (Teheran) *Genetic Psychology Monographs* 94: 177-226.

Hurwitz, Jacob I., Zander, Alvin F. and Hymovitch, Bernard, 1953. Some effects of power in the relations among group members, in Cartwright, Dorwin and Zander, Alvin, eds. *Group dynamics: Research and theory*. Evanston, Ill.: Row, Peterson.

Jaffee, Lester D., and Polansky, Norman A., 1962 .Verbal inaccessibility in young adolescents showing delinquent trends. *Journal of Health and Human Behavior* 3: 105-111.

Jourard, Sidney M., 1961. Age trends in self-disclosure. *Merrill-Palmer Quarterly* 7: 191-97.

Jourard, Sidney M., and Landsman, Murray J., 1960. Cognition, cathexis and the "dyadic effect" in men's self-disclosing behavior. *Merrill-Palmer Quarterly* 7: 178-86.

Kardiner, Abraham, 1945. *The psychological frontiers of society*. New York: Columbia University Press.

Kardiner, Abraham and Linton, Ralph, 1939. *The individual and his society*. New York: Columbia University Press.

Katan, Anny, 1961. Some thoughts about the role of verbalization in early childhood, in *The Psychoanalytic Study of the Child. Vol. 16*. New York: International Universities Press.

Kaufman, Irving, 1962. Stages in the treatment of the juvenile delinquent. *Proceedings of the Third World Congress of Psychiatry*. Montreal: McGill University Press.

Kaufman, Irving, 1963. Psychodynamics of protective casework, in Parad, Howard J. and Miller, Roger R. eds. *Ego-oriented casework: Problems and perspectives*. New York: Family Service Association of America.

Kelley, Harold H., 1951. Communication in experimentally created hierarchies. *Human Relations* 4: 39-56.

Kelly, Joan B. and Wallerstein, Judith S., 1976. The effects of parental divorce: Experiences of the child in early latency. *American Journal of Orthopsychiatry* 46: 20-32.

Kernberg, Otto, 1966. Structural derivatives of object relationships. *International Journal of Psycho-Analysis* 47: 236-53.

Kernberg, Otto, 1967. Borderline personality organization. *Journal of the American Psychoanalytic Association* 15: 641-85.

Kernberg, Otto, 1968. The treatment of patients with borderline personality organization. *International Journal of Psycho-Analysis* 49: 600-19.

Kernberg, Otto, 1972. Early ego-integration and object relations. *Annals of the New York Academy of Science* 193: 233-47.

Khan, M. Masud, 1960. Clinical aspects of the schizoid personality: Affects and technique. *International Journal of Psycho-Analysis* 41: 430-37.

Klein, Melanie, 1932. *The psycho-analysis of children*. London: Hogarth

Knight, Robert P., 1953. Borderline states. *Bulletin of the Menninger Clinic* 17: 1-12.

Knight, Robert P., 1954. Determination, freedom and responsibility, in Knight, Robert P. and Friedman, Cyrus R., eds. *Psychoanalytic psychiatry and psychology*. New York: International Universities Press.

Koestler, Arthur, 1941. *Darkness at noon*. New York: Macmillan.

Kogan, Leonard S., 1957. The short term case in the family agency. *Social Casework* 38: 366-74.

Kohut, Heinz, 1971. *The analysis of the self*. New York: International Universities Press.

Kounin, Jacob S. and Gump, Paul V., 1958. The ripple effect in discipline. *Elementary School Journal* 59: 158-62.

Kris, Ernst, 1952. *Psychoanalytic explorations in art*. New York: International Universities Press.

Lauer, James, 1980. *The role of the mental health professional in child neglect and abuse*. Washington, D.C.: National Center on Child Abuse and Neglect, D/HHS.

LeBon, Gustave, 1903. *The crowd*. London: F. Unwin.

Levy, David, 1943. *Maternal overprotection*. New York: Columbia University Press.

Lewin, Kurt, 1936. *Principles of topological psychology*. New York: McGraw-Hill.

Lewin, Kurt, 1937. Psychoanalysis and topological psychology. *Bulletin of the Menninger Clinic* 1: 202-12.

Lewin, Kurt, 1951. *Field theory in social science*. New York: Harper and Row.

Lindemann, Erich, 1944. Symptomatology and management of acute grief. *American Journal of Psychiatry* 101: 141-48.

Linton, Ralph, 1945. *The cultural background of personality*. New York: Appleton-Century-Crofts.

Lippitt, Ronald, 1940. An experimental study of authoritarian and democratic group atmospheres. *University of Iowa Studies in Child Welfare* 16: 43-195.

Lippitt, Ronald, Polansky, Norman and Rosen, Sidney, 1952. The dynamics of power. *Human Relations* 5: 37-62.

Lowenstein, Rudolph M., 1961. Introduction. *Journal of the American Psychoanalytic Association* 9: 2-6.

Mahler, Margaret S., Furer, Manuel and Settlage, Calvin F., 1959. Severe emotional disturbances in childhood psychosis, in Arieti, Silvano ed. *American Handbook of Psychiatry*. New York: Basic Books.

Mahler, Margaret S. and LaPerriere, Kitty, 1965. Mother-child interaction during separation-individuation. *Psychoanalytic Quarterly* 34: 483-98.

Mahler, Margaret S., Pine, Fred and Bergman, Anni, 1975. *The psychological birth of the human infant*. New York: Basic Books.

Maslow, Abraham H., 1943. A theory of human motivation. *Psychological Review* 50: 370-96.

Maslow, Abraham H., 1971. *The farther reaches of human nature*. New York: Viking Press.

Masterson, James F., 1976. *Psychotherapy of the borderline adult: A developmental approach*. New York: Bruner/Mazel.

Maurois, Andre, 1965. *Prometheus: The life of Balzac*. New York: Harper and Row.

McDougall, William, 1932. *The energies of men: A study of the fundamentals of dynamic psychology*. London: Methuen.

Mead, George H., 1934. *Mind, self and society*. Chicago: University of Chicago Press.

Mead, Margaret, 1935. *Sex and temperament*. New York: William Morrow and Co.

Meerloo, Joost A. M., 1952. *Conversation and communication*. New York: International Universities Press.

Moreno, Jacob L., 1946. *Psychodrama Vol. I*. New York: Beacon House.

Moreno, Jacob L., 1958. Fundamental rules and techniques of psychodrama, in Masserman, Jules H. and Moreno, Jacob L., eds. *Progress in Psychotherapy Vol. III*. New York: Grune and Stratton.

Morris, Marian G. and Gould, Robert W., 1963. Role-reversal, a necessary concept in dealing with the "battered child" syndrome, in *The neglected/battered child syndrome*. New York: Child Welfare League of America.

Muggeridge, Malcolm, 1969. Books. *Esquire* 71: 74-84.

Newcomb, Theodore M., 1950. *Social psychology*. New York: Dryden Press.

Nooney, James B. and Polansky, Norman A., 1962. The influence of perceived similarity and personality on verbal accessibility. *Merrill-Palmer Quarterly* 8: 33-40.

Parad, Howard J., ed., 1965. *Crisis intervention: Selected readings*. New York: Family Service Association of America.

Perlman, Helen H., 1957. *Social casework: A problem-solving process*. Chicago: University of Chicago Press.

Perry, J. Christopher and Klerman, Gerald L., 1978. The borderline patient: A comparative analysis of four sets of diagnostic criteria. *Archives of General Psychiatry* 35: 141-50.

Piaget, Jean, 1937. *The construction of reality in the child*. New York: Basic Books.

Pincus, Lily ed., 1960. *Marriage: Studies in emotional conflict and growth.* London: Methuen.

Polansky, Norman A., 1965. The concept of verbal accessibility. *Smith College Studies in Social Work* 36: 1-48.

Polansky, Norman A., 1975. Theory construction and the scientific method, in Polansky, Norman A. ed. *Social work research.* Chicago: University of Chicago Press.

Polansky, Norman A., 1980. On loneliness: A program for social work. *Smith College Studies in Social Work* 50: 85-113.

Polansky, Norman A., Boone, Donald R., DeSaix, Christine and Sharlin, Shlomo, 1971. Pseudostoicism in mothers of the retarded. *Social Casework* 52: 643-50.

Polansky, Norman A., Borgman, Robert D. and DeSaix, Christine, 1972. *Roots of futility.* San Francisco: Jossey-Bass.

Polansky, Norman A., Borgman, Robert D., DeSaix, Christine and Sharlin, Shlomo, 1971. Verbal accessibility in the treatment of child neglect. *Child Welfare* 50: 349-56.

Polansky, Norman A. and Brown, Sara Q., 1967. Verbal accessibility and fusion fantasy in a mountain county. *American Journal of Orthopsychiatry* 37: 651-60.

Polansky, Norman A., Chalmers, Mary Ann, Buttenwieser, Elizabeth and Williams, David P., 1981. *Damaged parents.* Chicago: University of Chicago Press.

Polansky, Norman A., DeSaix, Christine, Wing, Mary Lou and Patton, John D., 1968. Child neglect in a rural community. *Social Casework* 49: 467-74.

Polansky, Norman A., DeSaix, Christine and Sharlin, Shlomo, 1972. *Child neglect: Understanding and reaching the parent.* New York: Child Welfare League of America.

Polansky, Norman A. and Kounin, Jacob, 1956. Clients' reactions to initial interviews. *Human Relations* 9: 237-64.

Polansky, Norman, Lippitt, Ronald and Redl, Fritz, 1950. An investigation of behavioral contagion in groups. *Human Relations* 3: 319-48.

Polansky, Norman A. and Weiss, Erwin S., 1959. Determinants of accessibility to treatment in a children's institution. *Journal of Jewish Communal Service* 36: 130-37.

Polansky, Norman A., Weiss, Erwin S. and Blum, Arthur, 1961. Children's verbal accessibility as a function of content and personality. *American Journal of Orthopsychiatry* 31: 153-69.

Polansky, Norman A., White, Robert B. and Miller, Stuart C., 1957. Determinants of the role-image of the patient in a psychiatric hospital, in Greenblatt, Milton, Levinson, Daniel and Williams, Richard eds. *The patient and the mental hospital.* New York: Free Press.

Racker, Heinrich, 1968. *Transference and countertransference.* New York: International Universities Press.

Rapaport, David, 1950. On the psychoanalytic theory of thinking. *International Journal of Psycho-Analysis* 31: 161-70.

Rapaport, David, 1951. *Organization and pathology of thought*. New York: Columbia University Press.

Rapaport, David, 1959. A historical survey of psychoanalytic ego psychology. Introduction to Erikson, Erik H. *Identity and the life cycle*. (Psychological Issues Monograph 1) New York: International Universities Press.

Rapaport, David, 1960. *The structure of psychoanalytic theory: A systematizing attempt*. (Psychological Issues Monograph 6) New York: International Universities Press.

Rapaport, David, 1967a. Edward Bibring's theory of depression, in Gill, Merton M. ed. *Collected papers of David Rapaport*. New York: Basic Books.

Rapaport, David, 1967b. Some metapsychological considerations concerning activity and passivity, in Gill, Merton M. ed. *Collected papers of David Rapaport*. New York: Basic Books.

Redl, Fritz, 1942. Group emotion and leadership. *Psychiatry* 5: 573-96.

Redl, Fritz, 1948. Resistance in therapy groups. *Human Relations* 1: 307-13.

Redl, Fritz, 1949a. New ways of ego support in residential treatment of disturbed children. *Bulletin of the Menninger Clinic* 13: 60-66.

Redl, Friz, 1949b. The phenomenon of contagion and shock effect in group therapy, in Eissler, Karl ed. *Searchlight on delinquency*. New York: International Universities Press.

Redl, Fritz and Wineman, David, 1951. *Children who hate*. Glencoe, Ill.: Free Press.

Redl, Fritz and Wineman, David, 1952. *Controls from within*. New York: Free Press.

Reich, Wilhelm, 1949. *Character analysis*. New York: Noonday Press.

Reiner, Beatrice S. and Kaufman, Irving, 1959. *Character disorders in parents of delinquents*. New York: Family Service Association of America.

Rickers-Ovsiankina, Maria, and Kusmin, Arnold A., 1958. Individual differences in social accessibility. *Psychological Reports* 4: 391-406.

Rioch, Margaret, 1970. The work of Wilfred Bion on groups: *Psychiatry* 33: 56-66.

Ripple, Lillian, Alexander, Ernestine and Polemis, Bernice W., 1964. *Motivation, capacity and opportunity*. Chicago: School of Social Service Administration, University of Chicago.

Rosen, Sidney, Levinger, George and Lippitt, Ronald, 1960. Desired change in self and others as a function of resource ownership. *Human Relations* 13: 187-193.

Roth, Philip, 1969. *Portnoy's Complaint*. New York: Random House.

Ruesch, Jurgen, 1948. The infantile personality: The core problem of psychosomatic medicine. *Psychosomatic Medicine* 10: 134-44.

Runyon, Damon, 1941. *Take it easy*. New York: Triangle Books.

Russell, Bertrand, 1945. *A history of Western philosophy*. New York: Simon and Schuster.

Schachter, Stanley S., 1951. Deviation, rejection and communication. *Journal of Abnormal and Social Psychology* 46: 190-207.

Secrest, Meryle, 1979. *Being Bernard Berenson*. New York: Holt, Rinehart and Winston.

Seeman, Melvin, 1959. On the meaning of alienation. *American Sociological Review* 24: 783-91.

Segal, Hanna, 1974. *Introduction to the work of Melanie Klein*. New York: Basic Books.

Shapiro, David, 1965. *Neurotic styles*. New York: Basic Books.

Shapiro, David, 1970. Motivation and action in psychoanalytic psychiatry. *Psychiatry* 33: 329-43.

Shapiro, Edward R., 1978. The psychodynamics and developmental psychology of the borderline patient: A review of the literature. *American Journal of Psychiatry* 135: 1305-15.

Sharlin, Shlomo and Polansky, Norman A., 1972. The process of infantilization. *American Journal of Orthopsychiatry* 42: 92-102.

Sherif, Muzafer, 1966. *In common predicament*. Boston: Houghton Mifflin.

Siegal, Richard S., 1969. What are defense mechanisms? *Journal of the American Psychoanalytic Association* 17: 785-807.

Skeels, Harold M., 1966. Adult status of children with contrasting early life experience. *Monographs of the Society for Research in Child Development* 31: 1-65.

Skeels, Harold M., Updegraff, Ruth, Wellman, Beth L. and Williams, Harold M., 1938. A study of environmental stimulation: An orphanage preschool project. *University of Iowa Studies in Child Welfare* 15: 1-192 (whole No. 4).

Skinner, Burrhus F., 1969. *Contingencies of reinforcement: A theoretical analysis*. New York: Appleton-Century-Crofts.

Skinner, Burrhus F., 1971. *Beyond freedom and dignity*. New York: Alfred A. Knopf.

Solzhenitsyn, Aleksander I., 1978. *The Gulag archipelago*. New York: Harper and Row.

Spitz, René A., 1945. Hospitalism: An inquiry into the genesis of psychiatric conditions in early childhood. *Psychoanalytic Study of the Child Vol. 1*. New York: International Universities Press.

Spitz, René A., 1946a. Hospitalism: A follow-up report. *Psychoanalytic Study of the Child, Vol. 2*. New York: International Universities Press.

Spitz, René A., 1946b. Anaclitic depression. *Psychoanalytic Study of the Child, Vol. 2*. New York: International Universities Press.

Spitz, René A., 1966. Metapsychology and infant observation, in Loewenstein, Rudolf M., Newman, Lottie M., Schur, Max and Solnit, Albert J. eds. *Psychoanalysis — A general psychology*. New York: International Universities Press.

Stamm, Isabel L., 1959. Ego psychology in the emerging theoretical base of casework, in Kahn, Alfred J. ed. *Issues in American Social Work*. New York: Columbia University Press.

Stern, Adolph, 1938. Psychoanalytic investigation of and therapy in the borderline group of neuroses. *Psychoanalytic Quarterly* 7: 467-89.

Stern, William, 1914. *Psychologie der fruehen Kindzeit*. Leipzig: Quelle und Meyyer.

Stotland, Ezra, Zander, Alvin and Natsoulas, Thomas, 1961. Generalization of interpersonal similarity. *Journal of Abnormal and Social Psychology* 62: 250-56.

Sullivan, Harry S., 1940. *Conceptions of modern psychiatry*. Washington, D.C.: William Alanson White Psychiatric Foundation.

Sullivan, Mary, Spasser, Marion and Penner, G. Lewis, 1977. *Bowen Center project for abused and neglected children*. Washington, D.C.: Office of Human Development, D/HSS.

Taber, Merlin A., 1980. *The social context of helping: A review of the literature on alternative care for the physically and mentally handicapped*. Rockville, Md.: National Institute of Mental Health.

Taft, Jessie, 1933. *Dynamics of therapy in a controlled relationship*. New York: Macmillan.

Tarde, Gabriel, 1903. The laws of imitation. New York: Holt.

Tesser, Abraham and Rosen, Sidney, 1975. The reluctance to transmit bad news, in Berkowitz, Leonard ed. *Advances in experimental social psychology Vol. 8*. New York: Academic Press.

Tessler, Richard, 1975. Clients' reactions to initial interviews: Determinants of relationship-centered and problem-centered satisfaction. *Journal of Counseling Psychology* 22: 187-91.

Tessler, Richard C. and Polansky, Norman A., 1975. Perceived similarity: A paradox in interviewing. *Social Work* 5: 359-63.

Thorndike, Edward L., 1898. Animal intelligence: An experimental study of the associative process in animals. *Psychological Review*: Supplement No. 8.

Tolman, Edward C., 1932. *Purposive behavior in animals and men*. New York: Appleton-Century-Crofts.

Towle, Charlotte, 1945. *Common human needs: An interpretation for staff in public assistance agencies*. Washington, D.C.: Bureau of Public Assistance, Federal Security Agency.

Tucker, Gregory, 1961. A study of verbal accessibility in hospitalized paranoid schizophrenics in response to two styles of interviewing. Unpublished Ph.D. dissertation, Case Western Reserve University.

Turner, John B., 1959. A study of the block club: An instrument of community organization. Unpublished D.S.W. dissertation, School of Applied Social Sciences, Case Western Reserve University.

Voltaire, Francois A., 1930. *Candide*. New York: Arden Book Co.

Vygotsky, Lev S., 1962. *Thought and language*. Cambridge, Mass.: The MIT Press.

Wallerstein, Judith. 1977. Responses of the preschool child to divorce: Those who cope, in McMillan, Mae F. and Henao, Srgiom, eds. *Child psychiatry: Treatment and Research*. New York: Brunner/Mazel.

Wallerstein, Judith, S. and Kelly, Joan B., 1974. The effects of parental divorce: The adolescent experience, in Koupernik, Anthony, ed. *The Child in his family — Children at a psychiatric risk Vol. 3*. New York: Wiley

Wallerstein, Judith S. and Kelly, Joan B., 1975. The effects of parental divorce: Experiences of the preschool child. *Journal of the American Academy of Child Psychiatry* 14: 600-616.

Wallerstein, Judith S. and Kelly, Joan B., 1980. *Surviving the breakup. How children and parents cope with divorce*. New York: Basic Books.

Warner, William S., 1960. Behavioral contagion and social power: An experimental study. Unpublished Ph.D. dissertation, Case Western Reserve University.

Wasserman, Sidney L., 1974. Ego psychology, in Turner, Francis J. ed. *Social work treatment: Interlocking theoretical approaches*. New York: Free Press.

Weber, Ruth, 1963. Children's verbal accessibility as a predictor of treatment outcome. Unpublished DSW dissertation, School of Applied Social Sciences, Case Western Reserve University.

Wechsberg, Joseph, 1973. *The glory of the violin*. New York: Viking.

Weisman, Avery D., 1955. Silence and psychotherapy. *Psychiatry* 18: 241-60.

Werner, Heinz, 1957. The concept of development from a comparative and organismic point of view, in Harris, Dale B. ed. *The concept of development*. Minneapolis: University of Minnesota Press.

Williams, David P., 1979. A critical review of selected positions on the borderline personality. Athens, Ga.: University of Georgia. Photocopied.

Winnicott, Donald W., 1953. Transitional objects and transitional phenomena: A study of the first not-me possession. *International Journal of Psycho-Analysis* 34: 89-97.

Winnicott, Donald W., 1954-55. Metapsychological and clinical aspects of regression within the psychoanalytical set-up. *International Journal of Psycho-Analysis* 35-36: 16-26.

Winnicott, Donald W., 1955. The depressive position in normal emotional development. *British Journal of Medical Psychology* 28: 89-100.

Wodarski, John and Bagarozzi, Dennis A., 1979. *Behavioral social work*. New York: Human Sciences Press.

Wolff, Peter H., 1960. *The developmental psychologies of Jean Piaget and psychoanalysis* (Psychological Issues Monograph 5) New York: International Universities Press.

Wolpe, Joseph, 1973. *The practice of behavior therapy*. New York: Pergamon.

Woollams, Stanley, Brown, Michael and Huige, Kristyn, 1976. *Transactional analysis*. Ann Arbor, Mich.: Huron Valley Institute.

Yablonsky, Lewis and Enneis, James M., 1956. Psychodrama theory and practice, in Fromm-Reichmann, Frieda and Moreno, Jacob L. eds. *Progress in psychotherapy Vol. 1*. New York: Grune and Stratton.

Zander, Alvin, Stotland, Ezra and Wolfe, Donald, 1960. Unity of group, identification with group and self-esteem of members. *Journal of Personality* 28: 463-78.

Zeligs, Meyer A., 1961. The psychology of silence: Its role in transference, countertransference and the psychoanalytic process. *Journal of the American Psychoanalytic Association* 9: 7-43.

Zwerdling, Ella and Polansky, Grace H., 1949. Foster home placement of refugee children. *Social Casework* 30: 277-82.

Name Index

Subject Index

Abreaction 292, 306
Acting out 343
Addictive personality 108
Affect 34, binding of 306, as defense 50, 137, as discharge channel 36, 278, inhibition 146, 217, 222, 233, 273, flatness 231, 234, primitive 280, tracing 318-19
Aggression 10, in borderline states 154, as instinct 33, 202, 231, object of 198, in psychodrama 280, turned against the self 147, 148
Aggressiveness 166
Ahistorical causation 105
Alloplastic 60
All-or-none 110, 220
Ambivalence 192, 348
Anaclitic, choice 178, dependency 119, depression 177
Anal character 113-15
Anal-expulsive stage 106, 167, remnants in obsessive compulsives 129, -retentive stage 106, and shame, blame 114
Anxiety, commitment 237, and defense 45, ego 238, as energy 34, 36, existential 295, guilt 39, 334, persecutory 204, 328, release through uncovering 65, separation 50, 119, 228, signal function of 35, stranger 199, tolerance 118, 154
Apathy-futility syndrome 117, 235
As if personality 216
Attachment, behavior 237-242, object 239
Attention 75
Attitude, orienting 168
Authoritarian personality 204
Autism, childhood 178-79, as phase in development 182
Autonomy 155, development of 167, of the ego 165
Autoplastic 60
Auxiliary ego 278, 289, defined 276
Average expectable environment, defined 73, 161, in normal development 180
Basic assumption group 331
Behavior modification 320-21
Borderline personality 104, 217, 286, 151-56

Boundaries, ego 88, 104, 153, 359, 79-83
Burnout 195
Catharsis 39, in psychodrama 283-84
Cathexis 216
Censorship 46
Central person 327-28
Character, defense 101, 273, defined 100, 298, in differential diagnosis 104, disorder 117, 122, 273, 336, types 125, and verbal accessibility 298-301
Characterology, choice of 103, defined 100, traditional 105
Charisma 324-29
Childhood level of living scale 300
Choosing 356
Circumstantiality 260
Clarification 246, 274, 278, defined 64, 283, as ego support 92, function of 309, through psychodrama 283-86
Classical technique, basic rule 21, encouraging transference 190, 193
Closeness, fear of 225, 228, 231, 242, 281
Commitment, fear of 227-29, in identity formation 172, as reaction-formation 127
Communication, through action 274, 278, 301, freedom of 297, 301, 312-13, structure 323, verbal 302
Complex 39
Compulsion, defined 52, 126, elaboration of 66
Concept 7, inferred 9
Concrete mindedness 119
Condiction 103-04, 298
Conditioning, aversive 320, operant 347
Conflict 30, 37, 162, and concentration 74-75, defined 38, externalization of 137, 337, -free ego sphere 164, 301, invasion by 164, 241, 246, 301, resolution of 38, 309, 328, 336-37, about sexuality 135, 189
Consciousness 27
Consensual validation 142, 339
Construct, defined 9, as instinct 33, in object relations theory 207, and the unconscious 28
Contagion, behavioral 280, 292, 335-38, defined 335, and the initiatory act 328, and prestige 335

382

Mirroring 289
Modal personality 166
Motivation, for treatment 59
Narcissism, costs of 78, as defense 79, 150, 152, 260, defined 77, narcissistic character 151, primary 77, secondary 77, 230
Negativism 219, 223, 249
Neologism 80, defined 82
Neutralization, of affect 155, of energy 134
Nonjudgmentalism 315-16
Noogenic neurosis 361
Object, attachment 238, bad 236, constancy 198, 205, of drives 50, 196, 198, 328, good 232-33, as image 197-99, integrated 205 libidinal 196-98, 232, loss 94-96, 238, permanence 182, 198, relations 200, transitional 183, 248
Obsessive-compulsive 102, 140, personality 126-133, irresponsible 130
Obsession, defined 53, function of 126
Oedipus complex 4, 72, 82, 116, 179
Omnipotence, delusions of 143, 222, wishes 52, 182
Omniscience 144
Oral, -biting 106, 109, greed 150, -receptive 106, 167, remnant 107, 112, -sadistic 106, 234, supplies 109, 202
Oral character 108-13
Orgasmic 139
Overdetermination 41, 305, 353, defined 37
Pairing group 332
Paranoid, character 142-46, position 202-05, 235
Parsimony, rule of 10, 349, defined 8, overapplied 11, and the schismatics 12
Passive 272, -aggressive 148, 262
Perceived similarity 330
Perceptual balance 331
Perfectionism 109, 128, 266
Persecution, delusions of 142
Phallic, character 115-17, remnant 115, stage 106
Phobia 66, function of 128
Polarity 168
Practicing 183
Preconscious 27
Pride 78, 150-51

Primary process, in creativity 88, 292, in decompensation 152, defined 81
Producer-product relationship 353-54
Progression 122, 250, defined 50
Projection, 179, benign 330, defined 48, in hysterical personality 135, in paranoid character 143, in paranoid position 203
Projective identification 306, defined 195
Protagonist 273, 289
Protest 238
Pseudomaturity 50, 122, 291
Psychic energy, availability of 72, channels for discharge 35, loss in indecision 75-77, neutralized 73, use in defense 56, 77-79, use in attention 75
Psychoanalysis, clinical beginnings 24-27, determinism in 29, 347-48, schisms in 11-13, and social work 2
Psychodrama 271-93
Psychosexual stages 106, 168, 180
Psychosocial, approach 166-74, in casework 112
Psychosomatic symptoms, defined 54, in infantile personality 117
Rape fantasy 137
Rapprochement 183
Rationalization 48, 125, defined 51, of malfeasance 115
Reaction-formation 249, in character syndrome 110, 115, 116, defined 49, against immaturity 165, against inferiority 62, 116
Reality, relationship 191, -testing 118, 152
Reassurance 316-17
Reenactment 201, 344, in psychodrama 284
Reference group 339
Regression, defined 50, in ego development 182, 292, induced 272, 292, in psychosexual development 108, 248, in the service of the ego 81, 165, 174, 274, 292, in the service of resistance 332, transitory 194, 290-92
Reintrojection 203, 206
Reliability, and communicability 13, inter-observer 12
Remnant 62, 107

Reparation 205
Repetition compulsion 291, as coping 90, 205, 250, defined 52
Repression, and defenses 44, 47, defined 30, 48, and forgetting by disuse 163, in hysterical personality 135, in statu nascendi 49
Rescue fantasy 53, 205
Resistance 22, defined 332, in group therapy 332-35, in milieu treatment 333
Responsibility, function of avoiding 355, maneuvers to evade 257-59, 348
Restitution 96, 247, 249
Righteous indignation, functions of 137, in hysterical personality 136
Rigidity 143, 146, 152
Ripple-effect, defined 289, in psycho-drama 289-90
Role, re-enactment 206, 210, social 101, 170-71, 324
Schizoid, defined 217, dilemma 232 282, personality 221-231, position 231-37, spectrum 138, 216-17, 281
Screen memory 190
Script 211
Secondary process 292, 303, defined 81
Security maneuver, depressiveness 148, distancing 230, 235
Seduction 329
Self-abasement, as defense 51-52, 263, in depression 146, as security maneuver 149
Self-actualization 358-60
Self-analysis 69, 162
Self-disclosure 283, 300
Self-observation 48, 208, 272, capacity for 299, through ego-support 92, of infantile personality 121
Self-representation 183
Separateness, conflicts over 179, 185, 247, defined 181
Separation anxiety 50, and defense 56, and infantilization 121-22, and loss of attachment object 238, 248
Separation-individuation 182-84
Sexual drive 33, 189
Sexualization of relationship 135
Shame 129, 168, 260, 357
Shock-effect 337
Significant other 193
Silence 256, functions of 304-05, 308

Slip of the tongue 28, 30, 82
Somatization 54, 136
Speech, deficits in 310-12, facilitating 314-21, functions of 301-10, inhibition of 312-13, silent 304
Spiral of causation 310
Spite 46, 148, 232, 280, in negative identity 173
Splitting 192, 203-04, and all-or-none reaction 110, defined 286, in the ego 153, 234
Stimulus hunger 34, 210
Stroke 210
Structural, analysis 209-10, conception 31
Structure, defined 100, external 153, power 335
Stubbornness, of anal character 113, of obsessive-compulsive 127, of paranoid character 143, of schizoid personality 223
Sublimation, defined 51, and drive modulation 73, 134, 171, 231
Substitution, of affect 137, defined 50, of goal 336, of persons 196, of speech for action 306-07
Suggestibility 326
Superego 336, childish 120, 147, deficits in 83, defined 32, formation 84, function of 55, in infantile personality 120, rigid 147
Suppression 30, 48
Survival needs 34, 202
Survival value, of attachment 239, of instincts 33
Symbiosis 179, defined 181, as developmental phase 182
Symptom, choice of 60, defined 57-58, ego-dystonic 59, 343, ego-syntonic 59, 288, 343, etiology of 60, and secondary gain 89, as self-healing 69
Syndrome 104
Synthetic function, deficits in 153, in ego identity 174, facilitating speech 311-12, integrating motives 77, 172, supported by communication 302, 308, and the will 354
Talion principle 39-40
Thanatos 10, 231
Theory, classificatory 7, dynamic 7, of personality 14, in clinical work 6